Proceedings of the American Catholic Philosophical Association

Philosophy and Language

Volume 84, 2010

Edited by:
R. Edward Houser
Thomas Osborne
University of Saint Thomas

Papers for the regular sessions were selected by the program committee:
Nadja Germann
John Greco
Christopher Kaczor
Christopher Martin

Issued by the National Office of the American Catholic Philosophical Association
University of Saint Thomas
Houston, TX 77006

The *Proceedings of the American Catholic Philosophical Association* are published as an annual supplement to the *American Catholic Philosophical Quarterly* and distributed to members of the ACPA as a benefit of membership. The *Proceedings* are also available for purchase to libraries, departments, institutions, and individuals. For information regarding subscriptions and/or back issues, please contact:

Philosophy Documentation Center
P.O. Box 7147
Charlottesville, VA 22906-7147
Phone: 800-444-2419 (U.S. and Canada); 434-220-3300
Fax: 434-220-3301
E-mail: order@pdcnet.org
Web: www.pdcnet.org

The *Proceedings of the American Catholic Philosophical Association* are indexed in *Academic Search Premier, American Humanities Index, Catholic Periodical and Literature Index, Current Abstracts, Expanded Academic ASAP, Index Philosophicus, Index to Social Science & Humanities Proceedings, InfoTrac OneFile, International Bibliography of Periodical Literature (IBZ), International Philosophical Bibliography, ISI Alerting Services, Periodicals Index Online, Philosopher's Index, Reference and Research Book News*, and *Religious & Theological Abstracts*.
The *Proceedings of the American Catholic Philosophical Association* are also available in POIESIS: Philosophy Online Serials. The full text of the *Proceedings, American Catholic Philosophical Quarterly*, and *The New Scholasticism* are available online to libraries that subscribe both to the Proceedings and to POIESIS and to members of the American Catholic Philosophical Association. For more information, contact the Philosophy Documentation Center at order@pdcnet.org.

ISSN 0065-7638 (print)
ISSN 2153-7925 (online)
ISBN 978-1-889680-86-6
ISBN 1-889680-86-9

Published by the Philosophy Documentation Center, Charlottesville, Virginia.

Proceedings of the American Catholic Philosophical Association

Philosophy and Language

Volume 84, 2010

TABLE OF CONTENTS

Al-Fârâbî: An Arabic Account of the
Origin of Language and of Philosophical Vocabulary

Thérèse-Anne Druart

Abstract: The paper first presents the necessary background to appreciate al-Fârâbî's views and his originality. It explains the issues Anicent philosophers faced: the natural vs. the conventional origin of language, the problem of ambiguous words, and the difficulty to express Greek thought into Latin. It then sketches and contrasts the views of Christianity and Islam on the origin of language and the diversity of idioms. It argues that al-Fârâbî follows the philosophical tradition but develops it in sophisticated and original manner by telling the story of the origin and development of language and giving little place to the Islamic tradition. For al-Fârâbî language emerges naturally but develops by convention in three phases: (1) The constitution of utterances and crafts to ensure basic necessities; (2) The development of rhetoric, poetry, memorizing, writing, and the language arts; (3) the development of dialectic, sophistical reasoning and demonstration that leads to philosophy reaching its perfection with with Aristotle. Religion for him is posterior to philosophy and derives form it. As for al-Fârâbî philosophy in Islamic lands was imported from Greece, he includes rules to translate technical philosophical terms from one language into another.

We philosophers are looking for the "*logos*," the reasoned account expressed through a meaningful concatenation of "*logoi*" or propositions, each made of "*logoi*" or words. Language is at the heart of our ability to do philosophy and so early on philosophers did not use words and language simply to philosophize but also reflected on language and words, i.e., what they called "names" as names, be they proper or common, are the simplest referring words. Children first learn some names by ostension, as their parents both utter a name and point to the thing it refers to. Philosophers wondered about a host of issues, such as the origin of language, its evolution, its richness and ambiguities, the constitution of a technical vocabulary, and a philosophical one in particular, the multiplicity of tongues, and even the difficulty of translation. Things became still more complex when philosophy met Scriptures, be it the Bible or the *Qur'ân*, which give their own account of the origin of language and of the diversity of tongues. These scriptural accounts challenged philosophers to rethink or develop their views on language.

As we all know something about these topics in the Christian Greco-Latin tradition, I thought it interesting to examine something we know less, i.e., how a philosopher, steeped in the Greek philosophical tradition, confronted with the Qur'ânic text and the Islamic tradition, writing in Arabic, a language very different from Greek or Latin, and himself very aware of the diversity of tongues, as he was no native Arabic speaker, faces the same issues. My paper, therefore, will have three parts. In the first I shall outline some of the issues raised in Ancient philosophy. In the second I shall sketch some of the differences between the biblical account of the origin of language and the diversity of tongues and that of the *Qur'ân* as well as some implications of a different understanding of revelation. The third and more detailed part will explain and reflect on al-Fârâbî's own way of handling the issues he inherited from the Greek philosophical tradition and from the Islamic religious tradition.

I. The Ancient Philosophy Background

As only ancient philosophical texts written in Greek were translated into Arabic, and this at times through a Syriac intermediary, I shall focus on Greek texts with one exception: Lucretius both as transmitter of Greek Epicureanism and as fully aware of the difficulties to express it into another language, i.e., Latin.

In the *Cratylus* Plato discusses whether the correctness of "names" (*onomata*) rests on nature or convention. Were names established by a "*nomothetes*" (389d8) or giver of law or convention, who in fact is a "giver of names" (al-Fârâbî will not shy to use a literal translation of "giver of names")?

In *De interpretatione* Aristotle tersely tells us:

> Now spoken sounds are symbols of affections in the soul, and written marks symbols of spoken sounds. And just as written marks are not the same for all men, neither are spoken sounds. But what these are in the first place signs of—affections of the soul—are the same for all; and what these affections are likenesses of—actual things—are also the same. (1, 16 a3–8)[1]

Scripts and spoken sounds are conventional and differ among men, but the affections of the soul as likenesses of actual things and the actual things themselves are the same for all.

A few lines further Aristotle emphasizes the conventional aspect of "names" in contrast to animal noises, even if such animal sounds can be articulated and reveal something:

> A *name* is a spoken sound significant by convention, without time . . . I say 'by convention' because no name is a name naturally but only when it has become a symbol. Even inarticulate noises (of beasts, for instance) do indeed reveal something, yet none of them is a name. (2, 16a19–29)[2]

Origen, a Greek father of the Church (185–254), makes it clear that this debate kept going on during Hellenistic time:

> One should also say that a deep and arcane debate about the nature of names emerged: are names conventional, as Aristotle thinks; or natural, as the Stoics believe (for the first utterances imitate the things the utterances are applied to . . .); or are names natural, as Epicurus teaches—in a manner different from that of the Stoics, since the first men burst forth with certain sounds which were applied to things? (*Against Celsus* 1.24)[3]

Do not be surprised by my invoking a Father of the Church; most of the translators from Greek into Arabic, as well as the first philosophy teachers in Islamic lands, were Syriac Christians and so the Arabic tradition read Aristotle through the lenses of these translators and of the Greek commentators and, therefore, in an Hellenistic mode. Origen's statement is rather sketchy and oversimplified. So I shall spell out more the complex Epicurean view as al-Fârâbî too will present a naturalistic account with some similarities to that of the Epicureans. Epicurus in his *Letter to Herodotus* (75–76) details a sophisticated three step process for the origin of language. First, originally names "did not come into being by convention, but by the very nature of men"[4] and Lucretius adds that human beings used ostension.[5] Lucretius even compares human beings to the animals as animals too can indicate feelings by means of various sounds and this comparison strengthens the view that language at its origin is natural.[6] Second, later on, names were established "by a general convention in each tribe." Third, in each tribe people "who were aware of certain previously unobserved things introduced them [to their tribes] and with them handed over certain words [for these things]"[7] and so coined new words for the discovery of new things. This account implies that, though at its origin language is a natural phenomenon, it later on develops by convention. Besides, there always was a diversity of tongues as the development of language is specific to each tribe.

Aristotle in the *Sophistical Refutations*, chapter 1, makes two important points in order to explain why people are misled in arguments: one about the relation between names and things referred to and the other about the ambiguity of these names:

> The most prolific and usual [reason for mistakes] is the argument that turns upon names. It is impossible in a discussion to bring in the actual things discussed: we use their names as symbols instead of them; and we suppose that what follows in the names, follows in the things as well, just as people who calculate suppose in regard to their counters. But the two cases are not alike. For names are finite and so is the sum-total of accounts, while things are infinite in number. Inevitably, then, the same account and a single name signify several things. (165a5–13)[8]

Aristotle accepts as a fact of life that many words or names have more than one meaning and incites philosophers to beware of shifts of meaning in arguments He also once again indicates that names are symbols for things.

As for what concerns translation, we should return to Lucretius's famous poem, *De rerum natura*, in which he proudly claims to be the first to present Epicureanism in Latin and tells us:

> I am wide awake to the difficulty of the task of illuminating the obscure discoveries of the Greeks in Latin verse. The main obstacles are the inadequacy of our language and the novelty of my subject—factors that entail the coinage of many new terms. (1.136–39)[9]

II. The Scriptural Accounts

The Bible and the *Qur'ân* present accounts linking the origin of language to divine intervention and so fairly remote from those of the Ancient philosophers. Let us begin with the biblical texts. *Genesis* 2, the second account of creation, tells us:

> So from the soil Yahweh God fashioned all the wild beasts and all the birds of heaven. These he brought to the man to see what he would call them; each one was to bear the name the man would give it. The man gave names to all the cattle, all the birds of heaven and all the wild beasts. (19–20)[10]

This account emphasizes that God entrusted to Adam the responsibility of naming. So names do not arise by nature but rather are established by a namegiver, a "*nomothetes*" for language. Adam was entrusted with this task even before the creation of Eve and, therefore, before the very possibility of establishing names by convention among human beings. If such is the case, then originally there was only one language, maybe shared by God and man, and (1) the diversity of tongues needs explaining and (2) as this institution of language precedes original sin, one may wonder whether Adam spoke a perfect language, one without the possibility of ambiguity as for each thing or aspect of thing a single name would correspond and each name would refer to a single thing or aspect.

Let us begin with the need to explain the diversity of tongues. Curiously *Genesis* offers two very different accounts, which follow each other. The first account, often neglected, is a naturalistic one. Chapter 10, which details the descendants of Noah's sons and the origin of nations, indicates that the multiplicity of tongues arises after and from the geographical dispersion of human beings. There is no hint that this multiplicity is connected to any kind of punishment. The story of the Babel tower, which makes of the diversity of tongues a punishment inflicted by God, immediately follows this naturalistic account. The beginning of the story of the Babel tower emphasizes that up to that time all human beings were speaking the same language: "Throughout the earth man spoke the same language, with the same vocabulary" (11:1). People began to build the tower of Babel and God worried by the arrogance of the builders decided to do two things: (1) First, to confuse their language and so render them unable to complete their project and (2) to scatter them over the whole face of the earth (11:1–9). This latter account, which sees both the diversity of tongues and geographical dispersion as punishment, became dominant and people dreamt of a return to one and the same language.

If the institution of names came at the request of God himself and preceded the fault, then maybe God and Adam conversed in a language that must have been perfect. Needless to say, there were speculations to determine which kind of language it was and philosophers, who were less matter of fact than Aristotle about the ambiguity of names, dreamt of a perfect language either by trying to recover the original Adamic language or by creating artificially such a perfect language. This desire to return to a single language for all human beings seems surprising, as Christianity does not mind the diversity of tongues and privileges none. For Christians Scriptures are in two quite different languages, Hebrew and Greek, none of them the tongue spoken by Christ. At Pentecost the diversity of tongues is not suppressed but rather communication is restored, despite the diversity of tongues. Each of the people listening to the apostles was bewildered to hear them "speaking his own language" (*Acts* 2:1–13). Besides, liturgical rites in various languages quickly sprang up and in the Latin West the Latin translation of the Bible, known as the *Vulgate*, made around the year 400 by Jerome, after a time acquired some kind of canonical status.

Yet, in the Christian West ordinary people and philosophers remained fascinated by the dream of either a single language for all human beings in order to ensure universal peace, which in the nineteenth and early twentieth century led to the invention of such artificial international languages as *Volapük* and *Esperanto*, or the dream of a perfectly non-ambiguous language pursued by some philosophers in the seventeenth and eighteenth century, such as Leibniz. If you are interested in such topics Umberto Eco's *The Search for the Perfect Language*[11] is both informative and entertaining.

Of course, various interpretations, some highly allegorical, have been given to the biblical texts I have referred to but for the purpose of this paper I have opted for a fairly literal reading.

In the Bible, God entrusts Adam with the task of establishing "names." The *Qur'ân* too speaks of a "name giver," but this time the name giver is God himself as 2.31 tells us emphatically that "[God] taught Adam *all* the names" (wa 'allama Âdama al-'asmâ'a kullaha). Of course, interpretations of this Qur'ânic verse vary widely. Some of those I know go from the minimalist position that God simply gave the ability to speak to human beings, who then developed their own language, to the extreme one that God taught Adam Arabic in all its detail, including the famous late eighth-century grammar of Sibawayh (ca. 760–796/7).[12] Yet, if we can believe Michael G. Carter, commentators on the *Qur'ân* agree that the need for technical terms for new tools, etc, led to coinage by human beings.[13] Epicurus too had spoken of the need to coin terms for new discoveries in his presentation of the third step of the development of language.

The *Qur'ân* does not address the diversity of tongues but emphasizes that its text is clear because in Arabic. Besides, after some bitter and bloody disputes about the status of the *Qur'ân*, Islam adopted the view that the *Qur'ân* is "uncreated," that it to say, if you like, dictated to Muhammad by the intermediary of the angel

Gabriel. So it is literally the word of God as God himself says it and not a text written by a human being under God's inspiration. Inimitability became proof for its uncreatedness and often Muslims construe this inimitability as the impossibility for anyone to provide a text that would be more beautiful both in content and style. Hence, most Muslims grant a special status to one tongue, i.e., Arabic. For instance, according to strict Islamic law official prayers in the mosque, which comprise recitation of Qur'ânic verses, should be in Arabic.

The *Qur'ân* does not address the issue of the diversity of languages but the Islamic rulers often encouraged the use of Arabic, which became the "*lingua franca*" to such a point that fairly early on, i.e., the end of the eighth century the most famous grammarian, Sibawayh, a Persian, wrote his book as a help to non Arabic speakers.

Muslim theologians have held widely different interpretations of the Qur'ânic verse, but they generally considered language as a gift from God and not as something arising naturally. Besides, the privileged status of Arabic is emphasized by Islamic law, which prohibits translations of the *Qur'ân*, except to attract converts.

III. Al-Fârâbî

Before tackling directly al-Fârâbî's views I need to speak briefly of the complex question of translations from Greek into Arabic. Maybe because of the privileged status of Arabic, which did not encourage Arabic speakers to learn foreign languages, translators were foreigners and often Syriac Christians.[14] Their Arabic at times was fairly poor and, in order to translate some technical philosophical words or expressions, they coined rather barbaric equivalents, a feature al-Fârâbî does not endorse. Let me illustrate this barbaric aspect of early translations by means of the story of the famous encounter between Abû Bishr Mattâ ibn Yûnus, a Syriac Christian translator and one of the first teachers of philosophy in the Greek mode, and the grammarian Abû Sa'îd al-Sîrâfî. The encounter occurred in Bagdad around 938 at the invitation of the vizier Ibn al-Furât, who requested a discussion on the merits of logic and Arabic grammar, as some people wished to argue that logic had no universal value as it only was the grammar of Greek. The version we have presents a logician disputing in very broken Arabic full of coinages with a grammarian speaking beautiful Arabic and joyfully twisting around whatever the hapless logician said. In this version logic took a beating.[15]

Al-Fârâbî, who dislikes the *Mutakallimûn* or theologians, must (1) elaborate a naturalistic philosophical theory of the origin and development of language that eschews any kind of divine intervention and rivals or supersedes that of the theologians and (2) legitimize the Arabic translations of Greek texts in making them more palatable to Arab and contemporary ears. This was no mean task.

1. Did Language Originate by Nature or by Convention?

First, let us look at al-Fârâbî's position on the debate about whether "names" are by convention or by nature. Aristotle in his *De interpretatione* takes a position that implies that names are conventional and contrasts animals to human beings to bolster this view. Al-Fârâbî in his *Long Commentary* on this text concurs but spells out a contrast between convention and nature and substitutes to "names" a more encompassing and non-Qur'ânic term, "*lafz*," which I shall translate as utterance. He also grounds the convention of names in the diversity of languages taken as a matter of fact that does not require explanation:

> Aristotle wishes to make known what concerns utterances and that their signification is by imposition. . . . If utterances were natural for human beings, then they would be the very same for all nations as the intelligibles from the various languages are one and the same in all nations. The sensibles from which these intelligibles arise are also one and the same for all nations. How utterances signify the intelligibles is by imposition, convention, and legislation (*shari'at*). Utterance givers are also lawgivers. . . . The relation of the intelligibles, which are in the soul, to the beings outside the soul is a relation arising by nature, but the relation of the intelligibles to the utterances is a relation by imposition and plain legislation. (25, 15–17 and 27, 5–20)[16]

Al-Fârâbî also explains that just as law can emanate from the people or from one or few rulers, so utterances can emanate from the people or from one or a few rulers. We are far away from the Islamic theological view and seem far from a purely naturalistic approach. Yet, though "utterances" are conventional, al-Fârâbî's position turns up to be rather complex and closer to that of the Epicureans as his commentary on 2.16a27–29 shows. There he wishes to emend the text. He agrees that any name or noun (in Arabic the same word *'ism* means both a name and a noun) can only be by convention but "sound or voice (*sawt*) at times is by nature and at times by convention."[17] He refers to Aristotle's own *History of Animals*, II,11, 504b1–3: "Certain species of birds above all other animals, and next after man, possess the faculty of uttering articulate sounds; and this faculty is chiefly developed in broad-tongued birds"[18] and tells us:

> Yet we find in the *Book of Animals* that Aristotle says that many birds and other animals occasionally produce sounds composed of letters. And if utterances are composed of letters, the sounds these animals produce are utterances, even if [composed of] letters we do not happen to know. At the same time, we observe that many of the animals which live around us, such as goats and others, produce sounds—sounds they have been endowed by nature—which are composed of letters we do know. I am not thinking of birds like the parrot and the magpie, which can be taught utterances, but of those that produce sounds which they have been given by nature. Such sounds are utterances though they are not by convention. (31, 15–21)[19]

Fuad Haddad comments that goats naturally make sounds to communicate some feelings to other goats, such as fear, pleasure, or aggression, but such sounds are natural to the species and not established by convention.[20] As for parrots, though they imitate language, they do not really use "nouns" as they are not aware of their conventional meanings. Parroting lacks intentionality based on convention. Only human beings go beyond basic natural communication to language proper, which requires establishing "nouns" by convention. Communicating feelings by sound is natural to human beings and shared with some animals, as the Epicureans claimed, but language proper is typically human and requires conventional agreement. Therefore, even the articulate sounds of parrots do not really constitute a language. All goats naturally use the same sounds to communicate but as true language requires agreement, human beings developed various tongues.

The text known as the *Political Regime* or *The Principles of Beings*, a more personal work of al-Fârâbî, confirms our interpretation as it tersely tells us that "language (*lisân*) is conventional but has some basis in natural things" and specifies that by "language" (*lisân*, a Qur'ânic term), he means the "idiom" (*lughat*) used by people.[21] The shift from a Qur'ânic term, in need of clarification, as it means both articulate speech and the organ of speech and taste, to a non-Qur'ânic term may indicate an attempt to take discretely distance from the theological background.

2. The Origin and Development of Language

In order to get clearer about what al-Fârâbî meant by language "is conventional but has some basis in natural things," we need to move to the second part of the famous *Kitâb al-Hurûf* or *Book of Letters*.[22] In it al-Fârâbî presents a sophisticated and complex view of the development of language and of the various disciplines. He does not take into account the theological views but, in order to validate philosophy in the Greek mode, he insists on the necessity of maintaining the purity of the language and for that will refer to historical events concerning the development of Arabic. The detailed account is presented simply as a narrative. I have divided it into three successive or slightly overlapping stages and shall highlight the overt principles that ground it. Though al-Fârâbî nowhere refers or even alludes to it, it is clear that the first part of the narrative, which retraces the earliest development of language, is based on observing children's language acquisition.

Let us now look at the first stage of language development, which originally is natural. As for the Epicureans, there is an original diversity of tongues and in each nation the process begins with ostension followed by the establishment of some utterances. Later on, this uncoordinated multiplication of utterances will give rise to the need for conventional agreement.

First, to communicate human beings will use ostension and later on join speech-sound to ostension. Al-Fârâbî does not simply indicate that there is an immediate diversity of tongues but gives an explanation for it. The diversity of tongues stems (1) from the slightly different physical constitution of the organs of speech in the various nations and (2) from the natural inclination of human beings to select the easiest way to achieve one's purpose (115). This principle of the natural inclination of human beings to select the easiest path will recur in al-Fârâbî's explanation of other phenomena. So each nation will develop the speech-sounds easiest for it (116). Elementary speech-sounds develop in two phases. First, they will be used to call the attention of someone and to indicate that the person called is the one one intends to address; second, distinct speech-sounds will refer to the various things pointed to in ostension (116).[23] These speech-sounds already vary from one nation to another and "this is the first cause of the differences among the idioms of the nations as these first speech-sounds are the letters of the alphabet" (118). I think that by "letters of the alphabet" al-Fârâbî means phonemes and that he still holds the rather naïve view that each phoneme corresponds to one letter. As these phonemes used as signs are limited in number, people will begin to combine them and form utterances consisting of two [or more] letters. These first letters and utterances will be signs for sensibles one can point to or for intelligibles formed from these sensibles.[24]

Al-Fârâbî now needs to explain how, from sensible particulars pointed to, one moves to universals. Some speech-sounds are proper names, so to speak, whereas others are signs for universals as they are used while pointing to some sensible and any other similar sensible. Distinct utterances will be used for distinct intelligibles (119) and al-Fârâbî explains how such utterances are invented and then spread among a nation:

That is how the letters and the utterances stemming from these letters arise in some people.

> First, this comes from any chance person from among them. It happens that one of them uses some speech-sound or utterance to signify some thing around them. The listener will then use the very same utterance while addressing the original speaker . . . so the two of them will have adopted this utterance and agreed about it. They will then address others with it until it spreads among the group. (120)[25]

The process al-Fârâbî has just described is similar to the quadratic structure in children's language acquisition explained by Dr. Daniel Dahlstrom.[26] This process will continue and more chance persons will create utterances up to the time when someone begins to manage their affairs and to create utterances for things that had remained unnamed. This man will be the language giver, succeeded by other rulers who also will be language givers until utterances are set down for all life necessities (120). This process goes from adopting utterances for things, such as the sky, the earth and what is in them, through adopting utterances for activities[27] resulting from their natural powers to dispositions acquired through these activities, be they moral or relative to the crafts, and to what they all know through experience and infer from it. Finally, utterances are adopted for the tools, etc., specific to each craft.

Up to now al-Fârâbî has claimed, though indirectly, that there never was one and the same language for all human beings. In this he follows Aristotle and takes some distance from common theological views. Yet, he refines what his master had asserted in maintaining that the development of language for each nation is first simply a natural phenomenon of very basic communication, but, when becoming more complex, requires the establishment of a convention between at least two people. As some things have remained unnamed at some stage a succession of human "language givers," who all have some leadership role, have completed this first stage of the process so that utterances, covering both nouns and verbs, have been set down for whatever people need for the necessities of life. Up to now there is a single utterance for each signification and for each kind of thing, aspect of thing, or activity, etc. The focus is on the necessities of life and crafts necessary for survival. What al-Fârâbî describes applies to any nation.

The second stage now begins. It goes beyond the bare life necessities and institutes a parallel between developments in language and creation of some intellectual disciplines. Desiring to match the utterances with the various meanings, chance people or leaders begin to organize universal terms into genera and species, which signify some resemblance between sensibles. Besides, just as some meanings refer to something fixed and stable but endowed with changing accidents, utterances must reflect this distinction between stable and essential features, and changing accidents. The second master,[28] i.e., al-Fârâbî as he is called in the Arabic philosophical tradition, here refers to a particular feature of Arabic. Words in Arabic dictionaries are classified by roots. The root is the equivalent of the stable or essential aspect and the addition of specific prefixes, suffixes, and infixes, plus changes in vocalization according to set patterns add shades of meaning to the root and gives rise to derived words. To give an example, *fataha* means "to open." The set pattern for instrumental words requires the addition of the prefix *mi-* and some changes in vocalization. We then get the word *miftah* or "instrument to open," i.e., "key." The set pattern of the sixth verbal form indicates that an action is mutual. The root *katab* means "to write," but add the prefix *ta-* and lengthen the first vowel and you get *takâtaba*, "to correspond, to exchange letters." Add the locative prefix *ma-* to this same root and you get *maktab*, "a place where one writes," i.e., "an office." This systematic ordering of words around their root and a desire to organize further the utterances backfires and leads to establishing a single utterance for various quite different meanings. Equivocity has reared its ugly head (125). Metonymy, homonymy, and synonymy follow suit and so do metaphors and attempts at embellishments. Younger people learned proper usage from the elders and a certain level of language correctness has been reached. People are now ready to engage in the development first of rhetoric and then poetry.

The emergence of rhetoric and poetry is particularly important for al-Fârâbî, as he follows the Hellenistic philosophy school of Alexandria and considers rhetoric and poetry as parts of logic proper and, therefore, classifies them as syllogistic arts.[29] Al-Fârâbî is fascinated by logic. Rhetoric uses unexamined opinions and figures of speech. Poetry makes great use of metaphors, and the human natural inclination to pursue organization and order in everything leads to the discovery of meters. The rhythm of the utterances gives them a certain ornament, harmony, and organization in relation to the length of time required to utter them (129).

People then extend the range of speeches and poems in order to record historical reports. Poets and speech makers coin new terms and find expressions easier to articulate and more euphonious. Poems, speeches and historical reports, as well as moral teachings, are memorized and transmitted to new generations. A rich oral tradition develops. At this point, says al-Fârâbî, language has been perfected. Correct usage is grounded in oral literary works but they multiply so much that memory fails to retain them all and writing is invented.

The third stage begins: people reflect on language, lexicography emerges, and scholars will search for people who most correctly speak the language. Al-Fârâbî gives the example of the Arabs, who to preserve the purity of their language went to consult the Bedouins in the desert as Bedouins are not like city dwellers, who are meeting foreigners and whose language, therefore, gets corrupted under such influence. He even tells that if a nation regrettably from a linguistic point of view does not have deserts, then language scholars should consult country dwellers in the very center of the area since they are further away from contact with foreigners. Grammarians, such as those of Kufra and Basra in Iraq, discovered the rules of correct speech and needed to create technical grammatical terms, i.e., words of second imposition, for instance, to signify the parts of speech. In order to create words of second imposition scholars have a choice: either they coin new utterances or they transfer the meaning from a current utterance to another meaning, so that one and the same utterance will have two meanings. Both practices were common but al-Fârâbî favors transference,[30] particularly that using a primary meaning most similar to the new and still unnamed one. Thus scholars develop the linguistic arts, which can be taught and learned, and it becomes even possible to give a cause for everything they say (137).[31] Once again we have a mix of nature and convention as scholars set rules for what developed spontaneously. The Bedouins speak most correctly, even if they have not the faintest formal knowledge of grammar. This stage of development ends with a much more complex and rich language, but this language now, though much richer, has become a source of ambiguities. The early perfect match between thing, intelligible, and utterance has broken down, but this does not seem to bother al-Fârâbî, as he will use ambiguities for his own political purposes. He concludes his presentation of this second stage of language development by stating that it has given rise to five arts: rhetoric, poetry, memorization, writing, and the language arts, which we can add to the crafts discovered in the previous stage (138).

Now a third phase begins and philosophy proper finally can emerge as people wish to know the causes of things. So the syllogistic arts of rhetoric and poetry will yield precedence to dialectic and sophistical reasoning. With time, people discover and understand that sophistical reasoning is based on ambiguities and then sophistical reasoning will fade and dialectic will occupy center stage. Along with dialectic mathematics and political science develop and interest in demonstration begins. Al-Fârâbî claims that at this stage people have reached the time of Plato (142): dialectic has been perfected and demonstration takes its first steps. Culmination of the syllogistic arts and of philosophy comes with Aristotle who reaches certainty thanks to demonstrative syllogisms:

> [People] continue to be engaged in these matters until things become settled where they were during Aristotle's time. Scientific inquiry then culminates in distinguishing all the methods, and the whole practical and theoretical philosophy is completed with no room left in it for investigation. Philosophy becomes an art that is only learned and taught. . . . The instruction meant for the elite will be by demonstrative methods only,

while instruction for common people will be by dialectical, rhetorical, or poetical methods. (143)[32]

Al-Fârâbî concludes that this is the order in which the syllogistic arts emerge in nations from their own innate gifts and natural make-up, that is to say, when their philosophy is not imported from another nation. Now I need to make clear that al-Fârâbî has gone so far from theological positions that he proudly proclaims that "religion comes into existence after philosophy" (147).[33] For him religion is simply a watered down more imaginative or poetical version of philosophy, which uses metaphors and similes to translate technical philosophical notions into a language ordinary people easily grasp. This implies subordination of religion to philosophy. All along this story of the development of language and the intellectual disciplines religion had received the silent treatment.

3. How to Translate Philosophical Terms?

We have seen the narrative for the development of philosophy and demonstration inside a nation but al-Fârâbî needs also to address the development of philosophy and demonstration in a nation that had not yet reached it on its own and so imported it. He tells us that such is the case for the Arabs who imported philosophy form the Greeks. How does one translate philosophical terms? One can, of course, coin terms, but the second master does not recommend this process, as he prefers the use of ordinary language terms transferred to a philosophical level in order to be better understood and sound less foreign, and so ensure that logic be no longer confused with Greek grammar. Al-Fârâbî first presents his general principles for any translation of philosophy texts and then applies them to the specific case of translations from Greek into Arabic.

If a philosophical word in the foreign source language, which he calls the first language, is based on a transfer from a primary meaning to a technical one and the target or second language has the same ordinary meaning, then one should use the equivalent meaning in the target language (155). If there is no such equivalent, one should then select the most similar meaning. But what can we do, if no similar meaning can be found?

The general rules for transfer are detailed and take into account all possible cases, but it is a pity al-Fârâbî does not give instances of application of these rules. For each philosophical meaning that was already expressed in the source language by means of a transfer from an ordinary term:

(1) if both the source and target languages share the same ordinary meaning, then one should adopt it;

(2) if there is no real equivalent, but there is a similar ordinary meaning in the target language, then one should adopt it;

(3) if there is an equivalent, but the transfer would not lead to the most similar philosophical meaning in the target language, then one should substitute for it the ordinary meaning most similar to the philosophical one in the target language;

(4) if no suitable ordinary meaning can be found in the target language—
something that according to al-Fârâbî rarely occurs—then there are three
options: (1) an utterance may be coined respecting the phonetic and linguistic structures of the target language; or (2) any ambiguous utterance
can be adopted and transferred; or (3) a new utterance may be created by
means of transliteration but one should take into account modifications
required by the phonetics of the target language.[34]

Al-Fârâbî then moves to the specific case of translations from Greek into Arabic
and claims that the translators tried to follow these four principles. He then attacks
Arabic purists who require that there not be any transliteration. Here he gives an
example: the term " *'unsur*" was used to translate both element and prime matter.
This homonymy created confusion, wherefore he criticizes some translations that
led to homonymy, whereas transliterating the Greek word "*stoicheion*" or element
as "*ustuqus*"—notice the prosthetic aleph to get phonetic inculturation as in Arabic
no word can begin with two unvocalized consonants, so that, for instance, Plato is
transliterated as *Aflâtûn*—, and "*hyle*" or prime matter as "*hayûlâ*" avoids confusion (156).

Turning, then, to those who prefer literal translations, al-Fârâbî concedes that
using ordinary terms in order to express philosophical meanings may lead to some
confusion, if readers have not realized that there was a transfer and so understand
them in their ordinary meaning. Such people were favoring coinages and trans-
literations. Al-Fârâbî defends his own preference for transfers whenever possible,
claiming that they make it easier than jargon for beginners to have some grasp of
philosophical notions. Of course, a good teacher will make students aware of the
possible confusion (157).

Al-Fârâbî ends this section with an examination of how philosophical meanings
of one and the same word can be multiple though related to one another, such as
by "*pros hen*" equivocation (158).

As example of adopting a word of similar ordinary meaning one can point
to ch. 13 of the first part of this work, in which al-Fârâbî explains that translators
used the term "*djawhar*" to translate "*ousia*" in the technical sense of "substance."
Originally in Greek "*ousia*" means "wealth," that which one possesses. *Djawhar*, a
Persian word, imported into Arabic means something precious, such as the ore of
minerals or precious stones, and so is a good equivalent to the original Greek word.[35]

Once again al-Farabi uses the principle of facility as well as an emphasis on
using words familiar to Arabic speakers. He also indicates that, though coinages
could avoid confusion, they are generally to be avoided as they make life more
complicated for beginners in philosophy. Transference of meaning helps them to at
least have some basic grasp of philosophical notions.

IV. Conclusion

Al-Farabi's narrative of the origin and development of language in the context
of the development of various disciplines is certainly substantive and independent of

any religious origin or intervention and goes far beyond the Greek sources. Originally language is a natural phenomenon grounded in a basic ability to communicate some feelings, common to human beings and animals, but soon the desire to extend the field of communication requires the establishment of conventions arising through ostension. The diversity of languages is a given arising from the slight differences in the speech organs of various ethnic groups. There never was a unique language for the whole of mankind. Originally, too, idioms were unambiguous, as for each thing there was a single intelligible or meaning and a single utterance. The proliferation of the utterances necessitated some ordering and this ordering is purely conventional and linked to leadership power. The second master is very interested in maintaining the purity of language and to link the development of language to the development of the five syllogistic arts in the following chronological order, rhetoric, poetry, dialectic, sophistical reasoning, and finally demonstration. Recall that grammar and the language arts are posterior to the first two syllogistic arts. Though the text presents a universal pattern of development valid for any ethnic or linguistic group, it also exhibits signs of inculturation. Al-Fârâbî curiously puts a parallel between the system of "forms" typical of Arabic and the distinction between essential and accidental. He also describes how lexicography and grammar began in Arabic and required consulting the Bedouins in the desert. He takes this study of the language of the Bedouins as an example of attempting to preserve the purity of the language, whereas in fact Muslim scholars tried to recover so-called pre-Islamic poetry kept alive in oral tradition in order to explain Qur'ânic *hapax legomena*. Philosophy perfected by Aristotle uses demonstration, whereas religion that follows philosophy both chronologically and ontologically employs only dialectic in the case of theologians and jurists, though they constitute the religious elite, whereas ordinary believers limit themselves to rhetoric and poetry.[36]

Lucretius had complained about the inaptness of Latin to express Greek Epicurean philosophy, but al-Farabi far from complaining about an inaptness of Arabic to express Greek philosophical meanings, explains how to translate technical terms and indicates a preference for transference from ordinary meaning to technical meaning rather than coinage or transliteration. In fact in matter of Arabic usage he is very conservative and does not deplore the ambiguities inherent to Arabic vocabulary but rather uses them for his own philosophical and political purposes. His positions are sophisticated and present an attractive alternative to most theological positions of his own time and explain why he subordinates religion to philosophy.

The Catholic University of America

Notes

1. J. L. Ackrill's translation in *The Complete Works of Aristotle: The Revised Oxford Translation*, ed. Jonathan Barnes (Princeton, N.J.: Princeton University, 1984).

2. Ibid.

3. Brad Inwood and L. P. Gerson's translation in *Hellenistic Philosophy: Introductory Readings*, 2nd ed. (Indianapolis: Hackett, 1997), 93.

4. Inwood and Gerson's translation, 16.

5. 5.1028–32: at varios linguae sonitus natura subegit/ mittere et utilitas expressit nomina rerum,/ non alia longe ratione atque ipsa videtur/ protrahere ad gestum pueros infantia linguae,/ cum facit ut digito quae sunt praesentia monstrent.

6. 5.1056–62.

7. Inwood and Gerson's translation, 16. Further material about the views of the Epicureans on the origin and development of language as well as their criticisms of a purely conventional account can be found in *The Hellenistic Philosophers*, ed. A. A. Long and D. N. Sedley, 2 vols. (Cambridge: Cambridge University Press, 1987), vol. I, translation, 97–98; vol. II, original texts with comments, 98–101.

8. W. A. Pickard-Cambridge's translation in *The Complete Works of Aristotle*.

9. See also 1.832 and 3.260; Martin Ferguson Smith's translation in Lucretius, *On the Nature of Things* (Indianapolis: Hackett, 2001), 7.

10. *The Jerusalem Bible* translation. On this section see Thérèse-Anne Druart, "Islam and Christianity: One Divine and Human Language or Many Human Languages," *Journal of Religion and Society* 9 (2007): 1–13.

11. Umberto Eco, *The Search for the Perfect Language*, trans. James Fentress. Oxford: Blackwell, 1995.

12. See Druart, "Islam and Christianity." Curiously, scholars writing on al-Fârâbî's conception of language and its origin do not refer to the Qur'anic verse. The exception is André Roman, "Aperçus sur la naissance de la langue à partir du *Kitâb al-Hurûf* d'al-Fârâbî," *Studia Islamica* 92 (2001): 135–136. On various exegeses of *Qur'ân*, 2:31, see Henri Loucel, "L'origine du language d'après les grammairiens arabes," *Arabica* 10 (1963–1964): 188–208; M. J. Kister, "Legends in *tafsîr* and *hadîth* Literature: the Creation of Adam and Related Stories," in *Approaches to the History of the Interpretation of the Qur'an*, ed. Andrew Rippin (Oxford: Clarendon Press, 1988), 82–114. On the place of the language arts in the Arabic classifications of sciences, see Ahmad Hasnaoui, "Les théories du langage dans la pensée arabo-musulmane," in *Aristote aujourd'hui*, ed. M. A. Sinaceur (Paris/Toulouse: Erès, 1988), 218–240.

13. "Adam and the Technical Terms of Medieval Islam," in *Words, Texts and Concepts Cruising the Mediterranean Sea. Studies on the Sources, Contents and Influences of Islamic Civilization and Arabic Philosophy and Science Dedicated to Gerhard Endress on His Sixty-Fifth Birthday*, ed. R. Arnzen and J. Thielmann (Orientalia Lovaniensia Analecta 139) (Louvain: Peeters, 2006), 439–454.

14. On translations from Greek into Arabic see, Dimitri Gutas, *Greek Thought, Arabic culture: The Graeco-Arabic Translation Movement in Baghdad and Early 'Abbâsid Society (2nd–4th/8th Centuries)* (London and New York: Routledge, 1998); Cristina D'Ancona, "Le traduzioni di opere greche e la formazione del corpus filosofico arabo," in *Storia della filosofia nell'Islam medievale*, ed. Cristina D'Ancona, vol. I (Turin: Einaudi, 2005), 180–252 (includes an extensive bibliography); and Cecilia Martini Bonadeo, "Le biblioteche arabe e i centri di cultura fra IX e X secolo," in D'Ancona, *Storia della filosofia nell'Islam medievale*, 261–281.

15. On this famous debate, see Gerhard Endress, *Grammatik und Logik. Arabische Philologie und griechische Philosophie im Widerstreit* (Amsterdam: Grüner, 1986), 149–299; Abdelali Elamrani-Jamal, *Logique aristotélicienne et grammaire arabe (étude et documents)* (Études musulmanes, 26) (Paris: Vrin, 1983), 61–7 and 149–63; and Muhsin Mahdi, "Language and Logic in Classical Islam," in *Logic in Classical Islamic Culture*, ed. G. E. Grunebaum (Wiesbaden: Harrassowitz, 1970), 51–83.

16. *Alfarabi's Commentary on Aristotle's* ΠΕΡΙ ΕΡΜΗΝΕΙΑΣ *(De Interpretatione)*, ed. Wilhelm Kutsch, S.J. and Stanley Marrow, S.J. (Beirut: Imprimerie Catholique, 1960). The translation is mine. Complete English translation by F. W. Zimmermann in *Al-Farabi's Commentary and Short Treatise on Aristotle's De interpretatione* (The British Academy) (London: Oxford University Press, 1981).

17. Arabic, 31, ll. 14–15; my translation.

18. A. W. Thompson's translation in *The Complete Works of Aristotle*.

19. Zimmermann's translation with some modification.

20. Haddad pointed me to this interesting passage, even if I do not share fully his interpretation in "Alfarabi's Theory of Language," in *American University of Beirut Festival Book (Festschrift). Centennial Publications 1866–1966*, ed. Fûad Sarrû and Suha Tamîm (Beirut: The American University of Beirut, 1967), 327–351; and *Alfarabi's Theory of Communication* (Beirut: American University of Beirut, 1989), 46–47.

21. *Al-Fârâbî's The Political Regime (al-Siyâsa al-madaniyya also known as the Treatise on the Principles of Beings)*, ed. Fauzi M. Najjar (Beirut: Imprimerie Catholique, 1964), 70, ll. 6–7.

22. Thanks to Dr. Charles E. Butterworth's courtesy and kindness I was able to use Muhsin Mahdi's up to now still unpublished 2nd edition of this text (1st edition, Beirut: Dar el-Machreq, 1969) as well as to consult the draft of his and Butterworth's complete translation. Muhammad Ali Khalidi has published an English translation of the second part in *Medieval Islamic Philosophical Writings*, ed. Muhammad Ali Khalidi (Cambridge Texts in the History of Philosophy) (Cambridge: Cambridge University Press, 2005), 1–26; and José Antonio Paredes Gandia has published a good Spanish translation of this second part: *Abû Nasr al-Fârâbî, El libro de las letras. El origen de las palabras, la filosofía y la religión* (Pliegos de Oriente) (Madrid: Trotta, 2004). As both editions and the translations refer to the same division into brief sections, I shall simply refer to the number of these sections.

23. Al-Fârâbî even dedicates a full paragraph to the description of the organs of speech. Ibn Sînâ wrote a full treatise on phonetics recently edited and translated by Solomon I. Sara: Ibn Sînâ, *A Treatise on Arabic Phonetics* (Munich: Lincom Europa, 2009).

24. In his *Du Coran à la philosophie. La langue arabe et la formation du vocabulaire philosophique de Farabi* (Damascus: Institut Français de Damas, 1994), on 200–207, Jacques Langhade gives a detailed study of this passage (119) and indicates that in it al-Fârâbî takes distance from early and contemporary grammarians of Arabic. He concludes that for al-Fârâbî no language or alphabet or script, not even Arabic, has a privileged status.

25. My translation.

26. See the paper of D. Dahlstrom, "Towards an Explanation of Language," *Proceedings of the American Catholic Philosophical Association* 84 (this volume): 39.

27. The Arabic term is *fi'l*, which is both an activity or action and a verb in the grammatical sense. We have now moved beyond simply "names."

28. In the Arabic philosophical tradition the first master is Aristotle.

29. See Deborah L. Black, *Logic and Aristotle's* Rhetoric *and* Poetics *in Medieval Arabic Philosophy* (Islamic Philosophy and Theology 7) (Leiden: Brill, 1990).

30. See the very interesting article by Guillaume de Vaulx d'Arcy, "La *naqala*, étude du concept de transfert dans l'oeuvre d'al-Fârâbî," *Arabic Sciences and Philosophy* 20.1 (2010): 125–176.

31. In his *Enumeration of the Sciences* al-Fârâbî focuses its first part on the "science of language," 3rd ed., ed. Osman Amine (Cairo: Dar el-Fikr el-Arabi, 1949), 45–52, which is followed by a section on logic, at 53–74. Medieval Latin version with German translation: al-Fârâbî, *Über die Wissenschaften. Die version des Dominicus Gundissalinus.* Lateinisch-Deutsch, trans. and intro. Jakob Hans Josef Schneider (Herders Bibliothek der Philosophie des Mittelalters 9) (Freiburg: Herder, 2006), 122–127 and 128–140. French translation from Arabic by Ilham Mansour, Al Fârâbî, *'Ihsâ' el 'ulûm* (Beirut: C.D.N., 1991).

32. My translation.

33. See also *The Attainment of Happiness*, last line of (55), "philosophy is prior to religion in time," Muhsin Mahdi's translation in *Alfarabi's Philosophy of Plato and Aristotle*, rev. ed. (Ithaca, N.Y.: Cornell University Press, 1969).

34. "If in philosophy there are meanings for which in the second nation no ordinary similar meaning can be found in any way—although this rarely happens—then, they must do one of three things: 1. invent utterances from the letters of this nation, or 2. homonymously express other concepts with them in some way or another, or 3. they must use the utterances of the first nation after they are altered so to make their articulation easier to articulate for the second nation. This meaning will be very strange to the second nation, for they would not have had it before, or anything similar to it (155)." My translation.

35. See Thérèse-Anne Druart, "Substance in Arabic Philosophy: Al-Farabi's Discussion," in *Proceedings of the American Catholic Philosophical Association* 61 (1987): 88–97; and Langhade, *Du Coran à la philosophie*, 357–363.

36   On the link between al-Fârâbî's views on language and his political philosophy, see Emma Ganagé, "Y a-t-il une pensée politique dans le *Kitâb al-Hurûf* d'al-Fârâbî?," *Mélanges de l'Université Saint-Joseph*, 57 (2004): 229–257.

Introduction of the Aquinas Medalist
Alasdair MacIntyre

Mark C. Murphy

When the recipient of a high honor is introduced by a student of his or hers, the reaction of the audience is, or should be, disquiet and foreboding. Will the speaker seize the opportunity, and the microphone, in order to force the captive audience to submit to a variety of legends about the introducer's philosophical hero or minor anecdotes about moments in seminars or hallway conversations or mailroom encounters long past? So I immediately put your mind at ease. I will not use this opportunity to recount at length "How Alasdair MacIntyre broke up the Beatles," or "How Alasdair MacIntyre almost carried out the fatwa against Salman Rushdie," or "How Alasdair MacIntyre's house almost got TPed by a group of Notre Dame graduate students," or any of a legion of minor though I assure you true and intensely interesting stories. Listening to the recitation of such tales will remain on a volunteer basis, perhaps immediately after the banquet, in one of Baltimore's many fine nearby establishments.

Alasdair MacIntyre was educated at London, Manchester, and Oxford—he holds no doctorate, though, save honorary ones, so I recommend that you do not address him as "Dr. MacIntyre"—and taught at Manchester, Leeds, Essex, and Oxford before emigrating to the United States. Here he has taught at Brandeis, Wellesley, Boston University, Vanderbilt, Yale, and Duke. Just this year he retired from his post as senior research scholar at the Center for Ethics and Culture at the University of Notre Dame, and is now senior research fellow at the Centre for Contemporary Aristotelian Studies in Ethics and Politics at London Metropolitan University.

Professor MacIntyre has had a scholarly life marked both by tremendous range and by its sustained attention to a single problematic. He published his first book—*Marxism: An Interpretation*—at the age of twenty-four. Since then he has authored fourteen more books and nearly two hundred articles, on topics ranging from Freudian psychoanalysis to the nature of religious belief to power industry ethics to Confucian and Aristotelian understandings of the virtues to the recovery and reappropriation of the work of Edith Stein. The range of MacIntyre's work exhibits amazing learning both within the discipline of philosophy and outside it (his work draws upon literature, the history of social institutions, findings in contemporary ethnology, and so forth).

While diverse, MacIntyre's bibliography has been unified by devotion to a single project. MacIntyre's work—even the early writings from the 1950s and 1960s which he himself has described as "fragmented" and "messy"—exhibits a remarkable consistency in its direction, and from the late 1970s on he has been concerned to defend with great depth and completeness, and with attention to all of the possible rivals that he can confront, a specific view of morality and politics adherence to which would place one massively at odds with our present cultural condition. MacIntyre has always been centrally a moral and political philosopher, and his inquiries in other philosophical fields—philosophy of social science, philosophy of religion, along with studies of various individual figures in the history of philosophy—has been at the service of moral and political investigation. But this moral and political philosophy is itself put forward as a contribution to social criticism, to criticism of our prevailing social, political, economic, and cultural institutions.

From the beginning of MacIntyre's career, his inquiries were focused by three convictions: first, that moral and political thought must always remain firmly situated within social practices, that any attempt to engage in moral and political reflection untethered from the particularities of practice becomes mired in irresolvable conflict; second, that practical and theoretical questions inevitably arise within social practices, so that quietism is a non-option, and some standpoint for criticism is necessary; third, that the large-scale ideologies that modernity has to offer (Marxism, Freudian psychoanalysis, liberalism) all suffer from one or another deep rational deficiency. What makes his early writings appear heterogeneous and fragmented is that he takes up, aiming to understand and to assess, the wide variety of viewpoints on offer. These early studies are nearly unrelentingly critical in their appraisal of the very different viewpoints and are tentative and provisional in their suggestions with respect to the prospects for a reconstruction of a standpoint from which rational social criticism could take place. What makes his later writings, by contrast, much more obviously unified (despite their varied subject-matters) is that they are at the service of elaborating, defending, and modifying in response to criticism the positive account that he began to offer systematically in the great and massively influential *After Virtue* (1981) and continued to develop and modify in the subsequent *Whose Justice? Which Rationality?* (1988), *Three Rival Versions of Moral Enquiry* (1990), and *Dependent Rational Animals* (1999), along with the various articles he published in the 1980s, 1990s, and early 2000s.

What has MacIntyre taught us? He has taught us that a proper emphasis on particularity in ethics—of the historical and social situatedness of its problems and standards, articulated by MacIntyre in terms of the rationality of traditions—is necessary for theoretical progress and leads away from, rather than toward, relativism. He has taught us how the morasses of contemporary moral theory, both in metaethics and normative ethics, can be explained by the modern rejection of Aristotelianism. He has taught us that political life suitable for beings like us is possible only within a certain type of political community—not generic 'community,' but a very specific *type* of community—one in which commitment to and honoring the good of both the relatively able and the relatively disabled makes possible rational inquiry into the nature of the good life, both individually and in common. And he has taught us that the premier example of the recognition of these methodological, ethical, and political truths appears in the philosophy of St. Thomas Aquinas—philosophy that desperately needs to be understood, appropriated, furthered, and (in good Thomistic manner) corrected.

I present to you the recipient of the Aquinas Medal, Alasdair MacIntyre.

Georgetown University

On Being a Theistic Philosopher in a Secularized Culture

Alasdair MacIntyre

Charles Taylor has distinguished three ways in which a society may be secularized: first, by churches and other religious organizations losing their hold upon secular institutions, especially those of government; secondly, by the exclusion of religious belief and practice from the arenas of public life; and, thirdly, by belief in God coming to be considered just one option for belief among others and a problematic option at that. To this third aspect Taylor's great book on secularization is principally devoted. And no one could quarrel with his insistence on the importance of all three. Nonetheless I want to claim that what is salient in the ethos of *our* secularized culture needs to be characterized rather differently. Consider some defining features of that culture.

First, ours is a culture in which it is widely held that what theists and atheists disagree about and have reason to disagree about is the existence of God and only that. About everything else, about everything that comprises nature—that is, everything except God—there is, so it is widely believed, no reason to disagree. I contrast this view with what I take to be the theistic understanding of that disagreement, that it concerns some aspects of *everything*. To be a theist is to understand every particular as, by reason of its finitude and its contingency, pointing towards God. It is to believe that, if we try to understand finite particulars independently of their relationship to God, we are bound to misunderstand them. It is to hold that all explanation and understanding that does not refer us to God both as first cause and as final end is incomplete, and that foremost among the finite particulars of which this is true are we ourselves as human beings.

A second conviction of our secularized culture is that argumentative disagreement between atheists and theists is rationally unresolvable—neither party can supply a conclusive argument—and that *therefore* belief in God, as a matter of private nonrational determination, should receive no substantive recognition in the arenas of public life. The 'therefore' and the 'substantive' are important. The 'therefore' relates two of Taylor's three characterizations of the secular, by making one a justification for another. It is *because* belief in God has become problematic that it is to play no substantive part in public life.

Note that theistic belief in God is understood to be an expression of something called 'religion.' 'Religion' is an important classificatory label in secularized society, grouping together primitive animism, Greco-Roman and Hindu polytheisms, the theism of Judaism, Islam, and Christianity, Joseph Smith and Mary Baker Eddy, so that the contrast is between religion in all its various forms and non-religion, the secular. For aggressive unbelievers 'religion,' thus understood, is the name of an all-purpose trashcan, while some believers—consider Schleiermacher and Otto—and some unbelievers—consider Feuerbach—have searched earnestly for 'the essence of religion.' But this is not how genuine theists understand things.

For theists the basic contrast is between those who worship God and those who make the highest object of their devotion some finite object or state. So on this theistic classification primitive animists, Greco-Roman polytheists, and atheistic twenty-first-century professors and journalists with their finite objects of devotion all belong together, to be contrasted with practicing Jews, Christians, and Moslems. It follows that theists should have no particular interest in defending religion as such and have good reason for uneasiness when public discourse is framed in terms of a contrast between the religious and the nonreligious. But I put this line of thought aside for the moment, although I will take it up later.

Let me instead remark that it is also characteristic of our secularized society to believe that it is the *argumentative* disagreements between theists and atheists that are fundamental. What atheists assert is that theists need, but cannot provide compelling arguments, that it is on success or failure in *argument* concerning God's existence that everything turns. This contrasts with the theistic belief that at a fundamental level the differences between theists and atheists are of quite another kind. For theists what matters most is not the issue of God's existence or nonexistence, but the contrast between His presence and His absence, between those occasions when He manifests Himself in and through particulars and those dark nights of the soul when He withdraws from us. To someone engaged in prayerful practice of the presence of God, whether Hasidic Jew, or Ignatian Christian, or Sufi Moslem, the thought that perhaps God does not exist would be an idle thought, certainly not a thought to be responded to by philosophical argument any more than the fanciful thought that some human friend whom one only hears from at long intervals has perhaps never existed.

Of course some philosopher might say that, if there is indeed such a thing as genuine awareness of the presence of God, then the question of whether or not God exists should have been settled to everyone's satisfaction long ago. To which the only possible response is that of C. S. Peirce, in his reply to the objection posed to his own personalist theism, that "if there is a personal God, we must . . . be in personal communication with him. Now, if that be the case, the question arises how it is possible that the existence of this being should ever have been doubted by anybody." To which Peirce replied that "facts that stand before our face and eyes and stare us in the face are far from being, in all cases, the most easily discerned" ('The Law of Mind' in *Philosophical Writings of Peirce*, ed. Justus Buchler, New York: Dover Publications, 1955, 352). To discern them we need not argument, but to be open to those facts as Newman was open, when he perceived his own existence and that of God as "luminously self-evident."

I am not implying that philosophical argument about the existence of God is pointless, nor of course was Peirce or Newman. But its point, so far as theists are concerned, is not to reassure *us* as to God's existence, but to exhibit the groundlessness of atheism. So theists argue—and I take the argument to be sound—that if God did not exist, there would be only finite and contingent particulars, perhaps an infinite chain of them. But there could not have been *only* finite and contingent particulars, for nothing could have sustained such particulars, whether an infinite or finite set, in continuing existence. That is, if God did not exist, there would have been nothing. If God did not exist, there would be no atheists to say so. I do not need to rehearse the standard atheist's disgusted reply to this, a reply that matters more to her or him than it does to theists, since for theists less depends on the outcome of argumentative exchanges and nothing whatsoever with respect to the place that theistic practices and institutions should have in the arenas of public life. What then, on a theistic view, should that place be and why?

Newman as an historian remarked on the fact that the political establishment of the church has always been bad for the church, often very bad indeed. If we take this to be true—as I do—not only of the church, but also of Protestant churches, of mosques, and of synagogues, then we have a strong theistic reason for holding that in political society none of them should be politically established. So, although for a very different reason from the secularizers, theists can be and should be in favor of political forums in which a variety of theistic and other voices are all heard.

So far then I have identified two beliefs as characteristic features of our post-Christian society: a belief that disagreement between theists and atheists is about God, but not about nature, and a belief that the crucial disagreements between theists and atheists are argumentative disagreements. In each case what I have suggested is that theists reject or should reject this characterization of their quarrel with atheists. Let me now take the first of these a little further by clarifying the nature of the disagreement between theists and atheists over how nature is to be understood.

A widely held belief in our secularized culture is that the tasks of explanation and understanding are to be assigned to the natural sciences and to the social sciences just insofar as they approximate to the condition of the natural sciences. Explanation and understanding are correspondingly conceived so that only what can be explained by such sciences counts as explanation. The outcome is a proposition towards which atheists and theists take very different attitudes. Atheists assert that every type of particular, every event, and every state in nature can be explained by those sciences. To this the theistic reply is that, so long as you conceive of explanation as such atheists do, this is undeniably true. So about what then do we and they disagree? We and they disagree about how explanation is to be conceived.

What natural scientific investigations enable us to explain is how finite beings have come to be what they now are and how they will come to be what they will be. Such investigations begin from a recognition that some particular type of cause has produced some particular type of effect and our then asking how—how on earth!—we are to explain why and how such effects issue from such causes. The answer will be a more fundamental story of causal sequences that in turn invites explanation at a still more fundamental level. And at the same time we construct from the sequences provided by those causal explanations a narrative of the cosmos, from as near to its beginnings as we can get to as far into the future as we can predict. So we move from everyday narratives that begin with the planting of seeds and that end with the flowering and fruiting of apple trees to causal narratives that substitute for the beginning of this story an account of adjacent molecules and of chemical reactions between them, and finally to causal narratives that substitute for an account of molecules and chemical reactions an account of fundamental particles and their interactions. None of these stories is in itself incomplete. The relevant sciences can always supply an account of *what* happened and of *how* it happened. And no degree of complexity defies explanations in these terms. But every such explanatory narrative cries out for further explanation, for explanation of how *this* particular input would have resulted in *that* particular output, until—and here we approach the point at which theists and atheists disagree—what atheists take to be the final step, the step at which, having arrived at our narrative about quarks or leptons or bosons or whatever, it turns out that natural science has nothing more to add. But does this mean that nothing further requires explanation? Not at all. What still requires explanation is why the changes and chances of nature are such that they enable such striking transformations to take place. Consider one notable story about nature that we are now able to tell, a story, like all the others, of inputs and outputs.

The inputs with which this particular story, the story of the genesis of human beings, begins are a set of hadrons, leptons, and bosons. The outputs with which it ends are a set of opera-loving, James Joyce quoting, equation-solving atheistic physicists. This is amazing! What makes it amazing is not at all the improbability of the outcome. Any particular statistical distribution of fundamental particles is, given their past distribution and the nature of their interactions, going to be highly improbable. Nor is it a matter of our being impressed by degrees of or kinds of complexity. Nor is it that there is some explanatory gap in the step by step story of how it all happened. What is amazing is that, given *that* input, *any* step by step narrative should lead to *this* extraordinary outcome. How can this be possible? What could have made it the case?

Let me put those questions in another way. The account of the cosmos given by contemporary physicists has a place for hadrons, leptons, bosons, for strong and weak forces, for electromagnetism and gravitational attraction, and perhaps for strings and eleven dimensions. What it has no place at all for are physicists, nor indeed for any intentionality-informed agents. If what contemporary physics asserts is true, it is difficult to understand how physicists are even possible. Yet physicists are what in the end result from the interactions of particles. And that is not all. For physicists in the course of, say, bombarding protons and neutrons, in order to verify the existence of quarks, alter the course of those particles, so that they behave as the experimenters' intentions require and not as they would otherwise have done. Intentionally effective agents recurrently restructure this or that small part of the order of nature in accordance with their intentions. So here we have a story which both begins and ends with fundamental particles, but in which physicists are the transforming agents.

Science explains each of the steps in each of these stories. What it does not explain is why the stories have the structures and sequences that they do, why a universe that is at its physically fundamental level devoid of intentionality should, as it moves thermodynamically towards its own destruction, generate not just intentionality, but such technicolor examples of intentionality as those provided by opera-loving, James Joyce quoting, equation solving, atheistic physicists. Whatever might explain this, no yet to be told story about fields or forces or particles or strings as yet to be identified will provide anything like what is needed, for the problem just is that of explaining how *any* physical agency whatsoever could produce such an outcome. And here of course atheist and theist diverge. For atheists insist that there is no problem. They resolutely refuse to be amazed at their own existence.

The atheist says "That is just how it is. When explanation by physicists terminates, explanation terminates." Theists retort that, if, when explanation of causal sequences in the physical would was first proposed long ago, the response had been "That is just how it is," the scientific enterprise would never have been undertaken, and that there is no more reason to be content with "That is just how it is" now than there was then. And, so theists finally insist—after a further round of argument—that nothing can explain such relationships of input to output, nothing can make the workings of nature intelligible, except the will and purpose of some being whose intelligence, like His other powers, are not limited in the way that the powers of finite beings are limited, a being with unbounded abilities to astonish us.

The disagreement of theists and atheists then is in key part about explanation, about what it is that requires explanation, about what it is to provide an explanation, and about what it is for an explanation to be complete or incomplete. Disagreement about the existence of God is, among other things a consequence of disagreement about explanation. Are such disagreements about explanation rationally resolvable? If we take this to mean "Is there a prospect of atheists and theists agreeing upon what such a rational resolution would be?" then the answer is plainly "No." But this is not to concede that the issue is not rationally resolvable. For atheism involves a diminished and restricted conception of explanation and understanding and the onus is upon the atheist to justify the restriction, to show that our astonishment at the transformation of particles into physicists is not as much an expression of a legitimate demand for explanation as is our astonishment at the transformation of seeds into apple trees.

Note that I am not advancing an *argument* against the atheist, let alone an argument from premises that atheists accept. What I am pointing to is a disagreement about premises rooted in the atheist's incapacity for a certain kind of wonder. Atheists have no difficulty in appreciating aesthetically what are sometimes called "the wonders of science," such structures as those of the eye or the DNA helix. But they are quite inadequately astonished by some features of the cosmos. The nineteenth-century painter, J. M. W. Turner, while walking in the Welsh mountains suddenly and unexpectedly came upon a striking landscape. His response was to shout out

"Well done, God!" That was very much my own response, when I first came across Richard Dawkins. And it is the capacity to respond to nature in this way that is at the heart of theism, a capacity that tends to disappear as a culture is secularized.

Let me turn now to another very different feature of our secularized culture, its underappreciation of Nietzsche, its reduction of Nietzsche to just one more philosopher with one more set of theories, its domestication of Nietzsche. Theists owe Nietzsche an enormous debt. For Nietzsche was the atheist who understood far better than any other what and how much the atheist's rejection of theism involves. If God does not exist, then no point of view is privileged. There is only my perspective on how things are, your perspective, her perspective, their perspective. And that is to say, there is no such thing as how things are. We may choose of course to privilege this or that standpoint and we may construct a genealogy of this or that standpoint. But underlying all such projects are acts of self-affirmation expressed in our choice of standpoint.

Many philosophers before and after Nietzsche have denied that this is so and have insisted that there is an ordered reality independent of and prior to our perceptions of it and our judgments about it, some of them as persuaded of the truth of atheism as Nietzsche was. What Nietzsche claims is that such philosophers have failed to recognize that their belief in such a reality is a vestige of a theism that they have been unable wholly to discard. And indeed what followed in twentieth-century philosophy were a set of inconclusive debates between antirealists and realists with respect to a variety of subject-matters, so that, while any conception of "a God's eye view of things" was and is found unacceptable, yet at the same time a reluctance to discard realism remained and remains as powerful as it was when Nietzsche first identified it and tried to undermine it. So at the level of theory secularized philosophy inherits a set of unresolved and *de facto* unresolvable philosophical disagreements, while at the level of practice there is a tacit agreement to privilege certain standpoints and to ignore the arbitrary character of that privileging: the standpoint of science as such, the standpoint of morality as such, the standpoint of art as such, and sometimes even as a counterpart to these the standpoint of religion as such. What is missing here is any shared conception of an overall order of things and of the relationship of the particular findings of particular sciences, of the particular practical conclusions of ethics and politics, and of the particular makings of particular arts to such an order.

Consider in this light what is currently presented as the standpoint of morality as such. At the level of philosophical theory the key disagreements are those between quasi-Kantians, updated contractarians, and ever more sophisticated utilitarians and the disagreements are not only between the upholders of each of these theoretical points of view, but also between those who believe that to hold any one of these sets of positions commits one to rejecting the other two and those who hold that a great work of reconciliation between them is at least possible and may perhaps already have been achieved with the publication this year of Derek Parfit's *maximum opus, On What Matters.*

At the level of everyday moral practice however what we find is neither stark disagreement nor reconciliation, but rather an oscillation between on the one hand unconditional affirmations of inviolable rights of various kinds and on the other claims that this or that right can in this particular case be overridden in the name of the maximization of utility, perhaps the maximization of economic prosperity or that of national security or that of the therapeutic capacities of medical science. Rights that are in one context treated as inviolable are in another treated as not just open to being overridden, but such that we are required to override them. So economic progress may on occasion justify the destruction of types of neighborhood community, and national security may warrant the use of torture against terrorism. The resulting form of the moral rule in this culture is "Always tell the truth, always keep promises, always refrain from taking innocent life, except when . . . " The catalogue of exceptions is one that is open to indefinite further extension and revision. And alongside the categories of the required, the prohibited and the permissible we now find the category of the indefinitely debatable, that about which we are able to agree to disagree, not only with others, but sometimes with ourselves.

I took note already that many such disagreements are between those who on some particular occasion uphold the inviolability of someone's right to have or do or be free from such and such and those who hold that on this particular occasion our interest in securing this or that aspect of our well-being and our natural inclination to achieve our well-being are such that we ought to treat *this* case as an exception to an otherwise exceptionless rule. Since in the dominant culture there is available no shared impersonal standard by appeal to which such disagreements might be rationally adjudicated, they are in fact resolved, if at all, by some form of nonrational persuasion. Participants in such disputes often think of themselves as weighing a variety of relevant considerations, but the problem with this metaphor, as I have remarked elsewhere, is that there are no scales. Yet the thought that there are no scales is one that those participants rarely have an opportunity to entertain. And this is not the only thought effectively excluded by this conception of moral precepts and moral debate.

Imagine that someone were to attempt to intervene in contemporary public debate with a claim that we are unconditionally bound to obey a certain rule not in spite of our interests and natural inclinations, but because of them, that our nature is such that our end is such that we cannot achieve it except by respecting a law to whose giver we are accountable. What such a one had to say would inevitably go unheard. I do not mean to imply by this that such a view might not be entertained, even if briefly and curiously, in the arenas of purely theoretical discussion. But in the arenas of everyday public debate it would be too oblique to the terms of the controversies to secure a hearing and it would be treated as an irrelevant interruption. So another effect of secularization is to make theism morally irrelevant and often enough morally invisible. And this too has consequences.

"If God does not exist, then everything is permitted." The declaration that Dostoievski put in the mouth of Ivan Karamazov has often been misinterpreted. Karamazov was not saying, Dostoievski through Karamazov was not saying, that atheists are free from all moral constraints, that, if atheism is true, anyone is morally free to do anything at any time. What Karamazov *was* saying, what Dostoievski through Karamazov *was* saying, was that, if we take atheism to be true, then there is no type of action, no matter how horrifying, of which we can be sure that we could never find good reason to perform it, that it would never be overwhelmingly and overridingly in what we took to be the general interest to perform it. Dostoievski through Karamazov was not predicting Auschwitz or the Gulag. He was predicting the fire-bombing of Dresden and Tokyo, the saturation bombing of the Ruhr and the obliteration of Hiroshima and Nagasaki. He was predicting not the crimes of the obviously wicked, but the crimes of the apparently good, types of action that it is rational to prohibit unconditionally *only* if one is a theist. But it just this kind of position that will appear at best groundless, at worst unintelligible, to those whose presuppositions are those of our secularized culture.

It is worth remarking that in the attitudes and judgments characteristic of this kind of secularized morality there is not a trace of relativism. If by relativism we mean the doctrine that there is no appeal beyond the contingently established standards of one's own culture, then there are of course and have been some—a very few—philosophical relativists, most notably Richard Rorty. But I know of very few moral philosophers who have agreed with him—Gilbert Harman anticipated him—and everyday moral discourse is even more inhospitable to Rorty's doctrines than were and are his professional colleagues. So that when apologists for the morality of Catholic or Protestant Christianity or Islam lament what they mistakenly take to be the moral relativism of the contemporary world they add gratuitously in an unfortunate way to the misunderstanding of what it is that puts our secularized culture at odds with theism.

A much deeper misunderstanding is at the heart of the matter. It informs each of the three aspects of intellectual conflict between atheists and theists that I have considered so far, their disagreement about the place that arguments concerning the existence of God have in defining the issues that divide them, their disagreement about what it is to understand and to explain the natural world, and their disagreement about morality. In all three cases it is not just that atheists and theists disagree, but that they disagree about how to characterize their disagreement. And the debates between theists and atheists in the public arenas of our culture are generally and characteristically framed in terms that already presuppose the atheistic understanding of those disagreements.

Theists who imprudently enter into such debates equally generally and characteristically invite their own defeat. For they find themselves cast in the role of defenders of apparently untenable positions: to the atheist who requires of the theist a conclusive argument for the existence of God—conclusive, that is, in the atheist's terms—the theist has nothing conclusive to offer; to the atheist who demands that theology provide explanations of particular natural phenomena that are incompatible with and superior to those of natural scientists, the theists who accept that challenge—from Archdeacon Paley to contemporary intelligent design theorists—convince no one but themselves and the late A. G. N. Flew; to the atheist who insists that neither moral judgment nor moral action require belief in God the theist's reply seems to violate both the autonomy of the moral sphere and the autonomy of the moral agent.

Since the atheists' presuppositions in all three areas are widely shared in our secularized culture, it is not just atheists, but the spectators of these debates who generally find the theistic case unimpressive. But this does not necessarily result in any straightforward rejection of theism. For our secularized culture is happy to find a place for the intellectually defeated theist within an area of thought and practice that it distinguishes sharply from the areas assigned to the sciences, to technology, to the arts, to morality, and to law and politics, the area of religion.

What differentiates the sphere of religion from other spheres is that within it everyone is free as a private person to define their own position and no one is able to make effective claims for that position in any public sphere. Laboratories, engineering plants, museums and art galleries, law courts and political assemblies, and forums of institutionalized moral debate about rights and utility, these constitute the arenas of public life. Churches, synagogues, mosques, yoga classes, Zen Buddhist monasteries, New Age spirituality, all these belong elsewhere. Within the sphere of religion you may assert—almost—anything, including denials of the denial of the public relevance of religion. But you will effectively go unheard outside that sphere or rather you will be heard only insofar as what you say can be interpreted as a contribution to some other sphere, that of morality, say, or politics. And indeed there are those who think that a suitably attenuated theism can be a source of attitudes that are culturally valuable in those spheres.

We would therefore be making a mistake, if we supposed that a high degree of secularization and the survival and even flourishing of some kinds of religious belief and institution are incompatible. What matters is the emergence of a conception of religion that segregates religion from other concerns. In a theistic culture the question is inescapably posed in each area of human life of what it is to acknowledge God in the activities of that area and the answers that are given shape those activities, whether secular or religious, activities of philosophical and scientific enquiry, activities of artists and construction workers, activities of farmers and fisherman, activities of rulers and ruled. There are indeed in theistic cultures notable issues about the relationship of secular to ecclesiastical authority. But in such cultures the exercise of secular authority involves an acknowledgment of God quite as much as does the exercise of ecclesiastical authority. It is only with the cultural defeat of theism by secularization that the secular becomes secularized.

So finally the question is posed: *if* what I have claimed is by and large true, what are the tasks of a theistic philosopher who inhabits our present culture? The word "if" is important. I have in this brief time done no more than sketch positions and gesture at arguments. You almost certainly remain unconvinced and rightly so, but, if you were to be convinced, what would be the implications for those tasks?

Some of them would of course be what they have always been: to work within and extend our own traditions of philosophical enquiry, Jewish, Christian and Islamic, Augustinian and Thomist, phenomenological and analytic, entering into conversation and debate with each other as well as with such great critics of theism as Hume, Diderot, Feuerbach, Russell, and Sartre. But now we have to make ourselves more aware than we have been of the difficulty in framing the terms of debate in the current intellectual climate. We have to remain good listeners who are responsive to our critics, but not make ourselves into victims of those critics.

Instead we need to redirect the debates by focusing on the philosophical presuppositions of our critics and making *them and their position* rather than theism the matter for debate. We have to portray accurately and sympathetically the secular and secularizing cast of mind, so that we can exhibit ruthlessly the distortions, the weaknesses, the moral, scientific, and metaphysical vulnerabilities of that cast of mind. And this is something that we have so far by and large failed to do. Our most notable predecessors in this task were not by profession philosophers. I think especially of some of Chesterton's journalism and of some of Evelyn Waugh's novels. What we now need are thinkers who combine philosophical acumen and argument with the wit of Chesterton and the satire of Waugh. But that, you may say, would take a miracle! Miracles of course can never be ruled out. But what it would certainly take is a new kind of philosophical education. What kind of education would that be? Happily, that is a question for another occasion.

Towards an Explanation of Language

Daniel O. Dahlstrom

Abstract: After reviewing basic features of language, this paper reviews a central debate among twentieth-century philosophers over the proper analysis of linguistic meaning. While some center the analysis of meaning in language's capacity to be true, others locate meaning in the communicative intentions of the users of the language. As a means of addressing this impasse and suggesting its unfounded character, the paper draws on recent studies of language acquisition and relates them to existential dimensions of language.

καὶ Ἀμὴν λέγω ὑμῖν,
ἐὰν μὴ στραφῆτε καὶ γένησθε ὡς τὰ παιδία,
οὐ μὴ εἰσέλθητε εἰς τὴν βασιλείαν τῶν οὐρανῶν.

Matthew 18, 3

The following paper is an attempt to work towards a philosophical explanation of language and by that I mean an account of what is essential to language. What distinguishes this account is the fact that it is based upon consideration of some key conditions of language acquisition. I contend that this genetic turn is justified and suitable since, far from outgrowing these conditions, we—normal users of a natural language—realize them in existential uses of language.

The paper contains three parts and a conclusion. In Part One I give a preliminary sketch of what language is. In Part Two I consider a central and long-standing impasse among philosophers of language over the proper analysis of linguistic meaning. While some philosophers look for the source of linguistic meaning in the intentions of language users in communicating, others insist that meaning essentially depends on the truth or falsity of what is communicated. After drawing up the lines and stakes of this impasse, in Part Three I look to new, usage-based approaches to language acquisition for clues to resolving this impasse. In conclusion I suggest that the key to the essence of language is its existential dimension, not least because that dimension—the situation-based demand to speak and listen as authentically as we can—incorporates in a paradigmatic way the conditions of language acquisition, set forth by the new approaches discussed in Part Three.

I. What Language Is

Language is a means of communicating. I take 'language' here to designate our native tongue(s), *Muttersprachen* in the sense of both the languages of our respective mothers and the languages on which we have been nursed. Language under this description is a living language, a language natural to groups of native peoples and their descendants in the course of their evolution, in contrast to the more straightforwardly artificial languages of science, computers, or even music. Not every means of communicating is language, so construed. Other species communicate and we speak, more or less figuratively, of telecommunications, of intercellular and intracellular communication of information, genetic and otherwise, and so on. So to assert that language is a means of communicating is in no way to give, in the traditional sense, a definition of language. We have no specific difference; we have, at best, identified a genus and, indeed, a rather indeterminate one at that.

Yet from the commonplace that language is in some sense communication, we can infer that language always involves at least two parties, even if the speaker and the listener are in the same body. Communication in natural languages is a conversation, a dialogue, where each speaker has some understanding not simply of her words (what they say and what she is trying to say with them) but of how the listener is likely to take them. The understanding need not precede the utterances or come fully formed in advance of them, particularly in a running conversation, but even in the latter the conversant can usually give at least an *ex post facto* rationale for what she finds herself saying or to have said. That rationale, like the understanding and the communication itself, is locally and globally inter-subjective: local because it involves the two or more immediate, actual conversants; global because it draws its warrant from more potential subjects than the actual conversants themselves.

The speaker and the listener, I suggested, may be in the same body, agreeing with the Eleatic Stranger's observation in Plato's *Sophist* that thinking is an "inward dialogue carried on by the mind with itself without spoken sound."[1] Whether thinking is always and only an inner dialogue remains unclear to me, but it does seem right that most of the time thinking is a conversation that I am having with myself.[2] The point is controversial, to be sure, with Chomsky and maybe Husserl insisting for different reasons on sharply differentiating communication from thinking in the form of soliloquy.[3] But there are reasons to think that the difference is not an essential one. In the first place, whether talking with one another or talking with ourselves, we rely upon the same words and sentences to understand, make judgments, and come to conclusions about something. Moreover, even if we allow for wordless thoughts, "the use of language for self-addressed utterances is," as Dummet puts it, "an imitation of its use in linguistic interchange."[4]

This brief excursus into the controversial status of soliloquy brings to the fore the other salient dimension of language. In the conversation there is something communicated or at least an attempt to communicate something. The conversation is about something. If language is fundamentally intersubjective, involving a relation between subjects or between a subject and itself, it is no less objective, involving a relation between the subject or subjects and some object. Note that this aspect of language, what we might call its "disclosiveness," "aboutness," "inherent intentionality," or simply its "meaningfulness" is present not simply for declarative sentences, assertions, and judgments, expressed in the indicative mood, but also for questions, commands, and wonderings expressed in the subjunctive. It also bears noting that lots of things other than language can be about something else, can mean something in the sense of designating or denoting it. Pictures, signs, works of art, buildings, and arguably even some thoughts may mean something in the absence of language.

Like these other forms and objects of meaning, however, language is about things in particular ways that have been inherited and become established, making it possible to investigate the ingredients and structure of language itself. Here I have in mind what is explicitly said and heard, the words and word-combinations themselves, at arm's length from any particular user, usage and references. If we use words to speak about things, we do so in ways ordained by the grammars and lexicographies, the syntax and semantics, of our mother tongues.

II. How Language Is Able to Mean Something: The On-going Debate

Thanks to the rules of standard usage in our native language, we use words to designate things, i.e., to refer to them, and to do so in certain ways because the words have meanings that allow us to refer to things as this or that. As is well known to all of us, this semantic aspect of language has particularly exercised philosophers in the twentieth century. Seminal in this connection is the work of Frege who urged us to distinguish meaning from reference in order, among other things, to be able to make sense of identity statements where the symbols identified have the same referent but each mean something different, as in "The Evening Star = The Morning Star" or "7 + 5 = the number of Apostles."[5] In this tradition, Donald Davidson developed the basic insight that we understand a language when we understand what it is for a sentence to be true in that language. Putting Tarski's formal semantic definition of truth to work in the service of a theory of meaning, Davidson argued that "to give truth conditions is a way of giving the meaning of a sentence"; or, as he also put it, "we want to achieve an understanding of meaning or translation by assuming a prior grasp of the concept of truth."[6] Regardless of what a speaker intended or meant to say, we can trace the meaning of what is said, at least what is said in the form of a declarative sentence, by determining the conditions under which it is true or false.

Though this emphasis on formal semantic analyses of linguistic meaning seemed to come at the cost of considerations of communication, other philosophers of language midway through the last century were, of course, paying close attention to speech acts and conversation. On the view of these thinkers, the fact that syntactic and semantic rules of linguistic meaning can be formalized is less significant for understanding their role in language than the fact they are rules precisely for the purpose of communication. For Paul Grice, the meaning of a sentence is to be elucidated in terms of what the speaker of the sentence means and the speaker-meaning in turn is to be elucidated in terms of the speaker's intentions.[7] In other words, the way to understand a sentence's meaning is to understand what someone means by uttering the sentence. Notice the patent shift from the Davidsonian approach discussed earlier; speaker-meaning replaces sentence-meaning as the center of gravity for the understanding of language. Grice analyzes the speaker's meaning, i.e., what someone means by uttering a sentence, into an intention to elicit a response from a hearer or audience on three levels. The person uttering the sentence intends that the audience (a) has a particular response to the utterance, (b) recognizes that this response was the utterer's intention (or, more precisely, recognizes that the utterer intended the audience to have this response to what the utter said), and (c) has this reaction on the basis of this recognition. For example, Brutus's shame on hearing Caesar's words "*Et tu, Brute?*" is based upon the recognition that Caesar makes this utterance precisely to produce this response.

Of course, even when our fictional Caesar asks his questions, he's relying upon the conventional meanings of these words. We could imagine Caesar using the same words in happier times ("Et tu, Brute? Do you want come over to the house for a beer, too?"). Grice himself distinguishes between speaker meaning and word or sentence meaning. However, his insistence that the latter is founded in speaker meaning has continued to be controversial, not least because the words appear to retain a certain meaning, regardless of the speaker's intention on a certain occasion. Neo-Griceans, like Wayne Davis, have modified Grice's account to the effect that an expression is said to mean this or that if and only if it is conventional for people, i.e., the users of the language, to use the expression to mean this or that. Corresponding conventions regarding communication and interpretation must also be in place.[8] Grice's basic idea that meaning supposes ideas, beliefs, and intentions on the part of the users of the language remains in force. But understanding how conventions enable us to express ourselves allows for "the transition from speaker meaning to linguistic meaning."[9] At the same time, as Davis puts it, "The neo-Gricean analysis also enables us to explain why, despite the autonomy of word meaning, speaker meaning is the more fundamental phenomenon."[10] Sometime in the last thirty years, for example, people began to use the word 'spin' for public apologetics and that usage caught on, so that this meaning of the term is now conventional. A host of other terms related to the internet have similarly become conventional, through usage, but came into being because of speakers' intentions in using them.

In the past few paragraphs I have been glossing two different directions taken in the philosophy of language over the last half-century or so. Peter Strawson contended that the proponents of these two orientations were engaged in "a Homeric struggle" over what is essential or basic and what is inessential or derivative in language.[11] The formalists espouse the general idea that "the syntactic and semantic rules together determine the meanings of all sentences of a language and do this by means, precisely, of determining their truth-conditions."[12] On this formalist account, no recourse to communication is needed to determine these truth-conditions. By contrast, the "communication-intention theorists," as Strawson labels them, insist that the meanings of language can only be understood by reference to communication.

Forty years after Strawson's presentation of this conflict, the two approaches continue to resonate. In a 2003 study, Wayne Davis recognizes the truth-conditional analysis as the leading alternative to his Neo-Gricean analysis.[13] In "Arguments for the Truth-Condition Theory of Meaning," William G. Lycan defends this sort of theory against possible objections from positions he lumps together as "use" theories.[14] This past year, in an entry entitled "linguistic understanding" for *A Companion to Epistemology*, Christopher Peacocke calls the thesis that a sentence's meaning is given by its truth functions "the most influential idea in the theory of meaning for the past hundred years."[15]

The debate in short is long-standing and, while philosophers of language on both sides of the debate constantly refine its terms, the issue of explaining language at bottom in terms of its potential truthfulness or its potential to be communicated remains in force. If, as suggested at the outset, language is fundamentally both communicative and disclosive, the seeds of this debate are patent. As soon as we inquire into the relation between these dimensions, the prospect presents itself that one of them is more basic, at least for language.[16]

Of course, given the truism that language is both communicative and disclosive, there is a "specious" form of the debate, as Lycan puts it.[17] Consider two potential voters, hearing a candidate for re-election declare: "There were no scandals among my staff." Voter A takes the declaration at face value, its meaning is the meaning of the sentence; by contrast, Voter B takes the declaration as the candidate's attempt to set up a contrast between his staff and his opponent's; for Voter B, the meaning of the declaration is the speaker's meaning, what the speaker meant or intended by saying it. But there is no incompatibility here since the two voters are concerned with different meanings, sentence-meaning and speaker-meaning respectively. If one pounds on the table and insists that one of the two meanings is the *real* meaning, it is hard to see how that insistence reveals anything more than a preference for the interest of one or the other voter.

If, however, one argues, à la Neo-Griceans, that sentence-meaning and even the truth conditions for it, are grounded in "a complex function of possible speaker intentions," then there is a form of the debate that is far from specious. So, too, the debate is substantive if one maintains that truth-conditions characterize, not merely sentence-meaning, but what a speaker means in making an utterance on a particular occasion. On one side of the debate are those who take language's communicative function to be prior to its disclosive function; for those on the other side, the reverse holds.

Both sides of the dispute obviously have something right. Language is something that we do, more or less intentionally. It seems to fly in the face of our experience of using language to discount the fact that we intend something by what we say or to regard it as secondary to the formally determinable constraints on the semantics of the language we use to say it. On the other hand, whatever we intend to say and however we intend to say it piggy-back unmistakably on the possibility of saying the truth, a possibility that is given by conventionally instituted sentence-meanings. Intentions to lie, to dissemble, to suggest, to hypothesize, to express a belief, and so on by saying certain things suppose that saying those things or saying other things to which they are directly connected can be true. In light of such considerations, it would seem that the attempt to treat one of the two basic factors of language as more basic than the other is a mistake. But if it is a mistake, then some account must be given of their equally basic character and, indeed, in tandem with one another.

III. How Language Is Acquired

For some clues to such an account, I would like to turn to some relatively recent approaches to explaining language acquisition. Here, too, there is a feud instructively analogous to the philosophical debate we have just been reviewing. In the 1950s B. F. Skinner theorized that the way that children learn a language is through instrumental conditioning (based upon principles of association) combined with generalizations (based upon the requisite stimuli and principles of induction).[18] In 1959 Chomsky advanced an influential argument that the stimuli, on Skinner's theory, were too meager to account for what children learn when they learn a language. There is a "poverty of stimulus" available to children, as Chomsky put it, to account for their ability to acquire the correct grammar for their language. Since reliance upon induction from experience alone is incapable of providing a mechanism for determining which set of possible grammatical principles is the correct one, Chomsky infers that, in acquiring a language, children are guided by an innate, universal grammar.[19] Today Chomsky's basic argument for an innate, generative grammar continues to resonate positively with theorists of language acquisition.[20]

In the past decade, however, researchers have challenged this reigning approach to language acquisition on the basis of new research on early childhood development and new approaches to linguistics. Perhaps the most striking feature of the new research is a better understanding of children's pre-linguistic abilities to read others' intentions and to recognize patterns, auditory as well as visual. In contrast to the Chomskian tradition, Michael Tomasello argues that linguistic structure emerges from language use, such that "the essence of language is its symbolic dimension, with grammar being derivative."[21] Without denying by any means that humans are biologically prepared for language, Tomasello contends that language is a product of ontogenetic and historical processes of social interaction and the cognition entailed by that interaction.[22]

Tomasello puts forward specific and, as might be expected, controversial arguments against Chomsky-inspired approaches.[23] More important for our purposes are the new perspectives on the phenomenon of language that Tomasello's positive account of language acquisition yields. His account, it bears noting, is phylogenetic as well as ontogenetic. He claims that humans alone communicate symbolically because, in contrast to other animals, they alone attempt to direct or share the attention of others (their conspecifics).[24] Tomasello seems to me to be overreaching here and, for that reason, I pass over his phylogenetic arguments.[25] Yet, even if the difference between some nonhuman primate communication and human communication may in some regards be more a matter of degree than kind, Tomasello is certainly right to emphasize the overwhelmingly symbolic character of human communication. After all, humans have developed natural languages, systems of communicating through symbols, unlike any system of communication of any other animal, let alone primates.

In Tomasello's ontogenetic account of language, he stresses how, far from fitting the old Skinnerian-behaviorist model of isolated associations and induction, a child's process of learning a language is "integrated with other cognitive and social-cognitive skills."[26] By the time children are five months old, they have concepts, recognition of sound patterns, and capacities of associating different aspects of experience with one another. Yet they typically remain unable across cultures to produce or comprehend linguistic symbols at that age and, indeed, until after their first birthday. At around nine months, however, children develop capacities to act in ways that require an understanding of their social worlds. Tomasello hypothesizes that the social and cognitive development involved in acquiring these pre-linguistic capacities is precisely the place to look for the explanation of the subsequent language acquisition in children. Because there is an important sense in which we do not outgrow these capacities, I would like to take a moment to review Tomasello's account of them and the evidence for them.

The first such capacity is the capacity for joint attention. When a child learns to follow the gaze of an adult, it takes a crucial step forward by, in effect, learning to share a joint attentional frame. For example, when a child and an adult play together with a ball or building blocks, they jointly attend to the same objects and combinations of objects, ignoring other objects within the same perceptual field. This attentional interaction is not simply triadic (as Tomasello puts it), involving the partners in dialogue and the subject matter of the dialogue, but quadratic, since it also involves a common, perhaps undifferentiated intentionality. In other words, what is distinctive about joint attention is not simply a common frame of relevance but rather that a shared intentionality constitutes that frame, providing the background condition for communication generally.

The next key pre-linguistic, but language-enabling capacity is the child's capacity to differentiate the intentionality of others, to understand their communicative intentions within those shared attentional frames. It is one thing for a child to hear a parent's voice, even as indicating something, quite another to read an intention off that voice as the parent's intention. There is no doubt a progression to this ability of intention-reading. For example, a child may or may not come to recognize a parent's intention as the parent places it in a seated position. There is a higher level of complexity when the parent says to the child "Sit down" and the child recognizes the point of the command and acts on it. But there is an even higher level of complexity when the child *obeys* the command, i.e., acts on what it perceives is the parent's intention from what the parent says.

Joint attentional frames and understanding another's intention go hand-in-hand and not simply in early communication between a child and parent. To illustrate this dual-structure in an adult setting, consider the following two scenarios. In a foreign country whose language you do not know, a local asks you for directions to the train station; you do not have a clue what she is saying. By contrast, at a train station in the same country, you may manage to communicate to the ticket agent that you want a ticket to some well-marked destination. The difference in being able to communicate in the latter context is the common background provided by the setting (train station) and the roles and places of particular possible communicators in that setting (ticket agents, customers), allowing them to read off or at least guess each other's intention.

The third capacity crucial to a child's ability to communicate symbolically is the capacity for role reversal imitation. Imitation, Aristotle tells us, is "one of a human being's advantages over the lower animals" (*Poetics* 1448b6f) and, while children mimic adults very early, around nine months they begin to imitate adults' intentional actions on outside objects. Included in this mimicry is the use of tools, including the symbolic artifacts that form language. Tomasello cites two studies, albeit of children between 16 and 18 months old, which provide evidence of this capacity to imitate intentional behavior.[27] In the first study, one group of children witnessed adults successfully perform a certain action, while another group witnessed adults failing at the action; yet children from both groups subsequently reproduced the target actions equally well. In the second study, after watching adults perform certain actions that produced a desired result intentionally and other actions that produced it accidentally, children mainly reproduced the intentional actions.

However, it is not mere imitation but a certain kind of imitation that allows a child to learn a communicative symbol. In order to be able to use a symbol to communicate, the child must do more than simply imitate an adult when an adult says to it, for example, "Mama's over there." If it literally imitated the adult, the child would be saying this to itself. Instead, it must imitate by way of reversing its role with the parent, so that it directs the expression to the adult in the way that the adult directed the expression to it. In role reversal imitation, the child, formerly the addressee, exchanges roles with the adult who now becomes the addressee. Only at this stage of development does the child display an ability both to produce and consume a token of the language, to understand that speaking and listening go hand-in-hand, that one speaks because one presupposes a listener capable of a token of that same speech, albeit from her own position.

In this sense, language acquisition presupposes rudimentary forms of social-cognition from (a) joint attention (sharing attention toward some object with others) to (b) recognition of another's distinctive intention to (c) imitation of others through role reversal. Hand-in-hand with the development of these levels of social-cognition, children learn to grasp what others are attentively pointing at and to direct others' attention to distal objects by pointing themselves. Learning to point in this sense takes time; it is typically absent in infants before they are six months old, but present in most by the time of their first birthday. Tomasello identifies three levels of gestures, running from the non-symbolic to the symbolic, learned by children prior to learning language. The most elementary gestures are ritualizations, such as a child raising its arms as a sign that it wants to be picked up. Ritualizations are gestures that children and nonhuman primates have learned are effective. Ritual gestures are not symbolic; the child makes the gesture without the intention of affecting the intentions of the adult. The child makes the ritual gesture simply to be picked up. There is communication here, to be sure, but not via a shared communicative symbol.

The next level of gesture is indexical, holding up something or pointing to something in ways that are designed to focus someone else's attention on it. Not all such pointing involves this purpose, Tomasello notes, and in many cases pointing remains ritual gesture, performed simply to get something done, "not as an invitation to share attention using a mutually understood communicative symbol."[28] In order for a child to point in this way, it has to see and imitate, not simply what the adult does, but the adult's process of doing it to communicate an intention.

The third level of gesture is the referential gesture, via iconicity or metonymy, as when a child spreads its arms to indicate an airplane or blows to indicate something hot. Here, too, the outward character of the gesture may be the result of some ritualization. But the distinctiveness of these referential gestures is the fact that they involve role reversal as the child imitates the adult's use of them to direct the child's attention to the referent.

Referential gestures are clearly symbolic and a child's ability to communicate through such gestures appears to be an important precursor of its ability within a few months to learn language. Thus, in its first year, building on its capacities for joint attention and recognizing that others have intentions, indeed, communicative intentions, a child develops a capacity to imitate by reversing roles, enabling it to engage, not simply in ritual gestures, but in indexical and iconically referential gestures. With this development, the child learns to infer others' communicative intentions from their gestures and, through role reversal imitation, to use gestures itself for its own communicative intentions.

Allow me to summarize this gloss of Tomasello's theory of language acquisition, insofar as it depends upon the aforementioned key aspects of language acquisition. Children are able to learn a language, a symbolic form of communication, precisely by virtue of developing prelinguistic capabilities, each of which entails distinctive levels of social interaction and cognition. Co-operative communication does not depend upon language acquisition but rather language acquisition depends upon it.[29]

Conclusion

What does the ontogenesis of language tell us about the nature of language? Are there aspects of language acquisition that we do not outgrow? Conventions and the so-called deferential meanings of linguistic expressions no doubt allow us, quite efficiently, to bypass repeating the painstaking process a child goes through in learning to wield particular symbols for the purposes of communication and in general to communicate symbolically.[30] Moreover, conventions are not simply convenient but necessary, even despite the fact that all too often, thanks to the convenience of convention, talk is cheap, perhaps no more so than in our 24/7 media world and with the seemingly endless possibilities of communicating over the internet.

Nevertheless, there are cases, running from the exceptional to the quotidian, where we are called upon—sometimes by ourselves, sometimes by others, by the context or even the nature of the linguistic symbols themselves—to own up to our language. On one end of this spectrum are instances such as responding to a police inquiry, testifying in court, making marriage or priestly vows, confessing, speaking in the course of performing a sacrament, counseling and being counseled, speaking intimately, signing our names, and so on. On the other end, there is the situational use of indexicals and demonstratives, the use of 'you' and 'this' and other such context-sensitive expressions. In these cases I cannot rely on lexicography alone any more than I can when I make a vow. I have to authenticate my uses and, indeed, I have to somehow see to it that you take me as doing so. When I say 'you' here, I mean you, my audience, here and now, and this meaning can only hold thanks to our presence to one another in this situation, your presence to me as what I refer to when I say 'you' and my presence to you as the one using 'you' in just this way. Here the twin functions of language, to communicate and to refer, necessarily and happily coincide.[31]

The uses of language just glossed point to the fact that, despite the talk of use and usage, language is not simply a tool that we can pick up or put down as we wish. Instead in these uses of language we testify to who we are, the thoughts we think, the lives we live, and the worlds we inhabit. For this reason, I refer to such uses as existential uses of language, in keeping with a now familiar use of the term 'existential.' Language in this existential sense, symbolic communication that allows us to be responsible to the world and to one another, defines us but only insofar as it is the language we speak. Like a child's pre-linguistic pointing and gesturing, these existential uses of language are at once disclosive (i.e., referential and potentially true) and communicative. What I am proposing is that, for a philosophical explanation of language, for a determination of the essence of language, we look to the existential uses of language, the very uses that are grounded in human development, specifically, the sorts of social interaction and cognition that appear to underlie language acquisition. If we take language in this sense, we can continue to distinguish its disclosive (referential and alethic) dimensions from its communicative dimensions, but we can never separate them, never pretend to derive one from the other or construe one as more fundamental than the other.[32] From this existential and developmental vantage point, the debate between formalists and communication-intention theorists is, as Strawson aptly but incriminatingly dubbed it, a "Homeric struggle"—a struggle grounded in myth.

When we teach children how to speak, to listen, and to use language at all, our interest is in getting them to do so authentically. To this end, we avoid tropes and speak to them sincerely, straightforwardly, and simply; in this way, without conceit, we name, describe, and thereby communicate things to them. Of equal importance, they imitate us. So there are strong reasons to suppose that the early use of language is highly authentic—children are concerned with communicating effectively, and their teachers are generally concerned with helping them do so—and that our later inauthentic uses of language are parasitic upon learning how to do things, correctly, with words. What we find in these authentic uses of language are the two components mentioned at the outset—communication and world-disclosure—inseparably combined in a single intention.

Boston University

Notes

1. Plato, *Sophist* 263e; see *Theaetetus* 189e; Michael Dummett, *The Seas of Language* (Oxford: Clarendon Press, 1993), 184f.

2. Three difficulties with the thesis that soliloquy is communication deserve flagging here. The first difficulty is that of applying Grice's maxims to thinking. A second difficulty concerns miscommunication as a standing possibility of communication, something that is arguably precluded in soliloquy (thus, while I can misunderstand the content of someone else's utterance, it's hard to see how I could misunderstand what I myself meant in uttering it). A third difficulty is the regress that the thesis seems to set off. If I communicate what I think—my thoughts—to someone via language, then communication presupposes that I already have the thoughts. So if thinking were itself communication, then it would seem we need to communicate before we can communicate. While I suspect that these considerable difficulties are surmountable, I set them to the side since the main argument of this paper does not depend upon the interpretation or correctness of the thesis that soliloquy is communication.

3. Chomsky, *Reflections on Language* (New York: Pantheon, 1975), 71; Husserl, *Logische Untersuchungen*, II/1 (Tübingen: Niemeyer, 1968), §8, S. 35–36.

4. Dummett, *Seas of Language*, 185.

5. Gottlob Frege, *Grundgesetze der Arithmetik* (Hildesheim: Olms, 1962), § 32, S. 50–51; John McDowell, "On the Sense and Reference of a Proper Name," *Mind* 86 (April, 1977): 159. Challenging Frege's and Russell's descriptivist accounts of names, Kripke taught us that we have to understand names, not as definite descriptions, but as rigid designators, identifying the same reference in all possible worlds.

6. Donald Davidson, "Truth and Meaning," *Synthese* 17 (1967): 310 and "Belief and the Basis of Meaning," *Inquiries into Truth and Interpretation* (New York: Oxford University Press, 1984), 150.

7. Paul Grice, *Studies in the Way of Words* (Cambridge, Mass.: Harvard University Press, 1989), 91. Not to be overlooked in contributing to this shift in focus to what speakers do in using language is the influential work of J. L. Austin, with his differentiation of locutionary, illocutionary, and perlocutionary acts, critically taken up by Peter Strawson and John Searle; see J. L. Austin, *How to Do Things with Words* (Oxford: Oxford University Press, 1962); Peter Strawson, "Intention and Convention in Speech Acts," *Philosophical Review* 73 (1964): 439–460; and John Searle, *Speech Acts: An Essay in the Philosophy of Language* (Oxford: Oxford University Press, 1969). For a concise review of how differences within this group amount to different ways of developing Austin's approach, see Anita Avramides, "Intention and Convention," in *A Companion to the Philosophy of Language*, ed. Bob Hale and Crispin Wright (Malden, Mass.: Blackwell, 1999), 69.

8. Wayne A. Davis, *Meaning, Expression and Thought* (New York: Cambridge University Press, 2003), 163: "We will observe that conventions to use words to express or indicate certain ideas are correlative with conventions to use them to communicate those ideas and with conventions to interpret the words as expressing the ideas." See, too, ibid., 166–167 192–193.

9. Avramides, "Intention and Convention," 60 (see, too, Avramides's helpful review of Lewis's view of convention and her concluding remarks in ibid., 80–84). Of course, construing convention in this way can serve to underscore that a Gricean analysis remains essential to understanding language or that it is in fact dispensable, at best a ladder that can be kicked away. As Blackburn notes, even if Grice has given us a useful account of how, in the absence of language or some communicative system, one person manages to communicate with another (i.e., an account of the necessary conditions for that sort of communication), communication, once learned, can give way to conventions that dispense with the analysis of the intentions; see Simon Blackburn, *Spreading the Word: Groundings in the Philosophy of Language* (New York: Oxford University Press, 1984), 113.

10. Davis, *Meaning, Expression and Thought*, 194.

11. Peter Strawson, "Meaning and Truth," in: *Meaning and Truth* (Oxford: Oxford University Press, 1970), 104–105; see, too, the discussion of "Use Theories vs. Formal Theories," in Avramides, "Intention and Convention," 61–63.

12. Strawson, "Meaning and Truth," 107.

13. Davis, *Meaning, Expression and Thought*, 170.

14. William G. Lycan, "Direct Arguments for the Truth–Condition Theory of Meaning," *Topoi* 29.2 (2010): 99–108; Gabriel Segal, "How a Truth Theory Can Do Duty as a Theory of Meaning," in *Donald Davidson: Truth, Meaning, and Knowledge*, ed. Urszula M. Zeglen (London: Routledge, 1999), 45–52.

15. Christopher Peacocke, "Linguistic Understanding," in *A Companion to Epistemology*, ed. Jonathan Dancy, Ernest Sosa, Matthias Steup (Malden, Mass.: Blackwell, 2010), 492.

16. After noting language's two primary functions of being "an instrument of communication" and "a vehicle of thought," Dummett contends we are "impelled to ask which of the two is primary"; see Dummett, "Language and Communication," in *The Seas of Language*, 166.

17. Lycan, "Direct Arguments," 100.

18. B. F. Skinner, *Verbal Behavior* (New York: Appleton-Century-Croft, 1957).

19. Noam Chomsky, "A Review of B. F. Skinner's *Verbal Behavior*," *Language* 35 (1959): 26–58; see also, Chomsky, *Language and Mind* (New York: Harcourt Brace Jovanovich, 1968) and "Rules and Representations," *Behavioral and Brain Sciences* 3 (1980): 1–61. By the 1980s, building on Chomsky's work, many researchers set forth the continuity assumption, the notion that, throughout a child's development, the basic linguistic representations are the same since they stem from a single universal grammar.

20. See Stephen Laurence and Eric Margolis, "The Poverty of the Stimulus Argument," *British Journal of the Philosophy of Science* 52 (2001): 217–276. Laurence and Margolis defend a version of this argument against its philosophical critics, from the early challenges by Nelson Goodman and Hilary Putnam to more current objections by Fiona Cowie and others. Without any innate biases, Laurence and Margolis argue, children would be unable through induction

alone, based upon the data available to them, to come up with the principles of regularity governing the structure of language. "Not only are the data invariably an idiosyncratic finite sampling of an infinite set of sentences, but they're also degenerate" (Laurence and Margolis, "The Poverty of the Stimulus Argument," 230). Yet children overcome grammatical failures and infelicities that they hear. Moreover, they do so, that is to say, they grasp and incorporate into their use of language structures that are homologous across different languages, thus lending further support to the Chomskian contention that there is an innate language module, a universal grammar.

21. Michael Tomasello, *Constructing a Language: A Usage-Based Theory of Language Acquisition* (Cambridge, Mass.: Harvard University Press, 2003), 5.

22. Ibid., chap. 8, "Biological, Cultural and Ontogenetic Processes," 282–322.

23. Ibid., 288–290. Among other things, according to Tomasello, neither the universality of structure nor the poverty of stimulus (both supposed by Chomsky's theory) are in fact present and a combination of evolutionary and historical features of interpersonal communication adequately explain the development of grammars.

24. As Tomasello puts it, "nonhuman primates do not use communicative signals to convey meaning or to convey information or to refer to things or to direct the attention of others, but rather use them to affect the behavior or motivational states of others directly"; see ibid., 11.

25. While treatment of these arguments need not affect the central aims of the present paper, two issues in this connection may be flagged. First, there is the issue of how one goes about determining the negative in question, namely, that, in gesturing or making sounds, nonhuman primates and other species are not attempting to direct or share the attention of others. Second, while nonhuman primates may make sounds or may gesture, on Tomasello's account they do so primarily in the form of commands and to regulate dyadic interactions (grooming, play, sex, travel) rather than to refer to outside objects. As he puts it: "Most strikingly, nonhuman primates do not point or gesture to outside objects or events for others, they do not hold up objects to show them to others, and they do not even hold out objects to offer them to others" (ibid., 10–11). However, at least some commands or sounds regulating those interactions would seem necessarily to include information about the environment (hence, at least a triadic relation). Indeed, Tomasello seems to contradict the statement just quoted when, in discussing the most primitive level of gesturing in children, he observes: "This learning process is essentially the one by which nonhuman primates learn their gestures" (ibid., 32).

26. Ibid., 3.

27. Ibid., 26–27.

28. Ibid., 33.

29. In terms of the Homeric philosophical struggle over meaning discussed earlier, this account of language acquisition supports both sides of the debate. On the one hand, the child begins to communicate with a parent within a proto-Gricean framework for interaction, a shared intentionality. That is to say, the child develops an awareness that doing certain things will not simply produce certain behavior in the child's mother but will produce the behavior because the child knows that the mother understands or interprets what it is doing or saying and why, i.e., its intentions for doing or saying what it does. On the other hand, the child learns a language no less because its intention in communicating is also referential, aimed at—among other things—directing its mother's attention to something outside them both.

30. Gareth Evans, "The Causal Theory of Names," *Proceedings of the Aristotelian Society, Supplementary Volumes*, 47 (1973), 205: "Although standardly we use expressions with the intention of conforming with the general use made of them by the community, sometimes we use them with the *over-riding* intention to conform to the use made of them by some other person or persons. In that case I shall say that we use the expression *deferentially* (with respect to that other person or group of persons)."

31. Note that there are three dimensions to this claim, coinciding with the three dimensions of speaker meaning, sentence meaning, and truthfulness. In owning up to our use of language, we place ourselves under an obligation to match speaker meaning with sentence meaning, to mean what we say and say what we mean, correctly intimating our beliefs, desires, and so on in the process. But, under certain interpretations, a liar may be said to do as much; i.e., she says what she means and means what she says. So the obligation, in keeping with these paradigmatic uses of language, is also to the truth of what is said, to depicting and acknowledging—as faithfully as one can—the world as it actually is. The proviso 'as faithfully as one can' is necessary for anyone who, as a non-expert, is faced with the limitations of relying at times upon deferential word-meanings, where the most likely truthful story is a matter for an expert.

32. Language consists of seven elements: (1) a speaker, (2) a listener, (3) a set of symbols (conventional signs for intentional acts of meaning, referring to, questioning, commanding, exhorting, exclaiming, wondering, etc. some thing or some state of affairs), (4) a speaker's intention in speaking, i.e., using those signs, (5) a listener's recognition of the speaker's intention and/or the conventional significance from that use, (6) a communicative context, including a set of historically definite, background conditions, and (7) the truth or falsity of what is said or of what is entailed by what is said as a paramount background condition. Neither the communicative nor the referential and alethic aspects of language are more basic than the other. A suitable explanation of language should not attempt to reduce one to the other but recognize their equally fundamental status. A child points because there is something to which it is pointing and because there is someone whose attention it wants to direct to the object of its pointing and because it has learned that others use this gesture in an analogous way. Symbolic communication in the form of natural languages rests upon this pre-linguistic phenomenon.

Language and Philosophy in the *Essays* of Montaigne

Ann Hartle

Abstract: Montaigne chooses to write the *Essays* in French, the vulgar language, rather than in Latin, the language of the learned. He uses only the words that are heard in the streets, markets, and taverns of France. And he speaks about the body and the sexual in a manner that goes beyond the limits of propriety. The language of the *Essays* perfectly reflects Montaigne's philosophical project, the re-ordering of philosophy to the lowest rather than the highest, to the ordinary rather than the extraordinary. By bringing the private into the public, he frees the private from shame and creates the new, modern public space, i.e., society. The invention of the essay is the invention of society.

Montaigne's project is the restoration of philosophy to man. Like Socrates, who brought philosophy down from the heavens and into the cities of men, Montaigne brings philosophy down from the heavens and into the streets and markets and taverns of France. Montaigne's restoration is the re-ordering of philosophy and, at the same time, the re-ordering of human life as such.

I will argue that Montaigne re-orders philosophy to the human, rather than the divine; to the lowest, rather than the highest; to the weak, rather than the strong; to the imperfect, rather than the perfect; to what is, rather than what ought to be; to the particular, rather than the universal; to the domestic and private, rather than the political; to the ordinary, rather than the extraordinary. In the terms of the traditional hierarchy, this re-ordering looks like a mere "lowering" of the mind. However, I will argue that Montaigne's overcoming of the hierarchy is really a new kind of freedom, the freedom of the mind to order itself and to order the world.

The language of the *Essays* perfectly reflects Montaigne's philosophical project. I will begin with a brief discussion of several features of Montaigne's use of language. I will then set out Montaigne's understanding of the philosophical act. Finally, I will turn to his philosophical project and show how his use of language is integral to his project.

The Language of the *Essays*

Montaigne himself often draws attention to the language of the *Essays*, in particular the following four features. First, his writings are "purely human and philosophical, with no admixture of theology." He sets forth "notions that are human and [his] own, simply as human notions considered in themselves" (VS 323, F 234).[1]

Second, the *Essays* are written in French, rather than Latin (the language of the learned). Montaigne's first language was Latin. His father, who had formed certain unusual ideas about education, hired a tutor who spoke nothing but Latin with the young boy. In fact, the entire household joined in this project, so that Montaigne heard and spoke only Latin until he was six years old. As a young man, he was sent to the College de Guyenne in Bordeaux where he excelled in the study of Latin literature. Yet, Montaigne chose to write the *Essays* in French, giving only his quotations from the ancient philosophers and poets in their original Latin or, rarely, Greek. French, he says, is a "weaker idiom" than Latin (VS 440, F 320).

Third, not only does he choose the weaker idiom, Montaigne insists that he simply follows common usage in his writing (VS 796, F 604). He makes no attempt to dress up his thoughts in the manner of those who want to seek the world's favor. "In language," he says, "the search for novel phrases and little-known words comes from a childish and pedantic disposition. Would that I might use only those that are used in the markets of Paris!" (VS 172, F 127). He tells us that he does not avoid any of those words that are used in the streets of France (VS 875, F 667). And he asks: "Do we witness more of a jumble in the chatter of fishwives than in the public disputations of the professional logicians? I would rather have my son learn to speak in the taverns than in the schools of talk" (VS 926–927, F 707). The *Essays* are written in the language of the markets, the streets, and the taverns of France, not in the language of the schools or the courts. Further, in spite of the apparent disorder of the essays, Montaigne insists that it is order that he seeks above all. But this is "the order that we see everyday in the altercations of shepherds and shop boys," never among the learned (VS 925, F 706).

Fourth, Montaigne sometimes goes beyond the bounds of propriety in speaking about the parts and functions of the body and about sexual matters. And he defends what he calls his "excessive license" and his "immoderation" in speaking about the sexual (VS 845, F 642). He asks: "What has the sexual act, so natural, so necessary, and so just, done to mankind, for us not to dare to talk about it without shame and for us to exclude it from serious and decent conversations?" (VS 847, F 644). He disdains "those petty, feigned, customary, provincial rules" of propriety and ceremony that would keep him from presenting a complete portrait of himself to the public. And so, he concludes that "whoever would wean man of the folly of such a scrupulous verbal superstition would do the world no great harm" (VS 888, F 677).

These four features of Montaigne's language show the re-ordering of philosophy to the lowest rather than the highest, to the weak rather than to the strong. There are, however, at least two instances in the *Essays* where everyday language does not or cannot express precisely what he wants to convey. The first instance concerns Montaigne's intended audience. He asks himself: "For whom do you write?" The learned who pass judgment on books recognize only erudition and art and value only learning. Common and popular souls cannot recognize the grace and the weight of lofty and elevated discourse. These two types almost exhaust the possibilities. "The third type into whose hands you fall, that of souls regulated and strong in themselves, is so rare that for this very reason it has neither name nor rank among us" (VS 657, F 498). The third type has no name because it has no rank. In pointing to the fact that this type has no rank among us, Montaigne implies that his project involves a transcendence of the traditional hierarchy, the traditional order of high and low, strong and weak.

The second instance concerns a confusion in ordinary language. In "Of cruelty" Montaigne describes himself as merely innocent and good, rather than as virtuous. He is, therefore, lower in rank than both the perfectly virtuous whose rule over the passions is absolute and the imperfectly virtuous who must struggle with the passions. This third condition of goodness and innocence is, he says, "so close to imperfection and weakness that I do not very well know how to separate their confines and distinguish them. The very names of innocence and goodness are for this reason to some extent terms of contempt" (VS 426, F 310). Everyday language confuses goodness with weakness and imperfection. Montaigne, then, must overcome this confusion and articulate his overcoming of the traditional hierarchy while using only the everyday language that is thoroughly imbued with that hierarchy. He continues to use the language of perfection and imperfection, of high and low, strong and weak, but he radically alters the meanings of those terms to serve his own new philosophical project.

The Philosophical Act

For Montaigne, bringing philosophy down from the heavens and restoring it to man entails the replacement of contemplation by judgment. In the Aristotelian tradition, the end of philosophy is contemplation, the highest activity of the mind in which the mind beholds the first causes or principles of all that is. Contemplation is essentially receptive: the mind is like a blank writing tablet ready to receive the forms of all things. There is an essential harmony between the mind and the world such that the mind becomes what it knows.

Montaigne, however, presents the mind as generating and producing out of itself. This contrast between the traditional notions of knowing and contemplation as essentially receptive activities and Montaigne's presentation of the mind as generating and producing comes through clearly in his essay "Of idleness," a title intended to bring to mind the traditional idea of leisure as the condition for contemplation. Idleness is actually the opposite of leisure in the tradition, for leisure is time devoted to the divine in worship and contemplation: it is the highest activity, for it is "useless" in the best sense, i.e., it is not directed to an end outside itself but is an end in itself. Idleness, on the other hand, is useless in the worst sense: it is not good in itself but good for nothing, a waste of time.

In this essay, Montaigne tells of his withdrawal from the affairs of politics into the solitude of his study. He intends to let his mind "entertain itself in full idleness and stay and settle in itself," which he hoped it might do more easily now, "having become weightier and riper with time." But he finds instead that his mind "gives birth to . . . chimeras and fantastic monsters, one after another, without order or purpose (*propos*)." So he decides that "in order to contemplate their ineptitude and strangeness" at his pleasure, he will put these chimeras and monsters in writing, "hoping in time to make my mind ashamed of itself" (VS 33, F 21). Montaigne is playing on the traditional notions of leisure and contemplation, conflating leisure with idleness. Contemplation is not the beholding of form but of chimeras and fantastic monsters, "unformed" productions of his own mind. The activity of the mind in idleness is not the measuring of the mind by eternal being but the mind entertaining itself in time.

For Montaigne, the generative power of the mind is manifested in the capacity for "representation" which is one of the very few things that is said to be unique to man in the long comparison of man with the other animals that he draws in the "Apology." Representation shows that man is not constrained within the natural hierarchy. "If it is true that man alone, of all the animals, has this freedom of imagination and this unruliness in thought, that represents to him that which is, that which is not, and that which he wants, the false and the true, this is an advantage that is sold him very dear and in which he has very little to glorify himself, for from it springs the principal source of the evils that press him" (VS 459–460, F 336).

If the capacity to receive the intelligible forms of things were the distinctively human capacity, then man would remain within the order and limits of nature. His power of thought would be located in a continuous ascent from sensation, which he shares with all animals, to contemplation, which he shares with the divine. Representation, however, means the freedom and unruliness of the mind. "We have emancipated ourselves from [nature's] rules to abandon ourselves to the vagabond freedom of our fancies" (VS 58, F 39). Representation is the source of evils because it gives us both the true and the false, both what is and what is not. Representation is not the mind's reception of the intelligible forms of things but the production of the mind itself. If representation replaces the reception of form, then the mind is not naturally ordered to knowledge but must order itself. The mind's ordering of itself is judgment. As representation replaces the reception of form, judgment replaces contemplation.

Montaigne says that the *Essays* are the *essais*, the tests, of his judgment (VS 301, F 219; VS 653, F 495). In his essay on the education of children, he sets out the distinction between mere learning and true education in terms of the difference between simply borrowing from the ancients, which is only an exercise of memory, and forming one's own judgment. The student should be taught what to do with the pieces borrowed from others: "he will transform and blend them to make a work that is all his own, [that is], his judgment. His education, work, and study aim only at forming this" (VS 152, F 111).

Contemplation is divine; judgment is human, a purely human activity concerned only with the human. Montaigne encounters the human itself and as such. To judge within the traditional hierarchy is to judge by the standard of what is above.

Man is between the divine and the bestial and judges himself by the standard of the divine. Montaigne considers the human "purely," judging it as it is in itself, without relation to anything else. To judge man as he is in himself and to identify judgment as the distinctively human activity is to change everything about the traditional understanding of what it means to be human.

Within the tradition, contemplation is regarded as the highest human activity because in contemplation the mind escapes the temporal and is united with the divine, eternal, and unchanging: the human becomes divine. The essays are not directed to the divine, eternal, and unchanging, but to the human, temporal, and changing. Montaigne cannot stomach the contemplative ecstasies of Socrates. But he admires the Socrates "who brought human wisdom back down from heaven, where she was wasting her time, and restored her to man, with whom lies her most proper and laborious and useful business" (VS 1038, F 793).

Contemplation is the ecstatic beholding of the thing itself. Judgment is the subjecting of the thing itself, making it one's own. Montaigne's praise of Socrates for bringing philosophy back down from the heavens reveals the way in which contemplation has been transformed. "It is only for first-class men to dwell purely on the thing itself, consider it, and judge it. It belongs to the one and only Socrates to become acquainted with death with an ordinary countenance, to become familiar with it and play with it. He seeks no consolation outside the thing itself; dying seems to him a natural and indifferent accident. He fixes his gaze precisely on it, and makes up his mind to it, without looking elsewhere" (VS 833, F 632). To dwell on "the thing itself," to fix one's gaze on it, is not to contemplate it but to judge it and subject it.

Montaigne says that Socrates "raised himself . . . to the utmost point of vigor. Or, to speak more exactly, he raised nothing, but rather brought vigor, hardships, and difficulties down and back to his own natural and original level, and subjected them to it" (VS 1037, F 793). The Socrates of Montaigne's invention does not contemplate the thing itself; he judges it, subjects it to himself, by bringing it down and back, lowering it, to what is his own. He makes the thing itself his own, that is, he makes it familiar. That is what it means to restore philosophy to man.

Judgment looks like a lowering of the mind from the heights of contemplation, but it is actually a new kind of freedom. Freedom of judgment is the mark of the self-ordered soul which is "strong in itself." This strength is not measured by its perfection within the hierarchy but by its freedom of judgment: "Indeed there are few souls so regulated, so strong and well-born, that they can be trusted to their own conduct, and who are able, with moderation and without temerity, to sail in the liberty of their judgments beyond the common opinions."(VS 559, F 419–420). The self-regulated soul imposes order and measure upon itself. "Our mind is an erratic, dangerous, and heedless tool; it is difficult to impose order and moderation (*mesure*) upon it. And in my time those who have some rare excellence beyond the others, and some extraordinary quickness, are nearly all, we see, incontinent in the license of their opinions and conduct (*mœurs*). It is a miracle if you find a sedate and sociable one" (VS 559, F 419). Excellent minds, then, are inclined to be solitary, unsociable, immoderate, and dangerous. The miracle is the self-ordered soul that is sociable.

Montaigne's Philosophical Project

Montaigne describes himself as a philosopher only once in the *Essays*. He is "a new figure: an unpremeditated and accidental philosopher" (VS 546, F 409). He is an unpremeditated philosopher because he says the first words that come to his mouth, displaying the spontaneity of everyday language. His thoughts are "born with [him] and without a model," yet they resemble and are mistaken for the "humors" of ancient philosophy. His mores are weak for he has not called in any discipline to strengthen them. But when the desire to tell them seizes him, he calls upon the help of philosophy to express them so that he might go out a bit more decently in public. Then he marvels at just how much his weak mores conform, by accident, to so many of the teachings and examples of ancient philosophy. Montaigne uses ancient philosophy in order to go out in public a bit more decently. He is a common, private man who claims no great learning or great deeds but who emerges into the public wearing the fig leaf of ancient philosophy.

The private is the hidden and shameful, hidden because it is shameful. The actions of private life are the actions that are merely necessary, that is, unfree or servile, for they are associated with mere life. The deeds of great men, on the contrary, are great because they show contempt for mere life, a contempt that manifests itself most clearly in risking life in the face of imminent and violent death. The great philosophers too show contempt for mere life. This philosophical contempt manifests itself in the view that philosophy is the separation of the soul from the body, in the contempt that the philosopher has for the pleasures of the body, in the claim that philosophy is the highest activity of leisure which is freed from the servility of labor and work, in the philosopher's escape from the temporal and from this world to the eternal and celestial realm. But here is Montaigne, a common, private, and weak man, presuming to bring out into public view everything that the philosophers and the great despise. By bringing the private out into the public, into visibility, Montaigne is overcoming the shame of the private.

Montaigne emerges into the public as a particular. He emerges out of the anonymity of the common in his concrete particularity. Thus, he overcomes the anonymity and invisibility of the individual who is merely an undifferentiated part of the common herd. Without great deeds or learning, the particular is anonymous. But the essays are *The Essays of Michel de Montaigne*. Yet he presents himself as weak: his mores have not been formed by philosophy. It is the accidental conformity of his weak mores to the teachings and examples of philosophy that astonishes him. Philosophy allows him to see the weak, the private, and the shameful in a new light. Unpremeditated and accidental philosophy is the subordination of ancient philosophy to his desire for self-revelation, and the subordination of philosophy itself to the social. The emergence of the private into the public realm is the coming into being of a new, modern form of human association, that is, society, which is public but not political. For Montaigne, the social has the effect of limiting political power and of softening or weakening the political, for the invention of society means the shift from self-revelation through glorious deeds to self-revelation through speech.

The very first words of the *Essays* assert the primary significance of this emergence of the private into the public: "I have set myself no end but a domestic and private one. I have had no thought of serving either you or my own glory. My powers are inadequate for such a purpose." Montaigne's end is merely domestic and private. Once again, he presents himself as weak, not strong enough for the lofty goals of glory or public service. He simply wants to present himself in his "simple, natural, ordinary form, without striving." Thus, he concludes his address to the reader: "you would not be rational to spend your leisure on such a frivolous and vain subject" (VS 3, F 2). He is presenting his particularity, his weak and defective particularity, as it is in the realm of the domestic and private, not in the studied posture of the learned or of one seeking the favor of the world. Montaigne is reversing the Aristotelian order in which the domestic and private is imperfect and incomplete and finds its completion and perfection only in the political realm. This reversal is a "lowering" of the mind from the perfect to the imperfect, but it is also, at the same time, the end that he has freely set for himself. Setting his "end" for himself is his freedom from Aristotelian final cause.

Montaigne's particularity is articulated in relation to the condition of the domestic and private. It is the anonymous and defective private man who emerges into the public. Montaigne says: "Others form man; I tell of him, and represent a particular, very ill-formed" (VS 804, F 610). Those who "form" man are the philosophers and theologians, the "directors of conscience," who instruct us in accordance with the perfection of form. Montaigne, however, "represents" only a particular and that particular is very ill-formed, imperfect, and incomplete. When he says, in "To the reader," that he wants to be seen in his simple, natural, and ordinary form, without the striving of final cause, he explains why his defects will be an important aspect of his portrait (VS 3, F 2). The *Essays* do not conceal his imperfections any more than does his portrait which displays, not a perfect face, but his own face (VS 148, F 108).

Now it makes sense that particularity would appear first as imperfection, for any given particular would have to be seen as a kind of "falling off" from the perfection of form. Very few men attain the perfection of the human form. Montaigne estimates that only about a dozen men among the ancients have ever done so. The perfection of form is final cause and final cause is the good. Montaigne's re-ordering of philosophy is nothing less than the ordering of thought to what is, not to what ought to be. It is only by the standard of what ought to be that what is looks imperfect and weak.

Montaigne describes his decision to study only himself as a lowering of his mind: "Other men study themselves in order to elevate their minds and hoist them up tight; I to lower it and lay it to rest" (VS 821, F 623). The quotation that supports this claim is from Horace's *Odes* and illustrates the turn from the glorious enterprise of war to merely domestic concerns: "You sing of Aeacus' line and the wars beneath the sacred walls of Ilium: but you do not say how much I must pay for a jar of Chian wine, or who will heat my water on his fire, where I shall find shelter and when I shall escape from the cold of the Pelignian mountains" (III, xix, 3–8). But, this lowering to the domestic and private actually turns out to be a new kind of perfection.

Montaigne tells us that his purpose requires that he write the *Essays* "at home, in a backward region." There, no one knows enough Latin or French to correct him. He says: "I would have done it better elsewhere, but the work would have been less my own; and its principal end (*fin*) and perfection is to be precisely my own" (VS 875, F 667). The *Essays* are imperfect: they would have been better, more perfect, had they been written among the learned. Yet they are perfect because they are precisely and entirely his own, and they are his own because they were written at home.

Montaigne's new notion of perfection is set forth at the very end of the *Essays*: "It is an absolute perfection and God-like to know how to enjoy our own being rightly." We are ashamed to be merely human: we think we can be fully human only by achieving the divine condition. The enjoyment of our own being is an *absolute* perfection because it is taking joy in our humanity as such and in itself. Again, Montaigne points to the domestic and private as the human condition. "On the loftiest throne in the world we are still sitting on our own rump" (VS 1115, F 857). Thus, Montaigne says: "I set forth a humble and inglorious life; that does not matter. You can tie up all moral philosophy with a common and private life just as well as with a life of richer stuff. Each man bears the entire form of the human condition" (VS 805, F 611). Even the prince is essentially only a private and common man. "The judgment of an emperor should be above his imperial power, and see and consider it as an extraneous accident; and he should know how to find pleasure in himself apart, and to reveal himself like any Jack or Peter, at least to himself" (VS 1012, F 774).

Montaigne makes his mind ashamed of itself for its attempt to be divine, and by bringing the body and its everyday needs into the public, he overcomes the shame of the human. Thus he initiates a reform of the great and of the philosophers. In "On some verses of Virgil" he discusses the erotic and the sexual in a way that he admits goes beyond the limits of propriety. Then he clarifies the purpose of his open speaking: "God grant that this excessive license of mine may encourage our men to attain freedom, rising above these cowardly and hypocritical virtues born of our imperfections; that at the expense of my immoderation I may draw them on to the point of reason!" (VS 845, F 642). "Our men" are the nobility. Montaigne wants to lead them to freedom and reason through his bringing the private and hidden out into the public and overcoming the shame of the merely bodily and necessary. Overcoming the shame of the low is, at the same time, overcoming the pride of the lofty.

Pride is overcome through open speaking about oneself. Montaigne says that custom has made this open speaking about oneself a vice, but he finds more harm than good in this supposed remedy for pride. "The supreme remedy to cure it is to do just the opposite of what those people prescribe who, by prohibiting talking about oneself, even more strongly prohibit thinking about oneself. The pride lies in the thought; the tongue can have only a very slight share in it" (VS 379, F 274). Self-revelation in deeds is supplanted by self-revelation in words which both overcomes pride and compensates for pride because it is a new way of showing oneself in public. Greatness becomes openness; classical magnanimity becomes generosity. "If my heart is not great enough, it is compensatingly open, and it orders me boldly to publish its weakness" (VS 917, F 700).

Montaigne's project is not simply the lowering of the high but the subordination of the high to the low. In particular, the violence of great deeds is subordinated to the domestic and private. "When I see both Caesar and Alexander, in the thick of their great tasks, so fully enjoying natural and therefore necessary and just pleasures, I do not say that that is relaxing their souls, I say that it is toughening them, subordinating these violent occupations and laborious thoughts, by the vigor of their spirits, to the practice of everyday life: wise men, had they believed that this [the violent] was their ordinary occupation, the other [the everyday] the extraordinary" (VS 1108, F 850).

The order of the great and the everyday, the extraordinary and the ordinary is reversed: the lowest is higher than the highest. This reversal is so difficult to express because ordinary language is imbued with the traditional hierarchy. That is also why ordinary language confuses goodness and innocence with weakness and imperfection. Montaigne's subordination of the great to the everyday shows that we already possess the good, in the domestic and private. The good is not an end that we must strive for. It is already our own, "without striving," in the everyday. Enjoyment means possession. The good is not weak but strong because it subjects the strong and violent to itself.

The Theban general Epaminondas is the most outstanding man, surpassing even Alexander and Caesar, because in addition to his great valor in combat, his character and conscience are good and innocent. In the midst of the ferocity and violence of war, he turns aside from the friend whom he encounters in battle. Montaigne says of him: "Truly that man was in command of war itself, who made it endure the curb of benignity at the point of its greatest heat. . . . It is a miracle to be able to mingle some semblance of justice with such actions; but it belongs to the strength of Epaminondas to be able to mingle with them the sweetness and ease of the gentlest ways, and pure innocence." While others heard only the noise of weapons, "this man was not even kept from hearing the voices of civility and pure courtesy" (VS 801–802, F 609).

Montaigne invents society as a new form of human association and he invents the essay as a new form of philosophy. It might be said that he invents society by inventing the essay. David Hume, in his essay "Of essay-writing," argues that the essay form brings together what he calls the learned and the conversible worlds. "The separation of the learned from the conversible world," he says, "seems to have been the great defect of the last age, and must have had a very bad influence both on books and company." The social world suffers because, without the influence of philosophy, conversation is reduced to stories and gossip. But philosophy itself also suffers from this separation. Cut off from the world, philosophy becomes barbarous because it lacks "that liberty and facility of thought and expression which can only be acquired by conversation." Philosophy, Hume says, "went to wrack by this moaping recluse method of study, and became as chimerical in her conclusions as she was unintelligible in her stile and manner of delivery." Most important, philosophy suffers because experience, upon which philosophy rests, is to be found only "in common life and conversation."[2]

Montaigne re-orders the mind and thus philosophy itself to the familiar and the everyday, thereby overcoming the natural tendency of the mind to prefer the strange and extraordinary. Through the movement of Montaigne's thought in the *Essays*, the ordinary becomes extraordinary, the familiar becomes astonishing. "In my opinion, from the most ordinary, common, and familiar (*cogneues*) things, if we could put them in their proper light, can be formed the greatest miracles of nature and the most marvelous examples, especially on the subject of human actions" (VS 1081, F 829).

Philosophy allows him to see the everyday—to put the everyday—in a new light. The everyday is marvelous and miraculous because it subjects the extraordinary, rare, and strange to itself. (Alexander and Caesar would be "wise" if they considered the practice of everyday life to be extraordinary.) By re-ordering itself to the lowest rather than to the highest and subordinating itself to the everyday, philosophy becomes human. The philosophers' and theologians' attempt to separate the soul from the body in order to attain the divine and the eternal is a kind of violence to the man which makes him inhuman.

Reflecting on those Christian ascetics who despise the bodily pleasures of "that brattish rabble of men that we are," Montaigne says: "These are two things that I have always observed to be in singular accord: supercelestial thoughts and subterranean conduct. . . . They want to get out of themselves and escape from the man. That is madness: instead of changing into angels, they change into beasts; instead of raising themselves, they lower themselves. These transcendental humors frighten me" (VS 1115, F 856). That is why he approves of the legendary "theological drinking and feasting" at the Sorbonne (VS 1108, F 851).

Montaigne writes in French, the weaker idiom and the language of the vulgar; he uses the vulgar language of the streets, markets, and taverns of France; and he speaks with license and indiscretion about the body and the sexual because he is subordinating philosophy to the everyday. This act of subordination is the free act, the generous gesture, of the philosopher. Philosophy becomes merely unpremeditated and accidental. Montaigne himself is the miracle of the self-ordered soul that is sociable.

Emory University

Notes

1. References to the French text of the *Essais* are to the edition by Pierre Villey and V. L. Saulnier, 3 vols., 2nd ed. (Paris: Presses Universitaires de France, "Quadrige," 1992). The English translation is that of Donald Frame, *The Complete Essays of Montaigne* (Stanford, Calif.: Stanford University Press, 1943.) The citation (VS 323, F 234) refers to page 323 of the Villey-Saulnier edition and to page 234 of the Frame translation. In some instances, I have emended Frame's translation. I have also consulted the translation by M. A. Screech, *The Essays of Michel de Montaigne* (London: Penguin Press, 1991).

2. David Hume, *Essays: Moral, Political, and Literary*, ed. Eugene F. Miller (Indianapolis: Liberty Classics, 1985), 534–535.

William of Ockham and St. Augustine on Proper and Improper Statements

Stephen F. Brown

Abstract: William of Ockham discussed the fallacy of amphiboly twice in his writings. The first treatment was in his *Expositio super libros Elenchorum*, where he simply presents Aristotle's treatment, updates it with some Latin examples, and tells us it is not too important, since we do not often run into cases of ambiguity of this kind. Later, in his *Summa logicae*, however, he extends his treatment appreciably. He here includes under ambiguous statements philosophical and theological sentences which are improperly stated. Led by Aristotle, Augustine and Anselm, Ockham finds that in their writings they give us instances of improper statements which need to be restated properly before they can be evaluated as true or false. These leads provide for Ockham a key to unlocking the teaching treasures of the Ancients.

Aristotle, in chapter 4 of his *Sophistical Refutations*,[1] treats two particular types of fallacies: those that arise because of equivocation and those due to amphiboly. (Probably to set up a parallel likeness between 'amphiboly' and 'philology,' some ancient authors substituted for 'amphiboly' the extended form 'amphibology.') In speaking of 'amphiboly' or 'amphibology,' I could substitute a more familiar synonym: 'ambiguity,' which is the translation of ἀμφιβολία given in the Loeb edition of Aristotle's treatise.

However, as you might already realize, 'ambiguity' is ambiguous: there are ambiguous terms and ambiguous statements or propositions. Aristotle treats ambiguous terms in dealing with equivocation and ambiguous propositions when he deals with 'amphiboly' or 'amphibology' or 'syntactical ambiguity' ('syntactical' in contrast to 'lexical ambiguity' that belongs to equivocal terms). To put it all in simplified language: I am going to deal here with ambiguous propositions.

As we begin our discussion, let us ask some early commentators to explain Aristotle's warnings about ambiguous propositions. Following Aristotle, with the help of his Latin expositor, Boethius, Isidore of Seville, in his *Etymologies*,[2] where he divides or distinguishes ambiguous propositions, tells us that some propositions are ambiguous because they employ in Latin the accusative with the infinitive and it is at times hard to tell what the accusative is pointing to. For example, "Aio te, Aeacida, Romanos vincere posse." These words of Apollo to Pyrrhus, in Ennius's *Annales*, because of the two accusatives ('te' and 'Romanos') with an infinitive verb, could be translated in either of two ways: "I say that you, son of Aeacus, can conquer the Romans" or "I say that the Romans can conquer you, son of Aeacus."

In regard to ambiguous statements, Boethius himself tells us that each hearer has good reason to suppose that he is the one who has understood correctly. Using a similar example, "Audio Graecos vicisse Traianos," Boethius tells us that when someone says "I hear that the Greeks the Trojans have conquered," "one listener is entitled to understand that the Greeks have conquered the Trojans, while another may understand that the Trojans have conquered the Greeks, and given what the speaker himself factually said, each one has good reason for understanding what he does."[3] To clarify his meaning the speaker needs to make some adjustment.

Now ambiguous statements (and they can be due to causes besides accusatives with infinitives) can be avoided by a speaker in different ways according to Boethius: by addition, by subtraction, by division or by transposition. For the statement "I hear that the Trojans the Greeks have conquered," we could say more clearly: "I hear that the Trojans have conquered the Greeks" or "I hear that the Trojans have been conquered by the Greeks."[4] This is just one of Boethius's options for achieving clarity. For the present moment, we will not here detail his other manoeuvres for attaining clarity.

* * * * *

William of Ockham wrote a *Commentary on the Sophistical Refutations* of Aristotle (*Expositio super libros Elenchorum*).[5] In this work he essentially is just trying to understand and represent the teaching of Aristotle. He brings into his literal commentary some fresh examples to make his audience understand what the Philosopher is trying to teach. One such example is "Quod quis scit, hoc scit." Some would translate this as "That which someone knows is something that he knows." Others would understand it to be saying "That being which someone knows also is a being who knows."[6]

Ockham later brings on the scene bishops, priests and donkeys to gain the attention of his student listeners:

Quicumque sunt episcopi sunt sacerdotes

Isti asini sunt episcopi

Igitur isti asini sunt sacerdotes

When we say "Quicumque sunt episcopi sunt sacerdotes," 'episcopi' could be a nominative plural or a genitive singular, so it may be saying "Whoever are bishops are priests" or "Those who belong to the bishop are priests." When we say "isti asini sunt episcopi," 'episcopi' could also be nominative plural or genitive singular, with the resulting translations: "These donkeys are bishops" or "These donkeys belong to the bishop." The conclusion which can only mean "These donkeys are priests" could flow from the premises which are understood to say "Whoever are bishops are priests" and "These donkeys are bishops." The conclusion would then follow logically from the premises. However, since the premiss "These donkeys are bishops" is false, the conclusion flowing from it would also be false.[7]

Ockham, in his *Commentary on the Sophistical Refutations*, mentions such fallacies that may arise from accidents of speech (within propositions) related to case (nominative, genitive, etc.) and number (singular or plural), but comes to a quick conclusion that we would welcome: "Because we do not run into many instances of fallacies of this kind, I am led to move on."

* * * **

William moved on to other types of fallacies in his *Expositio super libros Elenchorum*. Later on, however, when he returned to a discussion of fallacies in his *Summa logicae*, his treatment of amphiboly or amphibology alone swelled to 23 pages, i.e., many times the size of his earlier treatment in his commentary on Aristotle's text. What has changed?

First, I would say that Boethius's *De divisione* plays some part in the expansion. Remember that he said that the ambiguity in the statement about the Greeks and the Trojans can be overcome by addition, subtraction, division and transposition. Ockham in his *Summa logicae* treatment works out each of these in detail—something he only mentioned generally in his *Expositio*. We can overcome the ambiguity by addition in saying "I heard that the Trojans conquered and the Greeks were conquered." We could clarify by subtraction by saying "I heard that the Greeks conquered." We could make the declaration clear by division if we said "The Greeks won; the Trojans lost." Finally, by transposition we could make things clear by saying "I heard that the Trojans conquered the Greeks."[8]

This adding of detail nonetheless only explains part of the extra treatment given to amphibolitic propositions in the *Summa logicae*. In the *Summa* Ockham spends a great amount of energy on the various modes of amphiboly. The earlier *Expositio* focused on the first mode of this fallacy. Attention in the *Expositio* was given to propositions which in their proper sense might have many meanings. The original proposition about the Greeks and the Trojans is a good example: no matter which way you would understand it, both understandings are understood in their proper sense.

In the *Summa logicae* Ockham attends also to a second mode of amphiboly or propositional ambiguity. In this mode ambiguity arises in a proposition where the statement is understood in one sense when it is taken properly, that is, in accord with its literal meaning, and in another sense according to its improper meaning. Some proverbs illustrate this well. For example, "Lupus est in fabula" properly signifies that a story is about a wolf; but in a secondary and improper or non-literal way the saying is telling us that there is an enemy in our midst. Similarly, when someone points to a salesman and says: "Iste vendit oleum," the primary and proper sense of the statement is that he sells a certain kind of liquid; however, secondarily and improperly this proverb means "This salesman cheats."[9]

Ockham here is not a collector of adages or proverbs; he is simply preparing to fish in deeper waters. In the works of the Fathers and the Philosophers he finds many propositions that speak improperly. He is not claiming a new insight or discovery; quite the contrary. He finds the same awareness in St. Augustine's *Confessions*. In chapter 20 of Book XI, Augustine says:

> But what now is manifest and clear is that neither are there future nor past things. Nor is it fitly said: 'There are three times: past, present and future.' But perchance it might fitly be said: 'There are three times: a present of things past, a present of things present, and a present of things future.' For these three do somehow exist in the soul, and otherwise I see them not: present of things past, memory; present of things present, sight; present of things future, expectation. If of these things we are permitted to speak, I see three times, and I grant there are three. It may also be said: 'There are three times: past, present and future,' as usage falsely has it. See, I trouble not, nor gainsay, nor reprove; provided always that that which is said may be understood, that neither the future, nor that which is past, now is. For there are but few things which we speak properly, many things improperly; but what we may wish to say is understood.[10]

Thus Augustine. On page after page in the *Summa logicae* we find a catalogue of propositions taken from the Church Fathers and Aristotle which, if taken properly, are not suited to express the true meaning. If taken improperly, nonetheless, we understand what they wish to say and we could express this correct meaning if we cast it in the form of another proposition.

We could start with Augustine in his *De Trinitate* where he tries to interpret the words: "Christ is the power of God and the wisdom of God." Augustine concludes a long discussion on how Christ is the wisdom of God with these words: "Therefore both the Father himself is wisdom, and the Son is in such a way called the wisdom of the Father as He is called the light of the Father, that is, that in the same manner as light from light and yet both one light, so we are to understand wisdom of wisdom and yet both one wisdom; and therefore also one essence, since, in God to be is the same as to be wise . . . and since in divine simplicity to be wise is nothing else than to be, therefore wisdom there is the same as essence."[11]

According to Ockham Anselm teaches us, in his *Monologion*,[12] that when we read in the Fathers "God has wisdom" or "God has justice," expressions that place a distinction between what the subject stands for and what the predicate stands for, then we have to clarify the expressions. If they are taken properly, and express a distinction between God and his wisdom or God and his justice they are false. Such propositions need to be taken improperly so that they are taken to mean the same as these properly stated propositions "God is wisdom," "God is justice." The same holds for propositions such as "Wisdom is in God" or "Understanding and Will are in God." Understood properly or literally, such propositions are false, since they imply a distinction between God and understanding and will. If they are understood improperly, i.e., not as stated, so that by these expressions "Wisdom is in God" and "Understanding and will are in God" the following propositions are understood: "God is wisdom" and "God is understanding and will," then they are true.[13]

But someone may object and say: "Why did the Fathers not say what they meant to say in a clear and proper way in the first place?" Ockham responds that there is no sure rule by which we can sufficiently know with regularity why an author speaks the way he does, since it depends upon his intention and his customary way of speaking. As a response, Ockham might just as well repeat the words of Augustine in the *Confessions*: "See, I trouble not, nor gainsay, nor reprove; provided always that that which is said may be understood. . . . For there are but few things which we speak properly, many things improperly; but what we may wish to say is understood."[14]

Ockham would note that it is not only the Fathers; even trained theologians of his own day at times speak improperly. E.g., they say things such as "God through His absolute power can grant eternal life to someone without grace but not by his ordained power." Such a statement, according to Ockham, is ambiguous. One meaning you could give to it is that "God by one power, which is absolute and not ordained, can reward someone without grace and by another power, which is ordained and not absolute, cannot reward him." This is to understand the original statement to mean that there are two powers in God and that he could reward by one and not by the other. This is a false interpretation. The original proposition, however, could also be understood to mean: "God could reward someone with eternal life without habitual or informing grace, because to do so does not include a contradiction, and nevertheless God has ordained that this will never happen." This is the true understanding of the original ambiguous proposition.[15]

Lest you might think that Ockham's *Summa logicae* is really only a logic and language guidebook for theologians, let us see how Ockham applies his logic of ambiguous propositions to philosophy. It might surprise you, but Aristotle himself also speaks improperly. However, more importantly, he criticizes others who speak improperly. In Book III of the *Physics* (and he is here followed by Averroes in comment 18), he examines the proposition "Motion is in the mobile body." He tells us that if you mean that 'motion' is in a mobile body as a distinct reality in a distinct thing," then you are wrong. You have to state it differently: "A mobile body is moving." Now it is stated in its true form.[16] Despite Aristotle's criticism of others, Ockham finds a dozen or more sentences from Aristotle's *Physics* where Aristotle himself speaks improperly. Given his own warning about "Motion is in a mobile body," we might in these cases be tempted to say: "Tsk, tsk. You contradicted yourself" or "You're not being consistent." Or we could say, as Augustine did above: "See, I trouble not, nor gainsay, nor reprove . . . . "[17] Why? Because I know what you really meant to say, though you expressed it improperly, and I accept your expression according to the meaning you intended it to provide."

The example that Aristotle used to criticize improper propositions, namely, "Motion is in a mobile" offers, I believe, a further insight into Ockham's deeper motive for expanding the treatment of amphiboly in the *Summa logicae*. If we want to follow why Aristotle preferred to translate this statement into its proper form, namely, "A mobile body is moving," it is because the improper form ("Motion is in a mobile") changes "is moving" into "motion is." The improper form thus substitutes a noun for a verbal expression and leads us to imagine 'motion' as some kind of reality or substance distinct from, although associated with, the mobile body. Ockham had a penchant to get rid of extra realities, though he knew that he could never get rid of the noun 'motion' or the propositions where it played the role of subject or predicate.[18] As Augustine said: "There are but few things which we speak properly, many things improperly." Yet if we want to understand the realities our often ambiguous propositions are speaking of, we have to translate them to their proper form and deal only with the realities they express.

The treatment of ampiboly in the *Summa logicae* of Ockham provides innumerable examples taken from Aristotle, Augustine, Anselm, and Peter Lombard of statements that need to be reshaped to get to their proper meanings.[19] Without a study of Ockham's way of reading these classic authors, it will be very difficult to understand his real debates with many of his contemporaries, especially Henry of Ghent, John Duns Scotus, Henry of Harclay and Walter Chatton. I think, in particular, it would be well worth the effort to go through the indices of Ockham's *Opera Philosophica et Theologica* and examine all his citations from Augustine to see how William reads these authorities, changing them to statements that more properly express the realities they discuss.

Boston College

Notes

1. Aristotle, *Sophistical Refutations* (ed. Bekker) 166a 6–23.

2. Isidorus, *Etymologiae*, I, 34, 13 (PL 83, 109): "Amphibolia ambigua dictio, quae fit aut per casum accusativum, ut illud responsum Apollinis ad Pyrrhum" (Ennius, *Annales*. 179): "Aio te, Aeacida, Romanus vincere posse . . . "

3. Boethius, *Liber de divisione* (PL 64, 889s; ed. J. Magee, 44): "In ambiguis enim uterque auditor rationabiliter seipsum intellexisse arbitratur, ut cum quis dicit, audio Graecos vicisse Trajanos, unus putat quod Graeci Trojanos vicerint, alius quod Trojani Graecos, et haec uterque dicentis ipsius sermonibus rationabiliter."

4. Ibid.: "Ambiguarum vero orationum facienda est divisio, aut per adjectionem, ut audio Trojanos vinci, Graecos vicisse; aut per diminutionem, ut audio Graeci vicisse; aut per divisionem, ut Graeci vicerunt, Trojani victi sunt; aut per aliquam transmutationem, ut cum dicitur, Audio Trojanos vicisse Graecos, ita dicamus, Audio quod Graeci vicerint Trojanos. Haec enim ambiguitas quolibet eorum modo solvitur."

5. Guillelmus de Ockham, *Expositio super libros Elenchorum*, c. 2 (Opera Philosophica III, ed. F. del Punta) (New York: St. Bonaventure University, 1979), 15–30.

6. Ibid., 18: "Secundus paralogismus est iste: quod quis scit hoc scit; sed aliquis scit grammaticam; ergo grammatica scit. Unde ista 'quod quis scit hoc scit' est distinguenda, ex eo quod li 'hoc' potest construi cum hoc verbo 'scit' a parte ante, ex vi personae; et sic est falsa, quia tunc denotatur quod illud quod est scitum, scit; et hoc est simpliciter falsum. Vel potest construi a parte post, ex vi transitionis, et tunc est vera, quia tunc non denotatur plus nisi quod illud quod est scitum ab aliquo, scitur ab eo."

7. Ibid., 30: "Est etiam sciendum quod praeter praedictos modos quibus potest fieri aequivocatio penes tertium modum, est unus modus quo eadem dictio potest esse unius casus vel alterius, sicut patet in hoc sophismate: quicumque sunt episcopi sunt sacerdotes; isti asini sunt episcopi; igitur isti asini sunt sacerdotes. Nam minor est distinguenda eo quod li 'episcopi' potest esse nominativi casus, et tunc est minor falsa et est discursus bonus; vel potest esse genitivi casus, et tunc est minor vera et discursus non valet."

8. Cf. supra, nn. 3 and 4.

9. Guillelmus de Ockham, *Summa logicae*, III-4, c. 6 (Opera philosophica I; ed. P. Boehner, G. Gál et S. Brown) (New York: St. Bonaventure University, 1974), 771: "Circa secundum modum amphiboliae est sciendum quod tunc est aliqua oratio multiplex penes secundum modum amphiboliae quando aliqua oratio proprie et ex sua primaria significatione seu impositione tantum uno modo accipitur, sed improprie et secundario potest aliter accipi et alium sensum habere. Sicut ista oratio 'Lupus est in fabula' primo et proprie significat quod fabula est de lupo, sed improprie et secundario significat quod inimicus accedit. Similiter ista oratio 'Iste vendit oleum' primo et proprie significat quod iste vendit talem liquorem, sed improprie et secundario significat quod iste adulatur. Et ita frequenter una oratio ponitur pro alia, quia si acciperentur proprie, nullam haberent convenientiam nec quantum ad significationes dictionum nec quantum ad significationes totalium orationum. Et talis sensus non contingit nisi ex usu loquentium, ponentium unam orationem pro alia."

10. Augustinus, *Confessiones*, XI, 20 (PL 32, 819): "Quod autem nunc liquet et claret, nec futura sunt, nec praeterita. Nec proprie dicitur, Tempora sunt tria: praeteritum, praesens et futurum; sed fortasse proprie diceretur, Tempora sunt tria: praesens de praeteritis, praesens de praesentibus, praesens de futuris. Sunt enim haec in anima tria quaedam, et alibi ea non video; praesens de praeteritis memoria, praesens de praesentibus contuitus, praesens de futuris exspectatio. Si haec permittimur dicere, tria tempora video, fateorque, tria sunt. Dicatum etiam, Tempora sunt tria: praeteritum, praesens et futurum; sicut abutitur consuetudo, dicatur: ecce non curo, nec resisto, nec reprehendo; dum tamen intelligatur quod dicitur, neque id quod futurum est, esse jam, neque id quod praeteritum est. Pauca sunt enim quae proprie loquimur, plura non proprie; sed agnoscitur quid velimus."

11. Augustinus, *De Trinitate*, VII, c. 1, n. 2 (PL 42, 935; CCSL 50-1, 248): "Quod si et Pater qui genuit sapientiam, ex ea fit sapiens, neque hoc est illi esse quod sapere, qualitas ejus est Filius, non proles ejus, et non ibi erit jam summa simplicitas,. Sed absit ut ita sit, quia vere ibi est summe simplex essentia, hoc ergo est ibi esse quod sapere. Quod si hoc est ibi esse quod sapere, non per illam sapientiam quam genuit sapiens est Pater, alioquin non ipse illam, sed illa eum genuit. Quid enim aliud dicimus, cum dicimus, Hoc illi est esse quod sapere, nisi, Eo est quo sapiens est?"

12. Anselmus, *Monologion*, c. 16 (ed. F. S. Schmitt, I, 30).

13. Guillelmus de Ockham, *Summa logicae*, 777: "Volo tamen de aliquibus orationibus multum usitatis a theologis exemplificare, et declarare quomodo penes istam fallaciam sunt multiplices. Unde dico quod omnes tales: Deus habet iustitiam; Deus habet sapientiam;

Deus habet intellectum et voluntatem; Deus habet essentiam; et omnes consimiles, in quibus ponitur aliqua dictio notans distinctionem inter illud pro quo supponit subiectum et pro quo supponit predicatum distinguendae sunt, eo quod possunt accipi proprie, et tunc sunt falsae; vel possunt accipi improprie, ut ponantur loco talium 'Deus est iustitia', 'Deus est sapientia' et huiusmodi, et tunc sunt verae. Et distinctionem talium innuit Anselmus, *Monologio*, cap. 16, ubi vult quod non proprie dicitur quod 'summa natura habet iustitiam', sed 'exsistit iustitia'. Et ita cum tales propositiones frequenter inveniantur in libris authenticis, oportet quod accipiantur improprie."

14. Cf. supra, n. 10.

15. Guillelmus de Ockham, *Summa logicae*, 779s.: "Item, talis propositio 'Deus per suam potentiam absolutam potest aliquem acceptare sine gratia sed non per suam potentiam ordinatam' multiplex est. Unus sensus est quod Deus per unam potentiam, quae est absoluta et non ordinata, potest acceptare aliquem sine gratia, et per unam aliam potentiam, quae est ordinata et non absoluta, non potest acceptare eum, quasi essent duae potentiae in Deo per quarum unam posset hoc et non per aliam. Et iste sensus est falsus. Aliter accipitur improprie, ut ponatur ista propositio pro ista oratione: Deus potest acceptare aliquem sine gratia informante, quia hoc non includit contradictionem, et tamen ordinavit quod hoc numquam est facturus. Et iste sensus verus est."

16. Guillelmus de Ockham, *Summa logicae*, 772: "Consimiliter sunt tales propositiones distinguendae 'motus est in mobili'. Unus sensus est iste 'aliquid importatum per motum, de quo verificatur motus, est in mobili sicut res distincta in re distincta', et hoc falsum est secundum opinionem Aristotelis. Alius sensus est iste 'mobile movetur', et hic sensus est verus."

17. Cf. supra, nn. 10 and 14.

18. For a more detailed study of proper and improper propositions of natural philosophy according to Ockham, see Stephen F. Brown, "A Modern Prologue to Ockham's Natural Philosophy" in *Miscellanea Mediaevalia, Band 13/1: Sprache und Erkenntnis im Mittelalter*, (1981), 107–129.

19. Cf. Guillelmus de Ockham, *Summa logicae*, 751–776.

Resurrection and Hylomorphism:
Moving Toward a Theory of Post-Mortem Survival Compatible with Catholic Doctrine

Paul Blaschko

Abstract: My paper raises the question whether there are any tenable hylomorphic theories of post-mortem survival and resurrection compatible with Catholic Church doctrine. After considering what it would mean for such a theory to be compatible with Church doctrine, I raise three objections to which a hylomorphic theory would need to successfully respond in order to be considered tenable. In the final section of the paper, I argue affirmatively, that there are tenable hylomorphic theories. I then consider two contemporary theories and offer reasons to prefer an alternative, non-reassemblist theory to others that are currently equally or more popular.

I. Introduction

In the recent literature of the metaphysics of post-mortem survival, there has been much debate as to whether or not hylomorphism is able to offer a tenable theory. Further, among those who argue in favor of such a theory are Catholic philosophers who maintain that such a theory need not come at the expense of Church doctrine. In this paper, I will examine two hylomorphic theories of post-mortem survival, the proponents of which believe them to obtain within the bounds of Church doctrine. The Catholic metaphysician will find this argument pressing because, if I am correct, there is only one (or at least one *kind* of) argument available to her. The secular philosopher should find this argument pressing for two reasons: first, if the argument succeeds, then there is at least one hylomorphic theory of post-mortem survival consistent with major contemporary objections, and secondly, because if such an argument is in fact compatible with Church doctrine, there is at least tenable hylomorphic theory of post-mortem survival that can consistently be held by Catholic philosophers.

In the first section of this paper, I will defend two principles as the criteria by which any hylomorphic theory of post-mortem survival needs to be judged. Any coherent theory consistent with Catholic doctrine, I will argue, will abide by the following:

(1) The theory must not obtain to the detriment or vast reconfiguration of the doctrines of death, particular judgment, purgatory, and the final resurrection.

(2) The theory must solve three objections that have been raised in connection with hylomorphic theories of post-mortem survival: the problems of non-unique replication, so-called gappy or intermittent existence, and the problem of the unjust God.

In section two of the paper, I will argue that a theory does not "obtain to the detriment or vast reconfiguration of" doctrine only so long as it affirms:

(a) that death is the separation of the soul from the body

(b) that it is the *immortal soul* that survives death and is particularly judged and subsequently sentenced to either eternal damnation or beatification via purgation (if necessary)

(c) that there is a some sort of *temporal period* between death and resurrection wherein a soul experiences beatification (via purgation if necessary) or eternal damnation.

I will then present arguments for the three objections mentioned in principle (2) and argue that all three arguments need to be answered in order for a theory to be tenable.

In section three of the paper I will present two contemporary hylomorphic theories of post-mortem resurrection, the traditional "reassembly" theory, and the so-called "alternative" theory, and critically examine each of them against the aforementioned criteria. I will conclude by suggesting that, because only the second theory, the "alternative" theory, can abide by both principles, it is the only tenable hylomorphic theory of post-mortem survival compatible with Church doctrine.

II. An Explanation of the Principles

If we expect to critically examine hylomorphic theories of post-mortem survival in light of the two principles given above, it is necessary to understand two things: first, what the doctrines named in principle (1) that such theories mustn't "obtain to the detriment or vast reconfiguration of" are (and what would count as "detrimental" or "vastly reconfiguring" in an appropriate sense), and, secondly, what the three objections contained in principle (2) are. To this end, I will briefly sketch the doctrinal positions of the Church relating to particular judgment, purgatory, the final resurrection and the last judgment, then I will present the three objections in the order in which they appear in principle (2).

In paragraph 997 of the *Catechism of the Catholic Church*, death is defined as the "separation of the soul from the body." In paragraph 1016, death is again said to be that process or event in which "the soul is separated from the body," and again in paragraph 336, the soul "separates from the body at death." Thus, it is clear that the body soul composite is not the sort of thing that survives through death, rather, it is the "[immortal soul]" that "does not perish when it separates from the body at death" (*Catechism of the Catholic Church* 1997).[1]

So the soul survives, but what about the body? It would seem that, in order for the doctrinal understanding of post-mortem survival to be *hylomorphic* the body would be, at least in some way, necessary. "[The soul] will be reunited with the body on the day of the resurrection of the dead," the Catechism tells us (*CCC* 1997). And again in paragraph 997, "God, in his almighty power, will definitively grant incorruptible life to our bodies by reuniting them with our souls." Finally, "by death the soul is separated from the body, but in the resurrection God will give incorruptible life to our body, transformed by reunion with our soul" (*CCC* 1997). Thus we can summarize the doctrinal position examined so far as follows: in death the soul separates from the body, at the resurrection of the dead soul and body will be reunited. But within this understanding of death and resurrection there are various complexities, not the least of which is the doctrines of particular judgment and the subsequent reward or punishment bestowed on the soul.

Aquinas explains particular judgment in the 57th section of the second book of his *Summa Contra Gentiles*[2] as follows:

> When the soul is separated from the body, it receives its reward or punishment immediately for those things which it did in the body. . . . In the providence of God, rewards and punishments are due to rational creatures. Since when they are separated from the body, they are immediately capable of both glory and of punishment, they immediately receive one or the other; and neither the reward of the good nor the punishment of the bad is put off until the souls take up their bodies again.

In a similar way, the Catechism explains that "each man receives his eternal retribution in his immortal soul at the very moment of his death, in a particular judgment that refers his life to Christ: either entrance into the blessedness of heaven—through a purification or immediately,—or immediate and everlasting damnation" (*CCC* 1997). Finally, in paragraph 1051, the Catechism reiterates this by stating that "every man receives his eternal recompense in his immortal soul from the moment of his death in a particular judgment by Christ, the judge of the living and the dead." Thus we can summarize the doctrines hitherto examined as follows: upon death, the separation of the body and the soul, each man received a particular judgment by Christ. Depending on the outcome of this judgment, the soul immediately receives either the rewards of heaven (by way of purgation if necessary) or the punishments of hell. In the final resurrection, an event that will occur sometime after death and particular judgment, beatified or damned souls will be transformed by God's granting them incorruptible life through reunion with their bodies.

In this way, we have arrived at a more complete understanding of the doctrines named in principle (1). In order for a hylomorphic theory of post-mortem survival to avoid "obtaining to the detriment or vast reconfiguration of" these doctrines (as was stipulated by this principle), it must affirm:

(a) that death is the separation of the soul from the body

(b) that it is the immortal soul that survives death and is particularly judged and subsequently sentenced to eternal damnation or punishment

(c) that there is a period between death and resurrection wherein a soul experiences beatification via purgation or eternal damnation

If any hylomorphic theory should appear to obtain while neglecting to affirm all three of these statements it will be to the "detriment or vast reconfiguration of" Church doctrine and, thus, it will fail to respect principle (1).

Having established what it would mean for a hylomorphic theory to be compatible with Church doctrine by respect principle (1), I will now raise three objections to which such a theory must adequately respond in order for it to be considered tenable (as defined by principle [2]). These objections, in the order I present them in principle (2), are as follows: first, the problem of non-unique replication, second, so-called "gappy" or intermittent existence, and, finally, the problem of the unjust God. I will now examine each of these objections in this order and show how the failure to resolve any one of them would render a theory of post-mortem survival untenable.

First, the problem of non-unique replication, as Richard Swinburne presents it, is that:

> if I come to live again, the question arises as to what makes some subsequent human me, for [at death] my body will be largely if not entirely destroyed. If the answer is given that (most of) the atoms of my original body will be reassembled into bodily form, there are two problems. First, many of the atoms may no longer exist; they may have been transmuted into energy. And second, what proportion of the atoms do we need? Sixty per cent, seventy per cent, or what? If it is mere atoms which make some body mine and so some living human me, then no body will be fully mine unless it has all my atoms. Yet some of my atoms, even if not destroyed, will have come from other human bodies.[3]

The argument, then, is as follows:

(1) Assume that upon dying my soul and body are separated and "I" cease to exist

(2) If I am individuated by my body and my soul and body are separated at death, then if any body other than the one made up of all and only my atoms is united to my soul at the resurrection it will individuate someone other than "me," and "I" will not be resurrected

(3) Therefore, if any body other than the one made up of all and only my atoms is united to my soul at the resurrection it will individuate someone other than "me," and "I" will not be resurrected

(4) But it is obvious that it is not that case that both propositions "if any body other than the one made up of all and only my atoms is united to my soul at the resurrection it will individuate someone other than "me," and "I" will not be resurrected," and "I will be resurrected are true" (because when I die, the

atoms of my body are spread throughout the biosphere and become energy and parts of other humans for whom the same principle would hold true).

(5) Therefore, it is either not the case that upon dying my soul and body are separated and "I" cease to exist, or it is not the case that "I" will be resurrected.

So theories of post-mortem survival are faced with the dilemma of either denying the resurrection, an impossibility for theories hoping to respect principle (1), or denying that human beings are individuated by their bodies and that the soul and body are separated at death, which is also an impossibility for those hoping to respect doctrine (1) and a hylomorphic conception of the person. Thus the problem of non-unique replication must be resolved in order for a hylomorphic theory of post-mortem survival to obtain.

The second problem that must be addressed is the very famous problems of intermittent existence. The problem hinges on two key assumptions: the first is that a thing cannot come into existence at more than one time. The second is that the doctrines of death and resurrection require a gap between these two events. Thus, the problem can be characterized as follows:

(1) Suppose it is true that a thing cannot come into existence at more than one time (that is, it cannot come to be, cease to be, and come to be once more)

(2) The doctrine of the final resurrection requires a gap in the existence of persons (as conceived as soul/body composites which separate at death and are reunited at the final resurrection)

(3) If the doctrine of the final resurrection requires a gap in the existence of persons between death and the final resurrection, then it would require persons to come into existence more than once

(4) Therefore, either the doctrine of the Church or the seemingly obvious principle that things only come to be once must be false.

Of course, we want to claim that neither of these is false, so we are faced with a contradiction. Just as in the case of our first problem, if this contradiction does not resolve in a theory of post-mortem survival it is to the detriment of that theory. Failure to account for apparent intermittent (or as it is sometimes known "gappy") existence is a failure to preserve (1), and, as such, nullifies the usefulness of theories to which it pertains.

Finally, the last objection to hylomorphic theories of post-mortem survival concerns how just and efficacious the purgation, beatification, or condemnation that occurs immediately after death is under theories purported to explain post-mortem survival. The Objection runs thus:

(1) If I cease to exist at death, then it is not "I" who am judged and sentenced to experience eternal punishment, purgation, or beatitude, but merely my soul

(2) If "I" am not judged and sentenced to experience punishment, purgation, or beatitude then "I" do not deserve the effects of punishment (hell),

purgation (heaven), or immediate beatitude (whole and complete vision of God), even though "I" receive them

(3) I cease to exist at death.

(4) Thus, I do not deserve these effects (hell, heaven, or immediate beatitude), even though "I" receive them

(5) If I do not deserve these effects (hell, heaven, or immediate beatitude), even though "I" receive them, then God is unjust

(6) Therefore God is unjust

This sort of problem, while treated by various philosophers including Eleonore Stump and Patrick Toner, has come to my attention through the works of David Hershenov (Hershenov 2006). Again, we can see how such an argument, if not diffused, is potentially damning for any hylomorphic theory of post-mortem survival.

Thus, for a theory of post-mortem survival to be both compatible with Church doctrine (that is to respect principle [1]) as well as useful (that is to respect principle [2]), it must solve the problems of non-unique replications, henceforth NR, intermittent or so-called "gappy" existence, henceforth IE, and the unjust God problem, henceforth UG. In the following section, I aim to offer three theories that attempt to resolve these problems while respecting principle (1). Finding a tenable position of hylomorphic post-mortem survival compatible with Church doctrine depends on finding a theory that is able to meet these conditions.

III. Two Theories of Post-mortem Survival

I will now present two theories that attempt to resolve the problems presented in principle (2) while respecting principle (1). I will first examine each theories' resolution to (2), that is, I will examine whether or not it plausibly resolves the problems of NR, IE, and UG, and then I will examine whether or not, should that theory provide answers to the three objections, it does so at the expense of principle (1). I will first examine the more traditional "reassembly" theory and then I will examine what Patrick Toner has called the "alternative" theory of Eleonore Stump and David Hershenov (Toner 2009b). Ultimately, I will argue that the first theory (even though it is by far the more common view) fails in vital ways to maintain both principles (1) and (2), and that the second, "alternative" theory is the only one that obtains in light of the conditions we have placed on such a theory's success.

Patrick Lee and Robert George present the first view, which they deem the "most traditional" view in their book *Body-Self Dualism in Contemporary Ethics and Politics* (Lee and George 2008). This view is commonly known as the reassembly view. It is distinguished from similar hylomorphic theories of post-mortem survival (such as the "alternative" position we will examine in a moment) because of a strict definition of person such that in order for a thing to be so defined, it must possess both a body and a soul without exception. "On this proposal," George and Lee explain, "God simply reassembles the matter, or much of the matter, that was in the human being at the point of his death and restores it to life by rejoining his immortal soul to it" (Lee and George 2008). The benefit of this view is that it most certainly respects principle (2). Under the view, (a) death is understood as the separation of the soul from the body, (b), it *is* the immortal soul that survives death and is particularly judged etc. and (c) there does exist period of time between death and resurrection. Quite clearly, then, the position presents no problems in its compatibility with Church doctrine. If there are difficulties at all, then, they are to be found in the answers such a position must provide for our three objections.

First, to the objection of NR, the argument seems to have no real way to defend itself. George and Lee attempt a defense, claiming "all that is required to answer this objection is to suppose that God has some principled way of parceling out the shared matter" (Lee and George 2008). But this defense should leave us unsatisfied. As Swinburne points out, "If it is mere atoms which make some body mine and so some living human me, then no body will be fully mine unless it has all my atoms." Without the possibility of accepting that my body will in fact be composed of all and only my atoms, and without the possibility of rejecting any of Swinburne's other premises, the theory fails to resolve the problem of NR.

Secondly, we must address the objection of IE. Perhaps the reassemblist could argue against premise one of this objection—that nothing can come into existence more than once. This argument, though strongly counter-intuitive may turn out to be the only plausible solution to the objection, and could be supported by famous analogies like the "repaired watch" scenario in which a watch is taken apart, cleaned, and reassembled (Merricks 2001). By and large, however, this seems to be an up-hill argument that we should avoid committing ourselves to if it is at all possible. After all, Aquinas seemed to believe intermittent existence utterly absurd, though, as Patrick Toner and others have argued, this may not mean that he wouldn't have upheld the reassembly theory.

Finally, the unjust God problem seems to plague this theory most fiercely. For a reassemblist—who believes that the human person goes out of existence when the soul separates from the body—there seems to be no solution to the problem unless she is willing to argue against premise six, "that if I do not deserve what "I" receive, then God is unjust." Patrick Toner tries to do just this when he claims that "It seems quite fitting and proper . . . [to allow] the soul to undergo punishment or reward for those acts—*when it is their source*." This conclusion depends on various distinctions he makes in an attempt to define the soul as a uniquely different kind of substantial part than any other we possess. However, I find the only plausible arguments for this conclusion to either lead directly to the absurdity that a just God could conceivably condemn a person to eternal damnation even though she has done nothing to deserve it, or to rely on manifestly non-hylomorphic assumptions (namely that it is the *soul* and not the *person* to whom justice is owed).

Thus far, we have examined the most common and the most promising hylomorphic theory of post-mortem survival that attempts compatibility with Church doctrine. I have argued, however, that it proves untenable because it fails to answer major objections. I will now present and defend a second theory of post-mortem survival, the "alternative" theory, that I believe provides answers to all three questions (as required by principle [2]), without obtaining at the expense of Church doctrine (as required by principle [1]). Because of this, I will claim that it is the view that the Catholic hylomorphist *must* adopt in order to maintain a metaphysically plausible account of post-mortem survival compatible with her tradition.

According to the "alternative" theory, human beings are naturally a hylomorphic composite of soul and body.[4] Upon death, however, the immortal soul just *is* the human person. That is, in the period following death and preceding resurrection (when the soul is presumably in purgatory, heaven, or hell) the human *person* really is present—though in an unnatural and bodiless way. Philosophers like Eleonore Stump argue for this position by claiming that the human soul is the person's "proper metaphysical part." Specifically, it is that part by which human beings function intellectually and will certain things (Stump 2006). Certainly, then, the soul is not the *whole* person—this would be dualism—rather, it is a unique and *constitutive* part of the human person. The uniqueness of the soul's relation to the whole of the person comes from the fact that *it* is what carries out the characteristic functions of the human being. Thus after death, the soul is able to think and will (just as the human being was able to do during his or her life) and thus is able to persist, and to do so under the category *rational animal*. But if the soul is one metaphysical part able to perform its characteristic functions (which are, coincidentally, the characteristic functions of the human person), we must affirm that it does in fact constitute a human person, even if this is an unnatural (and not its final) state.

It is easy to see, then, that such a theory fits seamlessly within Church doctrine regarding these matters. The theory affirms (a)—that earthly death is the separation of the body from the soul (though a proponent of this view would deny that "death" causes the human person to cease to exist). It affirms (b)—that it is the immortal soul (and actually the person) that survives death and is particularly judged and subsequently sentenced to eternal damnation or punishment. And it affirms (c)—that there is a period between death and resurrection wherein a soul (and, consequently, the person) experiences beatification via purgation or eternal damnation. The theory also provides explanations for several other somewhat vexing theological issues,[5] but, since we have shown these three to be the necessary doctrinal propositions, we need not address those here.

This theory also resolves the three objections. To NR, we are able to deny the second part of premise one, that "upon dying . . . 'I' cease to exist." If "I" never cease to exist, then there is no need to wonder how I am to be individuated at the resurrection. According to Stump's interpretation of St. Thomas Aquinas (whom she maintains was an "alternative" theorist), "the individuation of a substance is also a function of its substantial form. Any given thing is *this* thing just in virtue of the fact that the form which configures it is *this* form" (Stump 2006). Since the substantial form of the person just *is* the soul—the person is individuated at the resurrection by virtue of the continuity of personhood that has characterized the soul since the person's conception. So NR resolves. To IE, we can avoid the contradictory conclusion by denying that the alternative view requires anything to come into existence at more than one time (thus refuting premise one). As we saw in our resolution to NR, the human soul constitutes (even if unnaturally) the whole of the person between death and resurrection, so there is no need to explain any sort of second "coming to be" of the person. Thus IE resolves. To UG, we can deny premise four that "I cease to exist at death," and thus maintain that is it the whole person (constituted by the soul) that experiences particular judgment and beatification or condemnation. Thus God is just in bestowing the rewards or punishments that he does and the problem of UG resolves.

And so we see that, of these two theories presented, the alternative theory provides the only serious option of post-mortem survival for the hylomorphist who takes Church doctrine seriously. Because it is consistent with Church doctrine (as per [1]) and because it resolves the major objections facing such theories (as per [2]), it is the theory to which a philosopher of this sort *must* commit, and it is a theory which even a philosopher not committed to (1) must see as most promising.

IV. Conclusion

In conclusion, this view, the "alternative" view, is the only tenable theory for the Catholic hylomorphist to hold in light of the demands of post-mortem survival for two reasons: (1) because it successfully answers the objections raised in the second section of this paper and (2) it maintains the doctrinal demands of the Church. By setting up criteria with which a theory must be consistent, and raising three objections that any tenable theory must address, I have shown that if a hylomorphist wants her theory of post-mortem survival to cohere with Church doctrine, she has no choice but to adopt the alternative view.

University of St. Thomas

Notes

1. Henceforth the *Catechism of the Catholic Church* will be referred to as *CCC*.

2. The translation of this quote was taken from Eleonore Stump (2006), "Resurrection, Reassembly, and Reconstitution: Aquinas on the Soul," cited at the end of this work.

3. This is the passage as it is stated in Stump 2006.

4. My characterization and defense of this view owes much to Eleonore Stump and David Hershenov.

5. Take, for instance, the liturgy, wherein we are said to pray to "saints," and not merely to the "souls" of saints. Or, as Stump points out, the inconsistency that follows from claiming both that "St. Dominic's soul is beatified before the resurrection" and "St. Dominic will be beatified after the resurrection." "Something that God loves in union with him, the separated soul of Dominic, God ceases to hold in loving union with himself in heaven when Dominic is resurrected. For no fault on the part of the separated soul of Dominic, the bliss that the separated soul had in loving union with God terminates, never to be resumed." (Stump 2006).

Bibliography

Catechism of the Catholic Church. 1997. Washington, D.C. : USCCB Publishing.

Cooper, John. 2001. "Biblical Anthropology and the Body-Soul Problem." In *Soul, Body, and Survival,* ed. Kevin Corcoran, 218–228. New York: Cornell University Press.

Davis, Sephen T. 2001. "Physicalism and Resurrection ." In *Soul, Body, and Survival,* ed. Kevin Corcoran, 229–248. New York: Cornell University Press.

Fowler, Harold North. 1966. *Plato in Twelve Volumes,* Volume 1. Cambridge, Mass.: Harvard University Press.

Hershenov, David B. 2006. "Personal Identity and Purgatory." *Religious Studies* 42.4.

Lee, Patrick, and Robert P George. 2008. *Body-Self Dualism in Contemporary Ethics and Politics.* New York: Cambridge University Press.

Merricks, Trenton. 2001. "How to Live Forever without Saving Your Soul." In *Soul, Body, and Survival,* ed. Kevin Corcoran, 183–200. New York: Cornell University Press.

Parfit, Derek. 1984. *Reasons and Persons.* New York: Oxford University Press.

Ross, James F. 2001 "Together With the Body I Love." *Person, Soul, and Immortality,* American Catholic Philosophical Association. Charlottesville, Va.: Philosophy Documentation Center.

Rudder Baker, Lynne. 1995. "Need A Christian Be a Mind/Body Dualist?" *Faith and Philosophy* (October): 489–504.

———. 2000. *Persons and Bodies: A Constitution View.* New York: Cambridge University Press.

Stump, Eleanore. 2006. "Resurrection, Reassembly, and Reconstitution: Aquinas on the Soul." In *Die menschliche Seele: Brauchen wir den Dualismus?* Ed. Bruno Niederberger and Edmund. Runggaldier: Ontos Verlag.

Swinburne, Richard. 1999. "Soul, nature and immortality of the." In *Routledge Encyclopedia of Philosophy.* Ed. E. Craig. London: Routledge.

Toner, Patrick. 2009a. "On Hylemorphism and Personal Identity." *European Journal of Philosophy* 19.1 (forthcoming, March 2011); online, DOI: 10.1111/j.1468-0378.2009.00381.x.

———. 2009b. "Personhood and Death in St. Thomas Aquinas." *History of Philosophy Quarterly*: 121–138.

Van Dyke, Christina. 2007. "Human Identity, Immanent Causal Relations, and the Principle of Non-repeatability: Thomas Aquinas on the Bodily Resurrection." *Religious Studies* (2007): 373–394.

Wallace, W. A. 1996. "Hylomorphism." In *New Catholic Encyclopedia.* New York: McGraw-Hill, 237–238.

Catholicism, the Human Form, and Genetic Engineering

James J. Delaney

Abstract: In September of 2008, the Congregation for the Doctrine of the Faith published *Dignitas Personae*, which addresses several newly emerging topics in the area of biomedical ethics. One of these topics is genetic engineering, which we can define as the intentional manipulation of genetic material so as to produce some desired trait or characteristic. Genetic engineering is discussed in *Dignitas Personae*, but is done so relatively briefly. In this paper, I explore some of the metaphysical and ethical questions that are key in assessing the morality of this practice by examining other Church documents as well as philosophical literature. Ultimately, I will argue that aside from some instrumental restrictions, questions about the moral permissibility of genetic engineering, the distinction between therapy and enhancement, and what it means to be human are not as easily answered from a Catholic perspective as one might think.

Introduction

In September of 2008, the Congregation for the Doctrine of the Faith published *Dignitas Personae*, (DP) which addressed several newly emerging topics in the area of biomedical ethics. In a way this document served as a supplement to *Donum vitae*, which was published in 1987. At the heart of both documents is the emphasis on the intrinsic value of the human person. DP opens as follows: "The dignity of a person must be recognized in every human being from conception to natural death. This fundamental principle expresses a great 'yes' to human life and must be at the center of ethical reflection on biomedical research, which has an ever greater importance in today's world."[1]

It is fair to say, I think, that many controversial issues in biomedical ethics are closed when it comes to the Church's official position, abortion and active euthanasia for example. With other issues, however, there are central questions that we might say are at the core but to which we do not have answers. Genetic Engineering, which for the purposes of this paper I will define as the intentional manipulation of genetic material so as to produce some desired trait or characteristic, is one such issue. Genetic Engineering is discussed briefly in DP, and the core questions surrounding it are what I wish to explore in this paper. Ultimately, I will argue that (aside from some instrumental restrictions) questions about the ethical permissibility of genetic engineering, the distinction between therapy and enhancement, and what it means to be human are not as easily answered from a Catholic perspective as one might think.

I will proceed in three main parts. First, I will sketch the basic metaphysical and ethical tenets that form the lens of the basic Catholic perspective. In addition to DP, I will also rely heavily on the International Theological Commissions's declaration on *Human Persons Created in the Image of God* (HIG). Briefly, these tenets include a hylomorphic conception of substance with roots in the metaphysics of Aristotle and Aquinas; the fact that the Church endorses (and even recommends) the compatibility of this conception with evolutionary biology; the view that human persons with full dignity exist at conception; and the claim that certain violations of basic human goods are intrinsically wrong regardless of their potential benefits. Second, I will examine the Church's specific position on genetic engineering as given in DP and HIG. Though certain restrictions such as the maintenance of pro-creation through the conjugal act and appropriate safeguards for progeny must be preserved, both somatic and germ-line genetic engineering could be used in morally permissible ways. These primarily include therapeutic uses. Third, I will probe the question of genetic enhancement on a deeper level, distinguishing between two types of human enhancement, what I will call "individual enhancements" and "species enhancements." From a Catholic perspective, I will argue, we can easily identify some morally impermissible uses. However, I believe that we can also imagine some permissible uses (at least at the intuitive level) for both types of genetic enhancement. This leads to the conclusion that the significant moral questions may turn on matters other than whether or not we have intentionally modified genes. Specifically, these matters include the attitudes we take toward our offspring, and what we identify as the central basic human goods that constitute a Christian life. Corrupt attitudes and destruction of such goods, I will argue, are wrong regardless of whether they are carried out by genetic engineering or any other means.

I. Metaphysical and Ethical Foundations of the Magisterium

Before turning the question of genetic engineering specifically, it is necessary to sketch some basic foundational tenets that form the lens through with the Church examines biomedical ethical issues. In DP as well as other writings, the Church often uses the term "Human Person." This notion connects importantly with the hylomorphic understanding of the human soul, a view with its origins in Aristotle and Aquinas. The Church denies a strictly materialistic account of the universe, but also denies the view that human beings are *identical* to an immaterial soul that merely inhabits a body (the view advocated by Plato and Descartes). By contrast, the hylomorphic view understands the soul as the form of the body in the sense of an organizational principle; in living things, this organization is a principle of life. The form is prior to the matter, it informs the matter. By analogy we might think of it in the same way that the blueprints of a building exist prior to the materials that comprise it and informs them.[2] The hylomorphic view, then, is dualistic *in a sense*. And presumably, in humans, the soul can exist apart from the body in some capacity. However something important would be missing; the soul would exist in a privative state. The Church states:

> The view that bodiliness is essential to personal identity is fundamental, even if not explicitly thematized in the witness of Christian Revelation. . . . The central dogmas of the Christian faith imply that the body is an intrinsic part of the human person and thus participates in his being created in the image of God.[3]

Of course Aristotle and Aquinas were not aware of the existence of DNA; therefore, especially if we are interested in the ethics of genetic engineering, it is important to discuss the relationship between hylomorphism and modern genetics. The Church actually says we can make an analogy of the DNA to form: "Thus, for example, the DNA of the chromosomes contains the information necessary for matter to be organized according to what is typical of a certain species or individual. Analogically, the substantial form provides to prime matter the information it needs to be organized in a particular way."[4] The relationship of DNA to form can lead to two different interpretations of hylomorphism.

The first, for lack of a better term let us call it "Dualistic Hylomorphism," is the view that the soul is a purely immaterial entity that is not identifiable with DNA. There is some support in the literature for this interpretation. Immediately following the above statement in HIG, a word of caution is given so as to emphasize that this is merely an analogy; it should not be taken to mean that the substantial form *is* DNA: "metaphysical and spiritual concepts cannot be simply compared with material, biological data."[5] Especially in the context of genetic engineering, this is a crucial distinction. Though the Church's discussion here is not focused on genetic engineering, it can be said that even at the level of DNA, we are still talking about matter. It is somewhat difficult to know how we might understand the relationship of form to DNA however. Presumably, as long as the principle of life remains in the substance (or organism), the form remains. Even if very important functions are lost, even permanently, (though this might depend on the current state of medical technology) presumably we still have the same kind of organism. For example, from a Catholic perspective, a person whose body (matter) has been damaged in a particular way and who is now in a persistent vegetative state is still a fully human person. The same form actualizes the matter, though there is a deficiency. The person is no longer able to carry out many of the natural human functions. Interestingly, one could compare this privative state with that of the disembodied soul that exists after death which we mentioned above. At any rate, dualistic hylomorphism entails that changes in matter, so long as they do not kill the organism, could inhibit but not change the substantial form. If this is the case, then changes to an organism could never result in a substantial change. And, furthermore, if dualistic hylomorphism is correct, a change to DNA would be change in matter (since DNA is not the form strictly speaking), even radical changes in DNA brought about through genetic engineering could not change the form.

However, one might wish to say that the relationship between substantial form and DNA is more intimate than that which is entailed by dualistic hylomorphism. Let us call this alternative view "Genetic Hylomorphism." That is, the form of a substance can be changed in the same way the form of an artifact could be changed. Consider an artifact like a spoon. Presumably by radically changing the matter, I could change the form from one thing to another. I could melt the spoon down and then use the exact same matter to make a knife. My intuition, and I think everyone else's, would be to say that the spoon went out of existence and a knife came into existence. If substances are more like artifacts in this way, changing an organism's DNA would work similarly. Thus genetic hylomorphism differs from dualistic hylomorphism in the following way: genetic hylomorphism entails that radical changes in DNA brought about through genetic engineering could in fact change the substantial form.

To further this discussion, consider the following admittedly bizarre case. Suppose that in some future time when enormous progress in genetic engineering has taken place, I take an early stage human embryo and alter its DNA so that it is identical with a tiger's genome. Though the Church's position is that embryos (from conception on) ought to be treated as human persons, it does not take a stand on whether ensoulment (i.e., the form is present) happens immediately after conception or some time later. So in our example, suppose I wait until long enough in the development of the embryo that we agree the human form is present. Then I insert the genetically engineered embryo into the womb of an adult female tiger where it gestates and is then born. This organism, from an empirical perspective is indistinguishable from other tigers. Is this thing a healthy well functioning tiger or is it a severely malfunctioning human person? If we endorse dualistic hylompor-phism, it seems like it is a malfunctioning person similar to the case of a person in a persistent vegetative state. The embryo, at the stage at which we engineered it, is a human person in that it has a form organizing the matter; the genetic change is a change in the matter; the principle of life remains. However, if we endorse genetic hylomorphism, we would say that the human form was replaced by a tiger form. So what happened was that a person came into existence, and a short time later was destroyed and a tiger came into existence (just not the way tigers normally come into existence). This is because a change in DNA can produce a substantial change according to genetic hylomorphism.

What are we to make of this strange thought experiment? We might wish to say that the entire thing is moot because what I have proposed is biologically impossible. In fact, I posed this to a physician with some expertise in genetics; he did not think technology could ever get to that point. By analogy, he said, if you went to a Ford plant, gave all the workers the plans for Toyotas, and then told them "Now build Toyotas," they wouldn't be able to do it with the materials they had. The same might be true of genetic material too.[6] But if we endorse an evolutionary view of biology, and as we shall see below, the Church suggests that we should, then the notion that as DNA changes so forms change seems to follow. After all, genetic mutations happen gradually, but over a long period of time organisms do change from one species to another.

Let us return to Aristotle for a moment. Aristotle advocated sharp natural lines that distinguished species. For him, the species we currently observe (human beings, tigers, robins, oak trees, etc.) are the species that have always been. Interestingly he mentions Empedocles as posing something like an evolutionary theory, one that could potentially threaten his natural teleology.[7] But this objection is dismissed rather quickly, as he says that things must arise either coincidentally or for an end, and it cannot be the case that all the regularities in nature are mere coincidence. Aristotle's view of species would lend itself to the view that a substance could never go from one form to another (human to tiger for example) and is thus closer to the dualistic hylomorphism outlined above. This Aristotelian biology is of course at odds with current day evolutionary biology. On the modern view, species are not as neatly distinguished from another. Instead, given the view that species evolve from common ancestors, we must look at things like historical populations and breeding. At the risk of oversimplifying, we might say Aristotle thinks species are really "out there" in the world, whereas the modern view has us imposing species on the world as a useful way of categorizing. In fact, one's species membership could even be contingent on many evolutionary views.

While official Church doctrine, as we have seen, fairly straightforwardly endorses the hylomorphism of Aristotle and Aquinas as its view of soul and body, there is no such endorsement of Aristotelian biology. Neither is there an official rejection of Aristotelian biology either however. Catholics need not endorse Aristotle or evolution to be in line with Church teaching, though the Church certainly thinks scientific evidence weighs strongly in evolution's favor:

> Since it has been demonstrated that all living organisms on earth are genetically related, it is virtually certain that all living organisms have descended from this first organism. Converging evidence from many studies in the physical and biological sciences furnishes mounting support for some theory of evolution to account for the development and diversification of life on earth.[8]

At some point in the evolutionary process, human beings came on the scene. Pope John Paul II calls the emergence of humans an "ontological leap." We can understand this leap in one of two ways depending on which of the two versions of hylomorphim we endorse.

On the dualistic hylomorphic view, the leap would work in line with, that is, run parallel with biological "advances" (changes that could be scientifically observed). However, the human form/soul marks an important kind of intervening on God's part. God "ensouled" the first human persons, though presumably their immediate ancestors were not human persons. From this we could say that humans are genetically related to other non-human organisms but ontologically distinct in the way that Aristotle thought all species were. This would lead to the odd consequence that if we genetically engineered a bear into a tiger, we would get a healthy tiger; but if we genetically changed a human's genome to a tiger's, we would have an unhealthy human. Forms, then, for non-human animals should be understood on the genetic hylomorphic view and could be changed in the way that I could melt down a spoon and make it into a knife. But, according to dualistic hylomorphism, the ontological uniqueness of human beings distinguishes them from all others species. For someone sympathetic to Catholicism, this should not be too troubling. This might be an important aspect in which we are made in the image and likeness of God. If one endorses genetic hylomorphism, she would simply understand the formal relationships of humans to other substances to be no different than the formal relationships of non-human animals to each other. The ontological leap would be the genetic mutations that ultimately resulted in the present day human genome: a form that results in creatures like us who are able to relate to God in a unique way. But the leap is not identified with an immaterial form that ensouls the organism as dualistic hylomorphism asserts: a view that reduces the human genome to an accidental attribute. I see good arguments for both views of hylomorphism, dualistic and genetic.[9] However, in moving to the ethics of genetic engineering, I think the same basic conclusions follow with respect to moral permissibility. Therefore, I tentatively claim that in the absence of an official Church declaration, it is not imperative for us to pick one or the other in order to continue the discussion.

My treatment of the relevant ethical tenets of standard Catholic doctrine will be much briefer than the preceding account of metaphysics. Once again, following Aquinas, the Church often makes use of natural law theory, the view that our nature informs us of certain goods which we ought to pursue and reveals to us that such goods ought not to be violated. To take an action that intentionally aims at the destruction of a basic human good is wrong, even if there is some noble goal that is intended. This is primarily why the Church rejects consequentialist theories of ethics. For example, life itself is the one of the chief goods; therefore one cannot intentionally kill an innocent person even to promote some other good. I will follow John Finnis in saying that in addition to life, basic human goods include sociability and friendship, knowledge, practical reasonableness, religion, aesthetic experience, and play. Since the topics of reproduction and genetic engineering are our focus, we should also add the basic human goods of the family, the complimentary nature of man and woman, and the parent/child relationship. I will return to these in my final section on the permissibility of genetic enhancement.

II. The Church's Stated Position on Genetic Engineering

In this section, I want to briefly touch on the Church's explicit statements about genetic engineering. There are two types of genetic engineering, somatic and germ-line. Somatic genetic engineering (which is the type used in current gene-therapy treatments in humans) does not affect the sex cells of the recipient. A vector, often a modified virus, is used to repair targeted cells. This type of therapy is often used in adult patients, and because it does not affect the sex cells, does not affect the genes the adult passes along to offspring. It also has less a sense of permanence. The genetic changes will not become permanently encoded in the recipient's DNA. Germ line engineering is typically considered more controversial. Engineered traits that affect the sex cells would be passed along and permanently encoded in the resulting offspring. Germ line engineering is associated with being more permanent, and is usually envisioned as taking place very early on in development (either at the embryonic stage or even on the gametes before fertilization). At an intuitive level, many people find somatic genetic engineering permissible, but find germ line engineering impermissible.

Perhaps even more pressing in the ethics of genetic engineering than the somatic/germ line distinction, however, is the distinction between therapy (using genetic engineering to repair a disease or defect) and enhancement (using it to produce some desired trait or characteristic in an otherwise "normal" offspring). For many, using genetic engineering for therapeutic purposes would be acceptable, but using it for enhancement would be frivolous, vain, and dangerous; in short, genetic enhancement would be seriously morally wrong.

Based on these distinctions, we can think about four types of genetic engineering: somatic-therapeutic, germ-line-therapeutic, somatic-enhancement, and germ-line-enhancement. DP and HIG support the common attitudes outlined above, that the only one of these four that is permissible is somatic-therapeutic genetic engineering:

> Procedures used on somatic cells for strictly therapeutic purposes are in principle morally licit. Such actions seek to restore the normal genetic configuration of the patient or to counter damage caused by genetic anomalies or those related to other pathologies. . . . The moral evaluation of germ line cell therapy is different. Whatever genetic modifications are effected on the germ cells of a person will be transmitted to any potential offspring. Because the risks connected to any genetic manipulation are considerable and as yet not fully controllable, in the present state of research, it is not morally permissible to act in a way that may cause possible harm to the resulting progeny.[10]

What is important to note is that the Church emphasizes the impermissibility of germ line engineering "in its present state." The objection is not in principle to manipulating the germ line, which suggests that germ line manipulation as such is not an intentional violation of a basic human good (the foundational ethical tenet mentioned earlier). Rather, the impermissibility is based in instrumental concerns such as a lack of protection for progeny. Another such concern is the Church's view of the importance of the conjugal act in procreation, which could be threatened if genetic engineering were practiced in certain ways. HIG emphasizes this:

> Germ line genetic engineering with a therapeutic goal in man would in itself be acceptable were it not for the fact that it is hard to imagine how

this could be achieved without disproportionate risks especially in the first experimental stage, such as the huge loss of embryos and the incidence of mishaps, and without the use of reproductive techniques.[11]

These passages suggest that, so long as risks to progeny are reduced and procreation through the conjugal act are preserved, that germ line genetic engineering would be no more problematic than somatic genetic engineering.

The Church speaks to the therapy/enhancement distinction far more forcefully, and the prohibition against enhancement appears to be much more than an instrumental one. HIG states:

> Changing the genetic identity of man as a human person through the production of an infrahuman being is radically immoral. The use of genetic modification to yield a superhuman or being with essentially new spiritual faculties is unthinkable, given that the spiritual life principle of man—forming the matter into the body of the human person—is not a product of human hands and is not subject to genetic engineering. The uniqueness of each human person, in part constituted by his biogenetic characteristics and developed through nurture and growth, belongs intrinsically to him and cannot be instrumentalized in order to improve some of these characteristics.[12]

DP emphasizes additional concerns over genetic enhancement having to do with violations of justice: "such manipulation would promote a eugenic mentality and would lead to indirect social stigma with regard to people who lack certain qualities, while privileging qualities that happen to be appreciated by a certain culture or society; such qualities do not constitute what is specifically human."[13] Taking these passages, it seems that we can summarize the following as a Church position: For both instrumental reasons given the current state of technology and likely violations of justice, and more importantly the intrinsic evils depriving human beings of their essential form, germ line enhancement is morally impermissible. Nevertheless, I think this may be too quick, and so in my final section, I wish to probe the enhancement question more deeply and suggest that there may be forms of enhancement that would be in line with the general Catholic framework I have laid out to this point.

III. Further Reflection on Catholicism and Genetic Enhancement

Why probe this question more deeply given that the Church's answer is fairly straightforward? One reason is that to simply say that genetic therapy is permissible while enhancement is not is that the line between the two is not as sharp as it might seem at first glance. Certain practices such as curing Huntington's chorea are clearly therapeutic, and practices such as making someone 6'4" instead of 5'8" so he has a better chance of playing professional sports or making someone's sense of smell as acute as a Bloodhound's seem pretty clearly to be enhancements. But what about genes associated with intelligence, or as Jonathan Glover has suggested, those associated with being prone to depression? If having a significant deficiency in an area like this would be considered a defect, it could be therapeutic to intervene. How far do we go however; to the low end of the normal range, the middle of the normal range, the high end of normal? And wouldn't the normal range itself change if we treated those with deficiencies, suggesting that what is "normal" is fairly arbitrary? If the line between enhancement and therapy is blurred in many cases, then how might we treat the ethics of genetic engineering from a Catholic perspective, or any other perspective that takes that distinction to be morally significant?

I actually believe the Catholic metaphysical and ethical framework can deal with this question fairly well. First, we need to distinguish between two types of enhancement: let us call these individual enhancement and species enhancement (here I am not concerned with the Aristotelian vs. evolution question discussed above). Individual enhancement would include practices like my first example above of increasing height from 5'8" to 6'4". Being 5'8" is not a defect or a disease, so this is an enhancement. But the desired trait, being 6'4", is one that other human beings have. Individual enhancements would be those that aim to produce a trait that others have "naturally." Species enhancements, by contrast, would aim at going beyond the traits we observe in the human population. My second example, that of giving someone a sense of smell as acute as a Bloodhound's, would be a species enhancement. I should say that these are not hard and fast distinctions but rather helpful ways of categorizing. Presumably natural mutations could make some genetic engineering practices that are now species enhancements later become individual enhancements since some people would then have the traits "naturally." The Church recognizes that we can think about genes in either of these two ways:

> the genome has two dimensions: a general dimension inasmuch as it is a characteristic of all those who belong to the human species, and an individual dimension inasmuch as it is different for each human being, who receives it from his or her parents at the moment of conception: this is what it normally means to speak of the "genetic heritage" of a human being. It seems clear that this "heritage" should be given fundamental protection, since this "heritage" belongs concretely and individually to every human being.[14]

Let us consider individual enhancement first. If we stay with the current example, genetically engineering a child to be 6'4" to give him a better chance to be a professional athlete, I think many of us would disapprove. I also think the Church would consider this wrong. We can probe a bit deeper, however, and ask what it is about this enhancement that makes it wrong. I don't think we should say it is wrong *because* it is enhancement. Obviously we don't think enhancement is wrong in principle, we try to enhance our children all the time. We praise parents for "trying to give their children every opportunity." Where we disapprove, however, is when parents try to pressure their children, to take away from their autonomy, or in more Catholic language their "human dignity." So if I genetically engineer my child's height in the hope of making him a pro athlete, I think it is wrong in the same way that it would be wrong to force the child to play sports and pressure him to be a great athlete from the time he's five or six years old. This isn't to say that the same act, making a child taller, is made right or wrong purely by the intention; that is, it's right to do something to give the child every opportunity but wrong to do the exact same thing if the intention is to pressure him or her. Rather, the intentions are often helpful signs that reveal whether the child will be benefitted or harmed by a given intervention. Individual genetic enhancements could lend themselves to such abuses, and this is something to be on our guard against. But, given the blurred distinction between therapy and enhancement as well as the permissibility of manipulating the genome for the former, the question I think is a matter of our motivations. Are we enhancing the child to give him every opportunity in the way that we do environmentally as loving and supporting parents? Or, are we using the child as a means—to live our dreams through them, or to achieve fame or money, etc.? These questions, not simply *whether* or not the genetic engineering is an enhancement, are what are morally relevant. I would speculate that the reason therapeutic genetic engineering does not arouse the same worries as enhancement is because we easily grant that parents would be using therapeutic genetic engineering to give their children the best *for their own sake*. And this view towards our children seems to me to be perfectly in line with a Catholic moral framework.

Species enhancement raises some of the same moral questions, but additional concerns as well. Nevertheless, I think that from a Catholic perspective there is at least some room for discussion such that a categorical rejection would be premature. Our reaction to my example, creating a Bloodhound's sense of smell, is likely to be repugnance. And in one sense, I think this repugnance is like the kind we feel in the individual enhancement case. We immediately think of the child's dignity being violated. For why would we do such a thing other than with some goal in mind for the child to live a certain kind of life because *I* want it that way? With species enhancement, there is the added hubris that we think of the child as some sort of bizarre experiment just to see just what we are capable of doing. Clearly species enhancements with such a mentality are an affront to human dignity and morally wrong from the Catholic perspective.

Species enhancements are problematic for an additional reason. If we fundamentally changed our DNA and passed these changes on to our descendants, it could be that we severely limit and maybe even eliminate the ability of human persons to pursue basic human goods of the kind I mentioned at the end of the first section of this paper (family, knowledge, sociability/friendship, religion, play, etc.). On the dualistic hylomorphic view, future generations could consist exclusively of malfunctioning human beings. Another possibility (I do not know if it's better or worse) is that it could be that there is an ontological leap in reverse, so at some point the genome has been so manipulated that God no longer ensouls offspring and there are no more human persons. Although the phenomena will be explained differently, genetic hylomorphism would allow for the same catastrophes, namely severely deprived human persons and the inadvertent elimination of human persons altogether.

But would *all* forms of species enhancement *necessarily* lead to one of the problems just mentioned? I do not believe that the answer is obviously yes. Could we imagine our genetic make-up being different in such a way that it would not inhibit our ability to pursue basic human goods that are essential for our relationship to God and one another? Could these changes be brought about with a mentality to really benefit those we enhance for *their own good*, rather than our ulterior motives or hubris?

Would having an improved sense of smell beyond what humans now currently have inhibit our ability to pursue any basic human goods? Could we no longer have friendships, families, knowledge, or spiritual lives? I am inclined to say no. If we say that it is vain or pointless, imagine another species enhancement. Suppose we could significantly improve our immune systems, beyond what humans now currently have. This would go a long way toward eliminating disease and suffering, which we think are noble ends. I think it can be reasonably argued that, while it is a species enhancement, this practice would not conflict with the Catholic moral framework.

Conclusion

My goal in this paper has not been to say that Catholics should feel fine about pursuing genetic engineering as quickly as possible. Rather, it has been to sketch what I take to be the relevant metaphysical and ethical framework, and to do so relying on official Church documents. I ultimately suggested that in assessing whether or not a genetic engineering practice is permissible, we should be more concerned with questions about human dignity and basic human goods than with distinctions about somatic vs. germ-line or even therapy vs. enhancement. But it is important, before closing, to emphasize that this science is still in its infancy. We are still very far away from the kinds of practices I have used as examples in this paper. And as we progress, as with any technology, we need to carefully weigh risks against potential benefits, and never ignore how these risks might affect all human persons.[15]

Niagara University

Notes

1. Congregation for the Doctrine of the Faith, *Dignitas Personae* (Rome, Italy: Offices for the Congregation for the Doctrine of the Faith, 2009), 1.

2. One should of course be careful not to stretch the example too far. The soul is logically prior, though it is (unlike a blue print) not *existentially* separate from the matter it informs.

3. International Theological Commission, *Communion and Stewardship: Human Persons Created in the Image and Likeness of God* (Rome, Italy: Offices for the Congregation for the Doctrine of the Faith, 2002), 29–30.

4. Ibid., 30.

5. Ibid.

6. My thanks to Dr. David Martin of the Mayo Clinic for this example.

7. Aristotle, *Physics* II.8, 24–33.

8. International Theological Commission, *Humans in the Image of God*, 63.

9. In his comments on this paper, Samuel Condic suggests that the hylomorphism of Aquinas is identifiable with neither the dualistic nor the genetic versions I have laid out. The form can be affected by material change (presumably at the genetic level), but the human soul is also a subsistent being in its own right as an intellectual substance. So this would make it like the dualistic model in the sense of the "ontological leap" but like the genetic model in the sense that a change in DNA could result in a substantial change. I take it this is correct, but my construction of these two models still leaves us with the open question (which I intentionally leave open) that a case such as the one with the embryonic tiger is either a new substance or the same substance malfunctioning.

10. Congregation for the Doctrine of the Faith, *Dignitas Personae*, 26.

11. International Theological Commission, *Humans in the Image of God*, 90.

12. Ibid., 91.

13. Congregation for the Doctrine of the Faith, *Dignitas Personae*, 27.

14. Congregation for the Doctrine of the Faith, *Observations on the Universal Declaration on the Human Genome and Human Rights* (Rome, Italy: Offices for the Congregation for the Doctrine of the Faith, 1997).

15. My thanks to Samuel Condic for his very insightful and helpful comments on this paper at the ACPA meeting.

Bibliography

Aristotle. 1941. *The Basic Works of Aristotle*, ed. Richard McKeon. New York: Random House.

Congregation for the Doctrine of the Faith. 1987. *Donum Vitae*. Rome: Offices for the Congregation for the Doctrine of the Faith.

———. 1997. *Observations on the Universal Declaration on the Human Genome and Human Rights*. Rome: Offices for the Congregation of the Doctrine of the Faith.

———. 2009. *Dignitas Personae*. Rome: Offices for the Congregation of the Doctrine of the Faith.

Descartes, Rene, *Meditations of First Philosophy*, trans. Donald Cress. Indianapolis: Hackett Publishing Company, 1993.

Finnis, John. 1984. *Natural Law Natural Rights*. Oxford, N.Y.: Oxford University Press.

Glover, Jonathan. 1984. *What Sort of People Should There Be?* Harmondsworth, UK: Penguin Books.

International Theological Commission. 2002. *Communion and Stewardship: Human Persons Created in the Image and Likeness of God*. Rome: Offices for the Congregation for the Doctrine of the Faith.

Plato. 1997. *Phaedo*. In *The Complete Works*, ed. John Cooper. Indianapolis: Hackett Publishing Company.

Pope John Paul II. 1996. "Message to the Pontifical Academy of Sciences on Evolution." Message delivered to the Pontifical Academy of Sciences, Rome, Italy, October 22, 1996.

The Language of Rights:
Towards an Aristotelian-Thomistic Analysis

Michael Baur

Abstract: Alasdair MacIntyre has argued that our contemporary discourse about "rights," and "natural rights" or "human rights," is alien to the thought of Aristotle and Aquinas. His worry, it seems, is that our contemporary language of rights is often taken to imply that individuals may possess certain entitlement-conferring properties or powers (typically called "rights") entirely in isolation from other individuals, and outside the context of any community or common good. In this paper, I accept MacIntyre's worries about our contemporary language of "rights"; however, I seek to show that some of our contemporary language or discourse about "justice" and "rights" is not altogether misguided, but does—in fact—reflect a properly critical (Aristotelian-Thomistic) understanding of what is meant by "justice" and "rights."

I. Introduction:
The Problematic Character of our Language about "Rights"

In his ground-breaking work, *After Virtue*, Alasdair MacIntyre argues that our contemporary discourse about "natural rights," "human rights," or "the rights of man" is alien to the thought of Aristotle and Aquinas.[1] In fact, MacIntyre goes so far as to say that an Aristotelian-Thomistic thinker ought to regard "natural rights," "human rights," or "the rights of man" as fictions whose ontological status is no different from the ontological status of unicorns and witches:

> for the truth is plain: there are no such rights, and belief in them is one with belief in witches and unicorns. The best reason for asserting so bluntly that there are no such rights is indeed of precisely the same type as the best reason which we possess for asserting that there are no witches and the best reason we possess for asserting that there are no unicorns: every attempt to give good reasons for believing that there *are* such rights has failed.[2]

In some of his later work, MacIntyre seems to have moderated his position regarding "rights," limiting himself mainly to claims about the conditions under which talk about "natural rights," "human rights," or "the rights of man" might be possible within the context of virtue ethics:

> it is clear that from the standpoint of virtue ethics, rights would not primarily provide grounds for claims made by individuals *against* other individuals or groups. They would instead have to be conceived primarily as enabling provisions, whereby individuals could claim a due place within the life of some particular community, and the question of what rights individuals have or should have would be answerable only in terms of the answers to a prior set of questions about what sort of community this is, directed towards the achievement of what sort of common good, and inculcating what kinds of virtues.[3]

Based on these two quotations from MacIntyre, one might be led to conclude that MacIntyre has gradually come around—though somewhat reluctantly—to accepting the view that it might be possible to talk about "rights" and "natural rights" within the context of virtue ethics, but only if such talk is subject to rather rigorous restrictions or limiting conditions regarding what is meant by "rights."

In this paper, I do not aim to analyze the development of MacIntyre's thought regarding rights from the time that he wrote *After Virtue* (in 1981) to the time that he expressed what appears to be his more moderate view (in 1990). My aim, rather, is to make use of MacIntyre's difficult grappling with the language of "rights" as a starting point for my own reflections on what sense we can make of the term, "rights," within an Aristotelian-Thomistic context. As MacIntyre has shown us, it is important to exercise some degree of caution—or even suspicion—regarding the language of rights insofar as such language can easily be misunderstood to imply that individuals may possess certain entitlement-conferring properties or powers (typically called "rights") entirely in isolation from other individuals, and outside the context of any community or common good. Thus along with MacIntyre, I accept the view that "rights" are inescapably relational: to "possess a right," on the Aristotelian-Thomistic account I wish to explicate, is to occupy a place within an order or ordering of justice, according to which two or more individuals are related to one another as equals in some relevant respect.

But while agreeing with MacIntyre on the relational or context-dependent character of what we mean by "rights," I also wish to affirm that some of our contemporary language or discourse about "rights" is not altogether misguided. More specifically, I wish to affirm that at least some of our contemporary discourse does, indeed, reflect the Aristotelian-Thomistic view that justice consists in a kind of equality or commensuration between two or more individuals; and that the "rights" which individuals possess are not merely individual possessions, but depend—in a fundamental way—on what we might call "equality of due treatment." In short, I wish to affirm that we can meaningfully employ some of our contemporary language of "rights," even while denying (along with MacIntyre) that our language of "rights" refers to properties or powers that allegedly belong to individuals entirely apart from their relations to others or apart from their belonging to communities. On the Aristotelian-Thomistic account I wish to present, our language of rights must always be used in tandem with an understanding of justice, or equality of due treatment: if the proper equality or commensuration between individuals and their acts is observed, then we can justifiably say that (natural or positive) rights are respected; if the proper equality or commensuration is not observed, then we can justifiably say that (natural or positive) rights are violated.

II. Our Contemporary Language about "Rights," "Misfortunes," and "Injustices"

In contemporary discussions, the claim that a person (or, according to some, an animal) has a right is often taken to mean nothing more than that a person or animal ought to be treated in a certain way. Thus, when politicians and pundits argue that every American citizen has a "right to health care," they are taken to mean (and they often take themselves to mean) nothing more and nothing less than that every American citizen ought to be given health care. Similarly, when animal activists argue that animals have a "right to humane treatment," they are taken to mean (and they often take themselves to mean) nothing more and nothing less than that animals ought to be treated humanely. But for a critical-minded philosopher, this relatively straightforward equation of our language of "rights" and our language of "oughts" will simply not suffice. After all, I can believe with all due sincerity that books ought to be read and ought not to be burned, even though I do not hold that books have a right to be read or a right to be spared from the flames. Similarly, a person can believe that every American citizen ought to be given access to health care, or that animals ought to be treated humanely, even without believing that American citizens and animals, respectively, possess rights to these goods. If our language of "rights" does not simply mean the very same thing that is meant by our language of "oughts," then what precisely do we mean, when we make use of the language of rights?

In order to begin addressing this question, let us stipulate for the sake of convenience (after all, it is beyond the scope of this paper to provide complete justification for every relevant philosophical claim) that to be treated justly is to have one's right or rights respected; and to be treated unjustly is to have one's right or rights violated. Now let us ask: what do we mean, when we use the terms "injustice" and "misfortune" to refer to different kinds of happenings? Consider the following scenarios:

(A) While crossing an open meadow in the rain, I am struck and killed by lightning.

(B) While standing at an intersection, a stranger—without my prior knowledge or consent—suddenly pushes me, causing me to trip over the curb, fall to the ground, and fracture my femur.

Do the happenings described in (A) and (B) represent instances of injustice or misfortune? It is tempting to say that the happening described in (A) is a mere misfortune (a mere freak accident of nature), while the happening described in (B) is an injustice. But upon further reflection, it turns out that this immediately intuitive response is inadequate.

In scenario (A), it could be the case that the meadow which I am crossing is not an instance of *res nullius* (it is not a thing that belongs to nobody), but is in fact part of a large public park managed by a municipality that has been instructed repeatedly by state authorities to erect warning signs and a fence around the meadow, since (by virtue of its location and elevation) it is known to be an especially dangerous attractor of lightning strikes. Under those circumstances, my being struck and killed by lightning may turn out to be an instance of injustice, and not merely a misfortune or freak of nature. For in the scenario as it has thus been described in greater detail, at least one significant cause that contributes to my being struck and killed by lightning would be the municipality's negligent or intentional failure to erect a fence and warning signs, as required by the state authorities (for the sake of protecting individual citizens from risks about which they might otherwise be unaware).

In a similar vein, we can think of scenario (B) as illustrating an instance of a mere misfortune, rather than any kind of injustice. In scenario (B), it could be the case the stranger who pushes me and causes my femur to be fractured was (1) insane and compelled to push me on account of his insanity (let us call this scenario B.1), or (2) sane but acting with the intention of moving me quickly out of the path of an oncoming car and thus saving my life (let us call this scenario B.2). In scenario B.1, the harm caused to me (in the form of my fractured femur) is not an unjust harm, since the stranger who pushed me was not acting as a free and responsible agent (his action may have been caused—beyond the scope of his free agency—by a neurological or chemical condition). Since the harm that befalls me in this case is not traceable to an agent that I might hold responsible, the fact that this harm has befallen me is not an injustice but a misfortune (akin to the kinds of harms that are traceable only to natural causes, whether these causes have to do with lightning strikes and earthquakes in the world outside the bodies of human beings, or neurological debilities or chemical imbalances within the bodies of human beings). In scenario B.2, the harm caused to me (in the form of my fractured femur) is not an unjust harm, since the stranger whose actions brought about this harm was acting with the intention of saving my life. The stranger may have believed that he could push me out of the path of the oncoming car, without knocking me down and injuring me; in that case, my falling and sustaining a fracture would have not only been unintended by him, but also unforeseen. Alternatively, the stranger may have realized that his pushing me away from the oncoming car also carried with it the substantial risk of knocking me down and causing some non-fatal harm to me. But even if the stranger foresaw the harm to be caused to me, the harm itself (my femur's being fractured) is something that fell outside the scope of his intention when he pushed me, and thus the harm that he caused would be justifiable under the circumstances.

Now the traditional "doctrine of double effect" is relevant here, and it offers a credible explanation of precisely *why* the stranger's action was justified; for according to the "doctrine of double effect," the stranger's act of pushing me down in order to save my life would be justified, even if he foresaw the non-fatal harm that he would cause me, since the causing of this non-fatal harm fell outside the scope of his intention, and the good at which he was aiming in the act of pushing me (namely, the good of preserving my life) was sufficiently weighty to justify the causing of the lesser, unforeseen harm. A full explanation of the relevance and defensibility of the "doctrine of double effect" in the present case is beyond the scope of this paper.[4] But the important point, for our purposes here, is that the harm caused to me on account of the stranger's act of pushing me to the ground may, under certain circumstances, be properly characterized not as an instance of injustice, but as a mere misfortune. The fact that the harm caused to me is a misfortune, and not an injustice, is grounded on the fact that the harm caused to me is either (a) not traceable to any voluntary act of a free and responsible agent (e.g., if the stranger did not and could not reasonably have foreseen the harm that would befall me as a result of his act of pushing me), or (b) traceable to the voluntary act of a free and responsible agent, but in a case where the agent's achievement of some greater, intended good (e.g., the saving of my life) was apprehended by the agent as inseparable from the causing of some other, lesser harm (e.g., the fracturing of my femur). In both of these cases, the harm would be said to be a misfortune rather than an injustice, insofar as the harm as such is something that (a) falls altogether outside the scope of what the agent does voluntarily, or (b) falls within the scope of what the agent does voluntarily but outside the scope of what the agent does intentionally, even though the harm (given the way that circumstances in the natural world present themselves) is bound up with (is not separable from) what the agent aims at intentionally.[5] In either case, the fact that harm befalls me is properly traceable not to the causal efficacy of any moral agent acting for the sake of some intended end, but rather to the natural causality of things and circumstances in the world (after all, the brute fact that a particular intended good happens to be inseparable, given the way the world is, from an unintended but foreseen harm, is a function of natural and not intelligent causality); and thus the harm caused to me under these circumstances (my fractured femur) is properly characterized as a misfortune rather than an injustice.[6]

What emerges from the two scenarios that we have been considering is the following lesson: the question of whether a particular scenario is to be properly understood in terms of a "misfortune" or an "injustice" (i.e., a violation of rights) depends not simply on the nature or character of the harm done to some individual person; it depends rather on whether or not the harm done is properly traceable to (or attributable to) the free and responsible agency of some other individual person or persons. The lesson, in other words, is that the question of whether or not an injustice has been done and a right has been violated, depends fundamentally on relations between two or more persons, and not merely on relations between a particular person and a particular harm done. This implies, furthermore, that our language of "rights" is language about that which is inescapably relational; it is about relations between persons or moral agents, and not merely about relations between persons and things, or between persons and harms. Our contemporary language regarding the difference between misfortunes and injustices does, indeed, reflect this important lesson. In the final section of this paper, I wish to make a start at showing how this lesson (about the relational character of justice, and thus the relational character of what we mean by "rights") can be understood and accounted for, from an Aristotelian-Thomistic point of view.

III. Towards an Aristotelian-Thomistic Account of "Justice" and "Rights"

Following Aristotle, Aquinas holds that the virtue of justice directs the human being in his or her relations to others, and these others can be regarded (a) as individual others, or (b) as others in general, i.e., others as the whole community to which the human being belongs. When understood in this latter sense, justice can be regarded as lawfulness in general, in which case it is called "legal justice" or "general justice" (as distinct from "particular justice," which directs the human being in his or her relations to other individuals). Legal justice or general justice has the character of lawfulness in general, since it directs the human being to the common good of the entire community, and as a result may command any of the acts of the other virtues, since the good of any particular virtue can in principle be ordered to the common good of the whole community (*ST* 2-2, Q. 58, a. 5–7). Furthermore, Aquinas also holds that the proper aim or object of justice is "right" or "the right" (*ius*), which is a kind of equality or "something equal" in external things (*ST* 2-2, Q. 59, a. 2). For Aquinas, then, justice always involves the relation of an individual or individuals to some other or others (*ST* 2-2, Q. 58, a. 2), and we can talk meaningfully about "the right" only where there is some ordering or arrangement whereby the acts and/or works of separate individuals (or groups, which henceforth will be implied by the word "individuals") can be regarded as commensurate or equal with respect to one another in some respect (*ST* 2-2, Q. 57, a. 1–3; Q. 59, a. 2). Given the conceptual connections in Aquinas's thought between justice, lawfulness, and the right, it is no surprise that Aquinas's account of natural law has often been understood as implying an account of "natural rights" or "human rights."

It is worth emphasizing, however, that Aquinas himself never developed a theory of "rights" or "natural rights." He did sometimes talk about "the right" in ways that seem to imply that "rights" might belong to individuals. Thus, for example, we sometimes read in Aquinas about "the right of dominion" over things (*ST* 2-2, Q. 62, a. 1, ad. 2), "the right of possessing" things (*ST* 2-2, Q. 66, a. 5, ad. 2), "the right of rulership" over others (*ST* 2-2, Q. 69, a. 1, c.), and "the right of accepting" tithes (*ST* 2-2, Q. 87, a. 3, c.). Furthermore, Aquinas says that justice is fittingly defined as "the perpetual and constant will to render to each one his right" (*ST* 2-2, Q. 58, a. 1). But contrary to John Locke and others who think of rights as entitlements or powers that can be possessed by individuals considered in isolation from one another, Aquinas would hold that one can talk meaningfully about justice, the right, or "rights," only where two or more individuals are related to one another within the context of some arrangement or ordering whereby their acts and/or works can be regarded as commensurate or equal to one another in some relevant respect and in accordance with some common measure.

Consider, for example, a regime which recognizes what people today would call the right to own private property. For Aquinas, a defensible explanation or justification of this right would not appeal to any "natural," "self-evident," or "pre-existing" entitlements possessed by individuals as such (e.g., the entitlement to have dominion over one's own body or over the products of one's labor), but rather to the ends being served by the arrangement which allows for the ownership of private property. Thus, following Aristotle, Aquinas argues that it is reasonable for human beings to possess external things as their own, since in a society where some kind of private ownership is recognized, there will be less shirking of responsibility, less confusion, and less bickering in the way that people exercise dominion over external things (*ST* 2-2, Q. 66, a. 2). On Aquinas's account, to enjoy the "right" to own private property in such a society would be to enjoy equal treatment in accordance with the rules (whatever they may be) that allow for the acquisition, possession, and alienation of external things by private individuals. Significantly, Aquinas argues that in cases where one human being is in danger of perishing out of urgent and extreme need, it is licit for him or her to steal from another who possesses a surplus of wealth. Aquinas goes on to observe that this kind of taking, strictly speaking, would not even qualify as an instance of stealing (*ST* 2-2. Q. 66, a. 7). It is tempting to think that Aquinas's point here is that, in regimes which allow for the ownership of private property, individuals have a right to private property which may be violated in certain instances, such as in cases where someone is in danger of perishing out of extreme need. But to express the matter in this way is to commit a category mistake. Aquinas's point is not that the "right" to own private property can be violated in certain instances. His point, rather, is that in any instance where one person possesses a surplus of wealth and another is in imminent danger of dying on account of needs that could be remedied by taking from such surplus, there is (according to the "natural law" itself) no rightful ordering—and hence no "right" to own the surplus wealth—in the first place.

For Aquinas, we cannot speak meaningfully about "the right" or about "rights" if individuals are not related to one another in some way that allows us to regard their acts and/or works as equal to one another in some relevant respect. We might say that, on Aquinas's account, what we mean by "the right" or "rights" is inescapably relational: to possess a "right" is to occupy a place within some arrangement or ordering whereby two or more individuals are treated as equals in some relevant respect. Rights are respected when the proper equality between individuals is observed; and rights are violated when the proper equality between individuals is not observed. Of course, treating individuals as equals in one respect (e.g., in accordance with the rules that allow them to acquire, possess, and alienate property) is perfectly compatible with treating them as unequal in other, unrelated respects (thus those who acquire the largest sums of wealth in accordance with the rules of property law are not automatically qualified to win the most beauty contests or singing competitions).

Aquinas himself does not speak about "natural rights" or "human rights." But following Aquinas, human beings may be said to possess "natural rights" or "human rights" insofar as they can be regarded as equal to one another simply on account of their shared status as human beings, or on account of their shared membership in the natural kind, "human being." Thus even if two or more human individuals shared no common status within the context of some conventional or agreed upon ("posited") arrangement (and thus even if they had no "positive" rights with respect to one another), they may nevertheless be said to have "natural rights" or "human rights" with respect to one another. Thus it would be a violation of right or rights if such individuals were not accorded the kind of treatment that is (equally) fitting for them, given the sort of goodness and dignity that they possess simply as human beings. Notice, however, that to say that a certain kind of goodness or dignity exists wherever any human being exists, is not the same as saying that "natural rights" or "human rights" exist wherever any human being exists. When an isolated human being starves to death on a desert island, there is genuine harm or evil (namely, the loss of the unique goodness that belongs to a human life). But in such an instance, one cannot say that there has been a violation of right or rights, since the loss of human life on the desert island has not been the result of any sort of unequal treatment involving one human being and another. On the other hand, if a human being starves to death because his neighbors do not share with him their surplus wealth, then one can talk meaningfully about a violation of rights, and even a violation of "natural rights" or "human rights" (for Aquinas, it is a dictate of the natural law itself that the superabundant wealth of some should be used for the purpose of aiding those who need it; *ST* 2-2, Q. 66, a. 7). In the case of the stingy neighbors, the violation of "natural rights" would consist not in the loss of life as such, but rather in the neighbors' culpable failure to accord to another human being the sort of treatment that they can and do accord to themselves and that is (equally) fitting for all human beings, given the sort of goodness and dignity that they possess simply as human beings.

For Aquinas, the question of whether a particular being is or is not an instance of a certain natural kind is not to be settled by asking whether or not that particular being possesses or does not possess certain supposedly "essential" properties that are normally perfective for beings of that kind. After all, there are many individual human beings (instances of the natural kind, "human being") that remain human beings, even though they lack certain properties that are normally perfective for human beings (e.g., the properties of being able to engage in conscious activities, or to reason). For Aquinas, the question of whether a particular being is or is not an instance of a certain natural kind is to be settled by asking whether it is a being for which it is "natural" for it to have certain properties. More precisely, the question is to be settled by asking whether it is a being whose having of certain properties is to be explained by reference to some *internal* principle of the being itself, and whose lacking of those properties—if it does lack them—is to be explained by reference to some *failure* in its nature or some *extrinsic* cause of the lack (a cause such as a brain hemorrhage). Notice here that the question of whether a particular being is or is not an instance of a certain natural kind is not to be settled by attending to the individual being alone; for no amount of attending to an individual being alone can ever reveal which properties are essential, and which are inessential, to that being, given the kind of being it is.[7] Rather, the question of whether a particular being is or is not an instance of a certain natural kind is to be settled by relying on an account of what is natural to (what is expected for the most part of) the kind of being in question, even if particular instances of the being in question may lack the usual or expected properties on account of some interference with internal principles.

As a final note, it is worth emphasizing here that, on the Aristotelian-Thomistic account being presented, it remains the case that "natural rights" and "human rights" are inescapably relational. But it does not follow that respect for "natural rights" or "human rights" is reducible to respect for values or goods that are "merely relative" or "merely convention-based." While "rights" are inescapably relational (insofar as the very notion of rights pertains to "equal treatment" of two or more individuals in some relevant respect), it remains the case that the very foundation of "natural rights" or "human rights" (namely, membership in a community defined by a natural kind) is not "merely relative" or "merely convention-based." The crucial point might be illustrated through an analogy drawn from the physical sciences: the notion of "natural rights" stands to the notion of "human nature" as the notion of "weight" stands to the notion of "mass." According to the modern scientific understanding, a body does not have weight if there is no other body present to exert the gravitational force of attraction upon it; but while a body has weight only insofar as it stands in relation to some other body, a body is capable of having such weight only because it is a body which by its very nature has mass, and would continue to have mass even if it did not stand in relation to any other body. By the same token, a human being does not possess "natural rights" if his or her acts or works cannot be regarded as adjustable or commensurable to the acts or works of other human beings; but while a human being has "natural rights" only insofar as he or she stands in some relevant relation to one or more other human beings, a human being is capable of having such natural rights only because he or she by nature belongs to a certain natural (and not merely posited or socially-constructed) class of things, and therefore possesses what we call "human nature"; and furthermore, the human being would continue to possess this human nature (and would continue to possess all the value or dignity that properly belongs to beings of this nature), even if he or she did not stand in relation to any other human beings.

Fordham University

Notes

1. See Alasdair MacIntyre, *After Virtue: A Study in Moral Theory* (Notre Dame, Ind.: University of Notre Dame Press, 1981), 64–67.

2. MacIntyre, *After Virtue*, 67.

3. Alasdair MacIntyre, "The Return to Virtue Ethics," in *The Twentieth Anniversary of Vatican II: A Look Back and A Look Ahead: Proceedings of the Ninth Bishops' Conference*, ed. Russell E. Smith (Braintree, Mass.: The Pope John Center, 1990), 247–248.

4. For more on the doctrine of double effect, see G. E. M. Anscombe, "Action, Intention, and 'Double Effect,'" in *Proceedings of the American Catholic Philosophical Association* (Washington, D.C.: American Catholic Philosophical Association, 1982), 12–25; and T. A. Cavanaugh, *Double Effect Reasoning: Doing Good and Avoiding Evil* (Oxford: The Clarendon Press, 2006). For Aquinas's most famous articulation of the view that has come to be known as the "doctrine of double effect," see Thomas Aquinas, *Summa Theologica*, 2-2, Q. 64, a. 7. All subsequent references to Aquinas's *Summa Theologica* will be indicated parenthetically in the body of the text itself, using *ST* as the abbreviation for *Summa Theologica*.

5. Here, I am relying on the Aristotelian-Thomistic account of the difference between the voluntary and the intended (acts which are intended or intentional form a subset of those that are voluntary). It is beyond the scope of this paper to provide a full—or even adequate—account of this distinction. But what I mean by this distinction is the following: an agent voluntarily brings about some state of affairs, X, when the agent acts with knowledge and some degree of control over the coming to be of X; an agent intentionally brings about some state of affairs, X, when the agent not only acts voluntarily in bringing about X but also acts out of the desire to bring about X, insofar as X is deemed by the agent as being "good" ("good" either as an end in itself, or "good" as a means to some further end that the agent desires).

6. There is, of course, another way in which one can talk about moral agency and thus culpability, even in the absence of intention or voluntariness. That is, one can talk about moral culpability in cases of *negligence*: cases in which an agent ought to have known or ought to have acted in a certain way, but did not know or did not act in a certain way (or did not act at all). A fully satisfying account of negligence is beyond the scope the present paper; here I simply wish to say that the possibility of negligence is fully compatible with the account being articulated in this paper. For Aquinas on the possibility of negligence, see *ST* 1-2, Q. 6, a. 3, and Q. 71, a. 5.

7. This is another way of making the point—made famous in the twentieth century by Ludwig Wittgenstein—that there is no such thing as "ostensive definition," or definition that is settled simply by means of pointing to, or attending to, a particular, individual thing. For definitions always have the character of being universal, or "of a kind"; there is no such thing as the *definition* of a singular or particular entity as such.

Political Theology and Thomas Aquinas:
A Reading of the *De Regno*

Benjamin Smith

Abstract: Political life is and ought to be entirely autonomous from theology; religion belongs to the private sphere and political community is ruled by the sovereign power of the state in accordance with "secular reasons." This is commonly referred to as the modern settlement over the vexed relationship between politics and religious faith, and many have characterized it as one of the greatest legacies of the Enlightenment. Against this positive assessment, I shall argue that in his early *De Regno*, Thomas Aquinas offers compelling theological and philosophical reasons to doubt the coherence of the modern settlement and its compatibility with Christian tradition. According to this view, political practice must be reinterpreted according to a distinctly Christian understanding of the human person. Political life is not autonomous; rather it essentially requires theological reorientation.

Political life is and ought to be entirely autonomous from theology; religion belongs to the private sphere and political community is ruled by the sovereign power of the state in accordance with "secular reasons." This is the so-called "modern settlement" over the vexed relationship between politics and religious faith, and many have characterized this settlement as the one of the greatest legacies of the Enlightenment. However, since the late decades of the twentieth century a diverse group of thinkers have challenged the hegemony of the Enlightenment tradition. One effect of this challenge has been the reemergence of political theology, which disputes the value and coherence of the modern separation of theology from politics. One of the central questions of political theology is whether and how the Christian community has been made captive to the modern state and its mode of political deliberation, discourse, and practice. John Milbank, Oliver O'Donovan, Tracey Rowland, William Cavanaugh, and others—sometimes described as postmodern Augustinians—are especially critical of those Christian thinkers who have facilitated this process by reinterpreting Christian theology within the terms of classical liberalism.[1] In particular, these thinkers are critical of so-called Whig-Thomists who present a form of Thomism that supports the autonomy of politics from theology.[2] This interpretation finds its most comprehensive exposition in the work of John Finnis, who argues that because the basic goods of human flourishing are established in private life, politics must be limited to a minimal version of peace, security, legal protection, and economic prosperity—not too far different from J. S. Mill's notion of utility.[3] In contrast to this interpretation, I shall argue that Thomas's *De Regno* provides strong prima facie grounds for the legitimacy of political theology and challenges the substantive neutrality of political discourse in general, which is important, because neutrality is often invoked as a reason for excluding theological reasoning from political deliberation. Finally, I shall consider the practical application of these conclusions and explain why the phrase political theology ought to be discarded in favor of the clearer phrase "theological politics."

De Regno 1.1:
Nature, Authority, and the Common Good (1267)[4]

The *De Regno* (1267) is a practical treatise in moral theology that fits within the well-known genera of the mirror of princes. These works usually contained concise accounts of political community along with associated principles meant to guide Christian princes in the exercise of political authority. In keeping with the tradition of the genera, the *De Regno* addresses itself to a simple question: what pertains to the office of the good king? Following the norms of his education in medieval logic, in book 1, chapter 1, Thomas begins his enquiry with a treatment of the relevant principles: (1) man naturally belongs to political community and (2) the polis is ordered to the common good. Regarding the first principle, Thomas uses a dialectical form of argument appropriate for supporting first principles.[5] There are many things that the human person needs in order to live, e.g., sufficient food and shelter in season and out of season, associated tools, knowledge of the crafts needed for survival, etc. But for human persons these things are not available outside the context of social cooperation. Therefore it is natural for human beings to live in society with other men; the human person is naturally political. It is important to note right away that this argument is not the whole story; it is only intended to evince the basic naturalness of political community. So we are not justified in drawing any conclusions about the purpose of politics at this point.

Thomas's explanation of the community's ordination to the common good begins with an account of political authority. There must be a ruler over the political community, because the individual good and the common good are different, and therefore, require different causes. It is necessary that there be some cause that moves the whole to its common good over and above the individual goods of each part.[6] It is important to notice that this argument presumes that the polis as a whole is ordered to the common good—political authority is justified because of the primacy of the common good. In other words, Thomas's argument for the necessity of political authority treats the primacy of the common good as a principle rather than something to be demonstrated. Thomas expands on this point in chapter 2, wherein he takes up the question of good and bad order.

Now it happens in those things, which are ordered to an end, to proceed rightly or wrongly. Wherefore in the rule of the multitude both right, and wrong is found. But something is directed rightly when it is led to its due end; but not rightly when it is not fitting to the end.[7]

Therefore if the multitude of freemen is ordered by the king to the common good of the multitude, it would be a right and just rule, a condition that fits freemen. But if it is not ordered to the common good of the multitude, but to the private good of the ruler, it would be an unjust and perverse rule.[8]

In the *De Regno* Thomas does not gives us an explicit account of *why* the polis is directed to the common rather than individual good; rather, he simply states this as a matter of principle.[9] Perhaps at this point in his career Thomas merely assumed the primacy of the common good, or thought of it as self-evident, or perhaps the literary form of the work can explain the argumentative lacuna. I think the latter is the more likely interpretation, since the *De Regno* is meant to be a practical manual for governance in which principles are presented, explained, and expanded without necessarily arguing for the principles themselves. A good king does not necessarily need to know all the demonstrations that go with the practice of good governance.[10] At this point, Thomas has expounded two principles—the naturalness of political community and the primacy of the common good—and demonstrated one conclusion—the good for the king qua king is the ordering of his people to their common good. For Thomas, this conclusion is the definitive criterion for evaluating the practice of political authority. Nevertheless, at the end of book 1, the norm is under-defined. It only tells us that the king should seek the due end of the whole, rather than his merely individual end; it leaves unspecified the precise content of the due end of political community. Thomas takes up this topic in chapters 3 and 4 of book 2.

De Regno 2.3: The Order of Political Community

The argument in chapter 3 is somewhat complicated, and opens with a statement of the essential premise required for discovering the due end of political community. According to Thomas, the kingdom should have the same end as the human person in general: "now it is necessary for the judgment to be the same about the end of the whole multitude and of one man."[11] Throughout chapter 3 Thomas seeks to identify the political common good by considering the human end in general. To put it simply, the goal of politics is dependent upon the over-arching purpose of the human person; there is no definitive break between defining the good life and identifying the purpose of politics. Thomas next proceeds to consider alternative candidates for the end of the person and political community.

If therefore the ultimate good of man were the good of each existing in himself, it would be the ultimate end of ruling the multitude that such a good be acquired for the multitude and preserved in it. And indeed if the ultimate end whether of one man or the multitude were corporeal life and health of the body, the duty would be that of a physician; but if the ultimate end were an affluence of riches, the economic man would be king of the multitude; but if the good of the multitude were knowledge of truth, up to that which the multitude is able to acquire, the king would have the office of teacher.[12]

In keeping with the identity principle, Thomas rejects these possibilities.

However it seems that the ultimate end of the gathered multitude is to live according to virtue: for to this end men are gathered so that they might simultaneously live well, which each is not able to acquire living singly; now the good life is that which is according to virtue; therefore the virtuous life is the end of humans gathered together.[13]

The end of political life is the same as the end of the human person: to live well (*bene vivere*)—to live so as to actualize the person's intrinsic potential. At its most basic level, this life is formed by the practice of the classical virtues. In political terms, this means that the subjects of the well-governed kingdom are ultimately ordered to a shared life of solidarity in virtue. Hence, in his magisterial work on the common good, Louis Lachance claims that the political community—in its institutions and laws—brings to life the spiritual riches of the whole nation[14] and by doing so makes the human good concretely available to its members.[15] Similarly, when analyzing Thomas's commentary on Aristotle's *Politics*, Lawrence Dewan claims that insofar as the political community is ordered to virtue, it is in fact, ordered to imperfect beatitude.[16] Yet, Thomas knows full well that the human person does not find his full actualization simply in the exercise of acquired justice, prudence, temperance, and courage. He recognizes that the classical vision is incomplete; although the ancient philosophers knew of God, they could not reveal God as He is in Himself, nor teach us the way to communion with Him. Accordingly, the classical good life must be transformed by the more comprehensive vision of Christian theology. In conformity with the identity principle, Thomas applies this line of reasoning to political community.

But because man living according to virtue is ordained to a further end, which consists in the enjoyment of God, as we have already said, it is necessary for the same end to belong to the multitude of men which is of one man, the ultimate end of the gathered multitude is not to live according to virtue but through a virtuous life to come to the enjoyment of God.[17]

Thomas's argument could hardly be clearer. Since virtue is ordered to eternal beatitude and political community is ordered to virtue, it follows that political community is ordered (at least indirectly) to "the enjoyment of God." In other words, political community and the life of virtue are subordinate to the ultimate end as fully revealed in Christianity. This does not mean that Thomas is eliminating the distinction between the political community and the community of faith. We must recall that for Thomas the supernatural order perfects the natural order; it does not destroy or replace nature.[18] When the disciple is initiated into the mysteries of Christianity he does not cease to be human; he is still identifiably a human person and in many ways his life continues to be shaped by nature, reason, and the exercise of the classical virtues. Yet, at the same time, through the grace of the sacraments he has become a "new creation" with a new way of life. In a similar way, political theology must respect the naturalness and integrity of political order; politics continues to consist in framing laws for the common good, under the direction of justice and prudence. Nevertheless, theology (insofar as it is related to the ultimate end) reshapes the discourse of politics by introducing the conclusions of theology as principles in practical political deliberation, especially with regard to the theological virtues, the beatitudes, the reality of sin and its consequences, etc. Perhaps, above all, the introduction of Christian theology into political discourse requires a constant recognition that political authority is subject to the eternal law and the divine law, and that the eschatological "kingdom of God" finds its fulfillment beyond history and earthly politics.[19]

De Regno 2.4: The Practice of Kingship

How should the king direct his subjects to virtuous solidarity and ultimately, communion with God? Having established the order of political community, Thomas opens this chapter by arguing that it belongs to the king to make his subjects fit or congruous for the due end. And the reason is this: it belongs to whoever has care of a thing to lead the thing governed to its due end. Thomas's example is illuminating: the ruler should imitate the care provided by a weapon smith, who sees to it that the sword is constructed in such a way that it is made fit for combat.

> Now to whomever it belongs to perfect something that is ordered to another as an end, he ought to attend to this so that his work may be congruous to the end: as the maker so makes the sword that it accords with fighting and the builder ought so to dispose the home that is may be apt for living.[20]

One would think that this meant that political community should make its members "fit" for virtue and communion with God. Finnis has a very different interpretation.

> the group's—the political community's—good life is to be in line with (*congruit*) the "pursuing of heavenly fulfillment (*coelestem beatitudinem*)"; by promoting group good life in that way, rulers are like sword-smiths or house builders, whose role is to make an instrument suitable for others to put to their own good use.[21]

According to Finnis, the important point about this passage is that the sword-smith and the ruler make something, but leave it to others to put what is made to use. He concludes that the king should not "impose on individuals a legal duty to pursue their ultimate happiness."[22] One obvious difficulty with Finnis's interpretation is that it ignores the connection between chapters 3 and 4. Chapter 3 states that political life is ordered to virtuous solidarity for the sake of divine communion. This is the due order of political life, and as such, it is the governing political truth for understanding what Thomas has to say about the practice of kingship in chapter 4. In this latter chapter Thomas clearly says that the king's duty is to lead his community to its due end, and he has already defined the due end in chapter 3.

Furthermore, Michael Pakaluk has argued that Finnis's interpretation misconstrues the text of chapter 4 itself. Pakaluk offers the following account:

> Just as the sword-smith both (i) makes a sword, a definite and distinct kind of thing, but in doing so takes care that he (ii) make a sword adapted to a particular use, so that the king should both (i)' bring about "that virtuous life which we live at present," and (ii)' ensure that life is, furthermore, adapted to heavenly happiness.[23]

Pakaluk's point is that the movement of Thomas's argument proceeds from (i) to (i)' and from (ii) to (ii)'. Just as the sword-smith makes a sword, so the king makes virtuous life in the polis, and just as the sword-smith fits the sword for its ultimate end, viz., close combat, so the king directs our present virtuous life to eternal beatitude insofar as he is able to do so.[24] The text that immediately follows the sword-example affirms Pakaluk's interpretation:

> Therefore because the end of the life that we live well now in the present is heavenly beatitude, it pertains to the office of the king by reason to procure the good life of the multitude so that it conforms to the possession of heavenly beatitude, namely that those things which lead to heavenly beatitude are commanded, and the contrary of these—insofar as it is possible—be condemned.[25]

Thomas's argument is clear: the end of the polis is twofold and so is the task of the ruler. The polis is ordered to (i)' the good life, for the sake of achieving (ii)' heavenly beatitude. Likewise, the king's task is to establish the (i)' "good life of the multitude," in such a way that the communal practice of virtue conforms to (ii)' the attaining of heavenly beatitude. To this end the king is to enjoin the practice of virtue and forbid—"insofar as it is possible"—the vices that impede heavenly beatitude.

It is very difficult to avoid the conclusion that Thomas intends for lawmakers to consider not only the criterion of the classical virtues, but also the various norms expressed in Christian theology. The king is to establish virtuous solidarity—in keeping with the natural integrity of political life—but now informed by the further criteria of eternal beatitude. To this end, Thomas recommends that the king should learn about what is politically conducive to divine communion from ecclesial (priestly) instruction and the book of *Deuteronomy*.[26] Thomas supports his advice with a reference to Deut. 17:18–19, in which the king is enjoined to learn the law of God from the Levitical priests and the reading of the scriptures—these laws the king is expected to enforce.[27] Moreover, Thomas makes much the same point in his later *Summa Theologiae* (1271), wherein he says that the judicial precepts of the Mosaic Law, although no longer binding since the advent of the New Covenant, nevertheless serves as the pattern for political life.[28] This indicates what Thomas has in mind, viz., a form of political life directed by a theologically enriched deliberative process. In this process, theological reasons for action acquire a role in augmenting, extending, limiting, and reinforcing—without replacing—the natural priorities of political discourse and community and they do so by serving as principles for an enriched process of practical thinking about politics.

Analysis: the Political Theology of Thomas Aquinas

I have argued that Thomas's *De Regno* provides prima facie grounds for political theology and challenges the substantive neutrality of politics. This argument is rooted in three principles: (a) the naturalness of political life, (b) the primacy of the common good, and (c) the identity principle. The first principle provides an explanation of why political community is an essential part of human life and an unavoidable topic of reflection. Thomas's argument for this principle is taken directly from Aristotle: we can know that the person is naturally inclined to political life because he cannot live without political community. By the end of the *De Regno*, the full connection between political life and the human person becomes manifest: the human person cannot advance in the actualization of his nature without the cooperation and solidarity of his political companions. The second principle tells us that the task of the political ruler—whether one or many—is not to seek the private or individual good, but to seek the shared good of the whole. This is an important principle, but it does not define "the good of the whole." This all important question is answered by a consistent application of (c) the identity principle: the same judgment is to be made about the purpose of politics and the human person. This is the most important principle for determining the order of political community because it means that the object of human finality will also be the object of political order. Thomas, applying this principle consistently draws the inevitable conclusion (d) that political community is ordered beyond classical *bene vivere* to the ultimate end of divine communion. Principle (a) is supported by an Aristotelian dialectical argument, (d) is derived from (c), but principles (b) and (c) are not supported with argumentation.

It should be evident that principle (c) is the critical premise supporting Thomas's theological interpretation of political life. Thomas's argument and the identity principle can be recast in the following way without any violence to the text of the *De Regno*:

(1) The end of the human person is divine communion.

(2) The end of the political community is the end of the human person.

(3) Therefore, the end of political community is divine communion.

The minor premise of this argument (2) is only a slight reformulation of the identity principle. For Thomas, the major premise (1) is a truth of Catholic tradition, but on its own, it does not appear to offer compelling grounds for political theology. What forces the issue is the minor premise. If this premise is true then political theology rather than secular liberalism must become the standard of political practice, if we also accept premise (1). Indeed, if the minor premise is true, then Christian theology is the rival—in principle—of any attempt to construct a purely autonomous form of political life. After all, why should the Christian account of the ultimate end be excluded in favor of an alternative account? If politics is organized around an account of the ultimate end, then Christian theology is necessarily connected to politics. So, from the perspective of Christian faith, the identity principle provides strong grounds for political theology. In addition to this, the identity principle removes the reason most commonly invoked for excluding theology from political discourse, viz., the putative substantive neutrality of politics.

First, it must be recognized at the outset that there is nothing particularly Christian about the identity principle—in fact it comes directly from classical philosophy. Indeed almost every great political philosopher from Plato to Marx holds something like it at least implicitly. This is important because even the most ardent ethical subjectivist or Enlightenment adherent has, at least in practice, some account of the best sort of human life and how this ought to be pursued in politics. Whether these values have putative objective grounding is really irrelevant on the practical level. This means that politics is never neutral—it always expresses some narrative about the good life for the human person. The second premise of Thomas's argument could be replaced by any number of rival normative propositions without doing any violence to the logic of the argument. In fact it would only require a replacement of the minor term: for Marx, the overcoming of all forms of alienation; for Kant the kingdom of perpetual peace; for Mill, the maximization of utility; for Locke, individual liberty, etc. If this line of reasoning is correct, then the argument of the *De Regno* not only supports political theology, but calls into question modern claims to value-neutrality. If the identity principle is true then different conclusions about political order depend on different judgments about the ultimate end of the human person. Politics is not autonomous from comprehensive narratives of value. Excluding Christian theology from political life in the name of neutrality really means the replacement of political theology with a rival account of the human good. Thus, when the Christian community passively accepts or even endorses the modern settlement it is not settling for a neutral space—a simple cease-fire. Rather it is surrendering to a rival account of the ultimate end.[29]

What are the concrete implications of Thomas's political theology? On its own, the *De Regno* is too far removed from the circumstances of modern life to offer much guidance to the practice of contemporary politics. Nevertheless, I will conclude with a few practical suggestions. First, to use Aidan Nichols's terminology, we must begin by re-imagining Christendom. There is of course no question of returning to the medieval instantiation of political theology—this would not be desirable even if it were possible. Nevertheless, for political practice to become genuinely theological, the Christian community—especially its theologians and historians—needs to turn to the Bible, the liturgy, the Christian tradition, and even medieval civilization to craft standards and practices for creating new models for public life.[30] Consistent with this project, the Christian community must call into question and even reject some of the presuppositions and conclusions of Enlightenment political thought. This twofold task would make possible a Christian version of what Alasdair MacIntyre describes as authentic political community.

According to MacIntyre, political authority and practice should concentrate in local communities organized around a genuinely public discourse about our shared social life—one that seriously reflects upon and expresses a society's convictions about the good life. Needless to say, such a community would need to possess a degree of unity that would exclude radical and widespread pluralism, which means that a Christian version of this approach presupposes widespread theological solidarity—a Christian polity presupposes a Christian society. In such circumstances there would be no question of limiting legitimate political or legislative discourse to only "secular reasons." Rather, the theological doctrines of Christianity would be fully admissible to both formal and informal political deliberation. As I have already indicated, this theologically enriched discourse would not displace the natural priorities of politics, but balance them with practical principles derived from theology. The introduction of theology into political discourse distorts neither theology nor politics. Rather, theology enriches politics with additional principles, while leaving the essence of politics intact. Since in this model, theology enriches, but does not distort politics, and since there is no question (on this model) of politicizing theology, it would be preferable to replace the perhaps misleading phrase "political theology" with the clearer phrase "theological politics." This phrase more clearly reflects the fact that on the *De Regno* model theology transforms politics without seeking to replace it.

For example, when punishing criminals such a community would elect the most merciful and forgiving punishments consistent with justice.[31] Similarly, this kind of community would consider it legitimate to invoke charity and the beatitudes as reasons for going beyond the minimal demands of justice in assisting the poor.[32] Often, a theological political discourse could simply reinforce practices, which also have non-theological motives. For example, the doctrine of original sin and Augustinian versions of eschatology provide reasons for rejecting utopian policies, restraining government powers, and detaching from the greed, vanity, lust, and competitiveness that often distort political life. Finally communal support for institutions, practices, and endeavors inspired by Christianity would also be possible.[33] We should imagine small-scale communities, informed by a broadly shared Christian vision and imagination; because of their theological solidarity such communities would be capable of creating a form of political discourse and deliberation rooted in faith, hope, and charity.[34]

In concluding, I want to clarify what is and is not my thesis. First, I have *not* argued that theology replaces political prudence or the natural order of politics. Similarly, I have *not* argued that political rights, duties, or authority depend directly on sacred theology.[35] Rather, I have simply argued that the *De Regno* provides strong prima facie grounds for theological politics and for rejecting claims of substantive neutrality in politics. Furthermore, I have observed that theological politics will only be appropriate in circumstances where theological solidarity already exists on the ground.[36] Finally, I have tried to explain how—in certain limited circumstances— political discourse and deliberation can be elevated by incorporating theological conclusions as principles for practical reasoning.

Aquinas College, Nashville, Tennessee

Notes

1. See Aidan Nichols's discussion of Oliver O'Donovan in "Reimagining the Christendom State," in *Christendom Awake: On Reenergizing the Church in Culture* (Grand Rapids: William B. Eerdmans Publishing Company, 1999); John Milbank, "An Essay Against Secular Order," *The Journal of Religious Ethics* 15.2 (1987): 199–224; Tracey Rowland, *Culture and the Thomist Tradition After Vatican II* (London: Routledge, 2003); William T. Cavanaugh, "Killing for the Telephone Company: Why the Nation-State is not the Keeper of the Common Good," *Modern Theology* 20.2 (2004): 243–274; Richard John Neuhaus, "Political Theologies," *First Things* (2004): 72–78; Avishai Margalit, "Political Theology: The Authority of God," *Theoria* 106 (2005): 37–50; Peter Goodwin Heltzel and Corey D. B. Walker, "The Wound of Political Theology: A Prolegomenon to a Research Agenda," *Political Theology* 9.2 (2008): 252–255; Aristide Tessitore, "Political Theology and the Theological-Political Problem," *Perspectives on Political Science* 38 (2009): 5–12.

2. For a brief, but clear account of the leading proponents of "Whig-Thomism" see Rowland *Culture*, 16–17, and especially accompanying note 18. See also Kenneth Craycraft, "Was Aquinas a Whig? St Thomas on Regime," *Faith and Reason* (1994): 249–263.

3. John Finnis, *Natural Law and Natural Rights* (Oxford, U.K.: Clarendon Press, 1980), 154; for Finnis's association of Thomas with Mill: *Aquinas: Moral, Political, and Legal Theory* (Oxford, U.K.: Oxford University Press, 1998), 222 and 228. See also "Public Good: The Specifically Political Common Good in Aquinas," in *Natural Law and Moral Inquiry: Ethics, Metaphysics, and Politics in the Work of Germain Grisez*, ed. R. George (Washington, D.C.: Georgetown University Press, 1998).

4. For the authenticity of the *De Regno* up to book 2, chapter 8, see T. H. Eschman, "Introduction" to *On Kingship*, trans. G. Phelan (Toronto: Pontifical Institute for Mediaeval Studies, 1949), ix–xxx; Jean-Pierre Torrell, *Saint Thomas Aquinas: The Person and His Work*, vol. 1, trans. R. Royal (Washington, D.C.: The Catholic University of America, 1996), 169–171, 350; the Leonine Commission, in *Opera Omnia*, vol. 42 (Roma: 1979), 421–434. Early in his career—although he later changed his position—Eschmann pointed out that the *De Regno* is included in the oldest and most reliable bibliographies of Thomas's works and the only reason that its authenticity has been doubted is because of the additions made by Tolomeo of Lucca ("Introduction," xi–xv). Except where noted, I will be using the reformed Leonine organization of the text, which restores the older and authentic order, obscured when the *De Regno* was incorporated into Tolomeo's *De Regimine* (Eschmann, "Introduction," xiii–xv). For the date of original composition as 1267, see Torrell, *Saint Thomas Aquinas*, 169–171, 350.

5. Thomas Aquinas, *De Regno* (Roma: Leonine Commission, 1979), 1.1 (42:449). The latter set of numbers indicates the line numbers in the Leonine edition (henceforth: *DR*). Except where noted I shall use the Leonine texts and my own translations. See also: Thomas Aquinas, *On Kingship*, trans. G. Phelan (Toronto: Pontifical Institute for Mediaeval Studies, 1949), 1.1.

6. Ibid., 1.1. (42: 450). "Non enim idem est quod proprium et quod commune. Secundum propria quidem differunt, secundum commune autem uniuntur. Diversorum autem diverse sunt cause. Oportet igitur, preter id quod movet ad proprium bonum uniuscuiuque, esse aliquid quod movet ad bonum commune multorum."

7. Ibid., 1.1 (42: 450). "Contingit autem in quibusdam, quae ordinantur ad finem, et recte, et non recte procedere. Quare et in regimine multitudinis et rectum, et non rectum invenitur. Recte autem dirigitur unumquodque quando ad finem convenientem deducitur; non recte autem quando ad finem non convenientem."

8. Ibid. 1.1. "Si igitur liberorum multitudo a regente ad bonum commune multitudinis ordientur, erit regimen rectum et iustum, quale convenit liberis. Si vero non ad bonum commune multitudinis, sed ad bonum privatum regentis regimen ordinetur, erit regimen iniustum atque perversum."

9. Nevertheless, Thomas does illustrate this principle with an example, viz., the ship analogy. Just as the ship is moved by many winds and yet has one final destination, viz., the port. For the ship example, see *DR* 1.1 (47: 449). "non enim navis, quam secundum diversorum ventorum impulsum in diversa moveri contingit, ad destinatum finem perveniret nisi per gubernatoris industriam dirigeretur ad portum."

10. Eschmann, "Introduction," xiv–xv.

11. *DR* 2.3. "Idem autem oportet esse iudicium de fine totius multitudinis et unius." See: Aristotle, *Nicomachean Ethics*, 1.2 1094a8.

12. *DR* 2.3 (42: 465–466). "Si igitur finis ultimus hominis esset bonum quodcumque in ipso existens, et regendae multitudinis finis ultimus esset similiter ut tale bonum multitudo acquireret et in eo permanerat. Et si quidem ultimus sive unius hominis sive multitudinis finis esset corporalis vita et sanitas corporis, medici esset officium; si vero ultimus finis esset divitiarum affluentia, yconomous rex quidam multitudinis esset; si vero bonum cognoscendae veritatis tale quid esset, ad quod posset multitudo pertingere, rex haberet doctoris officium."

14. Father Pierre E. Lachance, O.P., "*L'humanism politique de Saint Thomas d'Aquin individu et état*" (Paris: Sirey, 1964), 237. "Il est considéré comme un organisme qui détient et conserve dans se institutions, ses lois, ses coutumes, ses traditions, toutes les rechesses matérielles et spirituelles, toutes les valuers de civilisations accumulées depuis de siécles, avec un soin diligent et pieux, par les initiatives de toute une nation." See also, 65.

15. Ibid., 65. "la cité apparait . . . comme la seule réalité concrete capable de produire le bien humain . . . ."

16. Lawrence Dewan, "St. Thomas, John Finnis, and the Political Good," *The Thomist* 64 (2000): 361: "Thomas conceives the completeness of the [political] community as a completeness that leads to virtue. . . . The common good of the city, so considered, seems very close to the ultimate end of human life. The imperfect "felicity" or "beatitude" possible in this life is seen by Thomas as primarily in contemplation of the divine, but secondarily in the operation of the practical intellect ordering human actions and passions." Of course, some of the elements of imperfect beatitude, e.g., the intellectual virtues, internal acts, etc.,

cannot be subject to human law, since the law only treats of external acts. For an excellent treatment of these points see Thomas M. MacLellan, "The Moral Virtues and the Speculative Life," *Laval Theologique Et Philosophique* 1956 (12.2): 175–232.

17. "Sed quia homo vivendo secundum virtutem ad ulteriorem finem ordinatur, qui consistit in fruitione divina ut supra iam diximus, oportet autem eundem finem esse multitudinis humanae qui est hominis unius, non est ultimus finis multitudinis congregatae vivere secundum virtutem sed per virtuosam vitam pervenire ad fruitionem divinam." Thomas goes on in the same chapter to argue that since it belongs to the Church to initiate disciples into communion with God, kings must be subject to ecclesial authority, which requires the re-conceptualization of political life in terms of the narrative, practices, and symbols of Christian faith.

18. J.-H. Nicolas, *Les Profondeurs De La Grace* (Paris: Beauchesne, 1969).

19. Matthew Levering, *Christ's Fulfillment of Torah and Temple: Salvation According to Thomas Aquinas* (Norte Dame: University of Notre Dame Press, 2002), 68–73, 130–134. See also Nichols, "Reimagining," 71–89. According to Thomas, since the Ascension all of human life—including political life—takes place under the reign of Christ the king, whose judiciary powers are fulfilled in his final coming to judge the living and the dead.

20. *DR* 2.4 (42: 467). "Cuicumque autem incumbit aliquid perficere quod ordinatur in aliud sicut in finem, hoc debet attendre ut suum opus sit congruum fini: sicut faber sic facit gladium ut pugnae conveniat, et edificator sic debet domum disponere ut ad habitandum sit apta."

21. Finnis, "Public Good," 182, quoted in Michael Pakaluk, "The Common Good of Political Society," *Review of Metaphysics* (Sept. 2001): 78.

22. Ibid., 182.

23. Pakaluk, "The Common Good," 78. We must not think of the virtuous life of the *polis* as merely instrumental; it is certainly ordered to a higher end, but it is choice-worthy for its own sake. In this sense, the communal life of virtue is an imperfect *bonum honestum*.

24. Ibid., 79.

25. *DR* 2.4 (42: 467). "Quia igitur vite qua hic in presenti bene vivimus finis est beatitudo celestis, ad regis officium pertinet ea ratione bonam vitam multitudinis procurare secundum quod congruit ad celestem beatitudinem consequendam, ut scilicet ea precipiat que ad celestem beatitudinem ducunt, et eorum contraria secundum quod fuerit possibile interdicat." Thomas argument seems to use the following analogy: (1) sword-smith:the making of the sword::king:virtuous solidarity, and (2) sword-smith:close combat::king:divine communion.

26. Ibid., 28–40.

27. Deut. 17:18–19. This passage is quoted by Thomas in *DR* 2.4 (42: 467).

28. *ST* 1-2.104.1 ad1 and 104.3. Among others, Thomas endorses the following judicial precepts: economic regulation to minimize greed and fraud, the regulation of marriage, the religious instruction of children, the slaying of unruly sons, as well as capital punishment for crimes against God, for incest, and for adultery. See *ST* 1-2.105. 2 co. and ad 9–10. See Levering, *Christ's Fulfillment*, 68–73, 130–134. Thomas explains that the king should establish communal virtue in three stages: through the establishment of the good life (bonam vitam), its preservation, and eventual perfection. Regarding the first, three things are

necessary: the establishment of peace, the legal enforcement of virtue, and the acquisition of necessary material goods. Regarding the second task, viz., the preservation of virtue, Thomas says that he king should follow the example of God, by punishing those who commit vice and rewarding those who are virtuous. *DR* 2.4: for the threefold kingly task see lines 42–47; for "bonam vitam," see 48–66; for the preservation of the good life, see 67–88. For all references see, 42–467. Of course ancient Israel represents a unique situation. Nevertheless, for Thomas it serves as the pattern for the Christian practice of politics.

29. See Nichols's discussion of Oliver O'Donovan, "Reimagining," 71–75. At this point, one might object that the theory of natural law provides a "neutral" standard for ordering politics. It is true that the natural law is not specifically Christian. Nevertheless, it is not neutral towards God, but has God as both its ultimate source and end. At a minimum a politics of natural law excludes political atheism or secularism. Moreover, from the perspective Christian faith, the natural law cannot be regarded as entirely autonomous from Christianity. This is true for two reasons: first, because natural law requirements regarding the virtue of religion cannot be fulfilled outside the order of grace; second, because the natural law is subject to the ultimate end of the human person—divine communion—which is the first principle in all matters of action. The natural law is a standard of evaluation applicable and available to those outside the Christian tradition. Nevertheless, it is intrinsically open to Christianity and, from the perspective of Christian faith, it is subordinated to man's true ultimate end and therefore, not autonomous.

30. See Nichols, "Reimagining," 71–87.

31. This leaves open the possibility that the just punishment of some crimes requires grave penalties, up to and including capital punishment. This does not contradict a Christian commitment to mercy, since a balanced Christian polity advocates a version of mercy that is consistent with justice.

32. Needless to say, such efforts would need to avoid committing other injustices.

33. Of course there is no question of coercing citizens into professing Christian faith. It is entirely possible for a community to tolerate non-belief *and* practice theological politics. Small communities, unified by shared religious beliefs are capable of a generous tolerance towards those who do not share their beliefs. Here are some examples of theological political practice that do not coerce non-believers: the social acceptance of explicitly theological thinking in public discourse, the communal promotion and support of Christian institutions and practices, the preservation of local customs inspired by Christianity, the public recognition of significant holy days, public forms of piety, the rejection of utopian policies, etc. Measures of this sort may either annoy or cause discomfort to a non-believer, but they do not directly coerce the non-believer into becoming a Christian. Of course, this sort political practice could only take place in a community in which Christian solidarity is present on the ground; there can be no question of imposing this form of practice from outside. This raises the question of feasibility, and it must be admitted that few places in the modern world could support this kind of politics. Nevertheless, it could still serve as a model for evaluating political practices and institutions. Furthermore, the facts of the contemporary world and the requirement of local solidarity, suggests that contemporary Christians should advocate radical political decentralization, so that practical political life can be relocated onto the local level where it is more likely that we will find—or be able to create—communities of organic Christian solidarity capable of naturally developing and supporting forms of Christian politics.

34. Alasdair MacIntyre, "Politics, Philosophy, and the Common Good," in *The MacIntyre Reader*, ed. K. Knight (Notre Dame: University of Notre Dame Press, 1998): 235–252.

35. In connection with these qualifications, I have not argued that temporal authorities are directly subject to ecclesiastical authorities. See *Sent.* L. II, dist. 44, q. 2, a. 3 *Scriptum super libros Sententiarum magistri Petri Lombardi episcopi Parisiensis*, t. 2., ed. P. Mandonnet (Parisiis: P. Lethielleux, 1929), accessed via corpusthomisticum.org, November 17, 2010. I am grateful to James Martin of St. John's University for pointing out this passage to me.

36. I do not think that every good political community necessarily practices political theology—political theology is not appropriate to every set of circumstances. Nevertheless, from the perspective of Christian faith and abstracting from concrete circumstances, political theology should be the case. In fact, even where circumstances impede the full practice of political theology, if Thomas's argument is correct, Christians should uphold political theology as the standard model of politics and bring theological reasoning to political discourse whenever it is possible and prudent to do so. I am grateful to Michael Baur of Fordham University for his comments on my article, which made it apparent that I needed to discuss the question of the circumstances required for the practice of political theology.

The Language of Being and the Nature of God in the Aristotelian Tradition

R. E. Houser

Abstract: Appropriate philosophical language for describing the nature of God took almost two millennia to develop. Parmenides first discovered the language of being. Plato then distinguished the world of changing beings from the world of true being and also from the good "beyond being." He refused to use being language for the Olympic gods. Aristotle understood a god as a substance (οὐσία). Avicenna described God, not as a substance but as "being," which transcends the categories, including substance. For Br. Thomas of Aquino, God was no longer an Aristotelian substance, nor even an Avicennian "necessary being," but is best described as "subsistent being itself" (*ipsum esse subsistens*). Here the Christian disciple brought to an even higher level of perfection the achievements of his Islamic master, achievements that far surpassed their beginnings in Parmenidean monism.

S ome commentators have thought that Avicenna's influence on Aquinas, while prominent in earlier works like *De ente* and his *Scriptum in Sententiis*, waned with the passing of the years, as he came to know Aristotle's text more closely than he had earlier in his writing career.[1] In this study I hope to show that even when he was writing the *Summa theologiae*, Br. Thomas's treatment of the divine nature, and the language he used about it, was much closer to Avicenna's than it was to Aristotle's. In order to show this, it will be necessary to trace the development of the language of being, and its application to the nature of God, back to its origins, looking at five philosophers: Parmenides, Plato, Aristotle, Avicenna, and Aquinas.

I. Before Aristotle

Parmenides: Aristotle did not invent out of whole cloth the metaphysical language he used to describe a god; he conceived himself as too much summing up the whole Greek philosophical tradition to do that. Plato and Parmenides, although they had little use for the Olympian gods, were the most important influences on Aristotle's language about god.

Parmenides's poem began with a goddess, opening with a mythic description of a horse-drawn chariot proceeding from the "house of night into the light" reminiscent of Apollo. But Parmenides's chariot belongs to an un-named "daimon" (δαίμονος), later called "goddess" (θεὰ). She tells Parmenides "you must learn *all things*, both the steady heart of persuasive truth, and the opinions of mortals, in whom there is no true trust,"[2] and then departs the scene.

In his effort to follow her directions, what struck Parmenides about the world studied by the earlier *physikoi* was that truth is found in propositions, such as "water is the source of things"[3]; for terms alone do not carry truth. The most basic propositions have a subject united to its predicate by the verb "is" (ἔστιν) or separated by "is not." There is an unbridgeable opposition between these verbs; water cannot both be and not be the source. Parmenides also used the participial form of "is" to describe any subject or predicate at the highest level of abstraction. 'This water' or 'water' is also "a being" (ἐόν, later ὄν), the opposite of "a non-being" (μὴ ἐόν).[4] And Parmenides used the infinitive "to be" (εἶναι) in order to point out the feature that "is" words, in all their variety, add over and beyond the meaning of more limited terms like "water" and "source." Parmenides bequeathed to his successors these three "is" terms, which would shape metaphysical understanding of God, because the opposition between "is" and "is not" is so radical.

His first conclusion was that intellectual thought about reality is conceived in the mind and set out in the language of being: "for it is the same thing to think intellectually and to be."[5] And when one thinks intellectually there are only two opposing roads to take:

> the one, *that is it and that it is not possible for it not to be*
> is the path of persuasion (πειθοῦς), for it attends upon truth;
> the other, that *it is not and that it is necessary for it not to be*,
> this I point out to you to be a path completely unlearnable;
> for you could not know a non-being (τό γε μὴ ἐόν), for that is not possible,
> nor could you point it out.[6]

Parmenides did not mean that only affirmative propositions are true. The problem with the path of "is not" is that it concerns "a non-being," something that does not exist and would be nothing, which is impossible to know. But the remaining route—"it is"—Parmenides finds weighted with consequences that assault our common experience. Based on insight into the nature of being (εἶναι) gained from its opposition to non-being, he concludes that "a being" cannot exist contingently, it must necessarily be. Yet we live in a world filled with things that seem to be contingent. And here he came to the crucial choice—whether to follow his mind in the direction of being or to follow his senses.

Parmenides drew out the logical consequences of the notion of "being" and followed them. Its message was that "being" is necessary, one, complete, and unchanging,[7] even though our senses tell us the reality we experience is contingent, many, incomplete, and full of change. Such is the tale of truth. But it so contradicts our experience that most turn away—not toward pure "non-being," which is impossible—but toward a middle ground: "At this point I stop for you my reliable account and intellectual thought / concerning truth; from here on, learn about mortal opinions (δόξας)." Among opinions one finds "two forms (μορφὰς)," "opposites"—"aetherial fire" and "dark night." The lesson: "I declare to you on this ordering all is 'likely' (ἐοικότα πάντα)."[8] This 'likely story' of change between opposites such as light and dark, heavy and light, though it might seem true to our experience, cannot be true knowledge, but only opinion (δόξα), because it violates the internal logic of "being."

Parmenides, then, stands at the head of Western metaphysical thought, holding out for a truth known by the mind and enunciated in the language of being, even though it is contrary to our experience. In choosing the mind over the senses he was not alone among the Greek "sages."

Plato: In order to understand reality properly, Plato sought to integrate three different traditions: Socrates's search for universal definitions (λόγοι) that manifest the "what it is" (τί ἔστι) or quiddity of things, the causes and principles (αἰτίαι καὶ ἀρχαι) sought by the φυσικοί, and a Parmenidean-style doctrine of being.

The constant theme of Plato's earliest dialogues is distinguishing examples of virtues from the definition (λόγος) of a virtue that is common enough to include all its examples. Even the *Republic* begins with Cephalus's definition of justice as "speaking the truth and paying whatever debts one has incurred," which is inadequate as a universal definition of justice, even if it does give some examples, though even here there must be qualifications, like not returning weapons borrowed from a man who has become insane (331c1–d1).

Plato dealt with the causes in Socrates's intellectual autobiography in the *Phaedo*, which manifests all four Aristotelian causes. "When I was young I was filled with wonder at pursuing the kind of wisdom they call natural science. For it seemed splendid to me to know the causes (αἰτίας) of each thing, why it is generated, why it is destroyed, why it *is*."[9] He wanted to know whether "we think by means of blood or air or fire"—material cause—and he "thought that ten was more than eight because two had been added," addition being a kind of agency.[10] Socrates later realized how wrong this approach was, as incorrect as "saying the reason why I am sitting here is because my body consists of bones and sinews." This would be to "neglect to say the *true causes* (ἀληθῶς αἰτίας), that when the Athenians decided it was *better* (βέλτιον) to condemn me, it seemed *better* (βέλτιον) to me to sit here." The true cause is *the good*, material and efficient factors are only conditions "without which the cause would not be able to act as a cause."[11]

After introducing the good, Socrates began his last argument for the immortality of the soul by "taking as an hypothesis" forms like "the beautiful (καλόν) itself through itself and the good (ἀγαθὸν) and the great (μέγα) and all the other" such forms.[12] In content, these causes contain the common and unchanging "quiddity" Socrates sought to define. In this way, the project of definition dovetails with the search for causes. The true causes are final and formal causes. There are three reasons why these are the "true causes." First, they explain how humans can know the abiding natures of things in the world of change. Second, they explain how two individual things can have formal traits in common, through "participation" in a common form. Finally, they explain the reason for the dynamic tendencies that lead individual beings to change; they change in order to become better by imitating more fully their perfect form.

In the *Phaedo*, then, Plato preferred formal and final causes to material and agent conditions, because they uncover the abiding quiddity Socrates had sought to define. He also introduced the Parmenidean issue of "being" into his argument. Formal and final causes have their "being" in the higher world from which the soul proceeds at birth and to which it returns at death.

In *Republic* 5 Plato squarely faced the third of the issues that characterize his mature thought—the Parmenidean doctrine of being. In Bk. 5-7 he ontologized, as it were, definition and causality, developing his own language of being and his own doctrine of being. His 'adjustments' to the Parmenidean doctrine of being begin with Socrates's argument to "the lovers of sights and sounds"[13] that the forms are real. To this end, Socrates distinguishes our subjective cognitive states from the kinds of things we cognize, in order to argue—against the non-philosopher—that there is a higher real realm of being that is the object of true knowledge, and also—against Parmenides—that there is a real realm of a lesser kind of being that is the object of opinion. "One who knows" has knowledge of "something," not "nothing," something described as "a being" (ὄν) rather than "not a being (οὐκ ὄν)." But "no matter how many ways we examine it, that which is fully a being, is also fully knowable (τὸ μὲν παντελῶς ὂν παντελῶς γνωστόν), and what is a being in no way at all, is also in every way un-knowable (μὴ ὂν δὲ μηδαμῇ πάντῃ ἄγνωστον)." In the face of the Parmenidean impasse, Socrates then breaks through to a middle ground, describing the object of "opinion" that he, unlike Parmenides, could embrace: "Now if anything is such as *to be and also not to be*, will it not be intermediate between what is purely a being (τοῦ εἰλικρινῶς ὄντος) and what in no way is a being (τοῦ αὖ μηδαμῇ ὄντος)?"[14] Such middle things "partake of both, of being and of non-being (τοῦ εἶναι τε καὶ μὴ εἶναι)," and "the many views of the many about the beautiful and the other things are that as intermediates they are rolling around between a non-being and a pure being."[15] This intermediate kind of reality is characterized by change, individuality, and a combination of perfection and imperfection.

The next step in Plato's program is found in the three great images of Bks. 6 and 7—the sun, divided line, and cave. The sun image is first of all designed to show us that the good (or beautiful) is a reality separate from ourselves—quite unlike the "many" who confuse it with pleasure, which only exists subjectively within us, and even the "few" (that is, the historical Socrates) who thought the good to be knowledge, which also exists subjectively within us, even though through knowledge we know things beyond us (505b3–4). Not just separate from ourselves, the sun is the highest reality and the highest cause, source of both the "sensible things" in the world and of our sensing them, for without light there would be no seeing and nothing to be seen. Analogously, the good is the separate cause not just of our knowing but of what we know—"the intelligibles." Plato, then, discerned three levels of things: changing individuals, the forms in which they participate, and the good, source of all.

Plato embellished the language of being in order to explain how truly separate are the forms and the good from everyday reality. In the divided line (6: 509d–511e; 7: 533d–534b), Socrates does not use the language of "being" to describe sensible, individual things, nor does he call them "partakers of being and not-being," as he had in Bk. 5. Rather, Socrates calls them "objects of opinion," "visibles," "living things," and "images." And when Socrates describes the intelligibles—the objects of διάνοια, νόησις, and ἐπιστήμη—he uses the language of formal causality—calling them "objects of knowledge" (νοητά), "form" (εἶδος), "idea" (ἰδέα), and 'X itself.'

The metaphysical language of being begun by Parmenides, however, was too valuable to be abandoned. So Plato separated Parmenides's ways of "truth" and "opinion" into two different ways of thinking, not about the same world—as Parmenides erroneously thought—but about *two different worlds*. As a linguistic sign of this division, Plato further developed Parmenides's language of being, making distinctions where the sage of Elea had not. So Socrates also calls a form "a being" (ὄν), "fully being" (τὸ παντελῶς ὄν), and "a beingly being" (τὸ ὄντως ὄν).[16] This cluster of being-terms is designed to distinguish the higher world of "beings" from the lower world of changing things. Forms are higher sorts of beings because they are common to all their participants; they are common because they are the unchanging quiddities in which visible "participate"; and they can be participated in because they are those quiddities in a completed (τίλειον) or perfect way.

In addition, Plato also uses the term οὐσία to describe a form. This term seems particularly chosen by Plato to contrast the form both from sensibles below it and "the good" above it. What does Plato mean by οὐσία? While earlier non-philosophical thinkers had used οὐσία, an abstract term formed off the feminine present participle, to describe things that "are" theirs, their possessions—which is the reason Aristotle will say one sense of οὐσία is matter—Plato understood οὐσία differently, as what we might literally translate as "being-ness."[17] In comparison with participants below it, then, οὐσία means the quidditative feature of an individual thing that is fundamental to its being and in a formal sense is the cause of it. If Socrates is a human by reason of sharing in the form "human itself," in English we can also use an abstract word like 'humanity' to describe that form, which never changes, even though Socrates was born and died.

The main reason Plato used οὐσία, however, seems to be in order to compare the forms with the good above them. "And for the things known now not only is their coming to be known seen to be (παρεῖναι) owing to the good, but also their being (εἶναι) and their being-ness (οὐσίαν) is seen to be due to that, though the good is not being-ness (οὐσίας), but more it is beyond being-ness (οὐσίας) *in rank and power*."[18] While each form is one, unchanging, and a cause, all forms are limited in their perfection; for dogs are not trees, green is not sweet, and courage is not temperance. The very first principle of all reality and of all knowledge, however, is *not limited* in its power and perfection, as the forms are. This is why it is "beyond being-ness," at least in its unlimited power and perfection.

The distance between Plato and the monotheistic philosophers of the middle ages is to be found in the notable fact that the gods—and by them Plato invariably meant the Olympians—are omitted from his metaphysical account. He never took what we might think an easy step—to identify the good with the one God—because the only gods he knew of were many, and not so good. His thought about the gods is difficult to determine, even in his myths, for Plato's critical attitude to the gods of his city and culture was deep-seated. His master, after all, had been executed in their name. With Plato, then, we are still two steps away from the connection between the one God and being that we will see among the medievals. While there is one highest principle of reality, its name is "good," not "being," and not "substance." And this principle is most definitely not a god.

II. Aristotle

In the long development connecting the language of being with God, Plato's pupil Aristotle took one step forward and one step backwards. About a god, Aristotle would use the language of being, even calling a god an οὐσία. But he would abandon Plato's insight that there is one ultimate principle of the universe. Aristotle's highest god will be highest only *per accidens*, because the unmoved mover of the highest celestial sphere.

If Plato had said there is one science of being (ὄν), which is a science of a higher world of forms, in the scrolls eventually labeled "the things after the physical things" (τὰ μετὰ τὰ φυσικά) Aristotle said "there is a science of being as being" (ὄν ᾗ ὄν). In this formula, the first "being" means metaphysics will consider any being, beginning with individual beings (ὄντα) in the physical world. The rider "as being" means metaphysics treats them from the perspective of their being, rather than change (as in physics) or quantity (as in mathematics). This perspective led Aristotle, like his master Plato, to approach beings with the Socratic question of definition in mind: "what is it? (τί ἔστι), that is, what is its quiddity? Unlike Plato, however, he found there is οὐσία in the world of change, for physical beings are composed of substance—the fundamental quiddity they have as independently existing things, like bronze—and accidents, quidditative features that depend upon substance in order to exist, like spherical.[19] But Aristotle quickly reduced the science of being to a science of its prime instance—οὐσία.[20] This reduction meant he concentrated on the "what it is" of individual substances (a 'this'), and there were three answers to this question because

> There are three senses of substance: 1) matter, being a 'this' in appearance . . . for example, fire, flesh, head, for all these are matter but the last is the matter of substance in the fullest sense [that is, an individual substance]; 2) the nature [or form], a 'this' and a kind of end state toward which motion proceeds; and 3) the third is the individual composed of them, for example, Socrates or Callias.[21]

That there are three kinds of substance (not just one, as for Plato), required Aristotle to make some choice among the three. Which is the most important? In order to answer this question, Aristotle took the Socratic definitional formula "what it is" (τί ἔστι)—which can apply to both substances and accidents—and developed a new technical term, limited to substances, that encapsulated his new question: τό τί ἦν εἶναι, which translates literally as "the what was being," to which a dative of reference is understood to be added 'for this,' say, a dog, human, or god. In a way, this formula is quite precise. It means 'the quiddity that is being' for a certain individual substance; and it is Aristotle's way of asking about a substance, which of the three senses of quiddity is foremost in describing its "being." Is it the composite, the matter, or the intrinsic form? Aristotle's answer is that it is the form. This is what substance is primarily, once it has been brought down from the Platonic heaven to the world of change; and this is what allowed Aristotle to do away with the world of forms. It is not surprising, then, that this formula would be rendered into Latin as *essentia*, the "being-ness" of something, in the sense of the primary aspect of its quiddity. Armed with these technical terms, in *Metaphysics* 7–9 Aristotle could analyze the kinds of substance found in that world of change. In *Metaphysics* Λ (12), however, Aristotle turned to consider a higher level of οὐσίαι: those "separate" from matter. He concluded that they do exist, they are spiritual, and they are causes of lower beings. And unlike Plato, he was perfectly willing to call such a substance "god" (θέος).

At 12, c.1–5, Aristotle laid out the principles needed to develop his theology in c. 6–10. The scientific "subject" under consideration is substance. The existence of sensible substance, both perishable and imperishable (the heavenly bodies) was not in doubt, only the existence of "immovable" or "separate" substance must be proven.[22] His argument for its existence takes off from his definition of change (μεταβολή): "everything changes from that which is potentially to that which is actually."[23] Change requires the internal principles of matter, form, and privation, as change "from potentially white to actually white" requires some matter that goes from non-white to white.[24] Form and matter exist only as intrinsic principles of things, not as beings in their own right: "For when a man is healthy, the health also exists; and the shape of a bronze sphere exists at the same time as the bronze sphere."[25] Substantial change also requires efficient and final causality. "Therefore analogically there are three elements and four causes and principles; but the elements are different in different things, and the proximate moving cause is different for different things. Health, disease, body; the moving cause is the medical art."[26] By the end of c. 5, the principles for dealing with eternal substances were set.

Aristotle devoted 12.6 to demonstrating the existence of separate substance, using a short two-step argument that draws out implications of his definition of change. The first step concerns matter. Change requires a pre-existing subject because change is actualization of a potency in something that pre-exists the change. It follows that sensible changing material substances can have no absolute beginning. Every presumed "beginning" would itself be achieved through a process of change, which would further require pre-existing matter. And these substances likewise could never be annihilated. So there always were and always will be perishable sensible substances. While earthly substances are eternal only in their species, the heavenly bodies are sensible substances eternal as individuals and in their species. The second step of Aristotle's argument concerns the fact that change requires a cause or "mover" (κινοῦν). An eternal physical world requires an eternal actual mover, or if there is more than one mover, an ultimate mover that is equally eternal with the effect. Aristotle here is primarily concerned with the cause of each of the distinct heavenly spheres that move continuously in a circle. But to be an eternal cause, an ultimate mover cannot be in any way in potency, it must be completely unmoved, "a principle whose very substance is actuality" (οὐσία ἐνέργεια).[27] This means "these substances must be without matter."

In c. 7, Aristotle turned to the nature of such a separate substance, and in c. 8–10 he tried to resolve three problems (ἀπορίαι) that arose from his description. C. 7 contains Aristotle's attempts to define separate substance. He began with an *extrinsic and causal consideration*. The eternal circular motion of "the first heaven" requires a mover that "moves without being moved, being *eternal*, *substance* (οὐσία), and *actuality* (ἐνέργεια)." He then immediately added: "And the object of desire and the object of thought move in this way; they move without being moved."[28] Separate substance, then, exercises *final* causality and is a kind of "good," as was Plato's good; but it is not "beyond οὐσία," it is οὐσία.

This substance "moves as the object of love, whereas the other [causes] move while being in motion."[29] This is why it cannot be a material cause, which would involve potentiality; nor can it be the substantial form or soul of a heavenly sphere, for then it would move at least *per accidens* along with the motion of its sphere; and it cannot be an efficient cause, since they introduce a form into some other matter and therefore change in exercising their causality. But as a final cause, "the first mover exists of necessity . . . and it is in this sense a *first principle*."[30]

Aristotle's second attempt at a definition in c.7 was to develop an *intrinsic* description of separate substance, drawn from its activities or operations. It is *living*, living the best life, the best we enjoy but for a short time, while it does so forever. This life is that of *intelligence*; but it is wholly separate from the world of change—separate intelligence because wholly immaterial. "And knowing in itself is about what is the best in itself, and knowing in the fullest sense is about the best in the fullest sense. And *knowing knows itself* through sharing in what is known . . . so that knowing and the object known are the same."[31] It was at this point that Aristotle used the term "god" for the first time in his argument, because knowing is an act of a person. And he then summed up his results this way: "We say, therefore, that a god (τὸν θέον) is living, eternal, best, so that life both ever present and eternal belongs to a god, for this *is* god."[32] Such a substance must be "separate from sensible things," it "can have no magnitude, but is without parts and indivisible."[33]

In the final three chapters of Bk. 12, Aristotle tried to solve three problems that arose from his definitions in c. 7. While Plato had one "good" but many "forms," Aristotle has many "gods," as many as there are heavenly spheres whose circular rotation they cause (c. 8), and each is good, but not "the [one] good." For gods the normal ontological distinction between first act—being a substance (οὐσία)—and second act—knowing—breaks down. And so, too, does the normal distinction between knower, knowing, and the object known; all are the same in a god (c. 9). Finally, Aristotle clarifies how "good" applies to a separate substance. Its goodness is neither purely separate from what it affects, like Plato's "good," nor it is purely immanent. "Its good is like that of the general of an army or the freemen of a household" (c. 10).

Aristotle, then, employed metaphysical language of being about a god, something Plato himself had studiously avoided. But he changed Plato's language and doctrine of being, and his doctrine of causality. An Aristotelian god is "a being" (ὄν). Its "being-ness" (οὐσία), in the sense of its intrinsic cause, is form without matter. But this fact also makes a god an οὐσία in the sense of a fully independent being, one whose whole being (εἶναι) and essence (τό τί ἦν εἶναι) is without matter, form alone. This ensures that a god is unchanging. As an extrinsic cause, a god is an unmoved "mover" of a heavenly sphere and indirectly of things on earth, in both cases as a final cause. Considered intrinsically, since a god is substance consisting only of form, he lives the happiest of lives, one devoted to theoretical understanding of himself. Since a god is a kind of substance, no god can be infinitely perfect, but is constrained within the limited categorical perfections that describe it—substance and action. This is why there can be many such gods, each a final cause but not a creator, living a life of thought oblivious of a world that depends upon it. In short, an Aristotelian god is an odd sort of general, one who inspires his troops while being unaware of them.

By reducing the study of "being" (ὄν) in its universality to a study of the highest kind of being—οὐσία—Aristotle immanentized οὐσία, bringing it down into the world of change, so that substance was no longer an abstract principle existing in a higher world of causes. But in order for the world of change to contain substance, Aristotle thought there must also be separate οὐσίαι that are the primary beings— the gods. On this point and in this way, the fundamental insight of his master Plato lived on in Aristotle and in the religiously motivated Aristotelianism to come.

III. After Aristotle

Avicenna: In the first of his four philosophical *summae*—*The Healing (al-Shifā'), Divine Science (al-Ilâhiyyât)*, also called his "metaphysics"—Avicenna (Ibn Sina) developed his first *ex professo* metaphysical treatment of the existence and nature of God, one that would be translated into Latin and have a profound impact on thinkers in the Latin world from Gundissalinus onwards. Here he drew on the way the Greek to Arabic translators had rendered Greek being-words into Arabic, which had no word for "it is" (ἔστιν) in the present tense because it does not use a copula in 'equational' sentences like 'the man is a believer.'[34] To render the Greek language of being into Arabic, the translators turned to the verb "to find" (*wajada*, he found). The concrete and substantive notion of "a being," captured in Greek by the active participle ὄν, they rendered by the passive participle *mawjûd* (literally, "the found"). The verbal noun *wujûd* signified more abstractly that aspect of a concrete thing which is its "to be" or "being" (εἶναι). But for οὐσία, they used a totally unrelated term, namely, *jawhar*, which emphasizes the importance of οὐσία because it also means "jewel."[35]

At *Metaphysics* 1, Avicenna sets out the "subject" and "principles" of metaphysics. Its "subject" is "a being" (*mawjûd*) considered in its universality. The common principles of metaphysics are the law of the excluded middle and the principle of non-contradiction, two features of one and the same axiom. Unlike Aristotle, Avicenna set out the proper principles of metaphysics quite explicitly. Its "definitions" are the most universal *notions* or concepts of thought: "a being" (*mawjûd*), "thing" (*shay*), "necessary" (*darûrî*) (along with "possible" and "impossible"), and finally "being" or "existence" (*wujûd*).[36] Its two "hypotheses" or fundamental *propositions* are: possible being is an ontological combination of thing (or quiddity or truth) and being; necessary being, that is, necessary in itself, is ontologically simple, only being.[37] The first hypothesis assumes one knows there are sensible things of our everyday experience, the second that, should it be proven that necessary being exists, it would have to be ontologically simple. Avicenna articulated his principles in the language of 'being' and its modes, quite different from Aristotle's causal principles. In Bks. 2–7, Avicenna drew conclusions about the ontology of possible beings or creatures, in Bks. 8–10 about "necessary being" or God.

In Bk. 8, chapters 1–3, Avicenna offered an argument for the existence of God that takes off from Aristotle, though not from *Metaphysics* 12 but from 2.2, where Aristotle had defended "scientific" knowledge by arguing that infinite regress in any of the four lines of causality is impossible. The first part of Avicenna's metaphysical argument for the existence of God concludes that there must be a "first," that is, a cosmic first cause, standing at the head of each line of causality. Avicenna then had to unify the "firsts," either by finding one of them that is God, the other "first" causes subordinated to God, or somehow identify all four "firsts" with God. Avicenna took the first option and, as we shall see, Aquinas will take the second. This part of his argument Avicenna set out in causal terms. But then he short-circuited full consideration of all four lines of causality, by beginning (and ending) with efficient causality: there is a first efficient cause of the universe. The reason he stopped here was because a first efficient cause clearly must be one and necessary, two criteria for necessary being (or God) that had been set out in the principles of his metaphysics.[38] One can readily sees that a first *efficient* cause must be a single and necessary being, whereas the other three 'firsts'—the first formal, material, and final causes—do not so readily 'fit' these criteria.[39]

Avicenna wasted no time but devoted the second half of c. 3 to clarifying what God is like. Here he concentrated on unity, conceived as a transcendental convertible with "a being" and "being," by contrasting the unity of God with the plurality found in creatures. The first efficient cause must be one, when considered extrinsically—it is one in number, different from all other beings—and when considered intrinsically—it has no ontological parts. By contrast, any possible being must be ontologically complex, and therefore requires an extrinsic efficient cause in order to exist. This is another way of saying that all possible beings must be created. The priority of God to creatures, then, is *ontological*, not temporal.

Avicenna recognized that there is an important difference between describing God's *intrinsic* nature, and describing God *extrinsically* in relation to creatures. So Avicenna he devoted Bk. 8, chapters 4 and 5, to God's *intrinsic* nature, *based on his own metaphysical principles*. This was something Aristotle had never done. Then in chapters 6 and 7, he turned to some *extrinsically* denominated divine attributes, focusing of God's knowledge, something Aristotle had done.

In c. 4, Avicenna laid out the primary features of God's nature. He began with the fact that "necessary being" is the first of all beings and is one. Avicenna then drew detailed conclusions using the language of being and unity. To understand them, we must distinguish three features of "a being" (*mawjûd*): the thing considered as an individual, such as Zayd; its nature or quiddity (*mâhiyya*), such as human; and its being (*wujûd*), for example, real or imaginary. When conceived as an individual, God is one with his quiddity. His quiddity is to be one in such manner that God is his own quiddity. In God, there is no distance between the individual subject he is and his quiddity, as there is in creatures, where an individual subject is not the same as its quiddity, as Zayd is not the same as humanity, though he has this quiddity.[40]

Second, in God there is no quiddity (*mahiyya*) other than his individual *inniyya*, a difficult word that can be translated either as individual quiddity or individual existence, depending upon context. This means that God does not have the kind of quiddity that can be multiplied in different individuals, because his own quiddity is unique. It also means that God's quiddity is being (or existence). This is why Avicenna says on occasion "the First has no quiddity other than his individual being."[41] In short, while Zayd's individuality, nature, and being are all ontologically *distinct* from each other, these three features in God are *identical with each other*.

Third, having a nature so different from every other being affects how we know God; for God is known metaphysically as "necessary being itself."[42]

Fourth, since there is no content to God's quiddity other than "necessary being," it follows that "the First has no quiddity (*mâhiyya*)," that is, the kind of nature that could be multiplied.[43] Several important conclusions follow from God's quiddity not being plurifiable: God fits under no common genus; God also fits under no species in common with other things; God has no differentia; and, most important, God is not a substance.[44]

These conclusions are very much at odds with the spirit and letter of Aristotle's view of god. They are set out in the language of being and unity; while substance, so central to Aristotle's conception of god, plays no role. As these topics are so important, Avicenna goes over them again in c. 5, as an exercise in negative theology. Between his argument for the existence of God and his more 'Aristotelian' causal approach to God's nature, in c. 4 and 5 Avicenna has inserted consideration of the intrinsic nature of God couched in the language of being, a considerable innovation in the history or metaphysics.

Avicenna, however, did not altogether neglect Aristotle's causal approach to God's nature. He developed that approach in cc. 6 and 7, describing God in relation to creatures and in terms of the divine operations. First, God is "perfect" and "more than perfect," which sets God at the top of the scale of reality.[45] Second, God is "pure good," which for Avicenna focuses on the "beneficent" side of goodness rather than the desirability of goodness. So goodness connotes in the first instance God as free "bestower of being" on creatures, rather than God as "end," which was the only way Aristotle had conceived of God.[46] Third, God is truth. For Avicenna, "truth" has an ontological sense, which is why it is a synonym for "thing" and "quiddity."[47] God's quiddity is that of "pure intellect." As such, God "knows himself," as Aristotle had said. But unlike Aristotle's gods, Avicenna's creative God "knows all things through knowing himself."[48] As intellect, Avicenna's God knows universals, to be sure, but he also knows particulars, albeit "universally."[49] Finally, again reflecting Aristotle, in God knower, knowing, and known are one.[50]

In c. 7 Avicenna looked at the objects of divine knowledge more carefully, in order to ensure that they not introduce multiplicity into God.[51] Avicenna ended with a brief consideration of joy and happiness in God. Since God's knowledge does not introduce multiplicity, the divine splendor, majesty, and glory characterize a joy and happiness that are undivided in God himself.[52] Such an end humans can only imitate, both in the present life and in the life rhwy might have upon "returning" to God.

About the nature of God, then, Avicenna incorporated some Aristotelian themes, such as God as unchangeable, good, a self-knower, and supremely happy. But far more striking are the ways Avicenna departed from Aristotle. The reason he did so was because Aristotle's principles were primarily causal, though he did develop the language of being in important ways, while Avicenna's principles focus on being and its transcendental attributes that go 'beyond the categories.' This is why Avicenna developed his most important conclusions in a completely original section (Bk. 8.3–5) inserted between his argument for God's existence and the more "Aristotelian" conclusions about God's nature developed in cc. 6–7.

Aquinas: In his *Summa theologiae* 1 (written 1265–1268), Br. Thomas of Aquino organized his theology "according to the order of the discipline." This led him to change how he treated God's nature, in comparison with his *Scriptum in Sententiis* (1252–1256) and his *Summa contra gentiles* (1259–1265). He conceived theology or "sacred doctrine" as an Aristotelian "science" that demonstrates conclusions from principles. From his *Scriptum* onward he recognized theology contains both demonstrations based on revealed principles and purely rational demonstrations. In his *Scriptum* he had set out both sets of principles explicitly. The revealed principles, the "articles of faith" contained in the ancient creeds, he introduces in the Prologue to Bk. 1.[53] Bk. 1, d. 8, q. 1, art. 1–3 contains the metaphysical principles he drew from Avicenna. At the outset of *Summa of Theology* 1, Aquinas again explicitly referred to the proper principles of theology—the articles of faith,[54] but as in the *Contra gentiles* he does not explicitly list the philosophical principles theology uses in its rational demonstrations. But in *De ente* he already had set out a simplified list of Avicennian *metaphysical* principles: "a being (ens) and essence are what are first conceived by the intellect, as Avicenna says in the first Book of his *Metaphysics*," to which Avicenna and Aquinas both added being or existence (*esse*). And in *On the Principles of Nature* he had laid out the principles of natural philosophy: potency and act, and the four causes. So following Avicenna, Aquinas couched his metaphysical principles in the language of being, while the principles of natural philosophy he set out in the language of causality.

To prove the existence of God, Aquinas employs Aristotle's argument from motion in his "first way," but the other four ways are modeled on the first step of Avicenna's argument from causality, proving that there is a cosmic "first" in each of the four lines of causality. The only category he changes is that "matter" is replaced by "possibility," its deeper metaphysical ground, in the third way. But where Avicenna left open the way these four "first causes" are related to each other, Br. Thomas argues in "ways" two through five that all four lines of Aristotelian causality lead inevitably to one and the same first cause—"and this we call God." God is the first efficient cause of all creation, the necessary being that all possible beings require in order to exist, the most formally perfect being, and the ultimate final cause of all creation. While *Contra gentiles* 1 had reflected a more "Aristotelian" order in treating the divine nature,[55] in the *Summa of Theology* Aquinas changed the order of topics significantly, and in an Avicennian direction. Intent on shining the lights of revelation and reason together, Aquinas treats first the nature of God as known through natural reason (Q. 3–26), then turns to the Trinitarian nature of God, based on revelation (Q. 27–43). Aquinas follows Avicenna's general plan for treating the divine essence, first treating God's intrinsic nature in Avicennian fashion (Q. 3–11), then treating God's "operations," where causal arguments come more into play (Q.12–25).

Aquinas begins just where Avicenna had begun, with divine simplicity (Q. 3). The terms of Br. Thomas's argument are being-terms: "a being" (*ens*), "essence" (*essentia*), "being" or "existence" (*esse*), and "one" (*unum*) conceived as a transcendental convertible with being. But there is a difference. Avicenna had begun with God's unity and rationistically drawn out the implications of this claim; but Aquinas follows a negative approach, denying various kinds of ontological multiplicity of God. He begins with greater complexity and proceeding to greater unity, a mode of argument intended to force his reader logically to recognize that God is not multiple in even a minimal way, but absolutely simple ontologically. God is not a physical body whose parts are extended in space (Art. 1). God is not composed of matter and form, as are all material substances (Art. 2). Conceived as an individual subject, God is same as his essence (Art. 3), unlike material creatures, where there are many individuals of one species. In God essence is identical with being (*esse*) (Art. 4), which was Avicenna's premier metaphysical claim about God. And since God does not have a quiddity or essence distinct from being, God has no genus (Art. 5), nor accidents (Art. 6). So ontologically God is completely simple (Art. 7). Finally, in no way enters into the composition of things, even though God is the direct efficient cause of the being of all creatures (Art. 8).

From the thoroughly Avicennian starting point in Q. 3, Br. Thomas develops a number of features of God's nature in questions 4–11, again following the order of *Metaphysics* 8.3–4. First, God is ontologically simple, he is "most actual, and therefore most perfect"; and as a creator, pre-possesses all the perfections of his creation.[56]

Second, God is not just good but "the highest good." Where Aristotle's highest god was the highest good only *per accidens*, because the final cause of the highest sphere, Aquinas's God, like Avicenna's, is not the highest good for some extrinsic reason, but "God alone is good through his essence, . . . for whom alone essence is his being." This conception of goodness as a transcendental attribute of being (*ens*), leads Aquinas to introduce a new kind of participation which makes "all things good by the divine goodness." For although

> it seems unreasonable to posit species of natural things subsisting separately through themselves [as Plato did and Aristotle rejected] . . . still it is absolutely true that something is first which, through its own essence is a being (*ens*) and good, which we call God. . . . Therefore, by the first, through its own essence a being and good, everything can be called good and a being, in as much as it participates in it by way of a kind of assimilation, albeit remotely and deficiently. . . . Therefore, in this way everything is called good by the divine goodness, as by a first principle that is the *exemplar, efficient,* and *final* cause of all goodness.[57]

Third, it follows that God is "essentially" and "absolutely" infinite, a status that can only be true of one God, who is beyond Aristotle's many gods since they were limited in perfection by the immaterial forms they were.[58] For Aquinas, Aristotle's many gods become many angels.

Fourth, God is omnipresent in creatures, "not as part of their essence, nor as an accident, but as an agent is present to that on which it works," for God "is in all things as causing the being (*esse*) of all things."[59] God does this directly, a departure from Avicenna's mediated creation.

Fifth, God is utterly unchangeable. Aquinas offers three reasons for this conclusion. First, God is pure act, without the admixture of any potency, an Aristotelian argument. Aquinas then adds two others: change requires composition, but "in God there is no composition, for he is altogether [ontologically] simple"; and since God is infinite, it would be impossible for him to acquire a new perfection through change, indeed, impossible to change at all.[60] Sixth, God is truly eternal, he does not merely persist through all time, as Aristotle thought.[61]

Finally, Aquinas completes this line of reasoning in q. 11, by returning to where it began in q. 3, with the unity of God. To his earlier consideration of divine simplicity, Aquinas now makes clear that in addition to "true" and "good," "one" is also a transcendental attribute of "being (*ens*)," so that God must be one to the highest degree, as he is being, true, and good to the highest degree. Aquinas offers three reasons for God's unity, which stand as a kind of coda for the "Avicennian" section of his treatment of God's nature. First, God must be one "from his simplicity," maximal ontological unity; second, "from the infinity of his perfection"; and finally, "from the unity of the world" which is bestowed by the "first" who "is completely perfect and through itself, not through another."[62]

While the four causes and the categories do enter Aquinas's arguments in questions 4–11, the language in which he couches his conclusions and arguments are fundamentally the language of being: "a being" (*ens*), "essence" (*essentia*), "being" (*esse*), and the three transcendental attributes of being—"one" (*unum*), "true" (*verum*), and "good" (*bonum*). The priority of being-language is reflected in the three reasons Aquinas give why the Biblical "who is" (*qui est*) is the "most proper name of God." First, "in its signification," the term 'is' "does not signify *some form*, but being itself (*ipsum esse*)." The second reason is due to "its universality." And the third reason is due to what is "signified along with" 'is'; "for it signifies being *in the present*," which is "most proper to God" who exists in an eternal present.[63]

In the second part of his treatment of the divine nature (Q. 12–26) Aquinas turns to divine "operation," which treats God's nature extrinsically. Here causal arguments predominate. But as a sign of the distance between Aristotle and Aquinas, let us consider what God knows. Where Aristotle had concluded that god knows only himself, nothing else, and Avicenna had said that God knows all of creation in knowing himself, but only indirectly, since the immediate created object of his knowledge is the one thing he immediately creates, the highest intelligence or first angel, Aquinas develops this line of reasoning one step further, saying that God directly knows all creation in knowing himself, because he creates directly, not through any mediation. The reason is that if God's knowledge is completely perfect, he must know not only himself but all the consequences that follow from himself as "the first efficient cause of all things." This conclusion "appears still more plainly if we add that the very being of the first efficient cause, that is, God, is his own act of understanding,"[64] an argument based on Aquinas's Avicennian doctrine of "being (*esse*)," as outlined earlier in Q. 3.

* * * * *

Appropriate philosophical language for describing the nature of God took almost two millennia to develop. Parmenides first discovered the language of being and used it to describe, not God, but the world of everyday experience, with the result that the truth about this world was incompatible with the way it appears. Plato distinguished the world of changing beings from the world of true being and the good "beyond being." To do so, he developed the vocabulary of being, introducing a new sense of οὐσία; but he refused to use that language to describe the Olympic gods, who were not worthy of it. And he also used certain causal principles—forms and ends—to describe the higher world. Aristotle 'brought the forms down to earth' by showing how to use the language of being about earthly things, yet he also was the first philosopher to use the language of being about the gods, whom he described as substances separate from matter. Even though writing in a language not well adapted to the Greek language of being, Avicenna used the Arabic language of being developed for philosophers, in order to describe God, not as a substance but as "being," which transcends all the categories, including substance. Br. Thomas of Aquino recognized how far beyond Aristotle the Persian had gone. Like Avicenna, he used the language of causality to prove the existence of God. But in nature his God is no longer an Aristotelian substance, nor even an Avicennian "necessary being," but is best described as "subsistent being itself" (*ipsum esse subsistens*), the *esse* which is only a principle in a creature now conceived as "subsisting" wholly on its own. Here the Christian disciple seems to have brought to an even higher level of perfection the achievements of his Islamic master, achievements that far surpassed their beginnings in Parmenidean monism.

Center for Thomistic Studies, University of St. Thomas, Houston

Notes

1. The secondary literature on God's nature in this tradition is vast. I list only the works from which I have learned most.

Languages: Charles H. Kahn, *The Verb 'Be' in Ancient Greek* (Indianapolis: Hackett, reprinted 2003); A.-M. Goichon, *Lexique de la language philosophique d'Ibn Sina* (Paris: Desclee, 1938); S. van Riet, *Avicenna Latinus. Liber de Philosophia Prima sive Scientia Divina, I–X, Lexiques* (Leiden: Brill, 1983).

Parmenides: Leonardo Taran, *Parmenides* (Princeton: Princeton University Press, 1965); David Gallop, *Parmenides of Elea* (Toronto: University of Toronto Press, 1984); Leonard Woodbury, "Parmenides on Names," *Harvard Studies in Classical Philology* 63 (1958): 145–160, reprinted in *Essays in Ancient Greek Philosophy*, ed. J. Anton and G. Kustus (Albany: SUNY Press, 1971): 145–162.

Plato: W. K. C. Guthrie, *A History of Greek Philosophy*, vol. 4 (Cambridge: Cambridge University Press, 1975); N. P. White, *A Companion to Plato's Republic* (Indianapolis: Hackett, 1979); Julia Annas, *An Introduction to Plato's Republic* (New York: Oxford University Press, 1981); C. D. C. Reeve, *Philosopher Kings* (Princeton: Princeton University Press, 1988); Allan Silverman, *The Dialectic of Essence: A Study of Plato's Metaphysics* (Princeton: Princeton University Press, 2002); Stephen Menn, "Aristotle and Plato on God as 'Nous' and as the Good," *Review of Metaphysics* 45.3 (1992): 543–573.

Aristotle: Leo Elders, *A Commentary on Bk. Λ of the Metaphysics* (Assen: Van Gorcum, 1972); Giovanni Reale, *The Concept of First Philosophy and the Unity of the Metaphysics of Aristotle*, trans. John R. Catan (Albany: SUNY Press, 1980); J. Owens, *The Doctrine of Being in the Aristotelian Metaphysics*, 3rd ed. (Toronto: PIMS, 1978); T. Irwin, *Aristotle's First Principles* (New York: Oxford University Press, 1990); Antoine Côté, "Intellection and Divine Causation in Aristotle," *Southern Journal of Philosophy* 43 (2005): 25–39; Lloyd Gerson, *Aristotle and other Platonists* (Ithaca: Cornell University Press, 2006).

Avicenna: A.-M. Goichon, *La distinction de l'essence et de l'existence d'apres Ibn Sina (Avicenne)* (Paris: Desclee de Brouwer, 1937); Michael E. Marmura, "Avicenna on the Primary Concepts in the Metaphysics of His *al-Shifā*,'" in R. Savory and A. Dionisius, *Logos Islamikos: Studia Islamica in honorem Georgii Michaelis Wickens* (Toronto: PIMS Press, 1984), 219–239; J. Jolivet, "Aux origins de l'ontologie d'Ibn Sina," in *Études sur Avicenne*, ed. J. Jolivet and R. Rashed (Paris: 1984), 19–28; D. Gutas, *Avicenna and the Aristotelian Tradition* (Leiden: Brill, 1988); M. E. Marmura, "Quiddity and Universality in Avicenna," in *Neoplatonism and Islamic Thought*, ed. Parviz Morewedge (New York: SUNY Press, 1992), 77–87; B. Mondin, "La metafisica di Avicenna," *Sapienza* 52 (1999): 257–279; Robert Wisnovsky, "Notes on Avicenna's Concept of Thingness (Shay'iyya)," *Arabic Sciences and Philosophy* 10 (2000): 181–221; Robert Wisnovsky, *Avicenna's Metaphysics in Context* (Ithaca: Cornell University Press, 2003): 173–180, 245–265; Peter Adamson, "On Knowledge of Particulars," *Proceedings of the Aristotelian Society*

105 (2005): 257–278; Thérèse-Anne Druart, "Metaphysics," in *Cambridge Companion to Arabic Philosophy*, ed. P. Adamson and R. C. Taylor (Cambridge: Cambridge University Press, 2005): 327–348; Amos Bertolacci, *The Reception of Aristotle's Metaphysics in Avicenna's Kitâb al-Shifâ'* (Leiden, Boston: Brill, 2006).

Aquinas: Etienne Gilson, *Thomism: the Philosophy of Thomas Aquinas*, trans. L. K. Shook and A. Maurer, from the sixth and final edition of *Le Thomisme* (Toronto: PIMS, 2002): 84–126; Jan Aertsen, *Nature and Creature: Thomas Aquinas's Way of Thought* (Leiden and New York: Brill, 1988); J. F. X. Knasas, *The Preface to Thomistic Metaphysics* (New York: Lang, 1990); Jan Aertsen, *Medieval Philosophy and the Transcendentals: The Case of Thomas Aquinas* (Leiden and New York: Brill, 1990); Norman Kretzmann, *The Metaphysics of Theism: Aquinas's Natural Theology in Summa contra gentiles I* (Oxford and New York: Clarendon, 1997); Brian Davies, *The Thought of Thomas Aquinas* (Oxford: Clarendon Press, 1992); Eleanore Stump, *Aquinas* (London and New York: Routledge, 2003); Benedict Ashley, *The Way toward Wisdom: An Interdisciplinary and Intercultural Introduction to Metaphysics*, Center for Thomistic Studies Series (Notre Dame: University of Notre Dame Press, 2006).

The influence of Aristotle and Avicenna on Aquinas: E. M. Macierowski, "Does God Have a Quiddity According to Avicenna?" *Thomist* 52 (1988): 79–87; J. F. Wippel, "The Latin Avicenna as a Source for Thomas Aquinas's Metaphysics," *Freiberger Zeitschrift für Philosophie und Theologie* (1990): 51–90; Rahim Acar, *Talking about God and Talking about Creation: Avicenna's and Thomas Aquinas' Positions* (Leiden, Boston: Brill, 2005): 79–130. See also, R. E. Houser, "The Real Distinction and the Principles of Metaphysics: Avicenna and Aquinas," in *Laudemus viros gloriosos: Essays in Honor of Armand Maurer CSB*, ed. R. E. Houser, Center for Thomistic Studies Series (Notre Dame: University of Notre Dame Press, 2007): 75–108.

All translations are my own.

2. Parmenides, Frag. 1. 3, 9–10, 22, 28–30 (ed. Gallup).

3. On Thales, see Aristotle, *Metaphysics*, 1.3 (938b6–27).

4. Heraclitus (frag. 7) and Empedocles (frag. 129) use τὰ ὄντα about the world of real things. See Liddell and Scott, *A Greek-English Lexicon* 9th ed. (Oxford: Clarendon, 1940), under εἰμί, A.II.1.

5. Parmenides, Frag. 3.

6. Parmenides, Frag. 2. line 3: ἡ μὲν ὅπως ἔστιν τε καὶ ὡς οὐκ ἔστι μὴ εἶναι. Line 5: ἡ δ' ὡς οὐκ ἔστιν τε καὶ ὡς χρειών ἐστι μὴ εἶναι.

7. Parmenides, Frag. 8: 1–6, 42–3:

> Now a single story of a way
> Is left, that it is (ὡς ἔστιν). On this way there are signs
> Very many: that a being (ἐòν) is un-generated and imperishable,
> Whole, of a single kind, unshaken, and complete.
> Nor was it once, nor will it be, since it is now, altogether,
> One, continuous. For what generation will you seek for it?
> . . . But since there is a furthest limit, it is complete,
> On all sides, like the bulk of a well-rounded sphere.

8. Parmenides, Frag. 8: 53–60.

> For they made up their minds to name two forms,
> of which it is not right to name one—in this they have gone astray—

And they distinguished things opposite in body, and established signs
Apart from one another—on one side, aetherial fire of flame, . . .
but on the other, that in itself
is opposite, dark night, a dense and heavy body.

9. Plato, *Phaedo*, 96a6–10.

10. Ibid., 96b4–e2.

11. Ibid., 98e2–99b4)

12. Ibid., 100b5–7. Plato does not use the phrase *to ontos on* in the Phaedo. But he does use the term οὐσία, as at 76d9: "If there are those things we always mention, a beautiful and good and every such kind of being (οὐσία)." The "beautiful itself" is the centerpiece of Diotima's speech in the *Symposium* (210e–211c).

13. Plato, *Republic* 5, 476b2–4.

14. Ibid., 476e7–b1.

15. Ibid., 478e1–2, 479d2–5.

16. Plato, *Republic* 6, 509d4–511e2.

17. See Heroditus, *Histories* 2.200, Sophocles, *Trachinian Women*, 911. See Liddell and Scott, *A Greek-English Lexicon*, entry οὐσία, I.

18. Plato, *Republic* 6, 508b6–10.

19. Aristotle, *Metaphysics* 4.1 (1003a21–6), W. D. Ross (Oxford, Clarendon Press: 1958), W. Jaeger (Oxford, Clarendon Press: 1957). Aristotle, *Metaphysics* 12.3 (1070a23–4).

20. Aristotle, *Metaphysics* 4.2 (1003b5–17); 12.1 (1069a1).

21. Aristotle, *Metaphysics* 12.3 (1070a10–14), with 19–21 inserted, following the critical editions.

22. Aristotle, *Metaphysics* 12.1 (1069a1).

23. Ibid., 12.2 (1069b16).

24. Ibid. (1069b16–18).

25. Ibid., 12.3 (1070a23–4).

26. Ibid., 12.4 (1070b26–8).

27. Ibid., 12.6 (1071b5–22).

28. Ibid., 12.7 (1072a26–8).

29. Ibid. (1072b4).

30. Ibid. (1072b11–12).

31. Ibid. (1072b14–22).

32. Ibid. (1072b27–28).

33. Ibid. (1073a4–7).

34. *Kâna* (root *kawn*) can be translated "it was (or is)," but in many contexts must be translated in the sense of "coming to be" (γίγνεσθαι), which makes it unacceptable for necessary knowledge claims and for describing God. Consequently, the Toledo translators sometimes rendered it by forms of esse, but at other times used forms of fieri. See Goichon,

Lexique de la language philosophique d'Ibn Sina, sec. 633; Van Riet, *Lexiques*, Arabic root 758 (kwn), under kâna, pp. 116–117.

35. Rough equivalents for the main being-words and causal words relevant to the nature of God:

English	Greek	Arabic	Latin
a being	οὔ	*maw......jûd*	ens
being/existence	εἶναι	*wujûd*	esse
it is	ἔστιν	[ ]	est
it comes to be	γίγνεται	kâna	fit
substance	οὐσία	jawhar	substantia
what it is	τί ἐστι	mâhiyya	quidditas
essence	τὸ τί ἦν εἶναι	dhât	essentia
principle	ἀρχή	mabda'	principium
cause	αἰτία	'illa, sabab	causa
form	εἶδος	ṣûra	forma
species	εἶδος	naw'	species
genus	γένος	jins	genus
matter	ὕλη	mâdda, hayûlâ	material
agent	κινοῦν, ποιητικόν	fâ'il	agens / efficiens
end	τέλος	ghâya	finis

36. Avicenna, *The Metaphysics of The Healing (Al-Shifâ')*, *Metaphysics (Al-Ilâhiyât)*, trans. and ed. Michael E. Marmura (Provo: Brigham Young University Press, 2005), 1.5, para. 1, p. 22, para. 8–9, p. 24.

37. Avicenna, *Metaphysics* 1.6–7, esp. c. 7, para. 13–14, p. 38.

38. Ibid., 1.7, para. 13, p. 38.

39. Ibid., 8.3, para. 5, p. 271.

40. Ibid., 8.4, para. 2, p. 273.

41. Ibid., para. 3–4, p. 274.

42. Ibid., para. 7, p. 274.

43. Ibid., para. 13, p. 276.

44. Ibid., para. 14–18, p. 277–278.

45. Ibid., 8.6, para. 1, p. 283.

46. Ibid., para. 2–4, p. 283–284.

47. Ibid., 1.5, para. 5, p. 23; para. 9, p. 24; 1.8, para. 1, p. 38–39.

48. Ibid., 8.6, para. 6–12, p. 284–287.

49. Ibid., para. 15, p. 287–288.

50. Ibid., para. 22, p. 290.

51. Ibid., 8.7, para. 1–9, p. 291–294.

52. Ibid., para. 12–16, p. 295–297.

53. Aquinas, *Scriptum in Sententiis*, "1. Prol," in Adriano Oliva, *Les débuts de l'enseignement de Thomas d'Aquin et sa conception de la Sacra doctrina: avec l'édition du prologue de son commentaire des Sentences* (Paris: Vrin, 2006). *Scriptum in Sententiis* 1.3.1c; 1.3.2 ad 2m, ed. Mandonnet (Paris: Vrin, 1947).

54. Aquinas, *Summa theologiae* 1.1.2c, 3c, 7c, leonine ed., 4–11 (Ottawa: Collège Dominicain, 1941). Hereafter *ST*.

55. Immediately after proving God's existence (*Summa contra gentiles* 1, c. 13), Aquinas began his treatment of the divine nature with a section devoted to understanding divine nature through Aristotelian causes: God is eternal (c. 15), an active power (c. 16), immaterial (c.17), incomposite (c. 18), and completely natural (c.19). Then Aquinas turned to the "Avicennian" features of the divine nature, ones that focus on God's being (c. 21–27). Aquinas then took up God's perfection and goodness (c. 28–41), followed by divine knowledge (c. 30–71) and will (c. 72–99), ending with divine beatitude (c.100–102).

56. Aquinas, *ST* 1.4.1c; 1.4.2c.

57. Ibid., 1.6.4c.

58. Ibid., 1.7.1c, 2c.

59. Ibid., 1.8.1c.

60. Ibid., 1.9.1c.

61. Ibid., 1.10.1c.

62. Ibid.,1.11.3.c.

63. Ibid.,1.13.11c.

64. Ibid.,1.14.5c.

The Aristotelian Epistemic Principle and the Problem of Divine Naming in Aquinas

Paul Symington

Abstract: In this paper, I engage in a preliminary discussion to the thorny problem of analogous naming in Aquinas; namely, the Maimonidean problem of how our conceptual content can relate to us any knowledge of God. I identify this problem as the First Semantic/Epistemic Problem (FSEP) of religious language. The primary determination of semantic content for Aquinas is what I call the Aristotelian Epistemic Principle (AEP). This principle holds that a belief is related to some experience in order to be known. I show how an examination of the extent the AEP engenders the problem and allows us to find a way out of the FSEP. For example, through such an analysis, we can see how the AEP relates to Aquinas's use of the distinction between the *res significata* and the *modus significandi*; the latter which includes the intension of being a created being where the former does not.

Thomas Aquinas envisioned philosophy as a handmaiden to theology; a way in which our purview is widened to accommodate and proportion the profundity of theological beliefs to limited human understanding.[1] As ordered to this Herculian task, perhaps there is no Thomistic doctrine more fundamental and controversial than that of analogy. Analogy is a semantic tool developed to provide epistemic security to the recondite and unwieldy doctrine of being and to provide justification for intelligible and true language about God.[2] There have been many involved studies attempting to present the semantics of analogy as a coherent and grounded theory.[3] It has also been the subject of many sustained criticisms, with one critic claiming that "*either* the doctrine of univocity is true *or* everything we say about God is in the most straightforward sense unintelligible."[4] To say the least, much criticism of the doctrine of analogy has arisen from deep interpretive problems and unclarity regarding the extent and nature of the doctrine itself. However, I believe that there are two preliminary ways of clarifying the doctrine and deflecting the force of its critics. The first is to pin-point and articulate the originating conditions that engendered the necessity for such a doctrine. Through this task, we can clearly see the conditions that need to be satisfied for the originating problem to be resolved.

Along these lines, we shall begin our discussion by identifying exactly how what I call the Aristotelian Epistemological Principle creates a need for constructing a semantic theory of analogy. The second is to identify and extricate a cluster of distinct issues—specifically, semantic and epistemic—that are grouped around Thomas's analogy doctrine in hopes of clarifying the problems surrounding the doctrine as a whole. In this paper, I identify one such preliminary problem, which I call the First Semantic/Epistemic Problem (henceforth, FSEP), and then present Aquinas's way of dealing specifically with it.[5]

Formally articulated and developed in the Western tradition by Moses Maimonides, the essence of the FSEP is familiar to students of Aquinas's thought.[6] The FSEP can be posited as follows:[7]

1. A positive judgment about extramental entities can only be true when the semantic content of this judgment pertains to, in some way, an extramental entity that is the subject of the judgment (Premise).

2. The only way that semantic content of a true positive judgment pertains to an extramental entity (or entities) that is the subject of a judgment is through acquaintance with that extramental entity (or entities) (Premise).

3. Only a created extramental entity is the kind of entity with which we can be acquainted (Premise).

4. Therefore, the only way through which the semantic content of a positive judgment can pertain to some extramental entity (or entities) is through acquaintance with the created entity that is the subject of the judgment (from 2, 3).

5. Therefore, a positive judgment about extramental entities can only be true when the semantic content pertains to the created extramental entity that is the subject of the judgment with which we are acquainted (from 1, 4).

6. In order for a positive judgment about God to be true, the semantic content of that judgment must pertain to an extramental entity with which we are acquainted (from 5).

7. However, God is not a created extramental entity (Premise).

8. God is an extramental entity (Premise).

9. Therefore, God is an extramental entity with which we are not acquainted (from 3, 7, 8).

10. Therefore, no positive judgment about God is true (from 4, 9).

11. Therefore, nothing positive can be known about God (from 10).

I need to address a few terms found in these premises. First, by 'positive judgment' is meant, in a broad sense, a non-negative judgment. A negative judgment is merely a proposition in which something is said to be not true of a subject. However, both negative and positive judgments each have logical and ontological meanings. A logical non-negative judgment pertains to the form of the judgment only, namely, that the term 'not' is not part of the predicate. But, in the ontological and narrower sense, a non-negative judgment asserts that the entity expressed by the subject itself possesses rather than lacks some real attribute.[8] For Aquinas, the model for understanding the nature of positive judgments according to its ontological sense is by appeal to common natures. A necessary condition for a common nature is that it is something that can exist either mentally as semantic content (as a universal), or extramentally as an individual essence of a being. Thus, a judgment is positive when the predicate asserts that that which is expressed by the subject term has a common nature (that can exist as an individual extramental essence) expressed by the predicate.[9] A vital role that common natures play for Aquinas is that they serve to ground the relation between our conceptual semantic content and the extramental things represented by them.[10] Regarding religious language, FSEP calls into question that any positive judgment—in which some real aspect is ascribed directly to God, such as 'Wisdom,' 'Joy,' 'Love'—can be truly predicated of God. This is very different from negative assertions of God in which God is said to lack some attribute, such as 'hatred,' or 'evil.'

Also, because I am using the term 'acquaintance' in a unique way, it needs to be identified. Underlying my use of the term is what can be cited generally as 'The Aristotelian Epistemic Principle' (henceforth, AEP), which asserts that a belief is related to some experience in order to be known.[11] In other words, some perceptual experience is a necessary condition for every instance of knowledge. Within the AEP I place the notion of 'acquaintance.' To be acquainted with x is to know x where x is some possible object of direct perceptual experience. It is important to note that the way that I use 'acquaintance' here is quite broad.[12] For example, insofar as I have had some experience of some dog, it is often enough for me to have some acquaintance with some other dogs that I have never directly experienced. This is because although direct perceptual experience is a necessary condition for knowing something, it is not sufficient. It is not sufficient (among other reasons) insofar as one has the cognitive ability to extend one's knowledge beyond an instance to a universal grasp of a kind. Thus, in virtue of the fact that from the necessary condition of some experience I can grasp a universal attribute in a direct perceptual experience, it is true that I am acquainted with some dog with which I have had no direct experience.[13]

With this in mind, in premise (2) of FSEP is the condition that in order to hold a true proposition one needs to be acquainted with that extramental entity which is the subject of one's judgment. In this case, it is sufficient that I be acquainted with what it means to be a dog in order for me to be acquainted with some dog with which I have no direct experience. So, when I know my belief that "The offspring of my dog Fifi will be a poodle," my knowledge arises from the fact that the semantic content of "poodle" possessed by me allows my acquaintance with the extramental entity that is the first-born offspring of my dog Fifi. This is true despite the fact that the first-born offspring of Fifi does not exist and so is not something of which I have had direct perceptual experience. In fact, due to the fact that knowing a kind allows us to extend our acquaintance beyond what we have experienced, we can be acquainted with things that are far removed and foreign to us. For example, I can be said to be directly acquainted with rationality through my experience of my own rational function and that of other human beings. Because I am acquainted with this property I can predicate this of entities with which I have no direct perceptual experience, such as Martians, and it is possible that such a judgment would be true because it does not trespass against the AEP.[14]

Premise (3) of the FSEP claims that any created thing is the kind of thing that can be known through acquaintance. As mentioned above, we are able to extend what we know in some direct experience beyond the scope of that given experience by identifying a universal kind or attribute in that experience. This allows us to extend our acquainted very broadly. However, (3) claims that the broadness of acquaintance is limited to the created order for the following reason: given the conditions of the AEP, it follows that the kinds with which we are acquainted in experience are themselves limited by possible perceptual experience. As a result, since created things are the only things with which we can be acquainted, created things function as a limit for knowledge.

This conclusion is supported by another principle that accounts for how one can be acquainted with those things with which one has had no direct perceptual experience. Namely, the reason why I can be said to be acquainted with the future off-spring of my poodle Fifi without direct perceptual experience of it is because of the relation of similarity between these two entities that are understood under a common kind.[15] However, this principle cannot be true of any created thing and an uncreated thing.

In addition, we need to point out that (3) asserts that if a thing is something with which we are acquainted, it is created, but it does not assert that every created thing is something with which we are, or can be, acquainted since it is possible that there are created things that are beyond the scope of acquaintance.

In short, FSEP asserts that since God—an extramental entity—is in no way related to the created order, and since the fundamental meaning for all of our concepts through which extramental entities are represented to us are given to us through acquaintance with things in the created order, it follows that our semantic content cannot represent God in any positive way. The argument asserts that our semantic content simply does not pertain to God, making God completely, and literally, inconceivable. FSEP is an appropriate name because a problem regarding the possibility of religious language is generated from a combination of epistemic and semantic conditions given in the AEP. Specifically, the epistemic conclusion, (11), follows from a complete semantic failure of our concepts to represent some positive aspect possessed by God.

If FSEP is sound, it would seem that our knowledge of God would have to be dependent on purely negative descriptions of Him. This certainly was Moses Maimonides's conclusion. Although Aquinas was influenced by Maimonides's claim that there is no relation of similarity between our concepts of things in the created order and those of God, Aquinas abandons neither positive, nor literal, expressions of God.[16] In fact, Aquinas argues that even negative knowledge of God runs into its own fatal epistemic problems.[17] Instead, Aquinas offers a way of resolving the

FSEP by rejecting some of its premises. Ultimately, Aquinas's answer to the FSEP is found in the doctrine of analogous naming; that we name God using non-univocal terms of God and creatures. Implicit in the doctrine of analogy are two views held in tension: (A) on one hand, only those concepts originally derived from experience are foundational for knowledge of God. (B) On the other hand, our knowledge is not limited to that with which we are acquainted, but rather the original concepts with which we are acquainted are adapted or changed to no longer pertain to the creaturely order but are made to correctly apply to God.[18] Thus, before one turns to the doctrine of analogy proper, one needs to address how Aquinas understands the possibility of maintaining (A) and (B).

To do so, we turn to question thirteen of the *Summa theologiae*. This question is entitled "The Names of God," and is a window into Aquinas's perspective on religious language and his attempt at resolving problems of knowing God in conjunction with the AEP and the concerns that generate the FSEP. Among other things, question thirteen analyzes the manner in which the semantic content of our concepts relate to God in our naming of Him. Much of the impetus for the question comes from the conclusion of question twelve: that God's essence can be known neither naturally by us nor in this life (which is expressed in [9] of the FSEP).[19] Given the FSEP, it is a question of considerable difficulty whether any name can be understood correctly to apply to God at all. As argued by Maimonides, any name predicated of God is tantamount to an idolatrous act.[20] This seems to follow from the fact that since the very concepts through which God is named are derived from, and ultimately about, the created order, understanding God through such concepts is equivalent to ascribing creaturely properties to God; and, to entertain such an idea is idolatrous. In other words, given the AEP, the creaturely origin of our names cannot be transcended to accurately name the Divine uncreated Being. So, when we say that "God is wise" we unintentionally are thinking of God in terms of the creaturely concept of wisdom—our concept of wisdom as we know it through our acquaintance with wise human beings.

But as identified in the FSEP, there are epistemic concerns specific to Divine naming that differ from concerns regarding the semantics of Divine naming, even though certainly the latter affects the former. The epistemological concern regards how we can know that God really is *P*, whereas the semantic concern involves our understanding of the incommensurability between the origin and meaning of our concepts and the reality of God. Yet, clearly the epistemic question cannot be answered unless the semantic one is resolved. To illustrate this, take the name 'wise' with respect to God. Certainly to know what "wisdom" means does not entail that we know that God is wise, and so this epistemological question stands alone. However, since any name has semantic content that is incommensurate with how God actually is, then it follows that we cannot know anything about God expressed by any of these names. As a result, an epistemic conclusion (11) follows directly from the semantic condition.

Aquinas takes up the issue about whether it is possible to give a name to God in the first article of question thirteen. In terms of the FSEP, Aquinas would definitely accept premises (7), (8), (3) and (1). (7) is a dogmatic teaching of the Church and obtained by Aquinas's proofs for God's existence. (8) merely states that God does not depend on some mind in order to exist (other than his own). (3) involves the AEP, which is firmly held by Aquinas since, following Aristotle, Aquinas is committed to the idea that all knowledge is derived from experience of the created world around us in conjunction with intellectual operation. (1) asserts that semantic content represents its extramental entity in some way, a position advocated by Thomas with his doctrine of common natures and his epistemic realism in which that which is represented by a concept stands in a relation of similarity to that concept.

However, Aquinas rejects premise (2) as such, although he would accept an altered version of it from which the conclusion of the FSEP cannot be implied. Regarding (2), although he holds that in general the words that function in the signification of things through a formed concept are made possible by the fact that there is a relation of similitude between concepts and things,[21] he does not think that a given concept needs to be limited absolutely to representing the original thing (or things) with which that concept had its original similarity. This is contrary to (2) which suggests that concepts are inflexibly fixed in semantic content to some specific type of extramental thing with which we are acquainted. From this, along with the assertion that God is not an extramental entity with which we are acquainted, it would seem to follow that it is impossible to know anything about God.

Certainly, Aquinas holds that all our concepts of extramental entities arise through experience with extramental entities but he also holds that there is a flexibility that semantic content has to the extramental things with which we are familiar. This flexibility allows for semantic content to apply to things with which we are not acquainted through a process of altering that original semantic content in some way. At the same time, Aquinas maintains that as a result of this alteration of semantic content, the distinctive similitude between our concepts derived from experience and God who is understood through such concepts is lost.[22] In other words, whichever concepts are used to represent God have to be dissimilar to those extramental things that they were originally formed to represent. One result of this process is that it is impossible to know God's essence in the same way that we know the essences of creatures because knowing something's essence involves, among other things, having a concept that has a relation of similarity with the invariant structure of a specific extramental thing.[23] For example, we know the essence of human beings through our concept of "human" because there is a relation of similitude between them. However, despite this limitation, Aquinas argues, we can still know God non-essentially through our knowledge of creatures both as the cause of creatures and negatively (by remotion).[24]

Aquinas's revision of (2) raises two further questions about how it is possible to alter the meaning of our concepts so radically to apply to something other than those original extramental things with which we are acquainted. First, even if it is possible to stretch the meaning of a concept to incorporate other entities with which we are not familiar (even if one is willing to countenance acquaintance with things like angels as being of the same generic kind as something that we perceive in experience, such as agency, reason or substance)[25] is it not beyond the capacity of our thought to represent a non-created entity! To wit, there is no possible point of comparison or similarity to bridge the semantic gap between what is experienced in the created order and God; even in its broadest possible conceptualization.

In light of this incredulity, in article three, Aquinas raises the objection that since all our concepts are derived from creatures, all language of God is merely metaphorical and not literally true of Him.[26] To dissolve this objection, Aquinas identifies two semantically relevant aspects in any instance of naming: the extramental attribute itself that is signified by the naming term, and its mode of signification.[27] The first semantic component is the specific content of the concept through which some extramental entity is represented and signified. The second semantic component is the way through which that content is expressed—its mode of signification, or the manner in which the content is expressed. The modes of signification of a concept are the attributes possessed by the semantic content beyond that expressed by the first semantic component that are peculiar to the individual person signifying that extramental entity. For example, take the semantic content of the concept "stone." When used to signify an extramentally existing stone, the first semantically relevant aspect is that component that directly represents the extramental stone. The second aspect is the way through which that stone is signified, such as "immaterially," "universally," "positively," or for our purposes here, "through acquaintance." These are all attributes of the semantic content of the person signifying the stone that go beyond the immediate semantic content of the concept. The importance of this distinction is in the fact that one asserts only the first semantic component of the extramental entity itself that is the subject of its judgment and not the second component. Regarding religious language, attributes expressed by the Divine Names are correctly understood to be possessed properly by God *via* the first semantic component, whereas the way through which God is signified by them is not relevant to the truth of the judgment. This is seen in the stone example: the first aspect is attributed to the stone but the second is not; one is not saying that a stone is itself universal, immaterial, nor something with which we are acquainted, even though this is an attribute of its mode of signification. Likewise, when we apply names to God, the mode of signification "something with which we are acquainted," (or, as Aquinas says, "a mode of signifying that is appropriate to creatures") is not attributed to God.[28] In this way, the limitation through which the semantic content fails to represent God is positively excluded from one's understanding of an attribute as it is applied to God. This also addresses the problem about how we can name God according to non-synonymous names in face of the fact that God is Himself absolutely simple.[29] The thing signified—namely, God—is accomplished through a complex mode of signification without undermining its truth.

The second problem that arises from Aquinas's alteration of (2) regards whether the content of the altered creaturely concept expresses anything at all. If we are not acquainted with the concepts through which God is understood how do we know that they are not just fictions or inherently unintelligible? How do we know that such semantic content has any reference at all (regardless of the fact that God exists) given the necessity of acquaintance for all regular knowledge? In answer to this, one need only point out that such a question follows from a confusion of semantic and epistemic concerns. The question is not how we can know that the semantic content of concepts with which are not acquainted is true or not about God (this question is one that we need not address here). The question at this point is whether or not the semantic content has proper signification; the question is whether or not the semantic content has sense and reference. Well, regarding sense, it certainly does, since one has altered an original concept with which one was acquainted to a new concept with a new meaning. Regarding reference, it seems that this is fixed independently of whether one has direct knowledge of the thing to which it refers; it is something external to us. Just because our first concepts are necessarily formed from those things with which we are acquainted does not mean that all our concepts refer only to those things with which we have acquaintance. There is no intrinsic limit placed on the reference of a concept from the fact that it is originally obtained through acquaintance with creatures, since this only constitutes its mode of signification and not the semantic content that identifies some extramentally existing attribute.

To conclude, there is much still left to be done to rehabilitate Aquinas's doctrine of analogy. However, I believe that the answer to providing a coherent view of it is dependent on discussing semantic and epistemic conditions that give rise to its need. I hope that in what I have presented here is a good beginning toward achieving this great task.

Franciscan University of Steubenville

Notes

1. Special thanks to Robert Miner for his very helpful and in-depth comments. I would also like to thank Michael Waddell for raising some important points relevant to the paper.

2. For seminal work on the prior influences on Aquinas's view of analogy, see E. J. Ashworth's, "Analogy and Equivocation in Thirteenth-Century Logic: Aquinas in Context," in *Mediaeval Studies* 54 (1992): 94–135; and E. J. Ashworth's, "Signification and Modes of Signifying in Thirteenth-Century Logic: A Preface to Aquinas on Analogy," *Medieval Philosophy and Theology* (1991): 39–67.

3. Some of the more influential and involved treatments on analogy in Aquinas include Tommaso de Vio, *The Analogy of Names and the Concept of Being*, trans. E. A. Bushinski and H. J. Koren (Pittsburgh: Duquesne University Press, 1953); G. P. Klubertanz, *St. Thomas Aquinas on Analogy: A Textual Analysis and Systematic Synthesis* (Chicago: Loyola University Press, 1960); H. Lyttkens, *The Analogy between God and the World: An Investigation of Its Background and Interpretation of Its Use by Thomas of Aquino* (Uppsala: Almqvist & Wiksell, 1952); R. M. McInerny, *Aquinas and Analogy* (Washington, D.C.: The Catholic University of America Press, 1996); R. M. McInerny, *The Logic of Analogy: An Interpretation of St. Thomas* (The Hague: M. Nijhoff, 1961).

4. Thomas Williams, "The Doctrine of Univocity is True and Salutary," *Modern Theology* 21 (2005): 579–580. See also, J. S. Morreall, *Analogy and Talking about God: A Critique of the Thomistic Approach* (Washington, D. C.: University Press of America, 1979).

5. Specifically, I focus on Thomas Aquinas, *Summa theologiae. Pars Prima et Prima Secundae*, ed. P. Caramelo, Leonine edition (Torino-Roma: Marietti, 1952) (henceforth, *ST*); *De veritate*, ed. R. M. Spiazzi, Leonine edition (Taurini: Marietti, 1949) (henceforeth, *DV*). Throughout I keep fairly closely to English translations in *St. Thomas Aquinas Summa Theologiae*, ed. Thomas Gilby, O. P., Vols. 1–61 (Cambridge: Blackfriars, 1964–1980); and *Truth*, trans. and ed. R. W. Mulligan, J. V. McGlynn and R. W. Schmidt, Vols. 1–3 (Chicago: H. Regnery Co., 1952).

6. Moses Maimonides, *Guide of the Perplexed*, trans. S. Pines, 2 Vols. (Chicago: University of Chicago Press, 1963).

7. Aquinas can be seen to be wrestling the basic problem involved in the FSEP. For example, Thomas Aquinas, *ST* 1.13.6: "Videtur quod nomina per prius dicantur de creaturist quam de Deo. Secundum enim quod cognoscimus aliquid, secundum hoc ilud nominanum, cum nomina secundum Philosophum, *I Perihermeneias*, sint signa intellectuum. Sed per prius cognoscimus creaturam quam Deum. Ergo nomina a nobis imposita per prius conveniunt creaturis quam Deo." Or, *ST* 1.13.1, "Praeterea, nomina significant substantiam cum qualitate, verba autem et participia significant cum termpore, pronomina autem cum demonstratione vel relatione. Quorum nihil competit Deo, quia sine qualitate est, et sine omni accidente, et sine tempore, et sentiri non potest ut demonstrari possit; nec relative significari, cum relativa sint aliquorum antedictorum recordativa, vel nominum, vel participiorum, vel pronominum demonstrativorum. Ergo Deus nullo modo potest nominari a nobis."

8. This view is essentially related to his inherence theory of predication. For central discussions on this, see Gyula Klima, "The Semantic Principles Underlying Saint Thomas Aquinas's Metaphysics of Being," *Medieval Philosophy and Theology* 5 (1996): 87–141; Gyula Klima, "Aquinas' Theory of the Copula," *Logical Analysis and History of Philosophy* 5 (2002); Allan Back, "Aquinas on Predication," *Aristotle's Peri hermeneias in the Latin Middle Ages*, ed. H. A. G. Brakhuis and C. H. Kneepkens (Groningen: Ingenium Publishers, 2003).

9. For example, Aquinas talks about predicates that signify things that fall under one of the ten categories of extramental things, and privations, which do not. See Thomas Aquinas, *Liber II Scriptum super librum Sententiarum*, ed. P. Mandonnet (Paris: P. Lethielleux, 1929), Vol. 2, d. 37, q. 1, a. 2.

10. In this way, common natures, or natures absolutely considered are a way of addressing the problem of universals. Aquinas and others thought that the doctrine of common natures saves epistemological realism without having to claim that universals are things that exist extramentally. See, his *De ente et essentia. Opera Omnia*, Leonine Edition (Roma: Editori di san Tommaso, 1976), Vol. 43.

11. It is, or course, not hard to come up with the basis of the AEP in Aquinas's texts. For example, in *ST* 1.84.7, Aquinas asserts: "Respondeo dicendum quod impossibile est intellectum nostrum, secundum praesentis vitae statum, quo passibili corpori coniungitur, aliquid intelligere in actu, nisi convertendo se ad phantasmata."

12. Admittedly, I use the notion in a way different from its normal use, following after Bertrand Russell's articulation of it in his, *Problems of Philosophy* (Oxford: Oxford University Press, 1912).

13. Although Aquinas does not use language of acquaintance, the general idea is held by Aquinas. For example, in *ST* 1.84.3, where Aquinas rejects the notion that there are innate species in the soul, Aquinas addresses the central issue of Plato's *Meno* in which it appears that all cases of learning is really only reminiscence (of innate species). His answer is revealing to the notion that we are in a way acquainted with individuals not directly known by us when we come to know a thing's species: "Ad tertium dicendum quod ordinata interrogatio procedit ex principiis communibus per se notis, ad propria. Per talem autem processum scientia causatur in anima addiscentis. Unde cum verum respondet de his de quibus secundo interrogatur, hoc non est quia prius ea noverit; sed quia tunc ea de novo addiscit. Nihil enim refert utrum ille qui docet, proponendo vel interrogando procedat de principiis communibus ad conclusiones, utrobique enim animus audientis certificatur de posterioribus per priora."

14. The reason why I am extending this notion of acquaintance to include such foreign things from our common or direct experience is in order to establish the absolute limit of our knowledge as those things in the created order. For example, through some experience we may come up with a species that includes some immaterial entity, such as an alien. Aquinas holds that even immaterial things like angels can be known through generic concepts logically in common with material entities; for example, both angels and humans logically fall under the genus of substance. However, this is the limit since no concepts are univocally common among God and creatures. For example, *ST* 1.88: "Ad quartum dicendum quod substantiae immateriales creatae in genere quidem naturali non conveniunt cum substantiis materialibus, quia non est in eis eadem ratio potentiae et materiae, conveniunt tamen cum eis in genere logico, quia etiam substantiae immateriales sunt in praedicamento substantiae, cum earum quidditas non sit earum esse. Sed Deus non convenit cum rebus materialibus neque secundum genus naturale, neque secundum genus logicum, quia Deus nullo modo est in genere, ut supra dictum est. Unde per similitudines rerum materialium aliquid affirmative potest cognosci de Angelis secundum rationem communem, licet non secundum rationem speciei; de Deo autem nullo modo."

15. For Aquinas, there is a relation of similarity between the thing outside of the mind and the thing as understood. Aquinas puts this notion as follows in *ST* 1.85.2, "Ad primum ergo dicendum quod intellectum est in intelligente per suam similitudinem. Et per hunc modum dicitur quod intellectum in actu est intellectus in actu, inquantum similitudo rei intellectae est forma intellectus; sicut similitudo rei sensibilis est forma sensus in actu. Unde non sequitur quod species intelligibilis abstracta sit id quod actu intelligitur, sed quod sit similitudo eius." However, not only is there a relation of similarity between things in the mind and outside of the mind, but also there is such a relation holding between two things existing outside of the mind that fall under the same species.

16. Aquinas was not only influenced by Maimonides in this respect, but also by Pseudo-Dionysius. See especially, *Pseudo-Dionysius: The Divine Names and Mystical Theology*, trans. J. Jones (Milwaukee: Marquette University Press, 1980).

17. Aquinas, *ST* 1.13.2: "Dicendum quod de nominibus quae de Deo dicuntur negative, vel quae relationem ipsius ad creaturam significant, manifestum est quod substantiam ejus nullo modo significant, sed remotionem alicujus ab ipso, vel relationem ejus ad alium, vel potius alicujus ad ipsum. Sed de nominibus quae absolute et affirmative de Deo dicuntur, sicut bonus, sapiens, et hujusmodi, multipliciter aliqui sunt opinati. Quidem enim dixerunt quod haec omnia nomina, licet affirmative de Deo dicantur, tamen magis inventa sunt ad aliquid removendum a Deo quam ad aliquid ponendum in ipso. Unde dicunt quod, cum

dicimus Deum esse viventem, significamus quod Deus non hoc modo est sicut res inanimatae; et similiter accipiendum est in aliis; et hoc posuit Rabbi Moyses, in lib. qui dicitur doctor dubiorum."

18. Given Aquinas's answer to the FSEP, we can see that John Duns Scotus misapprehends how exactly Aquinas's analogous naming is a possible resolution of the FSEP. For example, Scotus argues in *Ordinatio* 1, d. 3, pars 1, qq. 1–2, nn. 26–55, that it is not "worthwhile to distinguish between knowledge of God in a creature and in Himself, since if knowledge is had through a creature, so that discursive cognition beings from the creature, I ask in what term this cognition comes to a halt. If in God in Himself, I have the proposed position, since the inquiry concerns the concept of God in Himself. If it does not come to a halt in God, but in a creature, then the same will be the end and the beginning of the discursive process, and so no knowledge will be had of God." To this, in light of Aquinas's answer to the FSEP, Aquinas would answer that it is relevant to distinguish between knowledge of God in a creature and in Himself because the issue is not about whether it is God or a creature that is depicted (or is the term of the cognition) through a concept, for this is clearly the case. Rather, the issue concerns how it is possible for a concept, that always has a relation of similarity with created things can in principle represent God, with no relation of similarity between the concept and God. So, the relevance of distinguishing between the two is that in a sense, the term of the cognition is creatures (because there always remains a derivation and similarity with created things), and in another sense the term of the cognition of God (because God is known in some way through such a concept).

19. Aquinas, *ST* 1.12.4: "Dicendum quod impossibile est quod aliquis creatus intellectus per sua naturalia essentiam Dei videat."

20. Moses Maimonides, *Guide*, 1.56.

21. Aquinas, *ST* 13.1: "Dicendum quod secundum Philosophum, *1 Perihermeneias*, voces sunt signa intellectuum, et intellectus sunt rerum similtudines."

22. For example, Aquinas says that following in *ST* 1.13.2: "Unde quaelibet creatura intantum eum repraesentat, et est ei similis, inquantum perfectionem aliquam habet, non tamen ita quod repraesentet eum sicut aliquid ejusdem speciei vel generis, sed sicut excellens principium, a cujus forma effectus deficiunt, cujus tamen aliquaiem similitudinem effectus consequuntur."

23. *ST* 1.12.9: "Cum enim quaecumque uni et eidem sunt similia sibi invicem sint similia, virtus cognoscitiva dupliciter assimilari potest alicui cognoscibili. Uno modo secundum se, quando directe ejus similitudine informatur, et tunc cognoscitur illud secudnum se."

24. Aquinas, *ST* 13.1.

25. See note 13 above.

26. Aquinas, *ST* 13.3, obj 1.

27. Aquinas, *ST* 13.3: "In nominibus igitur quae Deo attribuimus, est duo considerare, scilicet perectiones ipsas significatas, ut bonitatem, vitam, et hujusmodi, et modum significandi."

28. Aquinas *ST* 1.13.3: "Quantum igitur ad id quod significant hujusmodi nomina, proprie competunt Deo, et magis proprie quam ipsis creaturis, et per prius dicuntur de eo. Quantum vero ad modum significandi, non propri dicuntur de Deo; habent enim modum significandi qui creaturis competit." One may take exception to the notion that acquaintance is a mode of signification. However, Aquinas says that creatures are signified according to a

mode distinct from how God is signified. This, as we defined above, is signification through acquaintance. So, with a specific semantic content according to the first semantic component it is signified through the mode of signification proper to creatures, namely, through acquaintance with things that are experienced. This is not true of these concepts that are expressive of God.

29. Aquinas, *ST* 1.13.4.

Bartholomew Mastrius (1602–1673) and John Punch (1599 or 1603–1661) on the Common Nature and Universal Unity

Daniel Heider

Abstract: The paper deals with the issue of the common nature (extramental universal) and universal unity (logical universal) in the theories of two of the foremost Scotists in the Baroque Era, the Italian Conventual Bartholomew Mastrius and the Irish Observant John Punch. They are in the scholarly community well-known for their antagonistic interpretations of the teaching of Duns Scotus. On the basis of the exposition of two representative places from Scotus's *Ordinatio* and *Questions on Aristotle's Metaphysics*, I claim that it is Mastrius's theory, which follows Scotus's model more tightly. Punch's theories are doctrines which are syncretically inspired by un-Scotist's sources (above all "Suarezian," "Thomistic," and "Ockhamistic"). The hermeneutical advantage of Punch's theory is that it remarkably mirrors the "Zeitgeist" of early modern academic philosophy, substantially determined by the Jesuit's exposition of Aquinas.

The doctrinal plurality of the school of John Duns Scotus is a recognized fact among the historians of Scotistic philosophy.[1] The poignant doctrinal controversy between two main representatives of Scotistic thought in the first half of the seventeenth century, sc. between the Conventual Bartholomew Mastrius, "the Princeps Scotistarum" (and his collaborator Bonaventure Belluti), and the Irish Observant John Punch is a controversy that is well-known to scholars of post-medieval scholasticism.[2] However, a treatment of the topic of universals and its striking doctrinal plurality and remarkable dynamics within the in the frame of "the Scotistic chronology" in early modern academic philosophy still remains, with a few exceptions, a project to be done.[3]

In this paper I want to bring in two substantially different interpretations of Scotus's claim "a common nature has less than numerical unity," which provide evidence that Scotus's doctrine of the common nature was the subject-matter of antagonistic interpretations in early modern academic philosophy. The two rival interpretations are the theories of the above-mentioned Punch and Mastrius.[4] The presentation of their expositions is also sought-after for systematic reasons. Apart from the demonstration in the already oldish monograph "Die Lehre des J. Duns Scotus von d. Natura Communis" by Johannes Kraus, in which Scotus's theory of the common nature is shown to be "the apple of discord" for the early modern and neoscholastic expositors of Duns Scotus, one can still observe a noticeable polarization today.[5] On the one hand, one gets the assessment that Scotus's theory of universals is the most realist account (more realist than that of Aquinas), still being in the frame of the moderate realism.[6] On the other hand, one finds the evaluation that Scotus's approach is remarkably economical. It must be taken into account, according to this interpretation, that Scotus says actually *nothing* positive about the extramental common nature. In fact, he *must* be reticent because one cannot get to know the world independently of one's mode of knowing, and that there are only two ways to conceive things in the world: the universal and the singular mode. Any reasoning about the third status of the extramental common nature "situated" between those two is precluded.[7]

I shall proceed in five steps: (1) On the basis of two representative passages I outline Scotus's basic claims about the common nature and universal unity.[8] (2) For the conceptual framework I sketch the typology of the various kinds of universals, in which both Scotists set their doctrines. (3) I present Punch's "economical" doctrine saying that Peter's nature denominated as universal disposes of no other unity than the unity of essential similarity. (4) In the context of the critique of Punch's concept, I introduce Mastrius's tenet of the so-called unity "per indifferentiam" of the extramental nature. (5) In the conclusion I shall claim that it is Mastrius's doctrine, which stands closer to the "littera" of Scotus's texts.

1. Scotus's Doctrine of the Common Nature and the Universal Unity (*Ordinatio* l. 2. d. 3. p. 1. q. 1 and *Questions on Aristotle's Metaphysics* l. VII, q. 18)

It is well-known that Scotus's response to the question in *Ordinatio* "Utrum substantia materialis ex se sive ex natura sua sit individua vel singularis" is decisively negative. He gives seven arguments to prove that the common nature possesses the real unity indifferent to the singular unity. In the third argument, especially relevant for Mastrius's critique of Punch's doctrine, Scotus states that the relation of similarity must be founded on the proximate foundation, which must be the unity lesser than numerical unity. Moreover, provided that one conceives a universal concept, it holds that if the extramentally existing natures were singular from themselves, one would have to apprehend them in a way repugnant to their extramental being. Thus the nature must be indifferent, sc. it cannot be contradictory for it to exist with some other haecceity other than with the current one. However, all that is made possible only by the nature having real unity lesser than numerical unity.[9]

When explaining its character, Scotus, in analogy to Aquinas, recurs to Avicenna's winged dictum "equinitas sit tantum equinitas," by which the Arabian philosopher claims that the nature in itself is neither many (particular), nor one (universal). However, as sufficiently mapped, one must bear in mind that Scotus's interpretation of Avicenna is different from that of Aquinas.[10] Whereas for Aquinas the expression "the nature *de se*" is connected exclusively with essential predicates in the first mode, for Scotus—on the basis of the application of the axiom: an entity is followed by some unity—the nature is necessarily accompanied by certain (transcendental) properties. It might be said that while for Aquinas what is denoted by the statement is ontologically "neutral," for Scotus it is the real metaphysical constituent of an individual thing, which is naturally prior to the individuation. It is not far-fetched to call Thomas's interpretation of Avicenna's claim "epistemological," and Scotus's adoption, tampering with the notion of the formal unity of the common nature, "ontological."[11]

Scotus remarks that the formal unity of the common nature is far from being the complete universal, commonly called the logical universal. Scotus considers the objection that if the universal were something real in a thing, then Averroes's claim that it is the intellect that produces universality in things would have to be refused. In answer to this objection Scotus brings in the central distinction between commonality and universality. Despite being common, the extramentally existing nature cannot be a fully-fledged universal (defined by Aristotle as "one in many" and "one of many")[12] because such a nature is not invested with the proximate, but only with the remote potency to be said of its supposits. Though it is not repugnant for it to be contracted by some other haecceity, that nature is far from being "the proximate object" predicable of inferiors by saying "this is this." If this extramental common nature were "numerically" the same nature, one would shamelessly incur the miracle of "divinis" in "creatis." Though it holds that three persons in the Trinity are distinct from the Divine nature by formal distinction in the same way as the common nature and haecceity, there is no numerically one and the same humanity in Peter, Paul and Francis as there is one and the same Divinity in the Father, the Son and the Holy Spirit.[13]

In the later *Quaestions on Aristotle's Metaphysics* (VII, q. 18) Scotus gives a useful summary of three types of universals.[14] Here he not only summarizes what has been said in the *Ordinatio*, but adds some important qualifications. The first type of universal, the complete universal, is to be taken as a second intention. A second intention must be identified with the relation of reason of a cognized nature to that of which it is predicated (its inferior natures). As such that intention is cognized by the reflexive act of the mind.[15] For the second kind of universal, Scotus introduces what is denoted by a first intention. However, a thing of the first intention can be taken twofold, sc. as what is denoted by this intention as the remote subject or as the proximate subject. Taken in the first way the nature is called extramentally common because it is not of itself "this." Envisaged in the second way one gets a universal, which, as positively indeterminate, is proximately predicable of every supposit. It can be said that this type of universal disposes of an ontologically stronger sort of indifference than the previous one. The last type of universal, designated also as "the contrary universality" (contrarily determinable by individual differences), naturally precedes the "relational," logical universality.[16]

2. The Typology of Universals in Mastrius and Punch

At the beginning of the last question of his 9th Metaphysical Disputation "Quid sit unitas universalis, et in quo statu naturae conveniat" Mastrius presents the analogical division of the universal as such. It can be seen that this division is similar to that of Scotus presented in his *Quaestions on Aristotle's Metaphysics*. He notes that the majority of scholastics distinguish the physical, the metaphysical and the logical universal, whereas only the last type is taken by the majority of authors (not by all) as the primary analogate. As regards the first type, the physical universal, he defines it as the extramentally existing nature, which retains its less than numerical unity. The nature under that condition represents the remote foundation for full-blown universality. The second type, the metaphysical universal, is the nature as denuded of individual differences, and in virtue of which the nature "puts on" the unity of precision. Thanks to this precision it comes to be positively and contrarily indeterminate in relation to the plurality of its instances. Owing to that affection it can be also directly contracted by individual differences. As such it constitutes the proximate foundation of universality. The last type, the logical universal, is the same nature now subjected to the second intention of universality, thanks to which the nature refers as something superior to inferiors.[17]

Using partly the same vocabulary, however, led by his parsimonious method-ological approach, Punch speaks only about two types of universal, sc. the metaphysical and the logical universal. The first one, defined as "the one able to be in many," is (to use Mastrius's nomenclature) identified with the physical universal. In other words, by considering different texts in Scotus than Mastrius (on his *Questions on Porphyry's Isagogé*, q.4, "Proemium"[18]), Punch replaces the division between the physical and metaphysical universal with the distinction between the universal "materialiter sump-tum" and "formaliter sumptum," applied both on the level of the metaphysical and the logical universal ("the one able to be predicated of many"). How does Punch describe those two aspects applied to the metaphysical and logical universal? As regards the metaphysical universal, he says that when taken materially one means the subject or the thing called universal. When considered formally it is the unity and the aptitude to be in many constituting a thing in its mode of universal's being. As for the logical universal, Punch typically identifies its material aspect with the metaphysical universal. As to the formal aspect he says that it is what makes the metaphysical universal the logical universal.[19] It should be seen that by the identification of the metaphysical and the physical universal Punch leaves out what Scotus in his *Quaestions on Metaphysics* calls "the contrary universality." Thus by reducing Mastrius's metaphysical universal to the physical universal Punch cuts out what "the Princeps Scotistarum" takes as the only candidate for the proximate foundation of the "relational" universality.

3. Punch's "Economical" Account of the Common Nature and Universal Unity

In contrast to Mastrius, Punch's theory is guided by an enormous effort to accommodate among Scotists, the rather infamous Ockham's razor without taking much care about loyally following Scotus's own theory.[20] Punch's reductive account can be observed in two main contexts within the complex issue of universals. The first one is concerned with (A) the metaphysical universal, the second one applies to (B) the logical universal.

(A) It has been already been shown that Punch defines the metaphysical universal as "something that is one and that has the aptitude (disposition) to be in many." Most of his third logical disputation "De universali ut sic" is devoted to parts of that definition, sc. to the unity and the aptitude to be in many. Since the question concerning the aptitude to be in many is substantially derived from the first issue, I shall only present Punch's thesis about the metaphysical universal with respect to the issue of the universal unity.

Within his exposition of the doctrine of the metaphysical universal, Punch presents four basic conclusions. He admits that the nature does not receive any unity from the intellect. If it did, then it could not be in many or said of many.[21] It may be said that by this claim Punch unambiguously refuses the claims of Hurtado de Mendoza and other Jesuit "confundistae," according to which the nature comes to be universally one by the confusive act of the intellect, which functions as an extrinsic denomination of the intellect.[22] The main reason for this refusal is Punch's claim that no fiction, necessarily deriving from that confusion, can satisfy the truth-conditions of essential predication. Each essential predication must be based on the assumption of the *real* identity of the subject and predicate, which cannot be the case with the claim of the "confundistae."[23]

After that Punch presents two, again negative, conclusions. In the first one he sets himself against the claim that on the arrival of singularity the specific nature gets deprived of some positive unity, which it would have had if the singularity did not come.[24] What he exactly means by this "privative unity" can be illustrated on Pedro Fonseca's theory of the unity of precision. According to Fonseca, universals before the mental operation, however prior to their being in things, must possess some kind of unity stronger than formal unity, which gets multiplied in individuals.[25] That kind of unity is called by him the 'unity of precision' or the 'unity mixed from the formal and numerical unity.' Like numerical unity, and in contrast to formal unity, that unity is not divided into its inferiors, but like formal unity it has an aptitude to be divided. The unity of precision is, for Fonseca, exactly what gives unity to the capacity for being divided into many and for being said of many without being really divided. The nature as such disposes of, prior to its contraction by particulars, the unity or indivisibility because it has the aptitude for being divided.[26]

Punch's main argument against Fonseca's thesis is based on the notion of a necessary property, which constitutes the main Scotistic device against the "episte-mological" interpretations of the Avicennian nature. If the extramental nature in the state antecedent to the oncoming of singularity had some positive unity, this unity would also have to belong to the nature as a property in the particularized phase, i.e., when constituting this or that individual. This contention is grounded on the axiom that unity is the necessary property of each being. As a property or essential predicate it could not be, as Fonseca suggests, revoked by the singularities at all. Therefore, one can conclude that the nature did not have and could not have Fonseca´s unity in that "pre-singular" state.[27]

In the next thesis, Punch refuses the opinion, according to which the specific nature is formally and positively one and the same in all individuals. Punch's arguments are based on the assumption, according to which the rejected claim inevitably slides down into the highly dubious interpretation "per inexistentiam."[28] What is meant by this interpretation? Like Mastrius, Punch is clear about the fact that according to this theory the common nature existing in the supposits possesses *entitative* and *physical* unity. However, contrary to Mastrius, there is no other possible alternative for Punch on how to understand the claim about the formal positive unity of the common nature, than as a claim about physical, numerical unity. However, that being supposed, the absurd consequence of this theory comes to be apparent. If the haecceities of Peter and Paul were separated from the given individuals (*per impossibile* if their inseparability is assumed), it would be right to say that the nature, which is in Peter, is entitatively the same as the nature in Paul.[29]

Punch's most idiosyncratic claim is his fourth conclusion. After he has excluded all possible types of unity in the extramentally existing nature, the Irish Observant comes to his conclusion. The nature denominated as universal which is found in Paul does not and cannot have any other extramental unity with the other nature existing in Peter, than the unity of similarity or representability by the same formal concept. Owing to this essential resemblance in individual essences of Peter and Paul, our formal concept (sc. the acts of intellection), which we have about Peter *qua* a man, can well represent Paul and other human beings. No other extramental unity can really make sense for Punch.[30]

The glaring inspiration by the teaching of Francisco Suárez is apparent.[31] Moreover, the further specification of that unity is the evidence that Punch, the Scotist, stands under the influence of Thomism as well. He avowedly acknowledges that the precisely taken nature of Peter possessing the formal unity is from itself neither the same (one) nor different (many). The human nature in Peter, as conceived by the intellect precisely in relation to its essential predicates, is neither the same nor a different nature from the nature in Paul. As such it has only the so-called negative unity, which is nothing more than the negation of essential division. Punch is sure about the fact that this "epistemological" interpretation does justice to Avicenna's dictum "equinitas est tantum equinitas." The only way to make any sense of Scotus's claim that "nature has a unity less than numerical unity," is to say that such a nature in itself is *not* able to provide the intellect with the occasion for the cognition of the nature as multiplied and distinct in each individual.[32] It is also not surprising that Punch consequently reinterprets Scotus's third argument for formal unity. When appealing to Aristotle, he affirms that the Philosopher does not say that similarity is grounded in common unity, but only that the extremes of the given relation are to be one formally. However, one must say that by being one formally they are one formally in a "Suarezian" way, i.e., in a way in which the metaphysical grades are not distinct formally "ex natura rei," but only conceptually with a foundation in a thing (the rather un-Scotistic conclusion).[33]

(B) Punch's statement according to which the extramentally existing nature has only the unity of representability by the same formal concept is, no doubt, of a Suarezian and Thomistic origin. However, it must be said that Punch himself does not care much about the labels ("Thomist," "Suarezian," "Herveist"), by which he is treated by Mastrius.[34] His doctrinal diversity is patent when taking into account the issue of the logical universal. In this context, Punch disavows himself not only from Mastrius, but also from Thomists and Suárez. It is well-known that Thomists, Suárez, but also Mastrius, with differences in detail, claim that the logical universal lies in the rational relation of the precised nature to its inferiors, from which it is abstracted. As such the logical universal becomes the second objective intention, which is to be identified with the being of reason with a foundation in a thing.[35]

Punch's theory of the logical universal or second intention is markedly different. It is not an exaggeration to say that the main methodological (not doctrinal!) inspiration for his doctrine comes from Ockham.[36] As it has been said, Punch defines the logical universal as "the one, which is able to be (proximately) predicated of many." When defining the ontological status of the logical universal Punch arrives at this striking conclusion: If essential predication is to be of the form "hoc est hoc," then the logical universal as the second intention must be something *real* and positive, having the *proximate* (sic!) potency to be formally predicated.[37] As it has been shown above, the logical universal is materially the same as the metaphysical universal, which amounts to the essential similarity of the individuals. The given identification is evidence that what Punch is after is as follows: an exposition of the logical universal by means of only two ontological constituents. The first one is the things with their essential convenience (particularized essences), which should be taken as an irresolvable state of affairs. The second one is the formal concepts (mental acts) denominating things either independently, or dependently of the comparative cognition. The predicates belonging to things without that dependence are called first objective intentions. The predicates pertaining to them with that dependence are second objective intentions.[38] The exposition of first and second intentions is the evidence that in the analysis of the ideogenesis of the various types of universals, Punch tampers only with two "elements," sc. with the essentially resembling individuals and with two orders of intellective acts, which give rise to the primary and secondary objective intentions, respectively.

4. Mastrius's Conception of the Unity "Per Indifferentiam" in the Context of the Critique of Punch

Mastrius's "ethos" in the elaboration of universals differs significantly from Punch's "conciliatory" attitude. From the very beginning of his disputation *De natura communi, seu universali* one gets an impression of Mastrius's delicate sense for doctrinal differences. Not only does Mastrius deny Punch's indulgence in parsimonious ontology, he also clearly demarcates the ideological line between an author who advocates the positive unity of the extramentally existing nature (Scotists), and those who support the negative unity of the nature before the intellect's operation

(Thomists). Again, I discriminate two doctrinal contexts in which Mastrius wages "Bellum scholasticum" with Punch: (A) The extramental common nature, (B) the logical universal.[39]

(A) To understand Mastrius's doctrine of the common nature and universal unity, one must specify two basic types of community proper to the physical and metaphysical universal. In direct line with Scotus, Mastrius distinguishes positive and negative indifference. Positive indifference pertains to the nature denuded of individual differences. Thanks to this indetermination, the nature is related to inferior natures in an equal or "conjunctive" way. Mastrius, like Scotus, remarks that this sort of indeterminacy can be also called "contrary" because it can be positively contracted by individual differences. On the other hand, Mastrius says that negative indifference is the property of the nature existing extramentally. He claims that by virtue of this indifference the nature relates to its own inferiors in a "disjunctive" way. What does he mean by the terms "conjunctive" and "disjunctive" community? The "conjunctive community" of a nature is explained by an analogy with the indeterminacy "per inexistentiam," which, nevertheless, in its extramental guise, is the target of Mastrius's critique. A nature having this type of community exists as liberated from the adjacent haecceity. Thus it can immediately exist in, or be predicated of its supposits. "Disjunctive community," by contrast, is a type of community with an individual "impediment;" Mastrius illustrates it with the aid of two types of modalities. The nature being now in Peter is of itself of such a nature that, according to the divided sense (*sensus divisus*), it could have constituted also Paul's substance. However *qua* already identified with Peter, i.e., according to the composite sense (*sensus compositus*), it is not possible for it to be Paul's part. Mastrius calls this weaker type of community the unity "per indifferentiam," whereas the previous one is called the unity "per inexistentiam."[40]

Mastrius does not get on well with Punch at all. According to Mastrius, Punch goes particularly astray in the statement that the extramental common nature with its own formal unity possesses only *per se* predicates in the first mode (essentials), never in the second mode (properties). Even though Punch is right that nature taken precisely is not accompanied by numerical unity and plurality, it does not mean that no transcendental properties can be ascribed to it on the essential plane. One of them is the property of (formal) unity. Formal indivision necessarily implies that the entity is *sui generis* and that its unity is *sui generis* as well.[41] That unity, however, cannot be taken as the entitative and physical unity because, as Mastrius admits together with Suárez and Thomists, it gets entitatively multiplied.[42]

When saying that Scotus in the "similarity-argument" did not argue for the real and positive common foundation of the real relation, but only aimed at the conclusion that each extreme of the relation must be one itself, sc. undivided in their essential predicates and representable by the same formal concept, Mastrius says that Punch substantially misinterprets Scotus's intention. What Punch does is nothing worse than the assimilation of Scotus's doctrine to the concept of Suárez and his followers.[43] Each comparison assumes a "tertium quid" or "species athoma," according to which the extremes of a relation can only be confronted. They are not compared by themselves. Punch's interpretation is equal to the statement that the extremes, e.g., two instances of the white color, are similar by their whole entity. However, the distinction 'by the whole entity' amounts to a numerical distinction, which represents the highest degree of dissimilarity. Thanks to the haecceities—the ultimate realities of the given entities—the two individuals can never be similar, but only fully dissimilar. Moreover, if one relinquishes the non-trivial explanation of similarity, one will not be able to explain why a white patch is more similar to another white patch than to a green patch.[44]

Mastrius is convinced that Punch's "Suarezian" claim about the unity of similarity also commits an offence against Scotus's claim that an object does not get its unity from a concept, but vice versa.[45] If an object got that unity from a concept, one would have to agree with Punch and Suárez that the objective definitions of Peter and Paul are actually two different definitions simply because of the fact that their extramental essences are different as well.[46] One would have to assent to the claim that there can only be the formal definition (based on the acts of the mind), which is based on the essential similarity of natures, and thanks to which the intellect, when representing the nature of a singular, can also represent the nature of another singular.[47] However, such a claim is utterly false.[48] Albeit in connection with the refusal of the unity "per inexistentiam," Mastrius accepts Punch's statement that whatever exists extramentally necessarily obtains numerical unity and plurality, however, he denies that on the metaphysical or essential level, it is not incompatible with actual existence (sic!), one is obliged to abandon any thought about essential or formal unity of a given species and thus to transform all unity-oriented to similarity-oriented discourse.

(B) To understand Mastrius's critique of Punch's theses concerning the logical universal, we must consider briefly the specifics of Mastrius's doctrine on the metaphysical universal, the logical universal, and his doctrine of predication. It has been said that for Mastrius the metaphysical universal is endowed with the unity of precision, by which the nature is objectively cut off from individual differences. Only a nature with this unity, contrary to Fonseca, existing only as abstracted and thus constituting a being of reason (namely an absolute being of reason),[49] can make up the proximate foundation for the logical universal. How does Mastrius conceive this logical universal? The "essence" of the logical universal is constituted not, as one would expect, by potential being in many, but by actual being in many.[50] Mastrius does not consider the logical universal to be the potential whole predicable of its subjective parts. If it were taken as the potential whole, one would be confronted with the question of how to link that nature with that unity together with the intentional contraction of the nature in individuals. It is just that intentional contraction, which constitutes for Mastrius the very logico-ontological basis of real predication.[51] By being intentionally identified with a given supposit, the potential totality necessarily gets lost. What Mastrius emphasizes is, therefore, the actual totality of the essential predicates of the metaphysical and logical universal. By taking into account this sort of actual whole, it cannot be said that the positive indeterminacy of the metaphysical universal gets inevitably revoked by being identified with many supposits. It is better to say that the metaphysical universal is placed in the second act. When envisaging predication in exercised act (*in actu exercito*), which is for Mastrius, in contrast to predication in signated act (*in actu signato*), considered as the metaphysically relevant type of predication not yet reflecting upon the first intention, predication must be seen as the statement about two already intentionally identified thought-objects.[52] The logical universal's being in many, is the *intentional* being of the nature in the way of being "per inexistentiam" in its supposits.[53]

The concept of predication, labeled as "intentional contraction," does not allow Mastrius to agree with Punch's two basic claims.[54] The first one is connected with Punch's statement about the sufficiency of remote predicability in the description of the logical universal. The second regards the issue of the ontological status of the logical universal. Punch's argument that the universal unity cannot belong to an abstracted nature predicated of inferiors (it necessarily implies fictive unity) is refused by the following rejoinder by Mastrius. Punch's thesis neglects the fact that the given rational unity of the metaphysical and logical universal is a being of reason *with* a foundation in a thing. He ignores that the logical universal is generated by the imitation of the extramental formal unity.[55] If the universal unity were to be identified with the being of real nature, then the identity-predication would be changed into the similarity-claims saying "Peter's nature is similar to Paul's nature."[56] What is of greater consequence is that Punch's claim, about the sufficiency of the remote foundation of logical universality, significantly deprecates the notion of beings with a foundation in things as such, which for Mastrius and the majority of other scholastics, except Punch, constitutes the proper object of Logic.[57]

5. Conclusion

When comparing both Scotists' doctrines on the issues of the common nature and universal unity with respect to their fidelity to the above-mentioned representative texts of Scotus, the upshot seems to be clear. There are at least three points on which Mastrius follows more closely Scotus's text[58]: (1) Punch's typological reduction of three kinds of universals is not fully authorized by Scotus. Due to this reduction, Punch comes to the conclusion that the only extramental unity of the common nature is the unity of essential resemblance. By advocating this thesis, the Observant embraces the Suarezian and Thomist doctrine leading to the overall suppression of the idiosyncratic features of the Scotistic synthesis. (2) By eliminating the middle type of universal, which Mastrius called metaphysical, Punch puts forth the thesis that the proximate foundation for the identical predication is the nature existing extramentally. Punch's refusal to ascribe the proximate foundation of the logical universal to the (abstracted) metaphysical universal brings Punch close to Ockham's doctrine of truth-conditions of essential predication. Without delving into that comparison in the body of the paper (see the note 52), it can be deduced that both Punch and Mastrius also disagree about questions concerning the theory of predication. (3) By his relegation of the proximate foundation of the fully-fledged universal to the extramental common nature, Punch comes to adopt the thesis that second intentions (at least materially) are real beings. Hereby Punch draws the conclusion that the logic does not deal with beings of reason, but with real beings.

On the other hand, if one is to evaluate Punch's doctrine not according to the criterion of his fidelity to Scotus's model, but according to his degree of creativity in mirroring the "Zeitgeist," one's evaluation radically changes. Punch's doctrine of the common nature and universal unity reflects a wide-spread tendency found in early modern academic philosophy in the second half of the sixteenth century and the first half of the seventeenth century. The given tendency is connected, above all, with the syncretical approach of the intellectual Jesuits, which since the very beginning of the order's existence aspired to absorb and reconcile various traditional schools. By incorporating the doctrines of Augustine, Aquinas, Scotus, Ockham, Biel, Gregory of Rimini and many other patristic, medieval, and Renaissance authors as well, into a doctrinal synthesis, the early Jesuits (Francisco Toleto, Suárez, Conimbricenses), together with the Thomists in the school of Salamanca (above all Domingo de Soto), paved the way, which was also later to be walked by Punch, the renegade Scotist.[59]

Faculty of Theology, University of South Bohemia; Institute of Philosophy,
Academy of the Sciences of the Czech Republic

Notes

I would like to thank Prof. Paul Richard Blum (Loyola University, Maryland) for his useful comments to my paper.

1. The paper has been elaborated with the support of the Grant Project no. P401/10/0080 "Univerzálie v raně novověké univerzitní filosofii" (Faculty of Theology, University of South Bohemia), Czech Science Foundation.

2. Cf. Stanislav Sousedík, "Der Streit um den Wahren Sinn der Scotischen Possibilienlehre," in Ludger Honnefelder, R. Wood, M. Dreyer, *John Duns Scotus. Metaphysics and Ethics* (Leiden: E.J. Brill, 1996) 191–204. See also Tobias Hoffmann, *Creatura intellecta. Die Ideen und possibilien bei Duns Scotus mit Ausblick auf Franz von Mayronis, Poncius und Mastrius* (Münster: Aschendorff Verlag, 2002), especially 263–304. As regards the various "layers" of their controversy see authoritative Marco Forlivesi, *Scotistarum Princeps, Bartolomeo Mastri (1602–1673) e il suo tempo* (Padova: Centro Studi Antoniani, 2002), 208–218.

3. By exceptions I mean mainly the studies on the conception of Francisco Suárez, whose doctrine has become the target of the competing interpretations. As for the moderately-realistic interpretation laying the emphasis on the item of the objective precision cf. José M. Alejandro, *La gnoseología del Doctor Eximio y la acusación nominalista* (Santander: Publicaciones anejas a "Miscelanea Comillas," 1948), 363ff.; José Hellín, *la analogiá del ser y el conocimiento de Dios en Suárez* (Madrid: Gráficas Uguina, 1947); Walter Hoeres, "Wesenheit und Individuum bei Suárez," *Scholastik* 2 (1962): 181–210; and "Bewusstsein und Erkenntnisbild bei Suárez," *Scholastik* 36 (1961): s. 192–206; Josef de Vries, "Die Erkenntnislehre des Franz Suarez und der Nominalismus," *Scholastik* 32 (1949): 321–344; Paul Descoqs, "Thomisme et suarezisme," *Archives de philosophie* 4.4 (1927), in particular 98. For the opposite interpretations charging Suárez with the alleged conceptualism based on the induction

as the only method of the intellect's generation of universality see Francisco L. Peccorini, "Knowledge of the Singulars: Aquinas, Suarez, and Recent Interpreters," *The Thomist* 38 (1974): 606–655; Peccorini, "Suárez's Struggle with the Problem of the One and the Many," *The Thomist* 36 (1972): 433–471; Wilhelm Kolter, *Die Universalienlehre des Franz Suarez*, Inaugural Dissertation, Freiburg, 1941, 151; León Mahieu, *François Suarez. Sa Philosophie et les rapports qu'elle a avec sa Théologie* (Paris: Desclée, De Brouwer, 1921), in particular 523; Carlo Giacón, *Guglielmo di Occam. Saggio storico-critico sulla formazione e sulla decadenza della Scolastica* (Milano: Vita e Pensiero, 1941), in particular 679–689; Giacón, *Suárez* (Brescia: "La Scuola" Editrice, 1943), in particular 29–49. As to the label "the realist conceptualism" cf. James F. Ross, "Suarez on 'Universals,'" *The Journal of Philosophy* 59.23 (1962): 736–748, in particular 747–748. There are also a couple of articles paying attention to Domingo de Soto and the Coimbra Jesuits. Cf. e.g., Ria Van der Lecq, "Domingo de Soto on Universals and the Ontology of Intentions," in *Medieval and Renaissance Logic in Spain*, ed. Angelelli Ignacio and Paloma Pérez-Ilzarbe (New York: Hildesheim, 2000), 309–325. As for the sketchy exposition of the position of Mastrius and Punch cf. also Ester Caruso, *Pedro Hurtado de Mendoza e la rinascita del nominalismo nella scolastica del seicento* (Firenze: La nuova Italia, 1979), 100–106. As regards the device of the objective precision in the critique of the Jesuit conceptualists cf. Michael Renemann, "Mastri on 'praecisio obiectiva,'" in *"Rem in seipsa cernere". Saggi sul pensiero filosofico di Bartolomeo Mastri (1602–1673)*, ed. Marco Forlivesi (Padova: Il Poligrafo, 2006), 399–414.

4. Because of the fact that it was only Mastrius, who finished "Metaphysics" of his later *Cursus Philosophicus* in Ravenna in early 1640s I shall refer further only to him. Cf. e.g., the brief paper from Bonaventure Crowley, "The Life and Works of Bartholomew Mastrius, O.F.M. Conv. 1602–1673," *Franciscan Studies* 8 (1948): 97–152, in particular 117.

5. Johannes Kraus, *Die Lehre des Johannes Duns Skotus O.F.M. von der Natura communis* (Freiburg, Schweiz: Studia Friburgensia, 1927).

6. Dónall McGinley, "Duns Scotus's Theory of Common Natures," *Filosofia Unisinos* 9 (2008): 64–83, 81. As for the emphasis on the strong parallelism between the intellect and reality in Scotus, presented with the aid of the analogy to the logical forms of Ludwig Wittgenstein see Allan B. Wolter, "The Realism of Scotus," *The Journal of Philosophy* 59.23 (1962): 725–736.

7. Cf., e.g., Girgio Pini, "Scotus on Universals: A Reconsideration," *Documenti e studi sulla tradizione filosofica medievale Late Middle Ages* 18 (2007): 395–409, 409.

8. That is also why I shall not make provision for Scotus's formulations presented in *Quaestiones in primum librum Perihermeneias Aristotelis*, where (so Gérard Sondag) Scotus apparently attributes to the extramental common nature features ascribed in *Ordinatio* to the fully-fledged universal. See Gérard Sondag, "Universel et *natura communis* dans l'*Ordinatio* et dans les *Questions sur le Perihermeneias* (une breve comparaison), in *John Duns Scotus. Metaphysics and Ethics*, ed. Ludger Honnefelder (Leiden: E.J. Brill, 1967), 385–391.

9. "Praeterea, illi cui de se convenit unum oppositum, ei de se repugnat aliud oppositum; igitur si natura de se sit una numero, repugnat ei multitudo numeralis . . . Obiectum in quantum est obiectum, est prius naturaliter ipso actu, et in illo priore—per te—obiectum est ex se singulare, quia hoc semper convenit naturae non acceptae secundum quid sive secundum esse quod habet in anima; igitur intellectus intelligens illud obiectum sub ratione universalis, intelligit ipsum sub ratione opposita suae rationi, quia ut praecedit actum determinatur ex se ad oppositum illius rationis, scilicet universalis," Ioannis Duns Scoti, *Opera omnia*, iussu

et auctoritate Rmi. P. Constantini Koser, tomus VII (Civitas Vaticana: Typis Vaticanis, 1973) *Ordinatio* II dist. 3 pars 1 q. 1, 392–393. Cf. also B. Ioannis Duns Scoti, *Quaestiones subtilissimae super libros Metaphysicorum Aristotelis*, libri VI–IX (St. Bonaventure, N.Z.: The Franciscan Institute, St. Bonaventure University, 1996), lib. VII, q. 13, 215.

10. As regards the clear discernment of the Thomistic and Scotistic interpretation of the Avicennian essence in respect to its being and unity see Joseph Owens, "Common Nature: A Point of Comparison between Thomistic and Scotistic Metaphysics," in *Inquiries into Medieval Philosophy: A Collection in Honor of Francis P. Clarke*, ed. James F. Ross (Westport, Conn.: Greenwood Publishing Co., 1971), 185–209.

11. In spite of the fact that Girgio Pini reserves those labels for two different versions of Aquinas's doctrine of universals discoverable in the author's doctrinal genealogy, I think that the given evaluative distinction can be *a fortiori* applied also on the "higher" level, i.e., between Aquinas, whatever versions he actually accepts, and Scotus, who speaks about the formal unity formally distinct from its haecceities. For Pini's two labels cf. "*Absoluta consideratio naturae*: Tommaso d'Aquino e la dottrina avicenniana dell'essenza," *Documenti e studi sulla Tradizione Filosofica Medievale* 15 (2004): 387–438, in particular 391. Cf. also Gabriele Galluzo, "The Problem of Universals and Its History. Some General Considerations," *Documenti e Studi sulla Tradizione Filosofica Medievale* 19 (2008): 335–369, 358–359.

12. For this Aristotle's definition of universality cf. *On Interpretation* VII, 17a39–b2, and *Posterior Analytics* II, 19, 100 a7–10.

13. ". . . universale in actu est illud quod habet aliquam unitatem indifferentem, secundum quam ipsum idem est in potentia proxima ut dicatur de quolibet supposito, quia secundum Philosophum I Posteriorum 'universale' est quod est unum in multis et de multis. Nihil enim . . . in re est tale quod secundum illam unitatem praecisam sit in potentia proxima ad quodlibet suppositum praedicatione dicente 'hoc est hoc' . . . Est ergo in re 'commune', quod non est de se hoc, et per consequens ei de se non repugnat non-hoc. Sed tale commune non est universale in actu, quia deficit illa indifferentia secundum quam completive universale est universale, secundum quam scilicet ipsum idem aliqua identitate est praedicabile de quolibet individuo, ita quod quodlibet sit ipsum . . . hoc enim ponendi, esset ponere quod aliqua natura creata non-divisa praedicatur de multis individuis praedicatione dicente 'hoc est hoc', sicut dicitur quod Pater est Deus et Filius est idem Deus," *Ordinatio* II dist. 3 pars 1 q. 1, 406–408.

14. On the significance of this division for Scotus cf. also Wolter, "The Realism of Scotus," 734–735.

15. As for Scotus's theory of second intentions in the context of rival theories in the second half of the thirteenth century (especially those of Radulphus Brito and Simon of Faversham) see Giorgio Pini, *Categorias and Logic in Duns Scotus. An Interpretation of Aristotle's Categories in the Late Thirteenth Century* (Leiden: E.J. Brill, 2002), in particular 99–137.

16. Joannis Duns Scoti, *Quaestiones subtilissimae super libros Metaphysicorum Aristotelis*, Lib. VII. Metaph., q. XVIII, 347–348: "Circa huius quaestionis solutionem, primo distinguendum est de universali. Sumitur vel sumi potest tripliciter: Quandoque pro intentione secunda quae scilicet est quaedam relatio rationis in praedicabili ad illud de quo est praedicabile, et hunc respectum significat hoc nomen 'universale' in concreto, sicut et 'universalitas' in abstracto. Alio modo accipitur universale pro illo, quod denominatur ab ista intentione, quod est aliqua res primae intentionis, nam secundae intentiones applicantur primis. Et sic accipi potest dupliciter: uno modo pro illo quod quasi ut subjectum remotum denominatur

ab ista intentione; alio modo pro subjecto propinquo. Primo modo dicitur natura absolute sumpta universale, quia non est ex se haec, et ita non repugnat sibi ex se dici de multis. Secundo modo non est universale nisi sit actu indeterminatum, ita quod unum intelligibile numero dicibile de omni supposito, et illud est complete universale . . . indeterminatio quasi contraria, qua 'homo' est sic indeterminatum, ut unica intellectione conceptum quidditative insit omni, praecedit naturaliter illam intentionem secundam, quae est universalitas logica sive habitudo de multis."

17. "Praeterea distingui apud omnes universale in physicum, metaphysicum, & logicum, per universale physicum intelligunt naturam in singularibus existentem cum sua unitate formali, quae est minor numerali, per metaphysicum intelligunt naturam, cum per opus intellectus abstrahitur, & exuitur differentiis, & induitur unitate praecisionis; denique per universale logicum intelligunt eandem naturam affectam secunda intentione universalitatis, per quam ad inferiora refertur in ratione superioris, & praedicabilis," Bartholomeus Mastrius, *Cursus philosophicus integer, Metaphysica* (Venetiis: Apud Nicolaum Pezzana, 1727), Disp. IX: "De Natura Communi sive Universali," § 201, 130 (henceforth, *Metaphysica*, § x, p. y). "*Dicendum tamen est, solum universale logicum esse universale vere & proprie dictum*," Mastrius, *Metaphysica*, § 203, 131.

18. As regards the "coarse" twofold distinction between the logical and metaphysical aspect of universals in Scotus cf. Timothy B. Noone, "Universals and Individuation," in *The Cambridge Companion to Duns Scotus*, ed. Thomas Williams (New York: Cambridge University Press, 2002), 100–128, in particular 106–107.

19. "sicut autem diximus quod universale metaphysicum est concretum dicens duo, unum materialiter, nimirum rem illam, quae dicitur universalis, & aliud formaliter nimirum ipsam unitatem & aptitudinem, qua constituitur in esse universalis: ita etiam de universali logico sentiendum est, quod dicat duo, unum materialiter, nimirum ipsum universale metaphysicum, & alterum formaliter nimirum illud, quod constituit & facit illud universale logicum," Ioannis Poncius, *Integer Philosophiae Cursus ad mentem Scoti in tres Partes divisus. Prima Pars Complectens Logicam* (Romae: Sumptibus Hermanni Scheus, 1642), "De universali ut sic," § 68, 216.

20. "In citationibus parcior sum," Punch, *Integer Philosophiae Cursus ad mentem Scoti in tres Partes divisus, Prima Pars Complectens Logicam*, "Ad Lectorem."

21. "Natura non recipit ullam unitatem ab intellectu, quae sufficiat pro universalitate, aut secundum quam natura vere possit esse, aut praedicari de multis . . . quia vel illa unitas quam reciperet natura humana, v.g. ab intellectu, est quid fictum attributum naturae per fictionem intellectus, vel est quid reale & verum collatum ipsi ab illo, vel est denominatio extrinseca desumpta ab actu aliquo, quo intellectus intelligit naturam illam; sed neutrum dici potest; ergo natura humana non recipit unitatem universalitatis ab intellectu . . . non fit quid fictum, quia ob unitatem fictam, quam haberet natura humana in Petro & Paulo per modum unius, ut est evidens," Punch, *Logic*, § 12, 189.

22. "Dico igitur, cognitionem universalem immediate terminari ad omnia singularia contenta intra speciem, vel genus; ut sunt similia in aliqua ratione; ratione cuius similitudinis per illum actum omnia confuse, & non collective noscuntur, nullum tamen in particulari: neque ex parte obiecti respondere formalitatem aliquam obiectivam distinctam ratione a singularibus, ut similibus." Pedro Hurtado de Mendoza, *Universa philosophia, in unum corpus redacta*, nova editio, quinque anterioribus tertia fere parte auctior, et ab ipso Auctore

ita recognita, et novum opus merito videri queat, Disputatio V.: "De unitate universali," (Lugduni,1624), 778.

23. ". . . illa natura sic concepta non potest praedicari vere de Paulo, praedicatione dicente, hoc est hoc . . . nisi sit in Paulo," Punch, *Logic*, § 14, 81.

24. "Natura specifica v. g. humana non est privata per singularitates aliqua unitate, quam haberet, nisi adveniret singularitates; nec si fuisset etiam, bene diceretur propterea esse privative una in suis individuis," Punch, *Logic*, § 21, 193.

25. For Fonseca's metaphysical theory of universal unity see João Madeira, "*Pedro da Fonseca's Isagoge Philosophia* and the Predicables from Boethius to the *Lovanienses*," dissertation, Katholieke Universiteit Leuven, 2006, especially 71–78.

26. ". . . debet esse privativa propria, nempe supponens aptitudinem rerum communium, nisi quatenus illae praecedunt contractionem sui ad particularia . . . Unitatem de qua est controversia, (quam nos aliquando, ut a formali distingueremus, praecisionis, praecisionis appelavimus) si ad generalem divisionem unitatis in numeralem & formalem revocanda est, etsi quodammodo mista ex formali & numerali dici potest: tamen numeralem potius appelanda esse. Cur autem praecisionis dixerimus, illa est ratio: quia non convenit rebus, quae denominantur universales, nisi praecise in eo prioritatis gradu, quo illae praecedunt contractionem sui ad sua particularia. Quoad autem quodammodo mista dici possit, ea ratione intellige: quia, quatenus convenit solis naturis communibus rationem participat formalis unitatis: naturae enim communes sunt modo suo formae rerum particularium: quatenus autem conficit numerum ipsarum naturarum communium, quem formalis unitas conficere non potest, numeralis quoque rationem habet: formalis enim, cum tam multiplicata sit in rebus particularibus, quam est ipsa natura communis, cuius est propria, certum numerum per se ipsum minime conficit . . . quemadmodum numeramus particularia, ita numeramus universalia, neque alia unitate, quam praecisionis: tum etiam, quia non est, cur ea negetur esse numeralis, quae est incommunicabilis pluribus. Ut enim communicabilitas seu multiplicabilitas in causa est, cur formalis unitas non dicatur numeralis, ita opposita incommunicabilitas in causa esse debet, cur unitas praecisionis, numeralis appelletur," Fonseca, *In Metaphysicorum*, cap. 28, q. 3, s. 2, p. 961. See also Mario de Carvalho, 2008, 538–539.

27. ". . . si illis naturis secundum se competeret unitas aliqua positiva, nisi advenissent singularitates impedientes illam, competerent illis tamquam predicatum essentiale aut proprietas, imo deberet competere tanquam proprietas in sententia communissima quod omnis unitas sit proprietas rei, cuius est unitas: sed si fuisset proprietas, aut praedicatum essentiale non posset tolli per singularitates, nihil enim potest tollere a re aliqua praedicata intrinseca, aut proprietates, ut patet: ergo non haberent istae naturae illam unitatem, etiamsi non advenirent haecceitates," Punch, *Logic*, §21, 82–83. For the similar criticism of Fonseca cf. also F. Suárez, *Disputationes Metaphysicae* 6 (no. of disputation), 3 (no. of section): "Utrum natura communis ex se habeat aliquam unitatem praecisionis extra individua, et ante mentis operationem," http://www.salvadorcastellote.com/investigacion.htm.

28. One of the adherents of the given theory in the era of the Second scholasticism was the Patavian Scotist Philipus Faber (Fabri) (1564–1630). When arguing for the entitative unity of the common nature in the context of the critique of Cajetan, Fabri introduces the distinction of the existential and the suppositional being. Fabri is convinced that the common nature disposes of the formal unity also on the existential plain. The main justification of this claim is based on the employment of the given distinction. If something exists by suppositional being, it exists outside its causes in itself (*per se*), and not in any subject (*in*

alio). As long as an entity exists in the way of existential being, it exists outside its causes and before the operation of the intellect. Fabri is clear about the fact that the second way of being is much more universal than the first one. The existential being belongs not only to all categories, but also to the substantial parts, e.g., to form and prime matter. In contrast to the entity possessing existential being, the entity having the suppositional being is entirely incommunicable because it is uninstantiable not only as an entity (*quod*), but also as "that through which" (*quo*). However, even though the entity with existential being cannot be shared as "that which," it can be quite well communicated as "through which." Exactly that is the case of the common nature. The parallel between the common nature and the physical principles of material composite seems to be the evidence that Fabri advocated the stronger form of the realism, which borders on the ultrarealism. Cf. Philippus Faber, *Philosophia naturalis Ioan. Duns Scoti ex quator libris Sententiarum et Quodlibetis collecta* (Parisiis: Apud Dionysium Moreau 1622), Theorema XCIII: "Natura communis habet esse praeter opus intellectus," 708–709.

29. "Natura specifica . . . quod distinguitur a singularitate, non est una formaliter positive in omnibus individuis . . . si secludantur haecceitates Petri & Pauli, esset verum dicere quod natura, quae est in Petro, est ipsamet natura, quae est in Paulo sine ulla prorsus distinctione . . . impossibile est quod idem indivisum & indistinctum creatum sit in pluribus individuis realissime distinctis: sed hoc sequeretur ex opposita sententia, quia eadem positiva natura humana esset simul in Petro & Paulo," Punch, *Logic*, § 23, 25, 194–195.

30. "Natura quae denominatur universalis v. g. natura humana quae reperitur in Paulo, non habet aliam unitatem a parte rei cum natura, quae est in Petro & aliis individuis eiusdem naturae, quam unitatem similitudinis & conformitatis aut repraesentabilitatis per eundem conceptum formalem; nec alia unitas requiritur ad hoc ut sit formaliter una illa unitate, quae requiritur ad hoc ut sit formaliter universalis," Punch, *Logic*, § 39, 201.

31. "sed est in rebus singularibus quaedam similitudo in suis unitatibus formalibus, in qua fundatur communitas quam intellectus attribuere potest tali naturae ut a se conceptae, quae similitudo non est proprie unitas, quia non dicit indivisionem entitatum in quibus fundatur, sed solum convenientiam, seu relationem, aut coexistentiam utriusque," Francisco Suárez, *Disputationes metaphysicae* 6, 1, 12.

32. "natura ex se & proprietatibus suis formaliter consideratis non habeat multiplicari, sed esse una formaliter, licet sit realiter multiplicata, quia scilicet ut sic considerata non potest determinare intellectum ad cognoscendum quod sit multiplicata, aut quod natura, quae est in uno individuo, v. g. Petro, sit distincta a natura, quae est in alio individuo . . . illam esse ita formaliter unam in pluribus, ut ex se non tribuat occasionem intellectui ad cognoscendum quod non sit una in pluribus . . . licet verum sit quod paries albus vel non sit albus, tamen non est verum dicere quod sit albus essentialiter, aut quod non sit albus essentialiter, neque enim albedo aut negatio albedinis non sit de essentia ipsius," Punch, *Logic*, § 43, 44, 203–204. Cf. also the Appendix, in which Punch gives the replies to Mastrius's sharp criticism: Punch, *Philosophiae ad mentem Scoti Cursus Integer* (Lugduni: Sumpt. Laur. Arnaud e Petri Borde, 1672); *Metaphysics*, "Additio: Circa naturam universalem," 960.

33. "Philosophum non dicere quod similitudo fundetur in unitate, sed quod illa sunt similia quae sunt una: qui modus loquendi non arguit, quod similitudo distinguatur ab unitate, aut quod unitas sit ratio fundandi similitudinem," Punch, *Logic*, § 41, 86. As for Suárez's refusal of the Scotistic formal distinction cf. *Disputationes metaphysicae* 7, 1, 13–15. From this point of view it does also make sense that Punch is fair-minded to a certain assimilation (at least on the base of the effects) of the formal distinction to the Thomistic

virtual distinction: "hanc distinctionem formalem vocari posse distinctionem virtualem . . . Potest etiam vocari distinctio rationis, non quod fiat per rationem, hoc est per intellectum, sed quod fit inter rationes obiectivas, quae possunt concipi seorsim ab intellectu," Punch, *Metaphysics*, §15, 941.

34. ". . . omnia argumenta Doctoris, quibus intendit loc. cit. probari dari unitatem naturae realem, quae sit minor numerali, ajuntque illa non probare, nisi hac puram unitatem similitudinis, & conformitatis, quae a parte rei reperitur inter plura individua ejusdem speciei, non autem aliquam naturae unitatem communem antecedentem, quae sit fundamentum similitudinis, & conformitatis, ut Scotus contendere videtur; quam doctrinam, & solutionem undequaque approbat, & recipit Poncius Scotista disp.3 Log. quaest. 2 concl. 4 ubi dicit naturam humanam, quae reperitur in Paulo non habere aliam unitatem a parte rei cum natura, quae est in Petro, & aliis individuis ejusdem naturae, quam unitatem similitudinis . . . Coeterum hoc est recedere a communi sententia Scoti, & Scotistarum tam Veterum, quam Recentiorum, & pedibus junctis ire in sententiam Nominalium, vel Thomistarum Hervaeistarum . . . ," Mastrius, *Metaphysica*, §141, 114.

35. "Tertia conclusio: Universale , tertio modo, quod logicum dicitur, quod in rationis relatione consistit, fit per actum reflexum, qui "notitia comparativa" dicitur . . . Universale, tertio modo, est ens rationis pro formali," Francisco Suárez, *De anima*, disp. 9, q. 3, § 26–27. ". . . omnis tamen secunda intentio formaliter sumpta, et non solum fundamentaliter, est relatio rationis," Johannes Poinsot, *Cursus Philosophicus Thomisticus*, Volume I.: *Ars Logica seu De forma et materia ratiocinandi*, ed. P. Beato Reiser O.S.B. (Hildesheim: Georg Olms verlag, 2008), Log. II. p. q. II. art. II, 291. ". . . ens rationis dividi in absolutum, & respectivum ad instar entis realis, ad modum cujus & concipitur, & dividitur; absolutum nempe est, quod concipitur, vel concipi potest ad modum entis ad se, respectivum vero quod concipitur per modum entis ad alliud, sicut sunt omnes secundae intentiones," Mastrius, Disp. VIII: "De Entis finiti essentia, ac existentia," § 20, 23.

36. "quando propositio verificatur pro rebus, si duae res sufficiunt ad eius veritatem, superfluum est ponere aliam rem tertiam," Guillelmi de Ockham, *Quodlibeta Septem*, ed. Joseph C. Wey (St. Bonaventure, N.Y.: St. Bonaventure University, 1980), Quodlibet IV, 472. However, there is no doctrinal identity. For Ockham the second intentions are the acts of intellect naturally signifying the first intentions, which stand for individual things (Quodlibet IV., 474). For Punch the second intentions are nothing else than the property "to be predicable of individuals" (or "to be predicated of individuals"), which is to be identified with the aptitude of a thing (its nature) to receive the extrinsic denomination. Cf. Punch, *Logic, De ente rationis*, Quaestio ultima: De primis & secundis intentionibus, 115–118.

37. "Nec prima nec secunda intentio formalis aut obiectiva dicit necessario ens rationis formaliter . . . si aliqua ex illis esset aut includeret ens rationis, potissimum intentio obiectiva secunda, ut omnes fatentur: sed illa non est nec dicit necessario ens rationis, ergo . . . esse genus nihil aliud est quam vel esse praedicabile, vel esse praedicatum de pluribus speciebus: & esse speciem nihil aliud est quam esse praedicabile vel praedicatum de pluribus individuis: sed esse praedicatum non necessario dicit aliud quam denominationem extrinsecam desumptam ab actu intellectus quo iudicatur aliquid de alio: & esse praedicabile non est aliud, quam aptitudo rei ad recipiendam talem denominationem: sed ex dictis constat huiusmodi denominationem extrinsecam esse quid reale, & nullo modo necessario sequi ad ipsam aliquid rationis," Punch, *Logic*, § 107, 118. "Ex quibus patet Universale logicum debere esse aliquid reale positivum per se unum, habens potentiam proximam, ut possit praedicari vere & formaliter de pluribus," Punch, *Logic*, § 68, 216.

38. Similarly, on the basis of the emphasis on the act-like character of our concepts, the first and second formal intentions are defined as follows: Whereas the act or the cognition, by which one cognizes the first type of predicates are the first formal intention, the act, by which one gets to know the second kind of predicates are the second formal intentions. Cf. Punch, *Logic*, § 104, 116. "Itaque illa praedicata, quae conveniunt rei independenter a cognitione comparativa, sunt & dicitur intentiones objectivae primae: Illae vero, quae conveniunt dependenter a tali cognitione, sunt intentiones objectivae secundae," ibidem.

39. As for the warlike terminology in the second scholasticism see also Jacob Schmutz, "Bellum scholasticum. Thomisme et antithomisme dans les débats doctrinaux modernes," *Revue Thomiste* Antithomisme. Histoire, thèmes et figures (2008): 131–182.

40. "Sed brevius explicari potest utraque indifferentia naturae, & communitas, ut positiva dicatur, quam habet natura ita ad plura individua indeterminata per abstractionem a differentiis individualibus, ut eademmet sit proxime potens, ut de illis praedicetur; communitas vero negativa dicitur illa, quam habet natura etiam quando est a parte rei per differentiam contractae; quia in tali statu . . . dici potest talis negative, quatenus licet sit haec, & singularis, id tamen ex se non habet, vel ex suis intrinsecis principiis, sed id ibi obvenit a differentia . . . humanitas namque Petri, quamdiu est sub Petreitate, aptitudinem habet remotam, ut sit in pluribus, dum vero cum nulla haecceitate est conjuncta habet proximam ad plura, quae aptitudines non sunt diversae, sed una, & eadem diverso modo scilicet impedita in statu contractionis, expedita in statu abstracto . . . hac naturae indifferentia . . . est ad plura disjunctim, quatenus natura, quae est in Petro, talis est conditionis, ut quantum est de se potuerit constituere Paulum," Mastrius, *Metaphysica*, §73–74, 96–97.

41. "Poncius recens Scotista . . . inquit, quod natura Petri, ut sic distincta formaliter a sua haecceitate, neque est una positive cum alia natura, neque positive distincta ab illa, nam ut sic praecise habet praedicata sua essentialia, inter quae non est nec unitas, nec distinctio . . . Haec solutio non satisfacit, & falsam continet doctrinam, naturae namque communi in statu essentiae consideratae, prout distinguitur a statu existentiae, non solum conveniunt praedicata essentialia primi modi, sed etiam secuni modi, idest praedicata, vel quae sunt de ejus quidditate, vel ejus necessariae passiones," Mastrius, *Metaphysica*, § 58, 93.

42. "Dico tertio unitas formalis, dum multiplicatur natura in individuis, non manet una indivisa in omnibus, sed ipsa etiam cum natura multiplicatur," Mastrius, Metaphysics, § 168, 121. The attribution of such predicates, which seems to be for some interpreters (cf. Pini, "Scotus on Universals: A Reconsideration") "speaking on credit," is for Mastrius, as far as I know, justified by the assumption of the formal or modal distinction between the essence and existence of finite beings ("Essentia realis & existentiae non distinguitur solum per intellectum, sed formaliter ex natura rei modaliter," Mastrius, *Metaphysica*, Disputatio VIII.: "De entis finiti essentia, & existentia," q. 2, art. 4, 46–48). It might be said that what is proved on the essential level (e.g., the formal unity), must be analogically assumed also on the existential level. Mastrius is convinced that it is far from being clear that the unity on the essential level immediately converts onto the unity on the physical level: "Resp. per essentiam ab existentia praescidentem non solum intelligi debere essentiam naturae in statu potentialitatis, antequam producatur, aut in esse objectivo apud intellectum abstrahentem, sed etiam in statu actualitatis, quatenus sub existentia manens adhuc ex natura rei formaliter, vel saltem modaliter ab ea secernitur . . . in hoc itaque sensu indivisio essentialis individuorum dicitur spectare ad essentiam, ut ab existentia praescindit, quatenus, scilicet convenit essentiae, sive existat, sive non; quo etiam sensu scientia dicitur abstrahere ab existentia, non quia de rebus existentibus haberi nequeat, sed quia indifferenter habetur, sive existant,

sive non; sic igitur in proposito talis unitas, & indivisio adhuc dicit potest realis, & realiter naturae convenit etiam existenti," Mastrius, *Metaphysica*, § 174, 123. As for the limiting case of the distinction *ex natura rei*, which is the distinction between *res* and its intrinsic mode (not to confuse with the extrinsic mode!) cf. Mastrius, Disputatio VIII., §124–135, 46–48.

43. "Item qualitates mediae inter extremas contrarias, ut color viridis aut rubeus inter albedinem et nigredinem, et liberalitas inter avaritiam et prodigalitatem, habent quamdam convenientiam et dissimilitudinem cum extremis; nam liberalitas comparata ad avaritiam differt ab illa et convenit cum prodigalitate in vi et propensione effundendi se et communicandi; comparata vero ad prodigalitatem, differt ab illa in moderatione et convenit cum avaritia in retinendo; vanum autem esset fingere in liberalitate varios gradus seu modos reales ex natura rei distinctos, propter has intellectus nostri comparationes et conceptiones quae (si res attente consideretur) fere possunt in infinitum multiplicari et vix possunt differentiae adeo simplices excogitari quas intellectus dividere non posset inveniendo in eis convenientiam et differentiam cum aliis rebus; ut in homine, quatenus rationalis est, invenit convenientiam cum angelo in intelligendo et differentiam in modo intelligendi; et sic de aliis," Suárez, *Disputationes metaphysicae*, 6,9,20.

44. "Primo, relationes primi modi idem, simile, & aequale, cum sint aequiparantiae fundantur super unum, sive super unitatem; ergo cum sint reales, unitas, in qua fundantur, & est ratio proxima fundandi illas, erit realis . . . duo individua in singularitatibus sunt omnino dissimilia," Mastrius, *Metaphysica*, § 140, 114. ". . . comparatio supponit aliquam similitudinem inter extrema comparata, quia comparatio sit in specie athoma ex 7. Phys. 29. sed comparatio supponit aliquam unitatem realem formae, in qua extrema comparatur, ergo etiam similitudo . . . Deinde quaero, quare unum album potius assimiletur alteri albo, quam unum viride . . . ratio cur unum album sit similius alteri, quam viride, est, quia utrumque participat albedinem in communi," Mastrius, ibidem, § 142, 114.

45. "Obiectum in quantum est obiectum, est prius naturaliter ipso actu," Scotus, *Ordinatio* II dist. 3 pars 1 q. 1, 394.

46. "ut natura possit definiri, hanc unitatem sufficere, quia definitio proprie non est in rebus, sed in ratione; et ideo non est una definitio communis, nisi quatenus mens concipit aliquid ut commune, separando illud a quolibet singulari, ad quod satis est unitas formalis quam natura habet in quolibet individuo cum similitudine omnium talium unitatum inter se, nam inde fit ut intellectus uno conceptu communi illam rationem formalem concipiat ac definiat," Suárez, *Disputationes metaphysicae*, 6,1,13.

47. ". . . si loquamur de definitione obiectiva, alia esse definitionem Petri, & aliam Pauli, sicut alia est essentia ipsius ab ipso, quamvis propter summam similitudinem, quam habet censeantur habere ut unam existentiam: ita etiam unam definitionem: si vero loquamur de definitione formali, qui est actus intellectus repraesentans formaliter definitionem obiectivam," Punch, *Logic*, § 32, 198.

48. ". . . falsum est, aliam esse essentiam unius ab essentia alterius, quamvis enim dici possit humanitatem Petri esse aliam ab humanitate Pauli, tamen cum veritate dici non potest essentiam Petri esse aliam ab essentia Pauli, & inter se differre essentialiter, quia cum illae humanitates sint entitates omnino ejusdem rationis," Mastrius, *Metaphysica*, § 127, 111.

49. "Dico 2. unitatem universalem non esse ipsam unitatem praecisionis, etiamsi haec ponatur esse rationis," Mastrius, *Metaphysica*, § 219, 135. ". . . ex vi unitatis praecisionis dicitur positive communis, quae communitas petit, ut sub tali conceptu natura nec ab intrinseco, nec ab extrinseco sit singularis, sed omnem prorsus singularitatem excludat, & omni

modo; ergo in statu existentiae talis unitas praecisionis nequit convenire naturae," Mastrius, *Metaphysica*, §190, 128. "sed natura communis, ut sic, aut repraesentata universaliter, aut expressa universaliter nullum habet esse reale realis existentiae, aut essentiae, sed solum esse extrinsecae denominationis, quod est esse secundum quid, & rationis . . . ergo unitas praecisionis, quae competit naturae, ut sic, non potest esse unitas realis, & competens naturae habenti esse extra animam," Mastrius, *Metaphysica*, §191, 129. The claim concerning the identity of the being of the extrinsic denomination and the being of reason constitutes, as far as I can see, a certain tension with Mastrius's statements in *Logic* (firstly published seven years before *Metaphysica*). When dealing in Logic with the extrinsic denominations in its relationship to the constitution of being of reason Mastrius affirms "ens rationis formaliter non consistere in extrinseca denominatione proveniente ab aliqua forma reali, neque ab actu rationis, sive hic exprimat rem, sicut est, sive aliter" (Mastrius, *Logic*, §15, 118) and "illud esse cognitum, quod est denominatio extrinseca, potius formaliter, & subjective esse in intellectu, quam objective . . . nam ex vi cognitionis directae non est objective in intellectu, sed solum formaliter, & subjective ratione formae denominantis, quam realiter dicit" (Mastrius, *Logic*, § 22, 119). The given tension is also confirmed by the contemporary research, which detects a certain ambiguity in Mastrius's doctrine of the objective concept. On one hand Mastrius is critical of Aureol (who, as some scholars say, lived through the renaissance in the Baroque Era, which can be confirmed by the following quotation from Mastrius´s "Ad Lectorem" in his *Metaphysica*: "Demum ex antiquioribus Aureolo praesertim respondere nitor, utpote qui in Metaphysicis acutissimus fuit, et principia jecit omnino contraria principiis nostri Doctoris," Mastrius, *Tomus quartus*), who puts forth that in the case of the objective concept one is to speak about the intermediary ontological dimension ("the third realm"), which is to be identified neither with the extramental thing, nor with the intellective act existing subjectively in the intellect. However, next to the rejection of Aureol's reification of the thing's being known, Mastrius makes amply use of the diversity of objective or intentional being when analyzing the notion of distinction of reason without the foundation in a thing. By that he seems to restore Aureol's ontology based on the key notion of *esse obiectivum*. As regards this duplicity in Mastrius's interpretation of the objective being cf. Sven K. Knebel, "What about Aureol? Mastri's Contribution to the Theory of the Distinction of Reason," in *Rem in se ipsa cernere*, ed. Marco Forlivesi (Padova: Il Poligrafo, 2006), 415–437, in particular 419–420, 432–436. Cf. also Marco Forlivesi, "La distinction entre concept formel et concept objectif: Suárez, Pasqualigo, Mastri," *Les Études philosophique* 1 (2002): 3–30, in particular 17–29.

50. ". . . universale in actu dici, dum est in potentia proxima, ut praedicetur de multis simul, sed numquam est in potentia magis propinqua ad sic praedicandum, nisi quando actu concipitur unum in multis, tunc enim immediate potest sequi talis praedicatio, nec unquam fieri potest talis praedicatio, nisi prius natura concipiatur, nedum apta, sed etiam actu existens in pluribus", Mastrius, *Logic*, § 47, 148. See also Mastrius., *Metaphysica*, § 225, 137.

51. ". . . universalis in ratione totius potestativi re vera consistit in indivisione ejus in partes subjectivas cum aptitudine ad sic dividi; verum notandum est universali duplicem habere praedicationem de suis inferioribus; unam signatam, aliam exercitam . . . in praedicatione signata praedicatur sub ratione totius potestativi, ut v.g. genus de pluribus speciebus, vel specie differentibus, in exercita vero per modum totius essentialis, & actualis, ut v.g. homo est animal, equus est animal, non enim ex hoc quod aliquod commune concipitur per modum totius potentialis, amittit ratione totius actualis", Mastrius, *Metaphysics*, § 226, 137.

52. As for this reading of Scotus's theory of predication cf. Richard Cross, R., "Divisibility, Communicability, and Predicability in Duns Scotus's Theories of the Common Nature," in

Medieval Philosophy and Theology 11 (2003): 43–62, in particular 44. As regards Mastrius's conception of the formal predication by which the predicate belongs to the subject in the way of inhesion see Marco Forlivesi, "The Nature of Transcendental Being and Its Contraction to Its Inferiors in the Thought of Mastri and Belluto," in *"Rem in seipsa cernere". Saggi sul pensiero filosofico di Bartlomeo Mastri (1602–1673)*, ed. Marco Forlivesi (Padova: Il Poligrafo, 2006), 262–337, in particular 305–310.

53. ". . . universale in actu a metaphysico praesertim definitur, & consideratur, ut praedicabile de inferioribus praedicatione exercita, dicitur enim esse illud, quod est in potentia proxima ad dici de multis praedicatione dicente, hoc est hoc; ideo in ordine ad talem praedicationem dicimus ejus unitatem universalem melius explicari per unitatem inexistentiae, & indivisionem praedicatorum essentialium, quam per indivisionem in partes subjectivas," Mastrius *Metaphysica*, § 226, 137. It is not accidental that Mastrius assimilates his theory of the logical universal existing intentionally "per inexistentiam" in its supposits to the way of being, by which the Divine nature exists in the three supposits. The only difference is that in the context of the logical universal Mastrius speaks about the intentional in-existence, in the context of the Trinity of the real in-existence. Whereas in the case of the in-existence of the Divine nature in the supposits one can doctrinally speak about the immanent Platonism, one should be far from being just to treat Mastrius's intentional in-existence of the "created universals" by the same label. As for the designation "the immanent Platonism" in the Trinity cf. e.g., Richard Cross, "Gregory of Nyssa on Universals," *Vigiliae Christianae* 56.4 (2002): 372–410.

54. In contrast to Mastrius whose effort is to lay the metaphysical ground for the essential predication in the way, by which a subject is identified with a predicate in the form of the intentional contraction of the "in-existing" predicate in the given subject, Punch seems to be satisfied with the more economical underpinning of that propositional identity. According to that Punch tampers only with the formal concepts and essentially similar individuals. I am sure about the fact that this Punch's ontological fulcrum draws the strong inspiration from Ockham's theory of the truth conditions. When analyzing the categorical sentence "man is animal" Punch says: ". . . homo est animal, quae propositio est essentialis, quomnis vox animal non identificetur homini, quia homo supponit pro re quae est animal rationale, & animal supponit pro re, quae est animal: sensus est, non quod vox animal identificetur homini, sed quod res illa, quae est animal rationale sit animal, & quod animalitas aliqua identificetur ipsi: ergo similiter natura humana Petri supposita pro natura simili potest praedicari de Paulo essentialiter quia quamvis ipsamet non identificetur illi; tamen natura similis, pro qua supponitur, identificatur ipsi," Punch, "Additio: Circa Naturam Universalem," 959–960. That statement is not far from Ockham, who says that a sentence is true if "the subject and predicate supposits a same thing." As for Ockham's theory of truth conditions cf. Calvin G. Normore, "Some Aspects of Ockham's Logic," in *The Cambridge Companion to Ockham*, ed. Paul V. Spade (New York: Cambridge University Press, 1999), 31–52, in particular 38–39. In the same volume see also Claude Panaccio, "Semantics and Mental Language," 53–75, in particular 61–63. The similar reinterpretation of formal predication (the type of predication, by which the denoted form signified by a predicate of a proposition is a form) by means of identical predication (the sort of predication, in which the thing signified by the predicate is the same as signified by a subject) can be found also in Domingo de Soto (1494–1560). Also Soto "shows some sympathy for Ockham's point of view" by claiming that the proposition "homo est humanitas" is true because "homo est res quae est humanitas." Cf. Ria van der Lecq, "Domingo de Soto on Universals and the Ontology of Intentions," 323.

55. ". . . [unitas universalis] habere tamen magis similitudinem cum unitate formali, quam cum aliis, unde cum ens rationis in universum efformetur ab intellectu ad modum entis realis, quod imitatur, ita in proposito unitas universalis, cum sit rationis, efformatur ad intellectu ad modum unitatis formalis, supra quam fundatur," Mastrius, *Metaphysica*, § 221, 136.

56. "unitas universalis debet esse talis, ut secundum eam possit universale proxime praedicari de pluribus predicatione dicente, hoc est hoc, sed unitas similitudinis ad hoc non sufficit," Mastrius, *Metaphysica*, § 217, 134–135.

57. ". . . in logica prout est ab Arist. tradita, non aliquid reale esse objectum, sed ens rationis," Mastrius, Logic, Proemium, § 24, 65. "Nec syllogismus, nec ullum aliud objectum ullius partis Logiace dicit per se formaliter ens rationis, & consequenter objectum Logicae formale non erit ens rationis ullum," Punch, *Logic*, Disputatio II: "De natura logicae," § 44, 140. Cf. Wilhelm Risse, *Die Logik der Neuzeit*, Band 1, 1500–1650, (Stuttgart-Bad Cannstatt: Friedrich Frommann Verlag, 1964), 432–433.

58. The same evaluation holds also for the issue of possible beings: "Mastrius mit seiner These der Abhängigkeit der Possibilien von göttlichen Verstand dem authentischen Sinn der scotischen Lehre im Vergleich mit Poncius doch näherkommt," Sousedík, "Der Streit um den Wahren Sinn der Scotischen Possibilienlehre," 198.

59. As for the striking similarity with Soto cf. Ria Van der Lecq, "Domingo de Soto on Universals and the Ontology of Intentions." The same setting of both authors can be seen, among others, in the claim that the major ontological economy denying the objective fictions in the mind does not *ipso facto* imply nominalism (Lecq, 313). That is also why I am far from saying that Punch's theory is to be evaluated as nominalism *purus et crassus*. As regards the "conciliatory" attitude in Francisco Toledo (1532–1596) in the issue of universals cf. "Possunt autem omnes opiniones [of nominalists, Platonists and moderate realists; D. H.] ex parte quadam conciliari: si dicamus esse universalia quaedam in voce; videlicet voces specificas, & genericas, & imo etiam in scripto simili modo: & esse etiam universalia in mente, conceptus videlicet intellectus, formales, specificos, & genericos, & quae possunt dici universalia forma-lia: esse praeterea universalia in rebus, rerum videlicet ipsarum genera & species realia & caet. quae possunt dici universalia obiectiva, quia sunt ipsarum cognitionum universalium obiecta. Nam protecto voces ipsae in voce praedicantur de pluribus & subiiciuntur: & conceptus in me se praedicatur & subiiciuntur & res ipsae per conceptus subiiciuntur, & praedicantur. Demum esse quoque separata a rebus alia universalia, scilicet, ideas in Deo ipso videlicet, & mente divina, ut aliqui Platonem interpretantur, atque ita omnia convenirent veritati" D. Francisci Toleti, *Opera omnia Philosophica*, In Librum Porphyrii, de quinque universalibus (Coloniae Agrippinae: in Officina Birckmannica, sumptibus Hermanni Mylii, 1615; repr. Hildesheim, N.Y.: G. Olms, 1985) 29.

Is Buridan's Theory of Abstraction Incompatible with His Nominalist Semantics? An Evaluation of Klima's Charge against Buridan

Joseph Hill, S.J.

Abstract: This paper addresses Klima's charge of inconsistancy against John Buridan in a book recently published on the subject. Klima argues that Buridan's theory of abstraction commits him to the aspectuality of substantial concepts. However, his semantics of absolute terms and concepts prevents him from accepting any aspectuality of substantial concepts. In light of this problem, the paper gives a detailed reconstruction of Buridan's account of abstraction, beginning with sensory perception and singular cognition and ending with the formation of substantial concepts that have a universal signification. Then, from this reconstruction, some Buridanian responses are given to Klima's critique, which explain at least why Buridan did not see the problem himself. Finally, the conclusion comes down in favor of Klima and, in light of the discussion, highlights some fundamental problems with the nominalist project.

I n a recent book on the philosophy of nominalist John Buridan, Klima argues that Buridan falls into inconsistency. He states that Buridan's theory of abstraction commits him to the aspectuality of simple substantial concepts, which is incompatible with his semantics because such concepts are said to be absolute and without any connotation to this or that aspect of a substance.[1] This paper intends to carefully analyze Buridan's theory of abstraction and substantial concept formation in order to assess the legitimacy of Klima's charge. So, the paper will begin with an exposition of Buridan's account of sensible and singular cognition, then of the process of abstraction. Then, there will be a discussion of universal representation of substantial concepts and the problem of indifference. Finally, in response to Klima's charge, I will attempt to explain why Buridan thought his theory of abstraction was compatible with his semantics. I will not exonerate Buridan from the charge but rather explain why he did not see the problem himself. In this way I hope to further the debate over whether the nominalists can have both concepts that signify many particulars and an ontology that excludes universals.

Buridan's nominalist program forces him to address two central problems. The first is the formation of simple substantial concepts. He accepts that we have such concepts, and that all our concepts are derived from sense perception. So, he must find a way to explain how these concepts are formed, because it seems that we only have access to accidental features of things through our senses. The second problem is how these simple concepts can have a universal signification. How can they represent and thus signify many singulars of a particular kind? Buridan maintains that humans have universal concepts. However, his nominalism prevents him from speaking of these universals being formed through the apprehension of common natures or substantial forms, as is found in moderate realist accounts of cognition. Instead, he must construe universal signification in a way that harmonizes with his nominalist ontology and semantics.

Buridan on the Formation of Substantial Concepts

The process of coming to a simple substantial cognition begins with the reception of sensible information from exterior objects through the five senses. Buridan maintains the standard Aristotelian empiricist account of knowledge. The five senses receive information and the common sense gathers it together to form a phantasm. He is insistent in several passages that understanding cannot take place if the sensible faculties, which include the imagination, are not functioning. He states, "we know by experience that in order to understand, we need an act of sensing with respect to either the exterior or interior sense; that is why we understand nothing when we sleep altogether dreamlessly."[2] This is how he interprets Aristotle's statement that the intellect must always turn to the phantasm.[3]

The second step in cognition is the presentation of this sensory information to the intellect. The intellect is presented with the phantasm, the sensible representation formed by the common sense and imagination. So far this follows the standard Aristotelian position. But Buridan then diverges from this account when he infers from his reasoning that the intelligible species and the phantasm are the same thing.[4] Buridan defines an intelligible species as, "that which by the mediation of sense is in the organ of the imagination or cogitative [power], or in the intellect, without which the intellect could not in the first place understand sensed or imagined things (just as an exterior sense could not sense without a species caused in the organ of that sense by an object)."[5] It is the phantasm as intelligible species that is the basis of all acts of the intellect. But why does Buridan equate these two that were previously understood as distinct?

The key to the answer lies in how Buridan conceives of the intellect as active and passive. For Buridan, the intellect is passive with regard to all objects, as he explains, "asked whether the intellect is a passive power as regards what is intelligible. I therefore propose a seventh thesis [T7]: that it is, because in whatever way it is acted upon, it is acted upon by some entity, and every entity is intelligible. Therefore, it is acted upon by what is intelligible."[6] So, the intellect is first a receiver of information.[7] Thus Buridan describes all entities as intelligible, for they are intelligible insofar as they can act on the intellect. The intellect only secondarily acts on these intelligibles.

What, then, constitutes the intellect's activity? Buridan identifies several ways in which the intellect is in act. With regard to cognition, the intellect is an agent in learning and understanding,[8] for otherwise these would not be able to take place. Although the intellect is passive with regard to what is intelligible, it is active in processing this information. On this point Buridan states, "it is necessary to grant that the intellect is actively disposed in compounding, dividing, syllogizing, and distinguishing."[9] Buridan does not distinguish the agent intellect as a special power and distinct from the possible intellect. Rather, his account describes how the intellect is active or passive in relation to different things. He is aware that, "something is said to be actual or in actuality in many ways."[10] So, the one intellect can be passive with regard to some things, such as intelligible objects, and active in processing those objects and reasoning from them, without the need to distinguish different powers within the intellect.

Why does Buridan think that the intellect is acted upon by what is intelligible and receives intelligible species?[11] The answer is twofold. First, Buridan does not associate materiality with individuality and immateriality with universality. Second, Buridan appeals to the argument from indifference in order to explain how simple concepts can signify many particulars, and indifference is described as a characteristic of sensible representations. So concepts must preserve something of their sensible content in order to be indifferent.[12] For within his nominalist framework, all substances are individual and in no need of a principle of individuation, even if they belong to a natural species. Furthermore, material conditions do not necessarily preclude a universal signification. He supports these points by showing that the intellect is able to cognize singularly,[13] and sense is able to cognize universally.

For Buridan, the intellect receives the objects of thought as intelligible species from the phantasms presented by the sensitive powers to the intellect. The next step is the formation of a vague singular concept. He argues that the senses cognize objects in a confused way. That is, they cognize something with all its accidents and location fused together in one representation. He states, "Therefore, even though exterior sense cognizes Socrates, or whiteness, or white, nevertheless this is only in a species representing it confusedly with the substance, the whiteness, the magnitude, and the location, in accordance with what appears in the prospect of the person cognizing it."[14] When one cognizes something *in prospectu* all its perceived characteristics are preserved in the single view. One cannot perceive only the whiteness of Socrates and not his shape when one is attentive to him *in prospectu*. This phantasm and species, then, is presented to the intellect, and from it the intellect forms a singular concept of the thing. He explains, "I say that when the intellect receives the species or intellection of Socrates from the phantasm with this type of confusion of size and location, making the thing appear in the manner of something existing in the prospect of the person cognizing it the intellect understands him in a singular manner."[15] This singular cognition becomes the basis for all other operations of the intellect.

From the singular concept the intellect is able to distinguish and abstract the substance from the accidents and thus form a simple substantial concept. Buridan describes the process of forming substantial concepts as a two-stage process. The first stage involves the comparison of several perceptions of the same object, from which the intellect is then able to distinguish the substance from the accidents.[16] Buridan states,

> The second way is that the senses first perceive both substance and accident in a confused manner, and afterwards the intellect, which is a superior power, differentiates between substance and accident. Therefore, if I see someone now to be white and later I see him to be black, and at the same time I perceive that he remains the same, I arrive at the cognition by which I notice that he is other than whiteness and likewise other than blackness. And thus, although substance and accident at first are apprehended by means of the senses in a confused manner, nevertheless given such sensitive cognition the intellect, which is the superior power, can arrive at the cognition of substance itself.[17]

The recognition of something permanent and distinct from the changing accidents allows the intellect to distinguish between the two. Something is seen to persist amidst change of accidental features. Significantly, Buridan maintains that information about the substance is communicated through the senses to the intellect with the perception of its exterior, accidental attributes. One is able to perceive substances, not just accidents.[18] It is also worth noting that several perceptions of a single object are needed in order to see the distinction. One must recognize the object that undergoes the change from its changing features.

For Buridan, the intellect forms simple substantial concepts by the activity of abstraction. After an *in prospectu* singular cognition of Socrates, and after recognizing accidental changes in Socrates and distinguishing Socrates from his whiteness and blackness, the intellect abstracts the substance of Socrates from his accidental features, thus forming a simple substantial concept. Buridan summarizes the whole process,

> In the third way, abstractively; as when I first have a concept that represents substance and accident together in a confused manner, for example, when I perceive something white, for I see not only whiteness, but something that is white, and then if I perceive the same thing to move and change from white to black, then I judge that this is something distinct from whiteness, and then the intellect naturally has the power to analyze that confusion, and to understand substance abstractively from accident, and accident abstractively from substance, and it can form a simple concept of each, and it is in the same way, by abstraction, that a universal concept is formed from a singular one, as one should see in bk. 3 of *On the Soul,* and bk. 7 of the *Metaphysics.*[19]

Abstraction is nothing more than the isolation of the substantial elements of the confused singular cognition from the accidental features. The result is a simple concept that represents the substance absolutely, with no connotation of accidents or anything else.[20] This is a natural process, for, as Buridan says, the intellect naturally has the power to sort out the confusion. It is not a discursive or conscious activity.[21]

What is the information content of this substantial concept? It is the information taken from the phantasm that corresponds to what is permanent. Buridan argues that it is the information corresponding to the individual substance apart from any accidental features. This seems fairly thin. It has been called a precursor to the 'bare particular' notion of contemporary philosophy.[22] Buridan does not elaborate on the nature of this content, but focuses rather on what it represents.

The question now turns to the representational content of simple substantial concepts and their mode of signification. Buridan argues that once the substance has been abstracted from the accidental features, although it is a concept of one thing, it has universal signification for all other particulars of the same species. But how can this be? He explains,

> Whenever the species (and likeness) of Socrates has existed in the intellect and has been abstracted from the species of external things, it will no more be a representation of Socrates than of Plato and other men; nor does the intellect understand Socrates by it any more than other men. On the contrary, the intellect understands all men by it indifferently, in a single concept, namely, the concept from which the name 'man' is taken. And this is to understand universally.[23]

How can a simple substantial concept taken from a perception of Socrates now be a common concept that represents all men? Buridan uses the argument from indifference to answer this question.

The representational content of simple substantial concepts are indifferent to many individuals and thus function as universal concepts. Buridan draws upon Ockham's argument from indifference at this point. For Ockham, sensible information is always indifferent, according to the natural similarity between sensible qualities. So, all representations of sensible things would be indifferent to whatever shares those similar qualities. For example, two individual instances of whiteness are sufficiently similar to be represented by a single white representation. Buridan accepts this point, and uses it to argue that two substances of the same species are so much alike that the only way to tell them apart is by extraneous considerations. He uses the example of two similarly looking stones to illustrate it.[24] In this way, although Buridan, on account of his nominalist ontology, holds that the there is a substantial difference between Socrates and Plato, because they have a different form and different matter,[25] their substances are so similar that they cannot be distinguished by comparing their substantial features. They have a natural similarity[26] and can only be distinguished by what he calls 'extraneous' considerations, that is, by their distinct accidents.[27] So, this translates into his theory of concept representation quite nicely. What makes cognition singular is the particular combination of accidents of a substance being perceived *in prospectu*. Once these accidents are stripped away and only the information about the substance remains, due to natural similarity, the representation content is indifferent to many individuals. He takes the indifference argument of Ockham and reapplies it here to satisfy his needs.

An Assessment of Klima's Objections

Buridan's cognitive psychology merges Aristotelian elements, especially with regards to abstraction, and Ockhamist-nominalist elements, in particular the argument from indifference. However, such a marriage has its problems. Does his position remain consistent with his nominalist ontology and semantics? Is Buridan, on account of his abstractionist theory, committed to the aspectuality of common concepts, and thus open to Klima's charge of inconsistency? Before I answer this question, the problem of indifference needs to be explained and assessed, because it is an important piece in Buridan's overall understanding of substantial concepts. It will provide clarity to one side of the inconsistency charge.

The attack leveled at Ockham is whether the indifference of representations is sufficient to account for genuinely universal signification of common concepts. Klima, in response to Panaccio's reconstruction and defense of Ockham's theory of concept formation,[28] argues that even if a cognition, cut off from its causal link to the object, is indifferent in representation to many other objects that are qualitatively similar, it is still not a universal representation.[29] The fact that two objects are similar and can be represented by the same concept indifferently, even if the concept is formed by means of a causal relation to only one of the objects, does not make it an actual representation of the second object. For example, if one takes a photograph of Michael, who has an identical twin named Jeremy, that image may be sufficiently indifferent in representational content to be able to represent both twins. However, the photograph is only an image of Michael. It is not an actual representation of Jeremy. To use another line of description, even if the phenomenal content of a concept, what it 'looks like' so to speak, allows the cognizer to identify both objects, the semantic content of the concept, what its information actually is, is only of one object and not many. So, if Buridan bases universal representation on indifference, which is how this reconstruction has interpreted him, then he is open to the same criticism.

One can give a tentative buridanian response to this criticism. For Buridan, "intelligible and intellect are not related to each other universally as active and passive, but as representable and that to which a representation can be made."[30] The intellect is able to have knowledge of everything that it represents through concepts. Concepts are similitudes of things, they represent them by being like them. He states, "things are understood not because they are in the intellect, but because their species, which are representative likenesses of them, are in the intellect."[31] This likeness between the representation and that which is represented is caused by the reception of information from the senses that is then processed by the sensitive powers and the intellect. If things existing singularly outside the intellect have a natural likeness to each other, then they can be represented by the same concept in the intellect, because this concept is a representational likeness of all of them. This is Buridan's basic argument on this point. On this reading, indifference is just a word he uses as part of his debt to Ockham, but what he means by it is representational likeness, not vague similarity. So, he provides a stronger account of universal signification than Ockham. But, he is still open to the charge that the concept does not semantically signify many individuals, but only the one individual thing from which the sensory information is received. In response to this line of argument, Buridan simply shifts the criteria for how a concept can signify a thing. He reduces concepts to representational likenesses of things and does not find it problematic if the information content of one common concept is taken from only one individual.[32] Why does this matter? As long as the concept is able to be a representational likeness of many particulars, who cares where the actual information content of this concept comes from? A photograph of Michael is sufficient to represent both twins.

This leads to the main objection. Is Buridan's theory of concept formation inconsistent with his semantics of concept signification? Klima argues as follows,

> the point in abstraction is precisely that by means of an abstract concept several things are represented *in respect of* what they resemble each other, disregarding what distinguishes them. Indeed, as we have seen in our discussion of universal concepts, it is crucial for abstraction to work, that is, for it to provide us with truly universal concepts, that the concepts acquired by abstraction represent the things observed in the process *in that respect* in which they do not differ from unobserved things of the same kind. . . . However, Buridan's absolute concepts are supposed to represent things absolutely, not in relation to something, that is, *not in any respect*. Therefore, it seems that they cannot really be obtained by abstraction in the way Buridan described, or if they are obtained in this way, then their representative function is not quite correctly described by him in his semantics.[33]

There can be no doubt that Buridan maintains the aspectuality of common concepts. In one passage he explains himself on the notion of similarity and representation in the following way,

> I again suppose that if there are any things similar to each other, whatever is a similarity for one of them, is, *in the respect in which* the two are similar to each other, a similarity for each of them. For example, if A, B, and C are similar with respect to whiteness because they are white, just as D is similar to A [in whiteness], it must also be similar to both B and C [in whiteness]. Therefore, it follows from the fact that representation occurs by means of likeness that that which was representative of one thing will be indifferently representative of others.[34]

There can be very little doubt from this passage that representation is understood as representative likeness of many singulars precisely under the aspect of which they are alike. But, if this is the case for simple substantial concepts, then their signification of substances is not absolute but rather according to the likeness that is represented. So Klima is correct. Absolute signification entails that the concepts denote a thing with no connotation of any other feature.[35] But, Buridan cannot hold both that substantial concepts, formed by abstraction, represent many particulars *in respect of* their likeness to each other, and that substantial concepts represent things absolutely, and not in relation to anything.[36] There is a conflict between Buridan's semantics and cognitive psychology.

Is there some way to reconcile this apparent contradiction? Why does Buridan think that there is no problem here? Here is my tentative answer to these questions. The simple substantial concept abstracted from the confusion of all the different features of a singular cognition of one substance signifies that substance in itself, and not with respect to this or that aspect. Buridan can hold that this simple substantial concept has an absolute signification with respect to the individual substance from which the concept was formed. That much seems consistent. The information is abstracted from the cognition of one particular substance and not many, as in a moderate realist account of abstraction, so it is a likeness of that particular substance. However, when Buridan makes the move to call that simple substantial concept universal in its representation, he falls into the problem that Klima identifies. For, how can an absolute concept, signifying a particular substance absolutely and not under any aspect, also signify other particulars absolutely unless there is some respect in which they are similar? There needs to be a principle of selecting and excluding particulars from this universal signification. But this principle must be that of the likeness between the particulars. Then this likeness is the aspect under which the concept represents and signifies those particulars. Therefore, the concept is not absolute.

It may be that Buridan conceived the substantial concept and its absolute signification of many individuals in this way. The substantial concept is a representative likeness of one substance and indifferently of many substances of the same species. The concept represents the substance according to that aspect by which they are alike. But, if the aspect by which they are alike is precisely their substance *qua* substance, disregarding all of their accidents, then the concept can signify the thing absolutely and not under any aspect, because the aspect that it signifies is nothing else than the substance itself. It signifies them absolutely and not under some extra aspect because they are similar in their very substances. So, if the 'aspect' of the representation is the bare substance, then signification is absolute and not connotative. This would save him from inconsistency.

However, this explanation will not do. It does capture the mind of Buridan, I believe, but it still falls short. For the process of abstraction entails aspectuality because it pulls out some information and forms a concept on the basis of that aspect and not any other. So the concept is a representation of the substance according to the aspect abstracted from the confused singular cognition. Even if this is a non-accidental feature, it is still an aspect. Buridan may have thought that as long as the concept represents the substances themselves and not their accidental features it can be absolute. But, as soon as one has the notion of likeness between individuals one implies an unlikeness as well, otherwise they would simply be identical or the same, which is tantamount to stating that they have a common nature. If there is both a likeness and unlikeness between individual substances, then the concept that represents the substances indifferently represents them precisely insofar as they are alike, prescinding from their unlikeness. But, this again implies the aspectuality of the concept's signification. Even if the unlikeness is due to accidental features and the concept's likeness represents the bare substance, one can distinguish between the substance and its representation and compare the relative likenesses between substances that are signified by a single concept, so the aspectuality of concepts that are representational likenesses of individual substances remains. It would seem from this reasoning that the very idea of a universal concept that signifies absolutely is questionable.

This conclusion has wider implications than simply Buridan's philosophy. It calls into question the cogency of the entire nominalist project. If the nominalists cannot give a cogent account of substantial concepts that signify universally, then they are in trouble of having a philosophy that is unable to explain some of the most basic terms and ideas that humans have. If they give up their semantics of absolute and connotative terms and concepts, then they are in danger of undermining their program of ontological reduction. Either option does not look promising.

Fordham University

Notes

1. Gyula Klima, *John Buridan* (Oxford: Oxford University Press, 2009), 265.

2. John Buridan, *Quaestiones de Anima* III, 9. 95–97 (hereafter *QDA*). "Experimur enim quod ad intelligendum indigeremus actu sentiendi vel secundum sensum exteriorem vel interiorem, propter quod nihil intelligimus quando perfecte sine somnis dormimus." All quotes from the *Questions on the De Anima* are taken from *John Buridan's Philosophy of Mind: An Edition and Translation of Book III of his 'Questions on Aristotle's De Anima' (Third Redaction)*, ed. John A. Zupko, Ph.D. diss., Cornell University, 1989, 2 vols. (Ann Arbor: University Microfilms International, 1990).

3. For the purposes of this paper, a detailed account of sense perception is not needed. the senses present information to the intellect and the intellect needs the sensible faculties in order to function.

4. Cf. *QDA* III. 15, 190–236. This comes after a long section in which Buridan argues that the intelligible species is not an intellectual habit. At the end of this passage Buridan explicitly states, "I say consequent to the third thesis advanced above, that the aforesaid intelligible species, that is, the imaginative apprehension, does not remain in the intellect once intellection has ceased [ego dico consequenter ad tertiam conclusionem prius positam quod praedicta species intelligibilis, id est illa phantastica apprehensio, non manet in intellectu intellectione cessante]" (*QDA* III. 15, 232–234).

5. *QDA* III, 15, 99–104: "Voco autem hic speciem intelligibilem quae mediante sensu sit in organo phantasiae vel cogitativae, vel in intellectu, sine qua intellectus non potest primo intelligere res sensatas vel phantasiastas (sicut sensus exterior non potest sentire sine specie causata ab obiecto in organo illius sensus)."

6. *QDA* III. 1, 109–113: "Et quaestio quaerebatur utrum intellectus sit virtus passiva ab intelligibili. Ideo ego pono septimam conclusionem: quod sic, quia quantumcumque patitur, ipse patitur ab aliquo ente, et omne ens est intelligibile. Ergo patitur ab intelligibili."

7. cf. *QDA* III. 1, 69–70, "because it receives intellections and intellectual dispositions, the intellect, like sense, is a passive power [quod intellectus sic et sensus est virtus passiva quia recipit intellectiones et habitus intellectualies]."

8. *QDA* III. 11, 68–73. One of the other ways in which the intellect is an active power is as the soul and form of the body. cf. *QDA* III. 3, 80–82; 7, 49–50.

9. *QDA* III. 1, 107–108: "Item necesse est concedere quod intellectus se habeat active in componendo, dividendo, syllogisando, et distinguendo."

10. *QDA* III. 7, 40: "aliquid enim esse actus vel in actu dicitur multipliciter."

11. This position is contrary to other accounts of abstraction, such as that of Aquinas, in which the intellect is active on the phantasms and passive in receiving the intelligible species that results. For example, *Summa theologiae* 1.79.3: "Nihil autem reducitur de potentia in actum, nisi per aliquod ens actu, sicut sensus fit in actu per sensibile in actu. Oportebat igitur ponere aliquam virtutem ex parte intellectus, quae faceret intelligibilia in actu, per abstractionem specierum a conditionibus materialibus. Et haec est necessitas ponendi intellectum agentem." Latin text taken from: Thomas Aquinas, *Summa Theologiae* (New York: McGraw Hill, 1964).

12. Buridan argues, following Ockham, that sensible information is sufficiently indifferent to several alike particulars that it can represent several like individuals. For example, Buridan states, "Alexander said that an extended power is indeed carried to its object in a universal way, just like the horse's appetite. For the thirsty horse desires water, and not determinately this water or that water, but indifferently any water at all. Therefore, it drinks whatever water it finds" (*QDA* III. 3, 161–165). [Ad quartam rationem dixisset Alexander quod virtus extensa bene fertur in obiectum suum modo universali, sicut appetites ipsius equi. Equus enim sitiens appetit aquam, et non determinate hanc vel illam, sed quamlibet indifferener appetit. Ideo quamcumque invenit, eam bibet.] The implication is simple, the horse cognizes only sensibly, not intellectually, but it can determine indifferently many particulars of the same kind, water in this example. Sensible apprehension can be sufficiently indifferent to particularity to allow for some universal application. This is the so-called 'argument from indifference.' Cf. Klima, *John Buridan*, 70. The question is, does uniformity of indifferent sensible information entail universality of signification? This question will be discussed later.

13. Buridan gives several arguments to substantiate the intellect's power to cognize singularly. For example, the proposition 'Socrates is a man' contains both a singular and a common term, Socrates and man, and the truth of such a proposition can only be determined by a power cognizant of the singular, the universal and the copula. This is the intellect (*QDA* III. 8, 180–190).

14. *QDA*, III. 8, 282–285: "Quamvis ergo sensus exterior cognoscat Sortem vel albedinem vel album, tamen hoc non est nisi secundum speciem confuse repraesentatem cum substantia et albedine et magnitudine et situ secundum quem apparet in prospectu cognoscentis."

15. *QDA*, III. 8, 357–361: "dico quod cum intellectus a phantasmate recipit speciem vel intellectionem Sortis cum tali confusione magnitudinis et situs, facientem apparere rem per modum existentis in prospectu cognoscentis, intellectus intelligit illum modo singulari." One can see hear that the distinctive confusion of information received from the senses renders the content of the concept singular. The confusion of the information is what Buridan often emphasizes. It is the particular combination of color, size, shape, place, all together that makes the perception singular, and thus the concept singular. Cf. John Buridan, *In Metaphysicen Aristotelis questiones* (Paris, 1518. Repr. Frankfurt am Main, 1964), lb. VII, q. 20:

"Similiter etiam in somnio bene res concipimus singulariter quia per modum existentium in conspectu nostro: sed sepeilli conceptus sunt ficti: quia non habent in re extra convenientem correspondentiam non est enim inconveniens quid sint conceptus singulares ficti sicut et communes" (hereafter *QM*).

16. Peter King, in his exposition of Buridan's theory of abstraction, fails to see the importance of this first stage in the formation of substantial concepts, so only mentions it in passing. Cf. Peter King, "John Buridan's Solution to the Problem of Universals," in *The Metaphysics and Natural Philosophy of John Buridan*, ed. J. M. M. H. Thijssen and Jack Zupko (Leiden: Brill, 2001), 15.

17. *QDA* lb. I, q. 5, pp. 207–208: "Secundus modus est quod sensus primo percipit simul confuse substantiam et accidens, sed postea intellectus, qui est virtus superior, ponit differentiam inter substantiam et accidens. Unde, si video aliquem nunc esse album et postea video esse nigrum, et cum hoc percipio quod ipse manet idem, ego venio in cognitionem qua cognosco hoc esse aliud ab albedine et similiter aliud a nigredine. Et sic, quamvis primo apprehendantur mediante sensu substantia et accidens confuse, tamen tali cognitione sensitive praecedente, intellectus, qui est virtus superior, potest venire in cognitionem determinatam ipsius substantiae." Translation taken from, Gyula Klima, "John Buridan on the Acquisition of Simple Substantial Concepts," in *John Buridan and Beyond*, ed. Russel L. Friedman and Sten Ebbesen (Copenhagen, The Royal Danish Academy of Sciences and Letters, 2004), 17–32, 28.

18. This point is very important in Buridan's refutation of skeptical arguments proposed during his time and in allowing him to avoid the problems that later the British empiricists fall into. Cf. Klima, "John Buridan on the Acquisition of Simple Substantial Concepts."

19. QiP, lib. I, q. 4, f. 5rb–va: "Tertio modo, abstractive; ut quia habeo primo conceptum confuse et simul repraesentantem et substantiam et accidens, ut cum percipio album—non enim solam albedinem video, sed album. Et si postea percipio idem moveri et mutari de albo in nigrum, iudico hoc esse aliud ab albedine, et tunc intellectus naturaliter habet virtutem dividendi illam confusionem, et intelligendi substantiam abstractive ab accidente, et accidens abstractive a substantia, et potest utriusque formare simplicem conceptum, et sic etiam abstrahendo fit conceptus universalis ex conceptu singulari, sicut debet videri in tertio De Anima, et septimo Metaphysicae." Translation taken from Klima, 'Buridan on the Acquisition of Simple Substantial Concepts,' note 19.

20. This fact is a rejection of the British empiricist account of substantial concepts as always a complex of simple sensible concepts. cf. Klima, *John Buridan*, 89–96.

21. It is clear from this reconstruction that this is not merely a filtration account of abstraction akin to Berkeley, as Zupko tentatively suggests in his work. For Buridan, the intellect grasps the substance apart from accidents. It is not just the pulling away of features, but the pulling out of what is permanent in all the perceptions, the substance. Cf. Zupko, *John Buridan's Philosophy of Mind*, 737–738.

22. Klima, *John Buridan*, 119.

23. *QDA* III. 8, 260–266. "quod cum species (et similitude) Sortis fuerit apud intellectum et fuerit abstracta a speciebus extraneorum, illa non magis erit repraesentatio Sortis quam Platonis et aliorum hominum; nec intellectus per eam magis intelligit Sortem quam alios homines. Immo sic per eam omnes homines indifferenter intelligent uno conceptu, scilicet a quo sumitur hoc nomen 'homo.' Et hoc est intelligere universaliter."

24. *QDA* III. 8, 241–250; *QiP* lb. I, q. 7.

25. *QM* VII. q. 17, "Dicendum est quod individua eiusdem speciei ut Sortes et Plato differunt substantialiter, scilicet per suas substantias tam per formas quam per materias, ex eo quod nec forma Sortis est forma Platonis, nec materia Sortis est materia Platonis. Sed tamen istam diversitatem non possumus iudicare nisi per differentiam extraneorum propter predictam causam."

26. On the reasons for this natural similarity, Buridan states, "Tunc accipimus quod res extra animam singulariter existentes de eadem specie vel de eodem genere habent ex natura sui similitudinem seu convenientiam essentialem maiorem quam illae quae sunt diversarum specierum vel diversorum generum" (*QDA* III. 8, 196–198). What accounts for this greater likeness and agreement among individuals of the same species? He gives three reasons for this greater likeness. First, the accidents in them agree naturally in their essences. Second, they come from the same or similar causes. Third, they belong to the same grade in the order of beings, or grades closer to one another (*QDA* III. 8, 232–238). Zupko interprets this likeness as nothing more than a kind of 'family resemblance.' (cf. Zupko, "Commentary on Q. III. 8.11," in *John Buridan's Philosophy of Mind*, 527).

27. *QM* VII. q. 17, rep. "Aliter distinguuntur Sortes et Plato quam nos possumus percipe eorum distinctionem, quia substantialiter distinguuntur etiam, circumscripta distinctione accidentium, sed nos non possumus distinctionem illam percipere nisi ex distinctione accidentium per quam tamen distinctionem accidentium nos bene concludimus quod Sortes et Plato substantialiter distinguuntur."

28. Cf. Claude Panaccio, *Ockham on Concepts* (Burlington, Vt.: Ashgate, 2004) 23–27, 127–129.

29. Gyula Klima, 'Is Ockham Off the Hook?' http://www.fordham.edu/gsas/phil/klima/FILES/Toronto.pdf

30. *QDA* III. 1, 119–121: "Ideo intelligibile et intellectus non referuntur ad invicem universaliter sicut activum et passivum, sed sicut repraesentabile et cui potest fieri repraesentatio."

31. *QDA* III. 8, 221–223: "res intelliguntur non propter hoc quod ipsae sint in intellectu, sed quia species earum, quae sunt similitudines repraesentivae earum, sunt in intellectu."

32. Buridan holds that the information content of simple substantial concepts is essentially the same content that the sensible powers of the soul transmit. The intellect is passive in its reception of information from the senses and only active in the processing of this information. So, again here concepts are indifferent to many particulars because their information content is essentially phenomenal, not an abstraction of a common nature.

33. Klima, *John Buridan*, 265.

34. *QDA* III. 8, 251–258 (emphasis mine): "Postea ego iterum suppono quod si sint aliqua ad invicem similia, quidquid est simile uni illorum, in eo in quo sunt duo in invicem similia, ipsum est simile unicuique illorum. Verbi gratia, si A, B, et C sint similia secundum albedinem quia sunt alba, sicut D est simili ipsi A, oportet quod sit consimili ipsi B et C. Ideo consequitur ex quo repraesentatio fit per similitudinem quod illud quod erat repraesentativum unius erit indifferenter repraesentativum aliorum."

35. Cf. John Buridan, *Summulae de Dialectica* (New Haven: Yale University Press, 2001), 2.1.3.

36. Klima, *John Buridan*, 265.

Linguistic Apprehension as Incidental Sensation in Thomas Aquinas

Daniel D. De Haan

Abstract: In this paper I will delineate the psychological operations and faculties required for linguistic apprehension within a Thomistic psychology. This will require first identifying the proper object of linguistic apprehension, which will then allow me to specify the distinct operations and faculties necessary for linguistic apprehension. I will argue that the semantic value of any linguistic term is a type of incidental sensible and that its cognitive apprehension is a type of incidental sensation. Hence, the faculties necessary for the apprehension of any linguistic term's semantic value will be the cogitative power and the intellect. The cogitative power, because it is the faculty of particular intentions, and the intellect, because it is the faculty of universal intentions.

Thomas Aquinas rarely treats at length philosophical problems on the relationship between thought and language.[1] But the very little he does say has generated a large body of literature from his commentators, especially due to the last century's so-called "linguistic-turn." Most of this literature treats such philosophical problems as how we are able to form sentences that express our thoughts,[2] how terms are able to supposit for things,[3] whether thought and language have intentionality,[4] whether linguistic terms signify thoughts or things,[5] and to what extent thought in itself is a "mental language" or has any "structural" parallels to semantics and syntax, i.e., is there some mentalese?[6] Within all this literature, however, I have not been able to find any extended discussion on the role of the cogitative power (*vis cogitativa*) in relation to language and thought.[7] Similarly, I have not been able to find any sustained treatment that addresses which cognitive faculties must be operative for such commonplace achievements as grasping the meaning of a friends' utterance or understanding words on a page.[8]

In this paper I will attempt to delineate the psychological operations and faculties required for linguistic apprehension within a Thomistic philosophical anthropology. This will require first identifying the proper object of linguistic apprehension, which will then allow me to specify the distinct operations and faculties necessary for linguistic apprehension.[9] I will argue that the semantic value of any linguistic term is a type of incidental sensible and that its cognitive apprehension is a type of incidental sensation. If this is true it entails that the faculties necessary for the apprehension of any linguistic term's semantic value will be the cogitative power and the intellect: the cogitative power because it is the faculty of particular intentions, and the intellect as the faculty of universal intentions.[10] I will note here at the beginning that the aims of this paper are primarily philosophical; however, I believe that the theses of this paper are not only consistent with the texts of Aquinas, but also provide the most plausible exegesis of the relevant Thomistic texts.

I. Linguistic-use Is a Property of the Human Person

Before taking up the central problem I must first distance this paper's interpretation of language-use from a number of problems and confusions other interpretations seem to have. It is important to note that while I agree with many Thomists who hold that language-use seems to be a distinctive feature of human beings, nevertheless I do not agree with the common presentation that language-use *only* reveals something significant to us about the intellect. As the extended treatments of Etienne Gilson, David Braine, Alasdair MacIntyre[11] and many others make clear, if language-use is distinctive of man, then it must reveal something about the *whole* human person, i.e., of his rational animality.[12]

It will be the contention of this paper that we cannot develop an adequate Thomistic account of the psychology of language-use without accounting for the linguistic functions performed by the inner senses, especially the cogitative power. Unfortunately, many interpretations tend to exaggerate the role of the intellect in language-use, which has resulted in a kind of bifurcation that is altogether foreign to Thomistic psychology.[13] This dualism is found in interpretations that segregate language-use to the intellect, which in turn entails that the sense faculties and their operations become irrelevant to what is internal to language-use, namely, semantics. Two difficulties emerge from this position, and I believe we can better understand them both if we look to the origins of this interpretation.

The source of this problem seems to rests in a misinterpretation of what exactly constitutes language-use by human persons *as* rational animals.[14] As is well known, Thomas Aquinas held that rationality, which is seated in man's intellect,[15] is the principle that differentiates man from other animals;[16] and since many philosophers today tend to identify language-use as the preeminent manifestation of this principle of rationality, the natural inference *seems* to be that we should place language-use solely within the domain of man's highest faculty, viz., the intellect.[17] Despite the popularity of this position the facts of language and a number of texts in Aquinas force us—both philosophically and exegetically—to think otherwise. To begin with, language-use cannot be a feature of the intellect alone for the simple reason that language necessarily consists in a material component. Now the intellect, according to Thomas Aquinas, is immaterial,[18] and this is because its proper object is a universal, immaterial intelligibility—which specifies its *per se* operations and consequently the ontological character of the power itself.[19] So even though this intelligibility is an abstracted quiddity found within material things,[20] *as* intellectually understood, it exists as an immaterial intentional being.

No one doubts that such universals are inextricable to the many predications used in forming sentences; it is quite clear that without universals man would be unable to have language. However, a word, i.e., a linguistic term, is not itself a strictly immaterial being like a universal conceived by the intellect. All linguistic terms are written or spoken publically or imaged privately—like, for instance, when I subvocalize or speak to myself. In other words, all linguistic terms must be in part a kind of visible, audible, or tactile sensible. Indeed, Aristotle tells us as much, he says that: "Voice is a certain sound of an animate being." And, "A noun is a vocal sound which is significant by convention."[21] Clearly these sensible media, whether spoken or written, are neither universal nor strictly immaterial. Considering these facts alone it is difficult to understand why so many Thomists are inclined to say something so very Cartesian. As putative as it might be to some philosophers that language-use entails the intellect, and is therefore in some sense immaterial, it should be just as obvious that language-use is always cast and expressed within various written or spoken sensibles, which are material things.[22] These are the facts which Gilson calls the "philosophical constants of language."

Now however problematic this latter difficulty might be, I think a second difficulty entirely undermines the philosophical plausibility of this line of interpretation. As we have mentioned, this position entails a kind of dualism because it attributes semantic apprehension exclusively to the intellect, and places the apprehension of linguistic expressions as visual, audible, and tactile sensibles entirely on the side of sensation. Now if the intellect alone is semantically involved, this entails that semantics are intrinsically and exclusively intellectual. But since the intellect is only directly concerned with abstracted universals, we are then forced to eliminate from semantics all meanings concerned with circumstantial singular things and events which are here and now. Hence, all singular or particular meanings become inherently impossible on this account of language-use. Clearly the consequences of this thesis are unacceptable, but not only are they philosophically untenable, they are completely inconsistent with Aquinas's own doctrine.

We only need to examine one text from the *Summa Theologiae* to confirm this exegetical point. In Ia.86.1, the first objection presents an argument which denies the thesis that our intellect only cognizes universals. The argument is based on the fact that we are clearly able to cognize and form the proposition "Socrates is a man." And since the term "Socrates" is singular, the intellect must be able to cognize the singular.[23] Aquinas's reply to this objection is assimilated into the body of the article's response; however, we need not consider his whole response since the most pertinent part for our purposes comes at the very end of the body.

Contrary to the objection, Aquinas maintains the thesis that the intellect only directly cognizes the universal, but adds the qualification that the intellect can indirectly cognize the singular in the phantasm. And it is in this indirect way that we are able to form the proposition "Socrates is a man."[24] But what does Aquinas mean here when he says that it is through cognition of the singular *as* by a phantasm that we are able to form a proposition with the singular term "Socrates" as its subject? Aquinas's reply to the second objection will provide us with a more complete answer to this question.

The second objection is similar to the first in that it tries to establish that the intellect does cognizes singulars because we do in fact form propositions with singular terms. The argument notes that the practical intellect is ordered towards action, and since action is singular, the intellect must therefore be able to cognize the singular. Aquinas contends that a singular conclusion cannot be drawn from a universal proposition without the medium of a singular proposition. But the latter, he qualifies, can only be formed by a particular apprehension. This particular apprehension is an operation which he attributes to the sensitive part of man. He then cites Aristotle's *de Anima* III. 11, in support of his answer.[25]

I believe Aquinas's two responses reveal that the objectors have made the same mistake which we considered before, namely, that of equating semantics use exclusively with the intellect and so making all meaning a proper object of the intellect. My interpretation to the contrary hinges in part on what Aquinas means by phantasms and the particular apprehension of the sensitive part.

According to Aquinas, following Avicenna and Averroes, phantasms are the particular cognitive items formed by the higher internal senses,[26] i.e., by the internal sensorium, in contrast to the external sensorium, which does not form phantasms. The external sensorium includes the five external senses along with the common sense faculty (*sensus communis*). The internal sensorium, for Aquinas, includes the imagination, the cogitative power and memory.[27] So which of the faculties of the internal sensorium does Aquinas have in mind when he makes reference to the phantasms that make possible our ability to form propositions with singular terms?

I think it is quite clear that when the *propositional term* "Socrates" is formed, we are not dealing with some kind of image formed by the imagination. One does not form an eidetic image or picture in their imagination for the subject of the proposition, and then form in their intellect the concept "man" for the predicate. The composition of the latter elements could only produce some sort of chimerical half-image half-conceptual proposition. As bizarre as that mental item sounds, I believe this is one of two positions entailed by the dualist interpretation introduced above.

Since the imagination has been eliminated as a viable option, it remains for us to discern whether the phantasms that are formed to serve as singular terms in propositions are formed in the memory or the cogitative power. Aside from the fact that the proper object of memory, viz., the intention of pastness, is irrelevant to at least the term "Socrates," the memory is itself identified by Aquinas as the retentive faculty of the cogitative power's apprehension.[28] So we are left with the cogitative power as the only viable faculty to fulfill this role.

When Aquinas states in his reply to the second objection that the singular proposition is formed by the particular apprehension of a faculty found in the sensitive part of the soul, we should understand this as a clear reference to the cogitative power. But if there was any doubt in the matter, Aquinas makes this connection explicit in his commentary on the *de Anima* passage, which was cited in his reply to the second objection, and also in such parallel passages as the commentary on the *Sentences* IV, d. 50, q. 1, a. 3, *On Truth* 10.5 and the commentary on *Nicomachean Ethics* VI. lt. 1, 7, and 9.[29]

This is significant because it also reveals that Aquinas's account of practical reason requires that there be an inner sense faculty, which he refers to as the "cogitative faculty," that is able to form singular terms and propositions. More germane to our own concerns is that it reveals that semantic notions are not restricted to the intellect alone but are also to be found in the cogitative faculty's formation of singular terms and propositions.

II. Three Senses of Verbum in Aquinas

Now that we have sufficiently cleared away a number of mistaken interpretations about the intellect's exclusive claim to semantic apprehension and expression, we can proceed to the primary aim of this paper. This task has been made easier now that I have eliminated a predominant misinterpretation and confusion surrounding the problem of linguistic apprehension and its concomitant counterpart in linguistic expression. In the next section I will attempt to make clear what the proper object of linguistic apprehension is.

It will be instructive to begin with an examination of what Aquinas has to say about words before we attempt to formulate our own account of the proper object of linguistic apprehension. Aquinas treats of the different senses of the term "word" (*verbum*) in a number of texts; overall his analysis consistently identifies three proper senses of *verbum*.[30]

1. Word of the Heart (*verbum cordis*)[31]
2. Interior Word; image of voice the likeness of the vocal word (*verbum interius; verbum . . . quod habet imaginem vocis verbum speciei vocis*)
3. Vocal Word (*verbum vocis*)

The "word of the heart" is also often identified by Aquinas as the concept, ratio, or intention formed by the intellect.[32] It is the term of the intellect's operation and is described as that by which (*quo*) and as that in which (*in quo*) the extramental thing (*res quae sunt extra animam*) is understood.[33] The "interior word" is described as being an image of the "vocal word." This is the word or audible image, formed by the imagination when we speak to ourselves; it is "the interior language, or interior word, that Thomas holds as the model according to which we think aloud."[34]

Finally, there is the "vocal word" which is spoken out loud in ordinary meaningful human utterances. This "vocal word," as well as the "interior word" of the imagination, signifies the concepts or words of the intellect, through which we grasp things.[35] In addition to this threefold distinction of *verbum*, we should also note that in his commentary on Aristotle's *De Interpretatione* Aquinas remarks that words have three modes of existence, one in the conceptions of the intellect, another in vocal utterances, and a third as written.[36]

Based on these texts we can see that Aquinas has distinguished four different kinds of words; that each word is proper to a different cognitive faculty; and that there is a hierarchy or proper order amongst these words. The "word of the heart" is proper to the intellect; the "interior word" is proper to the imagination; the "vocal word" is proper to voice for expression[37] but, in part, to the auditory faculty for apprehension; and the "written word" is proper to vision (or tactility, in the case of Braille).

Concerning the hierarchy of words, the "word of the heart" is the primary instance of *verbum*, which all other senses of *verbum* signify. It is this sense of *verbum* that is intrinsically meaningful in its intentional content, and is therefore necessarily required as the principle by which all other *verbum* are able to carry any semantic value.[38] Also, the "word of the heart" is the only sense of *verbum* that is properly used in theological discussions concerning the nature of God.[39] The other senses of *verbum* can only be used metaphorically in God-talk; this is because, as Aquinas notes, the "word of the heart" is the only sense that consists in the intellect alone.[40] That is to say, the other senses of *verbum* are all intrinsically are bound up with matter (*as* image, sound, written, and *hic et nunc*) and cannot properly signify the immaterial perfections of the transcendent deity.[41]

It is these latter derivative senses of *verbum* that will be the focus of the remainder of this paper. The word as spoken (publically or privately in images) and as written is what I shall call a "linguistic term." A "linguistic term" is any conventional sound (e.g., phonemes), visible symbol (e.g., graphemes), or tactile patterns (e.g., Braille) that, by human convention and use, contains or is imbedded with a semantic value.[42] Thematized hylomorphically, a linguistic term consists of a formal component, viz., a semantic value, and a material component, viz., some sensible media.[43]

III. The Proper Object of Linguistic Apprehension

This account of linguistic terms is sufficient to provide us with at least a quasi-proper object. Thus far we have established that the proper object of linguistic apprehension is a linguistic term, which is a material sensible informed by a semantic value. One should recognize immediately that there are a number of problems with this quasi-proper object of language. But it is these very difficulties which I believe illuminate for us a salient feature of language, which has been recognized by not a few philosophers and linguists. Gilson quotes one linguist who nicely captures for us the precise difficulty there is in attempting to ascribe to language a single proper object, operation, and faculty.

"Physiologically, speech is an overlaid function, or to be more precise, a group of overlaid functions. It gets what service it can out of organs and functions, nervous and muscular, that have come into being and are maintained for very different ends than its own." The appropriate function of teeth is to masticate, that of the palate is to taste; yet language superimposes on their natural functions that of contributing to the articulation of speech. One could truly say that a transcendent power "uses" the body for ends of a transcendent order akin to itself.[44]

This is not only true of language's ability to use organs and psychological faculties for its own ends, but of sensible media as well.[45] Language is able to "enrich" sensibles, i.e., material qualities which are natively semantic-less, with a fecundity of meaning.[46]

It is for this reason that there cannot be a proper object, operation, or faculty for the psychological apprehension and expression of language. Herein also resides the root of the confusion had by those philosophers that mistakenly place linguistic-use, notably semantic apprehension, entirely within the domain of the intellect. Language-use is a polyvalent ability that utilizes in concert material things, organs, and faculties, i.e., realities which have their own proper ends, and it uses all of them for its own linguistic ends. In other words, what we will have to look for is not a single proper object, operation and cognitive faculty, but a polymorphic object that is apprehended by the concurrent operations of various faculties for a synergic linguistic end, which is not to say a *sui generis* end. This also means that various faculties might have in common that their proper objects are often found in and through the apprehension of linguistic terms.

We are now in a position to begin delineating the operations and faculties necessary for linguistic apprehension. Since all cognition begins with the senses[47] we must begin our account of linguistic apprehension by explicating the sensible characteristics of linguistic terms before we can treat of their semantic values.

IV. Linguistic-terms as Essential and Incidental Sensibles

Aquinas's paradigmatic division of sensibles is threefold.[48] There are two kinds of sensibles which are sensed essentially (*per se*) and a third kind that is only said to be sensed accidentally (*per accidens*). The two sensibles that are sensed essentially are divided into the proper and common sensibles. Proper sensibles are uniquely sensed by a single external sense faculty, and are therefore *proper* to it alone. Common sensibles are essentially sensed, but are not exclusively apprehended by any one external sense faculty; rather they are able to be cognized by a number of different external senses.[49] For example, motion is sensed by vision, auditory, and tactile powers, hence, motion is a common sensible. Color, on the other hand, is not apprehended by any other sense faculty, and is therefore proper to vision alone.[50] Lists of proper sensibles typically include color, sound, odor, flavor, and tactile qualities (like thermals, textures, density, rarity, etc.). Aquinas's examples of common sensibles often include number, motion/rest, dimension, and shape.[51]

The proper sensibles common to most linguistic terms would be colors, sounds, and tactile sensibles, which are the proper objects of vision, auditory, and tactile faculties. We should not fail to note that each of these linguistic terms' proper sensible is also going to be inextricably constituted by some common sensible, like dimension, shape or number. Nevertheless, what is relevant to this paper are proper sensibles for they are able to specify distinct cognitive operations and faculties, whereas common sensibles by definition do not.

There should be nothing surprising in this analysis of the putative fact that linguistic terms are in part some kind of sensible, most likely a visible, audible, or a tactile quality. It seems that it is only overlooked because these sensibles are not the most salient aspect of our unified cognition of linguistic meaning as apprehended in conversation, reading, and writing. In other words, even though these sensibles provide the media that make linguistic communication possible, nevertheless, our conscious orientation is directed to the semantic value of linguistic terms and not to their distinctive characteristics *as* sensibles. This latter insight brings us to our next point.

Strictly speaking, sensibles are meaningless, which raises the question: how are we able to perform the ubiquitous operations of linguistic apprehension and expression through sensation if sensibles are in themselves entirely meaningless, and hence without any essential semantic value of themselves? Clearly linguistic apprehension is concurrent with sensation, but sensibles *as such* are devoid of any semantic value. What is it in material realities that admit of a semantic value and how is this apprehended through sensation?

V. Linguistic-terms as Incidental Sensibles

In order to answer these questions we will have to examine a third kind of sensible, namely, incidental sensibles. Aquinas gives us two conditions for something to be classified as an incidental sensibles. First, an incidental sensible must be accidentally connected with an essential sensible. For example, this man might be white, that dog might stink, this frying pan might be hot, and that moving object is alive. There is nothing intrinsic to sensibles like white, stinky odors, or heat that they be connected with cognoscible realities like man, dog, frying pan, or living concrete particulars. But it is the case that in *these* instances such cognoscibles are connected to *these* sensibles as concurrent with *these* sensations, and are thus incidental sensibles. The second condition is that the incidental sensible must be apprehended by the same cognitive agent that is sensing. Without this condition there would be no reason for saying that some cognoscible is also sensed incidentally.[52]

A key feature of incidental sensibles, strictly speaking, is that no external sense faculty can cognitively apprehend incidental sensibles. In other words, the external senses are unable to cognitively receive incidental sensibles, which is not to say that such sensibles are not received by the external senses at all. Aquinas makes this qualification to preclude a potential ambiguity in the term incidental sensible. Without this qualification, one could regard a sweet flavor as an incidental sensible to a colored red thing. To clarify the proper extension of the term Thomas qualifies that while in a broader sense it is true that redness is incidental to any flavor *qua* flavor, nevertheless, the salient feature of being an incidental sensible in the strict sense is that they are not *per se* sensed by any external sense faculty at all. Hence, even though red and sweet are incidental to each other, both color and flavor are *per se* sensibles in their own right.[53]

What the notion of incidental sensible reveals is that there are other cognoscible features of things in reality that are simultaneously apprehended through the essential sensibles of external sensation, but are not themselves apprehended by any external sense faculty. But if incidental sensibles are not cognized by any external sense faculty, are they cognized by some internal sense or are they apprehended by some non-sensory cognitive faculty? Further, and more importantly, what are these incidental sensibles essentially in themselves?

Answering the latter question first will provide us with a proper object for the former. Aquinas tells us that these incidental sensibles are in themselves essentially cognoscible realities, even though they are by definition accidental to sensibles *qua* sensibles. Following Avicenna, Aquinas calls these cognoscible realities *intentions*, as distinct from sensibles or sensible forms.[54] Cognoscibles like *this* man and man, Socrates, *this* beast and beast, *this tree* and tree, and living are all different instances of cognoscible intentions found in reality that are not sensibles apprehended by the external senses.[55] These cognoscible intentions also admit of a further division between those that are of the singular and particular circumstances and those that are abstracted from the here and now and are universal. It is this latter division between particular and universal intentions that Aquinas employs to specify two different faculties necessary for their apprehension. Aquinas asserts that universal intentions are apprehended and formed by the intellect, whose proper object is universal cognoscibles. The particular intentions are apprehended and formed by man's inner sense faculty, which, as we said above, Aquinas calls the cogitative power (*vis cogitativa*),[56] passive intellect (*intellectus passivus*),[57] or particular reason (*ratio particularis*),[58] and these particular intentions are the proper object of the cogitative power.[59]

VI. Summation

At this point it will be instructive to draw together and synthesize what this paper's three distinct lines of inquiry have revealed. At the beginning of this paper it was shown both philosophically and exegetically that semantic apprehension is not exclusive to the intellect, because there are putative instances of singular meanings that are apprehended and formed by the cogitative. Our explication of the different senses of *verbum* within Aquinas clarified the reason for the intentional primacy of the "word of the heart" over all other senses of *verbum*. In addition, this latter analysis from the second part provided the third part with a philosophically tenable quasi-proper object of linguistic apprehension, what I have called a "linguistic term." This third analysis revealed that linguistic terms are a polymorphous object composed of a formal semantic component and a material sensible component. In seeking to understand how these polymorphous linguistic terms can be apprehended psychologically, it has been helpful to analyze them in light of Aquinas's threefold division of proper, common, and incidental sensibles. Finally, our consideration of incidental sensibles has brought us back to the proper objects of the intellect and cogitative, namely, universal and particular intentions, respectively. This latter point has only shown further evidence that semantic values are not inherently intellectual, but are also grasped by the cogitative, which is a sense faculty.

VII. Concluding Remarks:
The *Verbum Cogitativae* and Linguistic Apprehension as *Incidental Sensation*

In light of the foregoing it should be clear that the singular and universal semantic values from the first section map nicely onto what, in the context of incidental sensation, Aquinas calls universal and particular intentions. Perhaps for the sake of clarity we should make the qualification that intentions should only be considered to have a semantic value if they are linguistically apprehended or expressed.[60] But where does the *verbum cordis*, that is, the "word of the heart" fit within this picture? I think a complete analysis of the Thomistic texts reveals that the *verbum cordis* is synonymous with the intellect's formation of universal intentions or concepts and universal propositions. What is different now, however, is that we have discovered another type of intention that is not strictly universal; a type of intention and singular semantic value that is grasped and formed in the cogitative, not the intellect. What relationship do these cogitative particular intentions and singular propositions have to the *verbum cordis*? Although I do not have time to argue for this here, I would suggest that we recognize another analogical and derivative sense of the *verbum cordis* that also applies beyond the intellect to the particular intentions formed by the cogitative, that is, a *verbum cogitativae* like the *verbum vocis*.[61]

Before concluding, one final point must be made concerning the particular and universal intentions apprehended by the cogitative and intellect. The apprehension of these intentions can only be designated as incidental sensation of incidental sensibles when these intentions are cognized by the cogitative or intellect simultaneously with acts of sensation of some one or more external senses.[62] But in the case of our apprehension of linguistic terms it seems there is always a simultaneous apprehension of a material and formal component. Hence, if semantic values are never apprehended independently of some material component, e.g., some sound or visual character, then linguistic terms are always apprehended as incidental sensibles. And it seems to me that if this is not globally the case, it is at least normative to linguistic apprehension.

In sum, I believe that this paper has sufficiently clarified a number of points about language-use and shown that, within a Thomistic psychology, semantics is not a matter which is exclusive to the intellect, that the cogitative plays an essential role in forming meaningful singular propositions, and finally, that it is philosophically necessary and fruitful to treat linguistic apprehension as a kind of incidental sensation.

Center for Thomistic Studies, University of St. Thomas (Texas)

Notes

A previous version of this paper was presented at the Center for Thomistic Studies Colloquium Series, at the University of St. Thomas, Houston, Texas; the comments that I received during that talk and at the ACPA conference were very helpful. I would like to thank Tony Lisska for his very kind and instructive commentary on this paper, as well as Mark Barker for the many stimulating conversions and correspondence which we have had on the *vis cogitativa* in Thomas Aquinas. This paper would not have been possible without his insightful work on the Angelic Doctor.

1. The *loci classici* seem to be: *Scriptum super libros Sententiarum* (Mandonnet, 2 vols., 1929) (henceforth: *In Sent*) I. d. 27.2.1.; *Quaestiones disputatae de veritate* (Leonine v. 22) (henceforth: *DV*) 4.1 and 2.; *Summa contra gentiles* (Leonine, manual ed., 1934) (henceforth: *SCG*) I. 53 and IV. 11; *Summa theologiae* (Marietti, 1950–1953) (henceforth: *ST*) I. 13.1; 27.1; 34.1; 85.2, ad. 3; I-II. 93.1, ad 2.; *Sentencia libri De anima* (Leonine v. 45,1) (henceforth: *In DA*) II. 8, lt. 18.; *Sentencia libri De sensu et sensato* (Leonine v. 45,2) (henceforth: *In Sensu*) I. c.1.; *Quaestiones quodlibetales* (Marietti, 1956) (henceforth: *Quod*) V. 5.2.; *Expositio libri Peryhermenias* (Marietti, 1964) (henceforth: *In PH*) I and II.; *Lectura super Evangelium S. Ioannis* (Marietti, 1952) (henceforth: *In Ioannis*) c.1, lect. 1.

2. Etienne Gilson, *Linguistics and Philosophy: An Essay on the Philosophical Constants of Language*, trans. John Lyon (Notre Dame, Ind.: University of Notre Dame Press, 1988) (henceforth: *Linguistics and Philosophy*); David Braine, *The Human Person: Animal and Spirit* (Notre Dame, Ind.: University of Notre Dame Press, 1992), c. XI, "The 'Objects' of the Mind in Speaking and Thinking," 398–446 (henceforth: *Human Person*).

3. Gyula Klima, "The Semantic Principles Underlying Saint Thomas Aquinas's Metaphysics of Being," *Medieval Philosophy and Theology* 5 (1996): 87–141 (henceforth: "Semantic Principles of Aquinas").

4. Anthony Kenny "Intentionality: Aquinas and Wittgenstein" in *Thomas Aquinas: Contemporary Philosophical Perspectives* ed. Brian Davies (New York and Oxford: Oxford University Press, 2002), 243–256; David Braine, *Human Person*, 345–479; From *Analytical Thomism: Traditions in Dialogue*, ed. Craig Paterson and Matthew S. Pugh (Burlington, Vt.: Ashgate, 2006), see: Stephen Boulter, "Aquinas and Searle on Singular Thoughts" chapter 4, 59–78; Anthony Lisska, "Medieval Theories of Intentionality: from Aquinas to Brentano and Beyond" in chapter 8, 147–170; and John C. Cahalan "Wittgenstein as a Gateway to Analytic Thomism" in chapter 10, 195–214.

5. John Haldane "The Life of Signs," *The Review of Metaphysics* 47.3 (1994): 451–470. John O'Callaghan, "The Problem of Language and Mental Representation," *The Review of Metaphysics* 50.3 (1997); *Thomist Realism and the Linguistic Turn: Toward a More Perfect Form of Existence* (Notre Dame, Ind.: University of Notre Dame Press, 2003); Bernard Lonergan, *Verbum: Word and Idea in Aquinas*, ed. David Burrell (Notre Dame, Ind.: University of Notre Dame Press, 1967) (henceforth: *Verbum*), 151–153; Harm Goris, *Free Creatures of an Eternal God: Thomas Aquinas on God's Infallible Foreknowledge and Irresistible Will*, Thomas Instituut Utrecht, 4 (Leuven: Peeters Publishers, 1996), chapter 5: "Psychology: Human Tensed Way of Knowing," 184–212 (henceforth "Tensed Way of Knowing"); Stephen Boulter, "Aquinas and Searle on Singular Thoughts"; Gilson, *Linguistics and Philosophy*; Braine, *Human Person*, X–XII, 345–479; and Klima, "Semantic Principles of Aquinas."

6. Robert Pasnau, "Aquinas on Thought's Linguistic Nature" *The Monist: Analytical Thomism* 80.4 (1997): 558–557; Haldane, "Life of Signs"; Gilson, *Linguistics and Philosophy*; Braine, *Human Person* X–XII, 345–479 (esp. 440–445); Lonergan, *Verbum*.

7. Braine and Goris are exceptions. Both of their accounts, however, are more focused on the imagination and only mention the cogitative power in passing. Nevertheless, I have learned a lot from both of their extensive treatments of language and Thomistic psychology,

and I have made a serious effort to make my account compatible with their work. Currently, I know of only three dissertations written in English on the cogitative power. But there is nothing substantial said about language and psychology in any of these works. Cf. Mark Barker, *The Cogitative Power: Objects and Terminology*, unpublished doctoral dissertation, Houston, University of ST, Thomas Center for Thomistic Studies, 2007; George P. Klubertanz, *The Discursive Power: Sources and Doctrine of the* Vis Cogitativa *According to St. Thomas Aquinas* (St. Louis, Mo.: Modern Schoolman, 1952); Leo A. White, *The Experience of Individual Objects in Aquinas*, Diss. CUA, 1997 (Ann Arbor: UMI [Microforms], 1997. Other treatments of the cogitative power also omit any direct account of its function with regard to language. Cf. Rudolph Allers, "The vis Cogitativa and Evaluation," *The New Scholasticism* 15 (1941): 195–221; Allers, "The Intellectual Cognition of Particulars," *The Thomist* 3.1 (January 1941), 95–163; Deborah Black, "Imagination and Estimation: Arabic Paradigms and Latin Transformations," *Topoi* 19 (2000): 59–75 (henceforth, "Imagination and Estimation"); John Deely, "Animal Intelligence and Concept-Formation," *The Thomist* 35.1 (1971): 43–93; Cornelio Fabro, "Knowledge and Perception in Aristotelico-Thomistic Psychology," *New Scholasticism* 12 (1938): 337–365; T. V. Flynn, "The Cogitative Power," *The Thomist* 16 (1953): 542–563; George P. Klubertanz, "St. Thomas and the Knowledge of the Singular," *New Scholasticism* 26 (1952): 135–166; Anthony Lisska, "A Look at Inner Sense in Aquinas: A Long-Neglected Faculty Psychology," *Proceedings of the American Catholic Philosophical Association* 80 (2006): 1–19; Julien Peghaire, "A Forgotten Sense, The Cogitative According to St. Thomas Aquinas (part I)," *The Modern Schoolman* 20 (1943): 123–140; Peghaire, "A Forgotten Sense, The Cogitative According to St. Thomas Aquinas (part II)," *The Modern Schoolman* 20, (1943): 210–229; Robert Schmidt S.J. "Unifying Sense, Which?" *The New Scholasticism* 57.1 (1983): 1–21; Michael Stock, O.P. "Sense Consciousness According to St. Thomas," *The Thomist* 21 (1958): 415–486; Leo A. White, "The Picture Theory of the Phantasm," *Tópicos: revista de Filosofía* 29 (2005) (Ejemplar dedicado a: Los comentadores árabes y latinos de Aristóteles):131–156; "Why the Cogitative Power?" *Proceedings of the American Catholic Philosophical Association* 72 (1998): 213–227.

8. David Braine in his *Human Person* presents the most extended treatment I have read. Other exceptions are Gilson and Kenny who make some remarks on this problem. Gilson, however, does not specify faculties, and Kenny develops his own doctrine of the imagination and fancy, which fails to properly articulate the points which will be the focus of this essay.

9. This contention assumes the Platonic-Aristotelian principle of faculty of differentiation (PoFD); a principle I cannot defend within this paper. Cf. Plato, *Republic*, V 477c–477e; Aristotle, *de Anima*, I, 1 403a1–20; II, 4. 415a18–21; Thomas Aquinas, *In III Sent.* d. 27.2.4.1ad3; *In DA* I. lt. 1; II. 4. lt. 6; III. lt. 8 n. 711; *ST* I. 77. 3; I-II.23.1; *DQdA*13. For Aquinas's Avicennian innovations and developments on the PoFD, see *DV* 15. 1 and 2.

10. Cf. *DV* 10.5; 15.1; *In DA* II. 6. Lt. 13.

11. Alasdair MacIntyre, *Dependent Rational Animals: Why Human Beings Need the Virtues*, The Paul Carus Lectures (Chicago: Open Court Publishing, 2001).

12. Although it would require a lengthy treatment of its own, it seems to me that linguistic-use is not an aspect of human being's specific difference, but rather is, like risibility, a property of being a rational animal.

13. Notable examples of this interpretation that I believe are guilty of this bifurcation are: Herbert McCabe, *On Aquinas*, ed. Brian Davies (London and New York: Continuum, 2008); and Pasnau, "Aquinas on Thought's Linguistic Nature," esp. n24; Pasnau, "The Turn

Toward Phantasms," in *Thomas Aquinas on Human Nature A Philosophical Study of Summa Theologiae, 1a 75–89* (Cambridge and New York: Cambridge University Press, 2002), 9.4. cf. 272, 284–295, (esp. 293–294); and Boulter, "Aquinas and Searle on Singular Thoughts." Anthony Kenny's numerous but brief treatments on the topic are difficult to distill. At times he seems to make language exclusive to the intellect, however, he also notes the importance of placing thought into a sensory context. Further, he does recognize the role of the imagination in forming mental images when we are "speaking to ourselves," and hence, that phantasms, in Aquinas, are not pictures but very often are words or inner utterances of the imagination. Nevertheless, the latter exercises of the imagination never carry any semantic value for Kenny. Finally, his entire account of language use is primarily introduced and treated in his chapters and discussions on the intellect. (cf. Anthony Kenny, *Aquinas on Mind*, 47–57, 93–99, and esp. 112–113; *Metaphysics of Mind*, 123–139.) We should also note that Kenny's treatment of the cogitative power is marginal at best, and he often attributes operations that are specific to the cogitative power to either the imagination or the intellect. Whatever his precise position is on the latter, he certainly has omitted what is the crucial thesis of this paper, namely, that linguistic apprehension is a kind of incidental sensation. For a sampling of some of Kenny's more extended treatments of these problems see: Anthony Kenny, "Intellect and Imagination in Aquinas" in *Aquinas: A Collection of Critical Essays*, ed. Anthony Kenny (London and Melbourne: Macmillan, 1969; Repr. Notre Dame, Ind.: University of Notre Dame Press, 1976), 274–296. cf. 291–296, Kenny, *Aquinas on Mind*, 36–40, 47–57, esp. 93–99 and 111–117; *The Metaphysics of Mind*, 20–26, 110–139, and 156–158; "Intentionality: Aquinas and Wittgenstein," 249–256.

14. Notable exceptions are David Braine and Alasdair MacInytre, who thematically reiterate similar points throughout their work on language and human persons. See also the work of Etienne Gilson and John O'Callahan.

15. Cf. *DV* 24.3ad1; *ST* I. 79.10.ad2. It is crucial to make this distinction between rationality and the intellect properly speaking, because the failure to do so often results in the kinds of confusions I have indicated. Lonergan also stresses the importance of this point. "Now, just as human intellect is mainly reason, because it operates from sense as a starting-point, so the quiddity known by the human intellect is different in kind from that known by the angelic" *Verbum*, 32. "[T]he pure Thomist theory of intellect is to be sought in the Thomist account of angelic knowledge, and from that account J. Peghaire rightly begins his investigation of Thomist notions of intellect and reason" ibid., 33.

16. Cf. *ST* I. 77.3.

17. "There is, then, a very close relationship between thought and words, between the operation of the intellect and the use of language. But it is important not to overstate this relationship. Aquinas believed that any judgment which can be made can be expressed by a sentence ([*DV*] 2,4). It does not follow from this, nor does Aquinas maintain, that every judgment which is made *is* put into words, either publically or in the privacy of the imagination. . . . The understanding of simples is related to the entertaining of judgments as the use of individual words is related to the construction of sentences," Kenny, *Aquinas on Mind*, 49–50. Kenny's account is far subtler then this quote reveals, however, it is still instructive of his general account of linguistic-use. Linguistic-use does require the inner senses, because, as Kenny asserts, the imagination must provide a sensory-context for reference; nevertheless, semantic apprehension, even of singular terms, is exclusive to the intellect.

18. Cf. *DQdA* 1; *ST*. I. 75.2

19. Cf. *DQdA* 1; *ST*. I. 85. 3. See the excellent article, Carlos Bazán, "The Human Soul: Form and Substance? Thomas Aquinas' Critique of Eclectic Aristotelianism" *AHDLMA* 64 (1997): 95–126.

20. Cf. *ST* I. 84. 7

21. Aristotle, *de Anima* II. 8, 420b8 (trans. Apostle) and *De Interpretatione*, I. 2. 16a20, (trans. Apostle)

22. Braine writes, "Indeed, in the inseparability of sentence and sense, we come upon the most extreme example of the unity of mind and body in an action, here not just the unity of intention and act in intentional action but the unity of understanding and speech in 'understandingly speaking.' And in 'understandingly hearing' we have the most unmistakable and rich example of the unity of the act of 'perceiving as' wherein what is perceived and how it is perceived (that is, not the means of perception but as what it is perceived) cannot be extricated from one another" *Human Person*, 352. Gilson writes, "The duality observed by the linguists in the words of language is but the reflex of that metaphysical duality of human nature and of the paradoxical condition of the human intellect. Man does not think without images. He ought therefore to have a body in order to be able to think. But the other animals have bodies and images; nevertheless, they do not think as man thinks. Seeing that they do not speak, their psychism ought to differ in nature from human psychism" *Linguistics and Philosophy*, 68. Cf. O'Callaghan, *Thomist Realism and the Linguistic Turn*, 297–298.

23. *ST* I. 81. 1, obj. 1: See Aquinas's more extended treatment of the same problem in *DV*. 10.5.

24. *ST* I. 86. 1c. To treat this problem adequately, moreover would actually require a full account of how we are able to have intellectual cognition of singulars. I cannot do that here. For some of the different treatments of this problem see: Cf. Rudolf Allers, "The Intellectual Cognition of Particulars," *The Thomist* 3.1 (January 1941): 95–163; George P. Klubertanz, "St. Thomas and the Knowledge of the Singular"; Francisco L. Peccorini, "Knowledge of the Singular: Aquinas, Suárez and Recent Interpreters," *The Thomist* 38 (1974): 606–655; Stephen Boulter, "Aquinas and Searle on Singular Thoughts," 59–78; Calvin G. Normore, "The Invention of Singular Thought" in *Forming the Mind: Essays on the Internal Senses and the Mind/Body Problem from Avicenna to the Medical Enlightenment* ed. Henrik Lagerlund, Studies in the History of Philosophy of Mind, Vol. 5 (Dordrecht, The Netherlands: Springer, 2007), chap. 6, 109–128. Another article, while not focused on engaging this problem, but nevertheless does so with erudition and brevity, is Klima, "Semantic Principles of Aquinas."

25. *ST* I. 86.1, obj 2. *ST* I. 86.1, ad 2. For Aquinas's comments on this passage from the *de Anima* see: infra n29.

26. 26. *SCG* II. 73. p. 173 (cf. Leonine, 1961. n. 14): ". . . sed a virtutibus in quibus sunt phantasmata, scilicet imaginativa, memorativa et cogitativa . . . ." Cf. *ST* I. 89.5; *In Mem.* III. 15.215-16.226; 16.274-275.

27. Cf. *ST* I. 78.4; *DQdA*. 13. I have taken this distinction between the external and internal sensorium from Anthony Lisska, who is the earliest writer I have come across to make this distinction. However, when I asked him if it was of his coinage he replied that he was not sure of its origins, but suspected that he got it from somewhere else. Cf. Anthony Lisska, "Thomas Aquinas on *Phantasia*: Rooted in But Transcending Aristotle's *De Anima*" in *Aquinas' Sources*, ed. Timothy Smith (South Bend, Ind.: St. Augustine Press, 2001) n27: "One needs here to distinguish the external senses from the internal senses, and the external sensorium from the internal sensorium. The former pair is distinguished by the location of

the sense faculties, while the latter pair is distinguished by the intentional act itself. The faculties of the internal sensorium—imagination, the *vis cogitativa* and the sense memory—all require phantasms."

28. *ST* I. 78. 4.

29. *In DA* III. 10 (434a16) 251.128–133. Also, *DV* 10.5, 309.94–99: Both in his commentary on this *de Anima* text and in *de Veritate*, Aquinas divides practical reason into "universal reason" and "particular reason," which is one of many ways in which Aquinas distinguishes the intellect from the cogitative power. Cf. *DV* 10.5 ad 2, 309.106–110. *In Ethics* VI. lt. 1, n. 1123; lt. 7 nn. 1213–1215; lt. 9, nn. 1247, 1249, 1253, 1255, and 1256. Compare these latter passages with *ST* II-II. 49. 2 and 5.

30. *DV* 4.1, 120.192–207. Aquinas makes the same distinctions in *In Sent.* I. d. 27. 2. 1, and in *ST* I. 34.1.

31. *In Sent.* I. d. 27. 2. 1.

32. Cf. *De Potentia* 8.1 and *SCG* I. 53. It is important to not confuse the terminus of the intellect's operation with its principle, as so many readers of Aquinas are prone to do. Aquinas is very clear on this point; (1) the word of the heart, concept, and intention of the intellect are all distinct from (2) the intelligible species, (*species intelligibilis*) which is the form and principle of the intellect's operation, (3) the intellect itself, and (4) the intellect's operation. The word, concept, and intention are all synonyms for the terminus of the intellect's operation. See: *Quod.* V. 5. 2., which explicitly takes up the question on, "*Utrum verbum cordis sit species intelligibilis.*" Aquinas concludes, "Unde necesse est quod species intelligibilis, quae est principium operationis intellectualis, *differat a verbo cordis*, quod est per operationem intellectus formatum." For an excellent study on this point see John F. Peifer, *The Concept of Thomism* (New York: The Bookman Associates, 1952). Later reprinted as *The Mystery of Knowledge* (New York: Magi Books, 1964) and again in *Modern Writings on Thomism*, ed. John Haldane (Bristol: Thoemmes, 2003).

33. Cf. *ST* I. 85. 2. Also, *In Ioannis*, c. 1, lect. 1 (26).

34. Gilson, *Linguistics and Philosophy*, 74–75. Pasnau holds a different interpretation of this sense of *verbum*. "Before giving voice to one's mental concepts one must formulate a kind of mental image of the utterance; one must mentally pick the very words one will use. This exemplar, this intermediary *verbum*, "is called the inner word that contains an image of the utterance," "Aquinas on Thought's Linguistic Nature," 555–566. In a note he writes, "Aquinas has in mind here the *De anima*'s claim that speech occurs "with some kind of imagination" (II 8, 420b32). (At *ST* 34.1c this connection is made explicit.) Evidently Aquinas does not understand Aristotle's claim in such a way that the inner sense of phantasia or imagination is involved: the operation Aquinas describes seems to be wholly intellectual" ibid. n. 24. Pasnau's interpretation is wrong. The context and examples given in *DV* 4. 1 and *ST* I. 34. 1 make it abundantly clear that Aquinas is referring to the inner sense of phantasia or imagination, and if there was any doubt it is unequivocally clear in, *In Sent.* I. d. 27. 2.1. Further, on Pasnau's interpretation Aquinas's conclusion in *ST* I. 34. 1, that only the word of the heart can be said of God in a non-metaphorical way, would not follow if "the operation Aquinas describes . . . [was] wholly intellectual." I also suspect a *homuncular* fallacy lies hidden within his remark that, "one must mentally pick the very words one will use." But perhaps he is innocently referring to the difficulty we sometimes have with selecting the best way to express a thought. Nevertheless, that is not what Aquinas is primarily referring to; though what he is referring to would be manifested in the latter phenomenon.

35. *In PH* I, lt. 2, 15 [5]. *ST* I. 13.1.

36. *In PH* I, lt. 2, 14 [4].

37. Technically, voice is not a faculty but a species of sound. Cf. *In DA*, II. 8, lt. 18.

38. John Haldane develops this line of argument at length in his, "The Life of Signs." He argues that speech-acts and various other kinds of linguistic terms only become semantically charged by the intentionality of mental states, and the latter, as Haldane shows, must be intrinsically intentional if we are to avoid an infinite regress. At the conclusion Haldane explains the reason how such mental states can be intrinsically meaningful. His answer follows closely Aquinas's account of formal causality in ideogenesis, in particular *SCG* I. 53, which accounts for the isomorphism between thought and reality. I am assuming Haldane's philosophical conclusions for the points being asserted here.

39. Cf. *In Sent.* I. d. 27. 2.1. and *ST* I. 34.1.

40. *In Sent.* I. d. 27. 2.1.

41. Cf. *ST* I. 13. ad. 1. For a comparison of the word in Aquinas's doctrine of God, angels and man see: Harm Goris, "The Angelic Doctor and Angelic Speech: The Development of Thomas Aquinas's Thought on How Angels Communicate," *Medieval Philosophy and Theology* 11 (2003): 87–105; "Theology and Theory of the Word in Aquinas: Understanding Augustine by Innovating Aristotle" in *Aquinas the Augustinian*, ed. Michael Dauphinais, Barry David, and Matthew Levering (Washington, D.C.: Catholic University of America Press, 2007), 62–78.

42. Of course, there are a variety of other forms of communication, even linguistic, through visual, auditory, and tactile mediums (perhaps even gustation and olfaction?). For the sake of brevity, this paper will only discuss language and linguistic terms as written and spoken.

43. It would require a work of its own to argue that language is actually hylomorphic, nevertheless I do believe there is some textual evidence that this is was Aquinas's position. Cf. *In Physics*, I. lt. 1, n. 5 and *In Physics*, II. lt. 5, nn. 183–184; *In Sensu* I. lect. 1.

44. Gilson, *Linguistics and Philosophy*, 47. The citation for the quote is Edward Sapir, *Language* (New York: Harvest Books, 1949 [1921]), 8–9. French translation: *Le langage* (Paris: Payot, 1967), 12.

45. Indeed, Aquinas makes this point explicit in the first chapter of his *In Sensu*, wherein he notes, following Aristotle, that we learn best through the hearing of sounds which can contain voice, i.e., significant intentions, and voice contains knowledge, nevertheless these intentions are themselves accidental to sound and hearing. *In Sensu* I.1.13–14.163–189. Also, *In Sensu* I.1.14.213–215. Also, *In Sensu* I.1.14–15.253–270, *In Sensu* I.1.15.273–303. Cf. *In Meta* I.1.

46. Cf. *ST* II-II.8.1.

47. Cf. *DV* 8.3; *SCG* I. 3, n. 4; II. 37, n. 2; IV. 55, n. 6; *ST* I. 1.9; 12. 12; 17. 1.

48. Cf. *In IV Sent.* d. 49, q. 2, a. 2c; *In DA* II. Lt. 13; and *ST* I. 17. 2.; 78. 3, ad 2.

49. *In DA* II. lt. 13. 118, 418a7–418a10.

50. A lot could be said concerning Aquinas's doctrine of external and internal sense faculties, but this would take us far beyond the scope of this paper. Unfortunately this forces me to present Aquinas's doctrine in a dogmatic fashion rather then defending it philosophically.

See the following articles which represent a sample of some of the best articles on sensation in Aquinas. Yves Simon, "An Essay on Sensation" in *Philosophy of Knowledge: Selected Readings*, ed. Roland Houde and Joseph P. Mullally (Chicago, Philadelphia, New York: J.B. Lippincott Company, 1960); Robert Henle, "The Basis of Philosophical Realism Re-Examined," *New Scholasticism* 56.1 (1982): 1–29; Paul MacDonald, "Direct Realism and Aquinas's Account of Sensory Cognition," *The Thomist* 71 (2007): 348–378; Debrah Black, "Imagination and Estimation"; Michael Stock, "Sense Consciousness According to St. Thomas."

51. *ST* I. 78.3 and *In DA* III. Lt. 1 n. 575: "the common sensibles are not sensed indirectly by any particular sense at all, but are directly sensed by many senses. Therefore the common sensibles cannot be the proper object of any particular sense" (my translation).

52. *In DA* II. 13, 120.164–170.

53. *In DA* II. lt. 13, 120.175–121.181.

54. The term *intentiones* was the Latin translation of Avicenna's term *ma'ānī* found in Avicenna's *De Anima*, IV and in his *Metaphysics of the Shifā'* (esp. I. 5, and V. 1). In Avicenna this notion is used with other terms like quiddity (*māhīyah, quidditas*) to help clarify thing (*shay', res*) which is one of Avicenna's three primordial metaphysical notions (cf. *Metaphysics of the Shifā'* I. 5). Deborah Black writes, "What is emitted vocally signifies what is in the soul, and these are what are called impressions (*āthāran*), whereas what is in the soul signifies the things, and these are what are called *meanings*, that is, the intentions of the soul." See Black, "Imagination and Estimation", n12 (my emphasis).

55. See *ST* I. 78. 4. It is important to note that intention here should not be confused with either intentional being (*esse intentionale*) and immutation which includes all objects and operations of cognition (e.g., images, memories, intentions, intelligible species, concepts, etc. cf. *ST* I. 78. 3 and *In DA* II, lt. 24), or with "intentions" as that which is a willed end (cf. *ST* I-II q. 11. a. 1). There is an underlying analogical similarity but important distinctions—like that between the cognitive and appetitive—must be kept in mind to keep all three meanings precise.

56. For further references to the *vis cogitativa* see: *In Sent* III. d. 26.1.2; *DV* 1.11; 10.5; 15.1 ad 9; *SCG* II. 60; 73; 76; 81.3; *Quaestio Disputata de Anima*, 13.

57. *In IV Sent.* d. 50.1.1.ad3. For further references to the *intellectus passivus*: *SCG.* II. 60 and 73; *ST* I. 79.2.ad.2; *DQdA.* 13; *DSC.* 9.

58. For further references to the *ratio particularis*: *In Sent* II. d. 24.2.1 and 3; IV d. 50.1.1 ad 3; *DV* 2.6; 10.5; 14.1 ad 9; 15.1; *SCG* II. 60; *In Nic. Ethic* VI. lt. 7; lt. 9; *In DA* II. lt. 16; *ST* I. 20.1 ad 1; 19.2 ad 2; 80.2 ad 3; I-II. 51.3.

59. *In DA* II. 13, 120.170–174. *In DA* II. 13, 121.182–183. *In DA* II. 13, 121.191–122.201.

60. This qualification would entail that intentions and semantic values are related asymmetrically. Every semantic value, whether universal or particular, is an intention, but not every intention as such has a semantic value. There also are important distinctions to be made concerning nominal and real definitions, intellectual insight into the meaning of a word (i.e., meaning as use), which signify the quiddities of material things, and then intellectual insight into quiddities.

61. As we have seen, Aquinas does have theological reasons for restricting the prime sense of *verbum* to our inner intellectual conceptions. Aquinas argues that the primary sense of *verbum* should not be attributed to our external words, but to that which has signifies

essentially and is intrinsically meaningful, namely, the preeminent *words* of our mind. What Aquinas wants to preserve is the Trinitarian analogy which employs the *verbum cordis* because it is a universal, immaterial, non-circumstantial expression of intellectual insight. This sense of *verbum cordis* is not diminished by Aquinas's analogical use of *verbum* to signify words spoken and imagined, and thus I see no reason why my suggestion to posit a *verbum cogitativae* should alter the Trinitarian analogy. There are commonalities between the word of the heart to the intention expressed by the cogitative, and these commonalities should be observed even when we are distinguishing them. The term *verbum cogitativae* aptly denotes what is distinctive of the cogitative's involvement in linguistic apprehension and expression.

62. *In DA* II. 13, 121.183–187. In other words, if the intellect forms a universal intention independent of any cognition of a sensible reality, this operation does not count as an incidental sensation. It only counts when the intention apprehended is cognized simultaneously with the sensation of some essential sensible. I might apprehend some particular intention like, "that is a puddle and I should walk around it," without actually expressing this apprehension and judged reaction in any linguistic manner at all. Anscombe's *Intention* is full of examples of this sort, which is not to confuse the fact that I am speaking of a cognitive intentions here, and she is treating appetitive intentions in her work.

Perception, Language,
and Concept Formation in St. Thomas

Alfred Leo White, Ph.D.

Abstract: According to St. Thomas, animals (both rational and non-rational) perceive objects in terms of goal-directed interactions. Repeated interactions give rise to *consuetudo* (translated custom or practice), a habit of sense memory that enables one to act skillfully. The interactive component of perception enables animals and humans to communicate. In humans, these perceptions are instrumental to the formation of concepts pertaining to life in society (such as law and liturgy) as well as to the understanding of human nature. But perception is able to perform this role only because it has been elevated by rational appetite. This elevation occurs in the context of practical reasoning, through which a kind of sortal awareness called "experience" (*experientia* or *experimentum*) is generated. Experience serves as the basis not only for our formation of concepts of things pertaining to life in society and human nature, but of other entities as well. In this way, the perceptual awareness of objects in terms of goal-directed interactions serves as the basis for the formation of all concepts.

Introduction

Whenever he lays out his theory of abstraction, St. Thomas Aquinas speaks of the agent intellect, possible intellect, phantasms, internal senses, material, and immaterial modes of being but never directly links these to speech or other practices. One who reads his works may think that since thoughts are one thing while interactions with one's environment are another, one may philosophically consider the former without the latter. Such an omission, however, would be a harmful mistake. In fact, as I will argue in this paper, when Aquinas says in the *Summa contra gentiles*[1] that custom and instruction are necessary conditions for being able to abstract concepts, he is mindful of how practices are embedded in the phantasms that play an instrumental role in the development of the intellectual virtues. I will argue furthermore that, since Aquinas assigns a central role to communication among human practices, this practice plays a preeminent role in the formation of concepts. Whoever denies these two theses, I will argue, renders

Aquinas's theory of abstraction incapable of giving an account of how one forms concepts of the natures of things as well as form concepts of those realities, such as law and liturgy, that are produced while seeking common goals. On the other hand, one who recognizes the role of practices (especially those related to communication) in abstraction opens the door to a fruitful path of philosophical discovery, one that integrates Aquinas's psychology with his understanding of man as a social being.

This paper consists of four parts. The first examines animals' perceptual awareness of their interactions with other animals, culminating with the examination of how this awareness functions in communicative acts. The second does the same for human perception and communication, this time with a focus on how rational appetite modifies sense perception. The third shows how the perceptual awareness of interactions serves as a kind of proximate matter for knowledge of the natures of things, with a special focus on how the perception of speech brings human nature to light. The fourth part proposes that the display of speech acts is integral to the formation of concepts regarding man's social nature.

Although this paper cites many passages in which the internal senses are mentioned, I do not discuss them at length in these pages. Instead, I mostly focus on perception as a whole. For those times when I do mention particular internal senses, however, the following brief synopsis will prove helpful. According to Aquinas, the five external senses terminate in one internal sense, called the common sense (*sensus communis*). The latter, says Aquinas, is cognizant of both the objects and operations of the five external senses; while another internal sense, called the estimative power (*vis aestimativa*) in non-rational animals and cogitative power (*vis cogitative*) in rational animals, is aware of whatever is beyond the external senses. To these two powers correspond the imagination and memory respectively: two powers that retain species previously apprehended so that the animal, be it rational or non-rational, can apprehend an object even in its absence.[2] As the highest internal sense power, the estimative/cogitative power synthesizes the objects of the other internal senses.[3] Its operation, therefore, corresponds to what a psychologist might call perception. When I speak of perception in this paper, I thus have in mind the operation attributed by Aquinas to the estimative power in brutes and cogitative power in humans.

I. Brute Perception and Its Role in Communication

According to St. Thomas, an animal that perceives an individual presently acting upon its external senses does not regard that object merely in terms of proper and common sensibles. Rather, it perceives through its estimative power what Aquinas calls *intentiones* or *per accidens sensibiles*. He explains what he means by these terms in his commentary on *De anima*, saying that a non-rational animal perceives its object as the principle or terminus of an action or passion.[4] He illustrates this point with the example of a lamb that perceives its mother as something to be nursed and grass as something to be eaten.[5] Aquinas speaks of the same kind of perception in the *Summa theologiae*'s discussion of the passions. Every animal movement, says St. Thomas, is caused by passion and passion is caused by perception.[6] For example, craving (*concupiscentia*) seems to be the passion that would cause a sheep to start eating grass. Animals are moved by this sort of passion only if they perceive something they love as absent, i.e., as not yet united to themselves. They love something, however, only if they are aware of that union with it as suitable to themselves. In other words, when the sheep sees grass, it imagines tasting it or (to put it in language more like that of St. Thomas) it imagines its union with grass.[7] This union seems suitable to the sheep; hence it loves grass.[8] When the sheep also perceives that the grass is absent (i.e., not yet in its mouth) the animal will be moved by craving to go to where the grass is and chew on it.[9] The perception that causes the lamb to crave and chew grass therefore has many components: the lamb senses the grass that lies before it, imagines tasting its flavor, perceives that it does not yet taste the grass, and imagines moving closer to the grass and chewing it.

The perception of the object of the irascible appetite is more complex than the perception that causes concupiscible passions like craving. To illustrate this sort of perception, St. Thomas offers the example of a sheep that fears a wolf. When it encounters this predator, says St. Thomas in the *Summa theologiae*, it perceives it as its enemy. That perception causes the sheep to be moved with fear,[10] and this fear causes the animal to flee. The sheep is moved with fear because it regards being attacked by the wolf not only as something unsuitable, but also as something difficult to avoid.[11] In other words, the sheep is cognizant of a difficult interaction, i.e., flight, as leading to the avoidance of a harmful contact with the wolf. Aquinas also offers another example of an irascible passion, this time of a dog that hunts a rabbit. Prior to hunting its prey, it sees it far away. According to Aquinas, the dog perceives the rabbit as attainable with difficulty and is moved by hope to pursue it.[12] The dog apprehends the hare in terms of two very different interactive processes—hunting and eating, one of which leads to the other.[13]

I propose that there is a kind of holism in Aquinas's descriptions of the perceptions that guide animal actions. That is, perception for Aquinas is a complex act involving many facets, each of which can be understood only by reference to the others. When describing the perception that leads the sheep to fear and flee the wolf, for example, he describes each of three sorts of awareness—i.e., the anticipation of a painful encounter with the individual presently before the senses, the awareness of the difficulty of avoiding this encounter, and the awareness of the individual presently acting upon its external senses as the source of pain—only in terms of the other two. For when speaking of the object of fear, he says that an animal fears the harm that it perceives as difficult to avoid; when speaking of the object of cognition, he says that the sheep perceives the wolf present to its senses as its enemy, i.e., as an imminent source of harm. And when one focuses on the sheep's awareness of its own act of avoidance, he says that it regards this as difficult. But this difficulty relates both to what the sheep perceives here and now and to the harm it anticipates, for the sheep finds it difficult to act here and now so as to avoid the anticipated harm. The fact that Aquinas describes each of these three components only in terms of the other two indicates that they are not three objects but rather three seamlessly interwoven aspects of one and the same whole.

Once one understands the complex yet unified nature of instinctive awareness, one is in a position to consider what Aquinas has to say about practices or custom (*consuetudo*) in animals. At first, his use of this term seems rather haphazard inasmuch as it lumps action, appetite and cognition together without explaining how these three cohere. This word refers, first of all, to practice or to the disposition that comes with repeated action.[14] As practice, *consuetudo* plays a key role in training animals how to act[15] and enables humans to react quickly, easily, and without deliberation.[16] *Consuetudo* is also related to appetite, for it causes one to find greater pleasure or joy in doing actions that one has done repeatedly in the past.[17] Because of its connection to appetite, Aquinas calls *consuetudo* a cause of virtue.[18] At other times, however, St. Thomas calls *consuetudo* a disposition in the memory that causes one to imagine things in a certain sequence.[19] In the *Summa theologiae*, he says that one can learn a language through study or practice (*per studium vel consuetudinem*).[20] Apparently, the latter has to do with acquiring skill in the use of that language rather than thinking about it as one does in a classroom. Finally, he uses the same term to refer to the shared practices of a society.[21] As this paper will show, all of these uses of this term are closely related to each other.

One can see how many of these different uses of *consuetudo* fit together once one has noted that memory retains and reactivates previous perceptions. For just as perceptions interrelate what is presently acting on the senses with the awareness of actions and goals, so too do acts originating from the memory. In fact, each of the three components pertaining to instinctive judgment are enhanced through custom or practice. *Consuetudo* enhances one's ability to size up the present situation and thereby make a quick judgment about what is to be done; it augments one's skill in action, making action less difficult or more pleasant, and increases familiarity with the goal, thereby increasing both the initial desire and later enjoyment.

In his commentary on the *Metaphysics*, Aquinas follows Aristotle in distinguishing three levels of cognition among animals: those with neither memory nor hearing, those with memory but without hearing, and those with both memory and hearing. The third level is the highest because this sort of animal can take instruction from a fellow member of the same species.[22] A complete account of animal cognition, therefore, must include communication, for while communicating one acquires judgments from others about how to act.

Aquinas does not spell out his entire theory of animal communication in any one text, but the hints that he leaves in many places are helpful. Aristotle points out, and Aquinas agrees, that only animal sounds accompanied by imagination are communicative acts.[23] He also says that animals communicate their concepts and passions.[24] Note, however, that by the use of the term "concepts" in this context he means the awareness of something particular rather than universal.[25] For example, the sheep that sees a wolf forms a concept of enmity inasmuch as it imagines that the individual it sees will chase and harm it: it does not form a notion of enmity as something common to many individuals at different places, for (as shown in the next section) such perceptual awareness is proper to humans. The other element in communication between non-rational animals is the display of passion: animals show different emotions by varying their pitch.[26] For example, a dog signifies anger through its bark, says Aquinas,[27] and a human signifies pain through his groans.[28] Besides showing passion, brutes also give directions to each other through their vocalizations. In fact, Aquinas even claims that brutes use different movements in their tongue to modify the messages that they are conveying.[29]

St. Thomas does not seem troubled with epistemological questions about how one animal could perceive another's emotional state. He takes it as a given that a barking dog *looks* angry and a groaning human seems to be in pain. This assumption is understandable if one recalls the earlier analysis of animal perception. A non-rational animal, says Aquinas, regards the individual before it in terms of the perceiver's own passions and actions. This perception brings actions and passions together in a seamless whole. The same is true of how an animal perceives other animals: it is aware of them as acting passionately. In other words, even before two animals that find themselves together have begun to communicate, they will already regard each other in terms of passionate interactions.[30] Communication merely adds specificity to this sort of awareness.

II. Human Perception and Its Role in Communication

The same power responsible for instinctive judgment in brutes operates differently in humans thanks to the influence of reason. As Aquinas's commentary on Aristotle's *De anima* points out, a brute's estimative power perceives its object only as the principle or terminus of an action or passion while the human cogitative power perceives "this human" as "this human."[31] This description is shorthand for the claim that a brute focuses on something only in terms of how the perceiver shall immediately interact with it, while human perception involves a kind of sortal awareness that involves no judgment about immediate pursuit or avoidance. This awareness in turn serves as the sentient basis of the intellect's grasp of the universal.[32] For example, the sentient grasp of "this human" enables the intellectual grasp of "human" as such.[33]

Reason somehow influences sense so that humans can perceive in a manner that seems analogous to reason—but how? One can answer this question by considering the interplay of appetite, action and cognition. One might say with Aquinas that the sense appetite of a non-rational animal is impetuous, for it does not allow for the suspension of judgment regarding action.[34] Upon apprehending a particular individual as suitable here and now, a brute is moved by passion to judge that it is to be pursued here and now.[35] When a human sees a particular good, however, he apprehends it as a particular instance of the universal good, and the will is moved by the particular good only inasmuch as it shares in the universal good.[36] Because the particular good does not encompass all that the rational appetite desires, reason is not constrained to judge that any particular instance of the universal good is to be pursued.[37] Rather, rational appetite overflows into the otherwise impetuous sense appetite, quelling it so that it no longer forces sense to judge that this good is to be pursued here and now.[38] With sense judgment suspended, practical reason is free to engage in a series of comparisons through which it determines how effective various means are in achieving an intended goal. Reason also compares the various courses of action with each other and eventually decides which one is to be undertaken.[39]

Perception plays an instrumental role throughout this process,[40] for the comparisons and judgments made during practical reasoning involve sentient comparisons of concrete means in relation to a concrete end.[41] These comparisons bring about a new kind of perception called "experience," which plays a critical role in conceptual development. Thomas illustrates experience with an example, borrowed from Aristotle, of a person who deliberates about how to treat someone who has a fever.[42] The would-be medic first recalls previous applications of various remedies and their results. He discovers that this sort of plant is anti-pyretic precisely by noting that the same plant has often alleviated the symptoms in question.[43] Experience is the perceptual component of this discovery: i.e., it is the concrete awareness of something as having had one or more antecedents. Note that the person who acquires this experience does not simply discover that there are many similar looking plants at different times and places. Instead, he discovers that in previous but similar situations, the application of this herb has cured those having a fever. In this way, the structure of this experience parallels the complex unity found in instinctive judgment, inasmuch as both relate the perceiver's interactions to the attainment of a goal. But the two also differ, thanks to the influence of practical reason. The medic perceives the patient as one upon whom he can act in the same way that he has acted in previous, similar situations, whereas the brute perceives the individual before it in terms of how it *will* act. In addition, the medic distinguishes the herb's capacity to bring about change from his own capacity to use it. In this way, the comparisons made while deliberating yield new perceptions of how things work, whereas instinctive judgment—even those enhanced by custom—never regard anything other than the ways in which the animal will interact with the individuals it encounters.[44]

Note also that one who has experienced an individual as having a characteristic common to many others is later able to perceive other individuals in the same manner without recapitulating the whole process of comparisons that led to the initial discovery. For example, the medic who has discovered the anti-pyretic properties of a plant will, upon seeing another person in a similar condition, recognize the patient's symptoms and be able to give a prognosis.[45] When he sees another, similar-looking plant, he will recognize it as something useful for curing fever, should the need occur. In both cases he will perceive something as familiar without having to recall when or where he has seen it before. In other words, perception acquired through experience is a kind of sortal awareness of individuals: Aquinas implies the same in his commentary on *De anima* when he says that the cogitative perceives individuals *sub natura communi*.[46]

Both human and non-human animals express their concepts as well as affections, but only humans intend manifestation as such.[47] Aquinas distinguishes what the two can do, saying that while a non-rational animal can produce a vocal sound (*vox*), only humans can produce speech (*locutio*).[48] One of the differences between the two lies in the number of concepts and desires they communicate. Brutes have only a few concepts and desires; hence their range of communication is inherently limited, in St. Thomas's opinion, to a few natural signs.[49] Another difference between human and brute communication lies in the spatio-temporal extent of their awareness. Brute awareness is harnessed to the here and now; hence animals desire to communicate only with individuals present to their senses about goods attainable through actions to be begun here and now.[50] Humans, however, are able to think abstractly, and for this reason, they are given to communicating not only with those whom they presently perceive, but also with those in remote times and places. This desire to communicate with those who are absent can give rise to writing.[51]

Aquinas sees thoughts as analogical to and concomitant with the use of words. He distinguishes the word of the heart (*verbum cordis*), which pertains to the intellect, from the spoken (*verbum quod voce profetur*) or external word (*verbo exteriori*) and imagined speech (*imaginatio vocis*). While discussing the Trinity in the *Summa theologiae*, he says that the intellectual word is the prime instance of a word: a vocalized sound is a genuine word only inasmuch as it signifies this interior word. But he adds in the same article that a vocalization cannot signify anything unless it proceeds from the imagination.[52] *Locutio*, therefore, is not a matter of just external sensation and intellection: it requires an intermediate cognitive activity that relates the universal known by the intellect to the particular toward which human actions such as speaking or writing are directed. Aquinas calls this activity the perception of particular intentions.[53] The perception of intentions pertains to the same power that prepares the phantasm for abstraction. Not only does the same power perform these two functions: it does so at the same time through one and the same act. In order to see how this is possible, consider the earlier argument that instinctive judgment is holistic inasmuch as brutes are aware of each of the three elements of perception (i.e., awareness of the individual presently acting upon the external senses, the anticipation of an encounter with that individual, and the awareness of its own interaction with the same individual) in terms of the other two. The same would seem to be true for animal communicative acts. Animals are not initially aware of an anticipated desirable interaction and then by some inference determine which communicative action they must perform in order to attain what they desire. Rather (at least in the case of cooperative behavior), they perceive their own actions and those of their cohort(s) as leading toward the same goal. Their gestures indicate to each other how each will act so as to get what both desire. The holistic nature of animal perception enables them to communicate without any inference from external sign to inner emotion or concept.

Human communicative acts add intellectual awareness to this mix, but they likewise proceed holistically—at least under normal circumstances. That is, the phantasm that serves as the "proximate matter" of abstraction interweaves the sentient awareness of the object of thought with the awareness of the human agent's own communicative activity. Humans do not typically first think a thought and then search for words to express it.[54] Instead, as Aquinas says, one thinks about something and speaks about it at the same time.[55] For this reason, Aquinas gives as an example of intellection the case in which a human being sees someone else talking or moving and immediately says that this person is alive.[56]

Human speech, as described by St. Thomas Aquinas, is a confluence of movements into and out of the soul.[57] The movement from things to the soul (*ad anima*) pertains to cognition,[58] while the movement from the soul (*ab anima*) to things pertains to appetite and self-movement, such as speech.[59] When one typically thinks of something and either speaks of it or sub-vocalizes, one is perceptually aware through the very same perceptual act of both the concrete features of the situation described in one's sentence and of the signifying act. Normally, one does not first think and then infer how one is to express one's thought. Rather, one's awareness of one's concrete expressive act permeates one's awareness of the matter being considered in a manner that relates the two to each other non-inferentially. The holistic nature of human perception allows for communication to take place in a manner analogous to how it does for brutes.

Aquinas was keenly aware of the unity of speech and thought, so much that he said in the *Summa theologiae* that speech is reason's proper operation,[60] and he even called the tongue the proper organ of the intellect.[61] That is not to say that all intellectual knowledge requires language as a necessary condition. For according to him, one is already in some way aware of first principles early in one's life, before one has begun to engage in any reasoning:[62] one begins to know before one speaks, but the perfection of the intellectual virtues is achieved only through the use of language.[63]

III. Practices and Knowledge of the Natures of Things

Thanks to reason's apprehension of the universal good, human perception takes on a structure that enables it to represent in some way the natures of the beings encountered in one's experience. To see how this is so, consider how nature is the principle of motion and rest, so that to perceive an individual as acting upon another is to have the sort of concrete awareness from which a concept of nature can be derived. Yet that is how even brutes perceive: as Aquinas says, they perceive individuals as the principles or termini of actions or passions. That is, they perceive individuals as sources of change. Experience brings perception to a new level, but it does not get rid of the awareness of individuals in interactive terms: it merely prescinds from judgment about how one shall act here and now, thus allowing one to focus on the way in which similar individuals have behaved various times in the past. The comparison of past instances gives the perceptual object a kind of generality which in turn allows its propensity for action to come to light. In other words, the generality that characterizes experience makes possible its focus on how things act. Aquinas's statement that the cogitative power perceives individuals *sub natura communi* can be taken as a kind of summary of this point, if one notes that *communi* accounts for the *natura*.[64]

Aquinas, following Aristotle, says that experience leads to art and art leads to science.[65] That is, practical involvement can eventually lead to speculative knowledge. One's initial experience gives a kind of know-how that serves as the basis of forming an opinion about how things work for the most part (*ut in pluribus*); this opinion in turn serves as the basis for making prudent judgments.[66] With more experience, opinion develops into art, the general knowledge of how to produce something.[67] Art exceeds mere prudent opinion because only art includes the knowledge of why some things work and others do not. Art can in turn become the source of *scientia*, or knowledge of the natures of things. One can understand how art leads to science if one considers how the items that function instrumentally in art perform those roles partially in virtue of their own natures. Nature is already somewhat apparent in art, but in a manner that is fused together with concern about the achievement of human goals.[68] One who seeks *scientia* no longer regards items in nature in terms of their instrumentality for human projects but instead seeks to understand them in terms of their own, inner teleologies.

While Aquinas makes it clear that practical involvements can aid one's acquisition of speculative knowledge, I propose that some sort of previous practical involvement is *necessary* for the acquisition of any *scientia*. Although science itself may prescind from the consideration of human interactions, the memory of such interactions serves as a necessary basis for the acquisition of science and other forms of speculative knowledge. One may object that humans do not thematize the object of scientific knowledge in terms of human interactions, so that such interactions are in no way integral to scientific knowledge: I would reply that in apprehending the natures of things, one regards them as principles of movement, and in order to do the latter, one must first perceive them as having the disposition to interact in one manner or another, and in order to perceive the latter, one must first have interacted with them oneself or with an analog thereof. Granted, there are many things in the world with which one has not directly interacted: in fact, it is simply impossible to interact with all but a few of them. In such cases, however, one grasps the natures of these things more removed from one's field of action on the basis of their similarity to those things with which one has been able to engage. Take, for example, the concept of "force" used by physicists: one understands this term on the basis of one's familiarity with one's own use of force as well as one's being subject thereto. Without such interactions as part of one's experience, one's concept of force would be empty, and without a host of such analogies, one would have no grasp whatsoever of the natures of many things in one's world. It follows, therefore, that one's interactions with things in one's environment—and the practices into which these interactions crystallize—lie at the root of one's consideration of the natures of things. Absent such a background of practices, the things one encounters in the world would appear merely as possessing certain proper and common sensible characteristics—hardly the likely source of an insight into their natures.

One who fails to acknowledge the cardinal role played by the awareness of practices in the formation of concepts of the natures of things will so impoverish one's concept of experience so that it will be unable to serve as the basis of abstraction. One will be forced instead to regard the intellect as imposing rather than receiving form—be it through Platonic reminiscence, innate ideas, or *a priori* structures. To preserve Aquinas's account of abstraction as the reception of form from a suitably prepared phantasm, one must recognize that practices are indispensable to the preparation of the phantasm for abstraction.

The role of practices in one's knowledge of human nature deserves special consideration. Consider how speech is the proper operation of man—so much so that Aquinas says in the *Summa contra gentiles* that the tongue is the proper human organ. If abstraction of the nature of something requires the representation of that thing performing its proper function, then the phantasm best representing human nature would be of a human as engaged in speech or some analogous operation.

One who accepts the notion that concepts are normally derived by abstracting from phantasms might propose that there is an exception in the case of knowledge of human nature, for humans seem to derive knowledge of their nature through self-awareness rather than by abstracting an intelligible species from a phantasm of something outside of oneself. I would reply that Aquinas's own discussion of self-awareness partially corroborates this objection, for he does say that in the act of judgment humans perform a kind of reflection (*per quandam reflexionem*)[69] upon their sentient and intellectual operations. Note, however, that reflection is not image-less introspection but is instead the awareness of oneself as both intellectually and sensorially active.[70] In fact, Aquinas states that one who is performing this reflection is cognizant of the operation of the very sensitive power responsible for directing self-movement (i.e., *vis cogitativa*).[71] It follows that this self-awareness cannot be divorced from one's awareness of oneself as interacting with others in one's environment. I propose, therefore, that both interactive and reflexive awareness contribute to the sort of experience that gives rise to the formation of concepts of human nature. Upon cooperating with others in the pursuit of a goal one recognizes oneself and others as seeking the same, universal good. This recognition is analogous to the recognition of an herb used at different times and places as capable of producing health. That cooperation takes place principally through shared deliberation about how to achieve a goal. In fact, Aquinas points out that *consilium*, his preferred word for deliberation, means sitting together in counsel.[72] Since humans deliberate together through speech, it follows that the paradigmatic example of self-awareness that gives rise to an understanding of human nature is our use of speech in deliberation.

One may object that various forms of non-linguistic bodily comportment likewise manifest rational appetite, so that a concept of human nature could be abstracted from the representation of these activities as well. The craftsman's use of a tool, for example, may manifest a desire for the universal good, yet it is not an exercise *per se* of the faculty of speech. I would agree that—to the degree that one can imagine oneself doing the same action—another's non-locutionary operations manifest the desire for the universal good and with them the human nature of those who perform them. But I would propose that such actions are even more intelligible when understood in terms of how they relate the doer to other members of a society, and that relation is conveyed by speech or one of its analogs. A landscaper, for example, does not just cut grass: he mows somebody's lawn for a fee that has been agreed upon. Thus, apparently non-locutionary behavior manifests human nature even more clearly when placed in the context of cooperation and communication.

The quest for speculative knowledge likewise illustrates how speech manifests human nature. Granted, some non-locutionary behavior, such as silent contemplation, could conceivably display the desire for knowledge and thereby serve as the basis for forming some concept of human nature. But words can convey this simple desire just as well, and in addition they manifest the pursuit of truth in a manner that could hardly be conveyed through non-locutionary gestures. That is because the desire for truth naturally leads one to discuss matters being inquired into with others. For this reason, Aquinas lists those arts that enable successful communication as a prerequisite to the acquisition of the intellectual virtues.[73] The initial desire to know and the subsequent effort to fulfill that desire are displayed just as well by speech as by any other behavior.

IV. Communication and Concepts Pertaining to Life in Society

Consider how one comes to form concepts pertaining to life in society, such as friendship, marriage, society, justice, law, money, and liturgy. One does not do so simply by forming a picture in one's imagination of a familiar person, group, judge, a dollar bill or a priest so that one's intellect can abstract a concept from that image. Instead, one comes to *experience* these realities through a process analogous to that by which one discovers that a certain plant alleviates fever. As with the medical discovery, this experience involves the interplay of the rational appetite's desire for a concrete goal as participating in the universal good with the awareness of many interactions directed toward the attainment of that concrete instance of the good. In these cases, however, cooperation itself is integral to the very object being considered. And rational appetite is displayed by speech because of the way in which cognition, appetite and action are interwoven. To understand this point, consider how, when examining animal communication, it was established that behavior displays appetite. The same is true for human cooperation, but in this case, the communicative behavior displays *rational* appetite (as well as directs its fulfillment). In fact, it is precisely by recognizing in speech and other cooperative acts the desire for a concrete, shared goal that interlocutors come to regard each other as friends, members of the same society, and fellow human beings.

One who wishes to give an adequate account of how the phantasm serves as a kind of object in the formation of concepts concerning social realities must be mindful of the holistic nature of human perception and communicative activity. For only such an approach can show how speech itself displays the appetite for the universal good, and only a phantasm displaying such an appetite can serve as the basis for abstracting concepts of human nature and action. One who is not mindful of the holistic nature of communicative acts will end up characterizing one's knowledge of other humans as relying upon an inference made from bodily movement to the existence of mental events in a soul—the sort of move one sees Descartes making in his *Meditations*. Nor will he be able to explain how humans come to form concepts of social realities such as friendship, justice, law and liturgy. For the formation of these and their like requires that one be perceptually aware of speech and other cooperative acts as directed toward a common goal just as the conceptualization of the "anti-pyretic" properties of a plant required the awareness of the past application of particular herbs.

Communities, laws, friends, etc. can be experienced only inasmuch as human actions, like speech, display the common pursuit of a concrete good, which is itself a participation in the universal good. One who has an inadequate understanding of perception will be unable to explain how humans form a concept of society. If he tries to describe the inductive process by which one comes to recognize and understand social realities, he is likely to conceive social wholes in atomistic terms, i.e., as the sum of their parts, atomistically conceived. Or perhaps he will regard society as rational construct imposed on otherwise self-seeking individuals. One who fails to grasp the holistic nature of human perception will face a dilemma, with a reductionist understanding of society on one horn and a dualistic understanding on the other.

Conclusion

Intellection is rooted in perception that is interactive, goal-directed, holistic and cooperation-enabling. It is precisely in virtue of its rich complexity that human perception, guided by rational appetite, is able to form experiences which in turn serve as the basis of one's forming concepts of the natures of things. The same elements of perception also enable animals to communicate and thereby cooperate with each other in the pursuit of shared goals. In humans, this cooperation and communication result in the formation of societies and in the production of everything from law to liturgy. These two roles of human perception—communication and the preparation of the phantasm for abstraction—overlap in the case of one's coming to understand human nature, for nothing manifests humanity more than the intentional manifestation of one's judgments and desires through speech and its analogs. The richness of one's conceptual life owes much to a sentient awareness, already enabling one to interact with one's surroundings in virtue of what it has in common with non-rational animals, that has been further animated by an "instinct" for the universal good so as to enable one to seek the common good.[74]

The alternative to including practices in Aquinas's account of human knowledge is to suppose that one can abstract intelligible species from a phantasm that represents individuals simply in terms of their proper and common sensible characteristics. Such an account fails to explain how humans come to know, and this failure leads either to the denial that we can know or to the denial that the forms are there to be known. Aquinas succeeds in part because he is attuned to practices, to the way in which reason is ever-engaged in the give and take of life.[75]

Morgan State University

Notes

1. *Summa contra gentiles* II, cap. 76, n. 8 (hereafter cited as *SCG*). All texts are from *S. Thomae de Aquino: Opera Omnia*, a website administered by Enrique Alarcón, sponsored by the Fundación Tomás de Aquino, published in 2009 and accessed on December 28, 2010 at http://www.corpusthomisticum.org/iopera.html.

2. *Summa theologiae* Iᵃ q. 78, a. 4, co (hereafter cited as *ST*).

3. In the following passages, Aquinas speaks in general terms about how higher cognitive powers perceive the objects of lower powers, but under a more universal formality: *ST* Iᵃ q. 3, ad 2, co.; *SCG* I, cap. 61, n. 5.

4. *Sententia libri de anima* II, lec. 13, n. 18

5. Ibid.

6. *Scriptum super Sententiis* II, d. 24, q. 2, a. 1, sol (hereafter cited as *SN*).

7. St. Thomas refers to the object of pleasure as the union (either bodily or cognitive) of the perceiver and perceived in *ST* Iᵃ-IIᵃᵉ q. 32, a. 1, ad 1; 33, a. 1, co.

8. *ST* Iᵃ-IIᵃᵉ q. 36, a. 2, co.; q. 45, a. 4, ad 2.

9. Note that even once an animal is eating, it continues to be moved by craving even though food is present in it's mouth. That is because, as Aquinas explains, not enough food is present: *ST* Iᵃ-IIᵃᵉ q. 33 ad 2.

10. *ST* Iᵃ q. 81 ad 3; *Sententia libri Metaphysicae* I, lec. 1, n. 8.

11. *ST* Iᵃ-IIᵃᵉ q. 41, a. 2, ad 3; q. 41, a. 4, co.; q. 42, a. 2, co.; q. 42, a. 4, co.

12. *ST* Iᵃ-IIᵃᵉ q. 40, a. 3, co.

13. Although brutes are not aware of ends and means as such, Aquinas notes how irascible passions involve a similar awareness. Hence he considers the perceptions causing these passions more of a participation in reason than those causing concupiscible passions. See *SN* III, d. 26, q. 1, a. 2, co.; *Quaestiones disputate de veritate*, q. 25 a. 2, co (hereafter cited as *De veritate*).

14. *Sententia libri Ethicorum* IX, lec. 3, n. 12.

15. *Sententia libri Metaphysicae* I, lec. 1, n. 12; *ST*, Iᵃ-IIᵃᵉ q. 50, a. 3, ad 2.

16. *Quaestiones disputate de malo*, q. 6, a. 24 (hereafter cited as *De malo*); see also *Sententia libri Metaphysicae* IX, lec. 4, n. 1; *SN* III, d. 33, q. 1, ar. 2, sc 1; and *SN* III, q. 1, ar. 2, co.

17. *ST* IIᵃᵉ-IIᵃᵉ q. 138, a. 1, ad 1; *SN* III, d. 23, q. 1, ar.4, co; *Sententia libri Ethicorum* IX, lec. 3, n. 12. The connection between *consuetudo* and appetite is apparent even in the etymology of this word, which means "with sweetness."

18. *Quaestiones disputatae de virtutibus* q. 1, a. 9, c.

19. *ST* Iᵃ-IIᵃᵉ q. 58, a. 1, co.; *De memoria et reminiscentia,* lec. 6, n. 10; *ST* Iᵃ-IIᵃᵉ q. 56, a. 5, co.; q. 50, a. 3, ad 5 and ad 7. In rational animals, *consuetudo* becomes the basis for reminiscence, a deliberate inquiry into the past that makes use of this sequentiality: see *De memoria et reminiscentia* lec. 8, n. 2.

20. *ST* Iᵃ-IIᵃᵉ q. 51, a. 4, co.

21. *ST* Iᵃ-IIᵃᵉ q. 97, a. 3, co.

22. *Sententia Metaphysicae* I, lec. 1, nn. 12–13.

23. *Sententia libri de anima* II, cap. 18, n. 12. When Aquinas says that an animal signifies with imagination (*cum imaginatione*), he may be referring to the operation of the estimative, imaginative and/or memorative powers. Imagination has this ambiguous meaning here because he is referring to Aristotle's understanding of imagination (*phantasia*), which is somewhat different from his own. Aristotle uses *phantasia* to signify any sentient

cognition that can occur when the individual causing it is no longer present (*De anima* III, chap. 3; 428a5–428b24). It therefore concerns not only proper and common sensibles, but incidentally sensible objects as well. As will be shown later on, incidentally sensible objects come into play in signifying acts.

24. *ST* I^a-II^{ae} q. 35, a. 8, co.

25. *De malo*, q. 6., ad 3; *De veritate* q. 22, a. 7, c.

26. *Sententia libri de anima* II, cap. 18, n. 3; *Sententia libri Politicorum*, I, lec. 1, n. 2.

27. *Sentencia libri De sensu et sensato*, lec. 2, n. 13.

28. *Expositio libri Peryermeneias* I, lec. 1, n. 5.

29. *Expositio libri Peryermeneias* I, lec. 2, n. 2; *Sententia libri de anima* II, cap. 18, n. 10.

30. *SN* III, d. 26, q. 1, a. 2, co.

31. *Sententia libri de anima* II, cap. 13, n. 398.

32. *In libros Physicorum* VII, lec. 6, n. 5.

33. *Expositio Posteriorum* II, cap. 20, n. 14.

34. *ST* I^a-II^{ae} q. 15, a. 2, ad 3; q. 13, a. 2, ad 2; q. 17, a. 2, ad 3. *De malo*, q. 16, a. 5, ad 4.

35. *Sententia libri Ethicorum*, I, cap. 10, n. 129; X, cap. 2, n. 1976.

36. *ST* I^a q. 80, a. 2, ad 2.

37. *ST* I^a-II^{ae} q. 10, a. 2, c.; q. 13, a. 2, c.

38. *ST* I^a-II^{ae} q. 31, a. 5, c. See also *De veritate* q. 25, a. 4, c.

39. *Sententia libri Ethicorum* VI, lec. 15; *Expositio libri Posteriorum analyticorum* II, cap. 20, n. 11, *Sententia libri Metaphysicae*, I, lec. 1, n. 19.

40. Aquinas assigns a role to the cogitative power throughout the whole process of practical reasoning. For that reason, he calls it the secondary subject of the virtue of prudence: II^{ae}-II^{ae} q. 47, a. 3, ad 3.

41. *Sententia libri de anima* III, lec. 16, n. 841. See also Aristotle, *De anima*, 433a25–433b25.

42. This paper will refer to the person who deliberates about how to alleviate fever as a medic, i.e., as one who does not yet possess the universal knowledge that characterizes the art of medicine, but is learning through experience how to apply remedies.

43. *Expositio libri Posteriorum analtyicorum* II, cap. 20, n. 11.

44. In *ST* II^{ae}-II^{ae} q. 173, a. 3, co., Aquinas notes that the formation of new concepts involves the creative use of the imagination. That is, humans form new concepts by recombining images in a manner analogous to how they combine letters to form new words.

45. *SN* II, d. 7 q. 2 a. 1, co.

46. *Sententia libri de anima* II, cap. 13, n. 398.

47. *ST* I^a-II^{ae} q. 35, a. 8, co.; II^{ae}-II^{ae} q. 110, a. 1 and 2, co.

48. *SN* I, d. 27, q. 2, ad 1, co.; *De veritate* q. 9, a. 5, co.; see also *Sententia libri de anima* II, cap. 18, n. 12.

49. *De veritate*, q. 9, a. 4, ad 10.

50. *Expositio libri Peryermeneias* I, lec. 2, n. 2.

51. Ibid.

52. *ST* I^a q. 34, a. 1. co.

53. *SN* I, d. 27 q. 2 a. 1 co.; *Sententia libri Ethicorum* III, lec. 19, n. 605.

54. At times humans get a flash of inspiration in which they "see" something without having found the words to express it. But it seems that the search for suitable words is itself a kind of deliberation that is carried out by sub-vocalization (*verbum imaginationis*). And it seems, likewise, that one can reason effectively about something only if one possess words that signify that about which one is reasoning.

55. *ST* I^a q. 63, a. 8, ad 1.

56. *Sententia libri de anima* II, cap. 13, n. 396.

57. *Sentencia libri de anima* II, lec. 18, n. 4.

58. *De veritate*, q. 10, a. 5, co.; *SN* III, d. 26, q. 1, a. 5, ad 4.

59. *Sententia libri de anima* II, cap. 18, n. 12.

60. *ST* I^a q. 91, a. 3, ad 3.

61. *SCG* IV, cap. 41, n. 13.

62. *ST* I^a q. 117 a. 1 co.; *De veritate*, q. 10 a. 6, co.; q. 11, a. 1, co.

63. In order to perfect the intellectual virtues, one must employ the liberal arts, which include the disposition to use language well: *ST* I^{ae}-II^{ae} q. 57, a. 3, ad 3.

64. Hence, as was noted before, Aquinas grants that this sensory power grasps its object "*sub natura communi.*" See *Sententia libri de anima* II, cap. 13, n. 398.

65. *ST* II^{ae}-II^{ae} q. 23, a. 7, ad 3.

66. *ST* II^{ae}-II^{ae} q. 47, a. 3, ad 2 and ad 3; II^{ae}-II^{ae} q. 49, a. 1, co.

67. In *Sententia libri Metaphysicae* I, lec. 1, n. 29, Aquinas distinguishes the mere opinion had by one who relies only upon experience with the knowledge of causes had by one who possesses art.

68. *De malo*, q. 5 a. 5, co. gives the example of an artisan who considers the nature of the material he is working with when making a saw. *ST* I^{ae}-II^{ae} q. 85, a. 6, co. uses the example of a craftsman making a knife to make the same point.

69. *ST* I^a q. 86, a. 1, co.

70. Imageless thought would seem more consistent with dualism than with Aquinas's hylomorphism.

71. *De veritate* q. 10, a. 5, ad 2.

72. *ST* I^{ae}-II^{ae} q. 14, a. 3, co.

73. *ST* I^{ae}-II^{ae} q. 57, a. 3, ad 3.

74. In *Estatic Morality and Sexual Politics: A Catholic Antitotalitarian Theory of the Body* (New York: Fordham University Press, 2005), 17, Graham McAleer says that for Aquinas, "matter is perpetually ecstatic in that it is intrinsically directed to form . . . ." In this spirit, one might say that the point of this essay is that human perception, as a kind of proximate matter of concepts, is estatic: its abilities to show how things work while at the same time engaging one with one's environment (especially through cooperation and communication) are brought to a still higher level by rational appetite and judgment.

75. I wish to thank my convention interlocutors for their helpful comments and challenges, especially Anthony Lisska and commentator Caery Evangelist.

Lies and Dishonest Endorsements

Alexander R. Pruss

Abstract: I shall discuss the problem of the definition of lying and the formulation of the duty of truthtelling. I shall argue that the morality of *assertion* is a special case of the morality of *endorsement*, and that a criterion of adequacy for an account of lying is that it handles certain cases of dishonest endorsement as well. Standard views of lying fail to do so. I shall offer an account of the duty of honest endorsement in terms of the intention to avoid falsehood. But, in the end, we may simply have reason to go back to the naïve view that lying is saying falsehoods.

1. Introduction

Lying is wrong. Some people think the wrongness of lying is only *prima facie* and in extreme circumstances it is permissible to lie. While I think this weaker view is mistaken, when I shall talk of the wrongness of lying, this should be understood as compatible with such views. Lying is, thus, at least *prima facie* wrong. Moreover, I shall take it that lying is always a form of dishonesty (so if lying is only prima facie wrong, dishonesty is only *prima facie* wrong).

But what is this forbidden activity and how shall we put the prohibition? This is surprisingly tricky to answer. In this paper, I shall in the end offer an account not so much of lying, but of the corresponding duty of honesty in assertion—or, more generally, of endorsement.

I should note that in all of the following, for strict precision, instead of talking of lying or asserting, we should be talking of lying or asserting to *some individual or group of individuals.*

2. Some Standard Views

Small children and persons enmeshed in partisan politics have a tendency to accuse anyone who disagrees with them of being a liar. The simplest view of lying is that:

(L1) A lie is a false assertion.

But most of us outgrow this simple view, thinking that the person who asserts sincerely is not lying, even if the proposition affirmed is in fact false. Still, maybe we'll have to go back to the naïve view once all the arguments are over.

A more sophisticated view is that lying is asserting something that one does not believe or maybe that one positively disbelieves. And some tack on to this the condition that one intends to deceive. The intention-to-deceive condition is, I think, unnecessary. Here is why. First of all, not every kind of deceit is relevant. If I know that the weather is cloudy, and I tell you that the weather is sunny in order to deceive you into thinking that I am my identical twin Fred, because Fred has a habit of telling you, regardless of the weather, that the weather is sunny, then this deceit does not have a sufficient connection with the insincerity to be relevant. When I lie to you that p, the relevant kind of deceit seems to be my deceiving you into thinking that p, or at least into being confirmed in thinking that p.

So, if we add on an intention-to-deceive condition, we get this:

(L2) To lie is to assert a proposition one doesn't believe (or positively disbelieves), in order to deceive the interlocutor in favor of the content asserted.

However, this is not correct. A common kind of lie is the lie of cowardice where one asserts a proposition that one's interlocutor already believes, not in order to deceive the interlocutor into thinking that the proposition *is true*, but in order to deceive her into thinking that *one believes it*, that one is part of the in-group, the smart folk. One might do this, for instance, with political or theological or scientific views.

So, perhaps, the right account is that

(L3) to lie is to assert something one takes to be false (Fallis 2009), or at least that it is to assert something one doesn't believe to be true.

But there are some rather out-of-the-way counterexamples to this, too. Here is one. I am a deaf person and I've been learning on my own to speak out loud by watching my oral muscles in the mirror. I believe that I haven't yet succeeded in vocalizing, but I also know that there is a small chance that I have. Now, I am alone with you. I know you don't know sign language or how to lip-read. You tell me what a pity it is that we can't have a conversation, and I lip-read that statement. So, I try to tell you: "I can speak out loud." I can try while yet believing that I won't succeed, though this time I do succeed. And while asserting that I can speak out loud, I still believe that I am not speaking. It is only when you say "That's great!" that I realize that I spoke. But there is no dishonesty, no lie, in what I have said, because when I say "I can speak out loud" to someone who can't lip-read, I say something that is guaranteed to be true if I manage to say it. And this conditional guarantee of truth, even absent unconditional belief in that truth, is all that honesty requires.

So it is possible to assert something one believes to be false and yet not be lying. Other similar cases can be manufactured, all of them fairly *outré*. I know almost no German. I am to meet a German philosopher tomorrow, and with much help from translation software, a grammar and a dictionary, I memorize a few German sentences containing my philosophical views. A couple of hours later, someone accosts me with an argument and convinces me that something I used to believe is false. Next day, I deliver my memorized address to my German counterpart, having forgotten that one of the memorized sentences (which are German to me, and that's worse than Greek!) states a view that I no longer believe. In so doing, I assert a proposition I disbelieve. But I am not being dishonest, just careless. If all lying is dishonesty, then I have not lied.

A full account of lying should take the outré into consideration, and doing so will force one to abandon the standard belief-based accounts of lying. But first, let us consider some cases which are on the borderline of assertion.

3. Endorsement

You write a letter to some entity. I co-sign it without having read all of it. Maybe I skimmed it or maybe you summarized the main points or maybe I haven't bothered to learn anything about the contents.

I may or may not have done the right thing. On one extreme, if I skimmed over the main points and agree with them, and I have reason to trust your expertise in the matter and hence to believe that the details are correct, I can honestly sign. On the other extreme, if I didn't read the letter at all, and I know that I tend to disagree with you and hence am confident that something important in the letter is false, but I sign out of cowardice (maybe you are on a hiring committee and I am applying for a job at your institution), then I have acted contrary to integrity.

Did I, in either case, *assert* the contents of the letter by signing? It seems difficult to say that I have done so when, in both cases, the letter has contents that I am quite ignorant of. I think a case can be made that I have in fact asserted all the contents of the letter. If so, then views of assertion that involve the communication of propositions that are in some internal sense grasped by the speaker need to be revised. But, in any case, there is a word that fits better than "assertion" with what I have done: I have *endorsed* the letter.

Another case. I make a local weather website. I program my server to pull in data from temperature, wind and other sensors, process the data and post statements about the current weather. There are two extremes here. I could be very careful in programming the server to post statements that are true. Or I could be very careful in programming the server to post statements that are false. In between these extremes are various cases of less carefulness or of deliberate inaccuracy.

When my automated website says "The current wind speed is 17.3 ± 0.5 km/h," have I *asserted* that the wind speed is in that range? I could be dead by the time the site is activated, and typically dead men don't speak, so it does not appear that I assert this content, though I do think the implausible claim that I assert it could actually be defended. But, in any case, by creating the website and its content I *endorsed* the content.

There does not appear to be a morally significant difference between single-authoring a letter that I know to contain falsehoods and co-signing such a letter (observe, too, that there is a continuum between these cases, as I increase the amount of material which I draw from other sources). Likewise, there is no morally significant difference between creating an automated website that gives incorrect information about the weather and manually updating a website with equally incorrect information. So any moral prohibition on lying had better extend to cases of endorsement as well.

In fact, cases of assertion are a special case of endorsement. When I assert, I do two things: I *express* a proposition, and I *endorse* it. The expression is responsible for the content, and the endorsement for the illocutionary force. In English, the endorsement is indicated by a combination of context, declarative mood and intonation. The letter-signing and website-production cases are cases where I do not express the propositions myself, but I nonetheless endorse them. My endorsement of the propositions does require the context to point out what the endorsed propositions are—the claims in the letter that lie above my signature or the claims on the website that I have created—but here I do not point out the proposition by directly producing a sentence that expresses them, as in cases of standard assertion.

Now, the prohibition on lying is tied precisely to the *endorsement* of the asserted proposition. In a lie, it is in the endorsement that one solicits the interlocutor's interpersonal trust while simultaneously betraying that trust. This trust-solicitation-cum-betrayal is identified by Jorge Garcia as the source of the wrongness of lying (Garcia 1998). Now, cases of endorsement of propositions other than in standard assertions involve the same solicitation of trust, and hence the same opprobrium should devolve on the betrayal of that trust as in standard lies. And this conclusion, I think, should hold for any reasonable view of lying, not just Garcia's (one way to see this is to reflect on the continuum between assertion and endorsement). Therefore, an account of lying should extend to an account of dishonest endorsement.

Before we look for such an account of lying, however, I need to distinguish two ways of endorsing a plurality of propositions—say, of the propositions expressed by sentences posted on my website or written in a letter that I've signed. I can endorse them *conjunctively* or *distributively*. If I endorse them conjunctively, I endorse their conjunction. If I endorse them distributively, I endorse each of them, but do not automatically endorse their conjunction.

The Preface Paradox shows that typical cases of endorsement of a plurality of propositions involve distributive endorsement. The Preface Paradox occurs when an honest author adds a preface to a book stating that something in the body of the book is false. This is paradoxical, because on the one hand, an honest author has good reason to think she's made a mistake somewhere, but, one the other hand, everything she says, including the disclaimer in the preface, she has good reason to say. Yet, as a result, she ends up making a contradictory body of claims, since the preface contradicts the conjunction of the propositions in the body of the book. To write a non-fiction book is to endorse it.[1] But it had better not be a *conjunctive* endorsement, since then the author who knows her fallibility typically will be knowingly endorsing a falsehood—and, if the disclaimer is in the preface, she will be knowingly endorsing a self-contradiction. And that would wreck any attempt to extend the morality of lying to cases of endorsement. Hence, standard cases of endorsement are distributive, though one can further specify one's endorsement to be conjunctive: "I agree that *everything* she just said is true."

It may be tempting to say that typical endorsement is neither distributive nor conjunctive, but for-the-most-part. In for-the-most-part endorsement of a body of claims, one is simply endorsing the proposition that a majority (or large majority) of the claims is true. However, typical cases of endorsement are not for-the-most-part but distributive. If endorsement was for-the-most-part, then in any book or letter or website whose contents were significantly more accurate than the "for the most part" condition requires, I could insert a deliberate falsehood and still honestly endorse. There is no slander in writing: "The majority of the following sentences are true: $2 + 2 = 4$. $3 + 3 = 6$. Our colleague George is a plagiarist." But there is a slander in signing a letter that says "$2 + 2 = 4$. $3 + 3 = 6$. Our colleague George is a plagiarist." And the slander would not disappear if one multiplied the true claims.

Now, a natural extension of standard accounts of lying to the case of endorsement would be something like this:

(E1) It is wrong to endorse a statement that I believe to be false.

However, this does not work. In a large body of propositions, whether in a letter, a book or on a website, there will likely be a falsehood. Thus, I may very well know that in endorsing that body of propositions, assuming that the endorsement is distributive, I will be endorsing a statement that is false, even though I am being perfectly honest. Thus, E1 is too strong.

Perhaps, though, I misinterpreted E1. Maybe it should be understood as follows:

(E2) It is wrong to endorse a statement that I *particularly* believe to be false.

If I am being honest, then presumably I don't know of a *particular* statement that is false. However, E2 is too weak. Suppose that I ask the primary author of the letter to insert a falsehood of her own choice and then I sign without reading, or I write code that at random times posts falsehoods on the website. In these cases, there is no endorsed statement that I *particularly* believe to be false. Moreover, the falsehoods might be such that I do not even believe them to be falsehoods. (The primary author of the letter might be asked by me to insert a proposition that she as an expert knows to be false but which I incorrectly believe to be true.)

So the belief-based accounts of lying not only do not handle the outré cases where whether one succeeds in speaking affects whether the content is true, but they do not handle more common cases of endorsement.

4. Back to the Naïve View?

The naïve view was that lying was assertion of falsehoods. Perhaps we should rehabilitate this. After all, it neatly extends to endorsements:

(E3) It is wrong to endorse a falsehood.

One problem, however, is that honest mistakes become wrongdoings. When students assert the wrong answer to calculus exam questions, according to E3 they are doing *wrong*. It might help to bite the bullet here to say that if they've studied hard enough, they're not culpable. But, still, the mere fact that they are doing wrong is problematic. For instance, it seems that we need very strong justification to put others in a position where they will likely do something morally wrong, even if the wrongdoing is non-culpable. But professors frequently set tests where it is very likely that a number of students will give the wrong answer and it is not clear that the justification is sufficiently strong.

A second problem is that even if it's not a lie on this view, it's still just as vicious to assert something you disbelieve even when it is, in fact, true. The defender of the naïve view can bring in conscience. Since almost all of us realize lying is wrong, the duty to follow conscience implies that it is wrong for us to say something that we *think* is a lie. And whenever we say something that we believe to be false, we are saying something that at least by our lights is a lie (perhaps we need to add some deceit conditions in, though—some people think these are required).

However, while bringing in conscience alleviates the problem for the naïve view, it does not remove it. For consider Frank who is in circumstances in which he believes himself to be morally justified in lying. Suppose, further, that Frank is mistaken about that: these circumstances do not in fact justify lying. Frank asserts p while disbelieving p. If p is false, then on the present view we can say that he is doing wrong, though his ignorance of the applicability of the prohibition of lying makes him non-culpable. So far so good. But suppose p is in fact true. Then, on the naïve view, Frank does *nothing* wrong, culpably or not, even though he says something he disbelieves in circumstances that do not justify lying. For he does not say anything false and hence does not violate E3. And he does not violate his conscience as he thinks he is in exceptional circumstances. But surely we should say that Frank *is* doing wrong here.

Despite these problems, the naïve account seems to do better than belief-based accounts. The belief-based accounts like E1 and E2 simply fail to provide correct advice to the agent in a number of cases, while this account does, and does so even in the cases where it doesn't correctly classify actions under the headings *right* or *wrong*. It advises the calculus student to avoid error and tells Frank not to speak falsely unless there should be a circumstance where lying is permitted.

5. The Intention View

I would bite the bullet and accept E3 if that was all that was on offer. But there is a better account available. When we dropped the deceit condition, we lost any explicit mention of *intentions*. And some of the endorsement cases can be seen as focusing our attention once again on intention. There is, surely, a difference between intentionally introducing errors into current-weather server code and simply being aware that the system sometimes fails.

One might focus on this aspect and say that what is wrong in the dishonest endorsement cases is intentional *deceit*. And certainly there is intentional deceit there. However, the moral prohibition against deceit is significantly weaker than that against lying. If I am escaping from a pursuer, I can set a false trail for the pursuer to follow, even if nothing at all momentous is at stake in my not getting caught. But even if lying is sometimes permitted, there should still be a very strong presumption against it. Why the difference? Recall Jorge Garcia's connection of lying with betrayal of trust. In asserting, or, more precisely, *endorsing*, a claim, I am soliciting your trust. But if I believe the claim is false, then except in outré cases, I am simultaneously breaking trust with you. However, when I lay a false trail, I do not solicit your trust in me, or give you any right to rely on the evidence. You do not have the right to complain: "But I trusted you!" But when I *tell* you that I took such-and-such a path, I give you the right to rely on my testimony, and to complain if my testimony deliberately led you astray.

The dishonest endorsement cases are more like lying than like putting down a false trail. One stands behind the endorsement, one guarantees it, while no one stands behind the false trail. So we should not consider the dishonest endorsement cases simply to be constituted by deception.

I suggest that instead of looking at what one should *not* do in these cases, it is helpful to look at what one *should* do. And here, then, is a rough proposal (there are some details of it that I am not yet happy with)—the Intention Principle—for an account of the duty of honesty in endorsement (and hence also in assertion):

(IP) In endorsing one or more propositions, one ought to be intending to be asserting or endorsing only truths.

Here, I stipulate that if one has not asserted or endorsed anything, one counts as having asserted or endorsed only truths.

When the honest person accidentally endorses a falsehood, it is reasonable to say that she has failed to do something she had set out to do. Thus, the honest person sets out to endorse only truths, and to set out to do something is to *intend* it. Hence, the honest person is, indeed, one who intends to assert or endorse only truths.

According to IP, intentions show up not just when we analyze what is the wrong thing to do, but also what the *right* one is. It follows that certain actions morally require certain intentions. A different example: To promise honestly requires that one intend to avoid non-fulfillment.[2]

IP works in the case of the deaf person who does not know she is speaking. Her statement is chosen so that if it is in fact asserted, it is true, and so the speaker has avoided—and intentionally so, we may charitably suppose—asserting a falsehood. She has intentionally asserted only truths, by the stipulative understanding of IP.

IP, at least typically, requires that one not believe one will be making a false statement. For, typically, if one believes the statement will be false, one is not intending to avoid making a false statement. For if one were acting on that intention, given the belief that the statement is false, one would simply keep one's mouth shut or say something else.

The person who creates a website and its content endorses the content by creating the engine behind it. But it is not possible to simultaneously intend that engine to insert errors while intending to endorse only something true. One cannot simultaneously act on such incompatible intentions, because intentions are not merely inner speeches,[3] but things that actually explain how one is acting. If one were really intending that the content be correct, one would not be inserting errors in it. If one disputes this judgment, we can modify IP by saying: "*consistently intend*" in place of "intend."

Similarly, if I endorse a letter while believing that it is mostly false, my action of endorsing it cannot have an intention of avoiding endorsing a falsehood. For if I were acting on that intention, I would refrain from the endorsement, or endorse only partly. Similarly (at least in ordinary circumstances where I can understand all the sentences in the letter), if I know of a *particular* statement in the letter that it is something I disbelieve, I cannot endorse that statement consistently with IP. But if the endorsement is distributive, then a mere belief that each individual statement has, say, a 1% chance of being false does not preclude endorsement with the distributive intention that one not endorse that statement if it's false.

IP has consequences over and beyond a mere prohibition on lying. As Heath White has pointed out to me in the case of a related principle, IP prohibits BS, namely speech where one simply does not care whether what one is saying is true or false. In BS, one does not intend to deceive. And one does not need to consider whether one believes the content or not. One simply speaks. If it turns out on self-reflection that one does believe the content, one has still engaged in BS. But if one follows IP, one will intend to endorse only truths, and hence BS will be forbidden. An analogue to BS is indiscriminate endorsement. One signs a letter because, say, one is expected to sign it, without caring whether the contents are true. This, too, violates IP. It violates IP even if in fact one believes the contents *are* true, just as BS is wrong even if one believes the claims are true.

Here is a somewhat difficult case. You believe that p_1 is true. Your credence is 99 percent. But there are two alternate, and mutually incompatible, hypotheses. There is probability 0.8 percent that p_2 is true, and a probability 0.2 percent that p_3 is true. For vicious reasons, you do not wish to assert p_1. Instead, you assert p_2. You claim that the intention to avoid saying something false was operative, and that's why you asserted the moderately unlikely p_2 instead of the exceedingly unlikely p_3. But, you add, the intention to avoid saying something false was mixed with an intention to assert either p_2 or p_3. There is, you claim, no violation of IP. Yet, surely you lied. However, this example seems to fail. For if I intended that q, then my action can be correctly described as *an attempt to bring it about that q*. But my asserting that p_2 cannot be described *an attempt to bring it about that I now assert only truths*, and hence my asserting that p_2 cannot have as an intention *to assert only truths*.

There is another difficulty with IP. It seems possible to intend to do things when one believes one will be unsuccessful. So perhaps I could intend to say something that I believe to be false, in the *hope* that it will, in fact, be true. In this case, I *intend* the statement to be true, but I do not believe that it is. Here is such a case based on examples of William James (James 1992). Unarmed, I face an armed enemy. I tell her, in a confident voice: "You will now think about the fact that, unlike you, I am unarmed. You could easily hurt me. But, instead, you will decide that it would dishonorable to do so." The last sentence is one that I do not believe to be true, and alas I am pretty sure it isn't. But I *hope* it is true, and *intend* that I be making a true assertion, because I hope to cause it to be true by making it. I do not, thus, violate IP.

If one thinks that this is a lie, and if it is indeed psychologically possible to intend something while disbelieving it will happen, then IP is insufficient to capture our intuitions about what makes lying wrong. I do not know, however, if this case is a lie. Certainly, there is no intention to deceive, and to the extent that the deceit intuition was plausible, we might think that here there is no lie. Moreover, the example is complicated by the fact that "you will decide that it would be dishonorable to do so" may not be simply an assertion. It may be a figure of speech that one might call a "hortatory declarative," where by using the form of assertion, one exhorts someone to act. It's like saying "Nice doggy" to the growling animal. Though perhaps the case can be modified so that it is *clearly* an assertion (maybe one is speaking a language that has no hortatory declarative).

Even if these examples work to the detriment of IP, IP still seems to capture much of our intuitions about the duties of truthfulness in language. It's just that there are *further* duties beyond those captured by IP.

IP does not give a definition of lying. And it appears rather difficult to give a definition of lying that correctly takes care of the outré cases. The simplest definition I can find that takes care of these cases is:

> (L4) *x* lies that *p* in an action *A* if and only if *x*'s endorsing the proposition that *p* is a successful performance of a part of *A* and *x* believed that the successful performance of that part of *A* would be such that there would be a proposition *q* such that (a) *x* would be endorsing *q* as the performance of that part of *A*, and (b) *q* would be false.

(If one prefers "lying" to be tied to assertion, one can replace "endorse" by "assert," or else replace "lies" by "lies in an extended sense.")

If one wants to give a condition that does not apply to outré cases, here is one:

> (L5) if *x* expected and intended to endorse that *p* and that expectation was fulfilled, and if the truth of *p* does not depend (causally, epistemically or constitutively) on whether *x* endorses it, then *x* lied in endorsing that *p* if and only if *x* believed that *p* was false.

It should, however, be no surprise that giving a precise definition of lying is harder than giving an account of what one should be doing. For there may be no natural kinds of violations of a duty like IP. What unifies all the violations is simply that they are violations of IP, but the violations come in different sorts—lies, BS, indiscriminate endorsement, etc.—whose mutual delineation is not particularly natural.

If, in the end, IP cannot be defended against objections, I will retreat to the naïve E3. It is a surprising fact that there is so much to be said for the naïve view.

Baylor University

Notes

1. The process of book composition is, in general, complex, and to model it on standard cases of assertion is often mistaken. The author may often pull various passages out of her notes (these days, simply copying and pasting), modifying them if necessary to fit new contexts. In those cases, it is not clear when a straightforward assertion of the author's has been made: when the notes were written or when the notes were modified? Moreover, the author is not fully committed to the content of the book until after the last proofreading. It is only when the proofreading is done and the manuscript (or maybe galleys?) is sent off that the book has been endorsed. It is plausible, thus, to see the endorsement as happening not so much in the writing, as in the *sending* of it. In fact, we can imagine a writer who writes a book while not being sure if the ideas in it will pan out. Then once she's written the manuscript, she reads it and circulates it tentatively to colleagues, to see if it is worth publishing. And she may well decide to the contrary, in which case nothing has yet been asserted.

2. John Searle (1969) thinks that the sincerity condition on promises is that one intends fulfillment. This could be too strong, if we think that three things could happen with a promise: it could be fulfilled, non-fulfilled or *mooted*. The last occurs in the case of a conditional promise whose antecedent never comes true. One might not want to say such a promise is non-fulfilled, but neither might one want to say it's fulfilled.

3. "The idea that one can determine one's intentions by making such a little speech to oneself is obvious bosh" (Anscombe 2000, 42).

Bibliography

Anscombe, G. E. M. 2000. *Intention*. Cambridge, Mass.: Harvard University Press.

Fallis, Don. 2009. "What is Lying?" *Journal of Philosophy* 106: 29–56.

Garcia, J. L. A. 1998. "Lies and the Vices of Deception." *Faith and Philosophy* 15: 514–537.

James, William. 1992. "The Will to Believe." In *Readings in the Philosophy of Religion: An Analytic Approach*, 2nd ed. Edited by Baruch A. Brody, 35–47. Englewood Cliffs, N.J.: Prentice Hall.

Searle, John. 1969. *Speech Acts*. Cambridge: Cambridge University Press.

The Indispensability of Tradition in the Philosophical Activity of Socrates

Jessy E. G. Jordan

Abstract: In this paper I argue that narratives concerning Periclean Athens have mistakenly imposed modern conceptions of enlightenment onto the Greek world, and have therefore been blinded to crucial aspects of Socrates's practice of moral reason giving. In contrast to the Kantian conception of enlightenment, which puts forth an image of the ideally enlightened person as an autonomous reasoner, one who refuses to be guided by another and who has the courage to throw off the chains of tradition and "think for oneself," I argue that Socrates provides us with a much different picture of the enlightened individual. Socrates's practice of moral reasoning does not take the form of autonomous rationality that is antithetical to tradition, but rather his practice recognizes the rightful authority of tradition and custom in moral reason giving. Thus, rather than characterizing Socrates through a Kantian enlightenment reading, this paper argues that we should study Socrates through the lens of the *sensus communis*, a humanist concept articulated well by Giambattista Vico and Hans Georg-Gadamer.

Whan properly contextualized against the backdrop of the threat represented by the new *paideia* of the Sophists in fifth-century Athens, Socrates emerges as a unique type of enlightenment figure.[1] The claim that Socrates is such a figure will hardly strike most readers of Plato as surprising; however, the characteristics of "enlightenment" outlined in what follows might. Socrates is not, as many commentators have argued, the sort of enlightenment figure who radically rejects the authority of tradition and instead establishes his philosophical positions on the autonomous exercise of a neutral rationality. He is not one more stage on the way to the successive conquest of *logos* over *mythos*;[2] he is not a proponent of "that critical philosophy which defies all authority, and which, in its search for truth, wishes to be guided by the glimmer of evidence alone;"[3] he is not a part of the "reasoned rejection of tradition which marked the middle of the fifth century."[4] These readings of Socrates owe more to the eighteenth-century German conception of enlightenment than to the actual activity of philosophy as practiced by Socrates within the Platonic dialogues. Although this autonomous, anti-tradition view of Socrates has been challenged by some recent scholars, it remains rather entrenched in the ways in which we talk, write, and think about him.[5] Kant's vision of enlightenment as the ability of an individual "to make use of his understanding *without direction from another*"[6] is not the Socratic picture. Instead Socrates's practice of philosophy reveals a thinker who recognizes and affirms the role of moral custom in his search for the good. Socrates should therefore be read as a figure who maintains the indispensability of tradition and authority in his search for wisdom.

In this paper I argue that Socrates should not be regarded as a Kantian enlightened thinker, but rather as a Traditionalist. This position, as I will demonstrate, is importantly distinct from the merely conventional morality maintained by either the conservative or the *hoi polloi*. In order to argue that Socrates is a Traditionalist, I begin by distinguishing between four possible positions that emerged out of the threat posed by the new *paideia* of the Sophists in fifth-century Athens and the central question confronting those concerned with the moral fragmentation present: namely, can virtue be taught? This question functioned as a litmus test, and one's answer to it could reveal one as a Liberal, a Conservative, an Autonomous Reasoner, or a Traditionalist. Next, I demonstrate that Socrates is best characterized as a Traditionalist, first, by providing an interpretation of the *aporetic* ending of the *Protagoras*, and second, by considering his strategy of consensus building in his conversational exchanges. Finally I conclude with the suggestion that Socrates's emphasis on the importance of solidarity, community, and the ties of political friendship offers further support for my reading.

Can Virtue Be Taught?: Four Positions

The moral crisis present in Periclean Athens is well known. The values of traditional society were crumbling, the sense of solidarity and community between individuals was vanishing, and appeals to traditional moral authorities such as Homer were often thinly disguised efforts at justifying self-interest. It is this context into which the Sophists stepped along with their new *paideia*, which promised to deliver success in public and private through the employment of rhetorical techniques that would enable an individual to win any side of an argument. As Protagoras claims in the dialogue of the same name, "What I teach is sound deliberation, both in domestic matters—how best to manage one's household, and in public affairs—how to realize one's maximum potential for success in political debate and action."[7] And it is this new *paideia* of the Sophists that represents the fundamental concern of Socrates, that occasions his philosophical activity, and to which his philosophical project is primarily addressed. After all, the rhetorical pedagogy of the Sophists enables any given student to manipulate argument into to the service of self-interest rather than truth, and Socrates and Plato rightly worry about the corrupting influence of this education. As P. Christopher Smith relays, "Plato is responding in the whole of what he says to a near-total moral dissolution in his society and to the concurrent sophistic rhetorical techniques that confound any real moral reasoning and substitute for it more or less disguised rationalizations of cupidity and the unbridled will to power."[8]

Many scholars have remarked on the centrality of the Sophist threat as the polemical context in which the philosophical activity of Socrates and the dialogical productions of Plato are to be understood. In fact one commentator speaking of Plato's philosophical work makes the bold claim that the "advent of sophism is *the* occasion for his thought;"[9] and another maintains, "The distinction between Sophist and philosopher dictated the orientation of not only his own thought, but Greek thought in general. . . . It is even fair to say that Plato's deep sense of that distinction stamped its imprint upon the whole of his thought."[10] One can gain an initial sense of the way in which Socrates and Plato articulate their positions in contrast to the Sophists by attending to the then much debated question as to whether virtue can be taught. The opening lines of the *Meno* are significant in this respect. Meno asks, "Can you tell me, Socrates, can virtue be taught? Or is it not teachable but the result of practice, or is it neither of these, but men possess it by nature or in some other way?"[11] In this passage Meno outlines four possible responses to the question as to whether virtue can be taught: (1) virtue can be taught; (2) virtue cannot be taught but it is the result of practice; (3) virtue is not taught but possessed by nature; and (4) virtue is acquired in some other unspecified way. Socrates notably refuses to answer Meno's question, appealing to his typical ignorance and drawing attention to his own difference from the reputed Sophist, Gorgias: "In particular, [Gorgias] accustomed you to give a bold and grand answer to any question you may be asked, as experts are likely to do. . . . But here in Athens, my dear Meno, the opposite is the case, as if there were a dearth of wisdom, and wisdom seems to have departed hence to go to you."[12] Socrates's playful caginess in response to Meno's question can be explained by his recognition that an answer one way or another would immediately land him in a particular partisan camp. This is most obvious with the first and third way of responding, for answering that virtue can be taught would reveal one to be on the side of the Sophists and answering that virtue was acquired by nature would reveal one to be on the side of the conservative ruling elites who were concerned with maintaining the status quo. As Jacqueline De Romilly points out, within traditional Athenian education values had been passed down by heredity and example, like any aristocratic city; now, for a price, the Sophists offered an educational program that would enable anyone to play a distinguished part in city life.[13] Taking a position on whether virtue was natural or acquired through education at the same time indicated whether one's sympathies were aristocratic or revolutionary. There was a power struggle between the claims of heredity and the claims of the self-made intellectual, and Socrates, by refusing to answer Meno's question, is refusing to be identified with the revolutionary Sophists or the aristocratic conservatives who were interested in maintaining the traditional power structures.

This power struggle is dramatically on display later in the *Meno* during Socrates's exchange with Anytus, the Athenian gentleman and obvious partisan for aristocratic interests. In response to Socrates's question as to whom Meno ought to be sent to learn virtue, Anytus asserts, "Why give him the name of one individual? Any Athenian gentleman he may meet, if he is willing to be persuaded, will make him a better man than the sophists would."[14] Anytus is clearly advocating for the claims of heredity over against the new *paideia* of the Sophists. Socrates ends up reducing Anytus to *aporia*[15] just as he had reduced Protagoras to *aporia* when Protagoras had claimed to be able to teach virtue,[16] and both cases again demonstrate Socrates's refusal to be identified as a Sophist or as an aristocratic conservative.

By process of elimination, we are left with two other possible responses as outlined by Meno to the question as to whether virtue can be taught: it cannot be taught but is the result of practice, and it is acquired in some other unspecified way. I want to suggest that the former position is closest to Socrates's own, and that the latter position could be specified along Kantian lines where the authority of moral custom and moral tradition are rejected in an attempt to ground reason autonomously. If I am correct, then what emerges from the *Meno* are four different possible views of moral rationality: (1) the Liberal, which corresponds to the Sophists; (2) the Conservative, which corresponds to the aristocratic ruling elites; (3) the Autonomous, which corresponds to the Kantian rejection of tradition; and (4) the Traditionalist, which I am arguing is Socrates's position of dependence on moral custom.

At this point it is helpful to think of the Autonomous and the Traditional views as responses to the inadequacies present within the Liberal and the Conservative positions. In response to the moral fragmentation and the loss of solidarity in Periclean Athens, the Sophists and the ruling elites developed moral positions that ultimately boiled down to manipulation and the will to power of one group over another. The Sophists flourished in Athens because Athens was a democracy, and one's success in a democratic polity is dependent on one's ability to argue persuasively and convince a majority. Protagoras's assertion that "man is the measure of all things"[17] is instructive here, for the conception of truth that emerges on this account is a democratic one: questions of truth are arrived at by vote of the majority. A clever manipulator of argument could convince the majority of his or her particular, private interest and thereby assert his or her will coercively on a potentially unsuspecting public. The conservative aristocrat, on the other hand, interested in maintaining the current power structures guaranteeing his or her interests, is concerned to defend the claims of heredity over against the majority. When unmasked by Socrates's *elenctic* activity, these positions both reveal themselves as arbitrary, coercive exercises of power. Might truly makes right, whether might be an exercise of the democratic majority or the aristocratic minority.[18]

In order to avoid these positions and to ground the truth of moral claims on a reality that transcends the mere vote of the majority or the coercive tactics of the powerful, the Autonomous and Traditional views are two potential alternative positions. The Autonomous view maintains that we need some extra human, community-transcendent foundation for our claims, or that we are indeed left with some version of the two positions. From this perspective, the authority of human tradition and moral custom is just one more institution that autonomous reason must rise above in its ascent to objectivity. Indeed, as we have seen, it can even be construed as "the reasoned rejection of tradition." Additionally, on the Autonomous account, there is no meaningful difference between the merely conventional morality of the *hoi polloi* and a morality grounded in the consensual norms embedded in the *sensus communis*.

The Traditional view, just like the Autonomous, challenges the Liberal and Conservative positions. However, the Traditional view does so by grounding the objectivity and rationality of moral claims on the authority of moral custom and, in general, the moral sense of the community. Rather than viewing tradition as a heteronomous imposition on the proper functioning of reason, the pre-given authority of tradition and moral custom themselves are the transcendental condition for the possibility of moral reasoning at all.[19] The Traditionalist thus offers a form of moral reasoning and rational justification as grounded in the "conformity to the consensual standards of sound judgment."[20]

My claim then, is that Socrates, in the face of the moral crisis evident in the war between the Conservative aristocrats and the Liberal Sophists, attempts to avoid the conclusion that the arbitrary will is the creator of value, not through a radical rejection of tradition in an attempt to ground reason autonomously, but rather through grounding moral rationality in the "consensual norms of valid reasoning"[21] present within his Athenian community. In other words, Socrates is not the ideally rational person as conceived by Kant, but rather much closer to the Traditionalist as described above. To support this claim, we first need to turn to the *aporetic* ending of the *Protagoras*.

Socrates as Traditionalist

The *Protagoras* and the *Meno* both take up the question of the teachability of virtue. We have already seen this in the case of the latter, but the former especially highlights this question in Socrates's direct confrontation with the Sophist threat in the person of Protagoras. The dialogue famously ends in *aporia*. As a result of their dialectical exchange, it emerges that Socrates and Protagoras both hold paradoxical positions that seem unable to be reconciled internally. Socrates outlines clearly how this is the case, speaking of Protagoras and himself in the third person:

> Socrates and Protagoras, how ridiculous you are, both of you. Socrates, you said earlier that virtue cannot be taught, but now you are arguing the very opposite and have attempted to show that everything is knowledge—justice, temperance, courage—in which case, virtue would appear to be eminently teachable. On the other hand, if virtue is anything other than knowledge, as Protagoras has been trying to say, then it would clearly be unteachable. But, if it turns out to be wholly knowledge, as you now urge, Socrates, it would be very surprising indeed if virtue could not be taught. Now, Protagoras maintained at first that it could be taught, but now he thinks the opposite, urging that hardly any of the virtues turn out to be knowledge. On that view, virtue could hardly be taught at all.[22]

In other words, on the one hand, if one holds the position that virtue is knowledge, then one ought to be committed to the teachability of virtue. On the other hand, if one holds the position that virtue is not knowledge, then one ought to be committed to the unteachability of virtue. Socrates, arguing that virtue is knowledge, but that it cannot be taught, and Protagoras, arguing that virtue is not knowledge, but that it can be taught, each hold internally inconsistent positions. Thus, in light of the fact that they have gotten "topsy-turvy and terribly confused," Socrates proposes that they "continue until we come through to what virtue is in itself, and then to return to inquire about whether it can or cannot be taught."[23]

Socrates's proposal is more than the mere suggestion that they need to start the conversation over in light of their ignorance. He indicates a very specific direction for further inquiry. Before they can properly answer the question as to the teachability of virtue, they must first be able to give an account of what virtue is in itself. I want to suggest that this is Plato's subtle hint at the end of the dialogue to reconsider the conception of virtue and knowledge that has been presupposed by both Socrates and Protagoras up to this point. If we ask this question, we see that Socrates and Protagoras are both working with a conception of knowledge that is based on *techné* as its paradigm.[24] Characteristic of *techné* as the paradigm for knowledge is that one can provide an account of what it is that one knows and that this knowledge can be taught to others in a relatively straightforward manner through a thorough training in the techniques of the craft in question. As Terry Penner sums up, conceiving virtue as technical expertise involves "the ability to 'give an account,' to explain to others, and to teach them; it is not just a matter of 'knowing how.' It does not involve any (propaedeutic) training of the emotions *independent of* the understanding to be reached by discussion."[25] The student comes to know this technical knowledge as a learned insight (i.e., *mathema*). He can now rely on that general knowledge for the exercise and teaching of his craft.[26] In short, technical knowledge is characterized by stability, reliability, and teachability. David Roochnik summarizes, moral *techné* is "a stable body of reliable knowledge able to tell us, in fixed terms readily teachable to others, how we ought to live."[27]

Many scholars, such as Penner and Terence Irwin have argued that Socrates holds a *techné* conception of moral knowledge, but, on my reading, Socrates assumes this paradigm in order to push his interlocutors beyond it by displaying its inadequacy.[28] My reading depends on a specific understanding of the function of the *aporetic* dialogues in general and a specific interpretation of the *aporetic* ending of the *Protagoras*. Commenting on the point and function of the "'negative' [or aporetic] dialogues" in Plato's *oeuvre*, Gadamer observes, "All the refutations which they contain of the preconceptions about arête that the interlocutors bring with them to the discussion . . . have a common character: no answer is found to the questions posed, namely, what this or that arête actually is, or whether arête can be taught or not, in view of the unclarity and deceptiveness of whatever particular thing is taken to be arête."[29] In other words, the main function of the *aporetic* dialogues is to deconstruct the common preconceptions about virtue. Gadamer further maintains what we have already seen from the *Protagoras*, that one of the main preconceptions targeted by Plato is an understanding of virtue through the paradigm of *techné*. The *aporetic* dialogues, then, can be seen to have a positive goal: they not only "demonstrate the inadequacy of the technē concept for attaining a clear concept of knowledge of the good and the nature or arête,"[30] as Gadamer details, but they also beckon us to find a model for the knowledge of the good other than the *techné* paradigm. In other words, the positive direction in which the negative dialogues point us is to some other model for the knowledge of the good than the *techné* paradigm. And as we see from the *Protagoras*, so long as Socrates holds to *techné* as the model for the knowledge of the good, he cannot consistently maintain both that virtue is knowledge and that virtue is unteachable. However, the *aporetic* ending of the *Protagoras* leads us to ask whether there is an alternative kind of knowledge that is not teachable in the way that *techné* is teachable, and, if so, Socrates may be able consistently to maintain that virtue is knowledge while not being teachable as a *techné* is teachable.[31] If we return to Meno's second possibility, namely, that virtue cannot be taught but is the result of practice, we get a clue to what this alternative model might be.

Here we begin to be pushed in a distinctly Aristotelian direction, especially his mature clarification of the difference between *techné* and *phronesis* in the *Nicomachean Ethics*, and his recognition of the role of habituation and moral character in knowledge of the good.[32] For Aristotle, *phronesis* requires more than the technical mental ability to achieve one's end by recognizing and employing the appropriate means, which, incidentally, is precisely the ability that we saw Protagoras promise to deliver.[33] Herein lay Aristotle's consequential distinction between mere cleverness and true prudence.[34] Prudence is not only knowledge of the means, but also proper insight into the ends worth pursuing; proper insight into correct ends necessarily depends upon virtue of character, which presupposes a good moral formation. Socrates recognizes this complicated relationship between *logos* and *ethos* in moral knowledge and moral reasoning, and therefore must reject any position on the knowledge of the good that ignores the role of moral formation and practice. One need only recall the centrality of character formation in the pedagogical program of the *Republic* to recognize the truth of this claim.[35] In the case of Socrates, I am not arguing that he rejects the *techné* model for the fully formed *phronesis* model of moral knowledge articulated by Aristotle, but rather that Socrates's rejection of the technical mode of reasoning begins to push him toward this Aristotelian position, and, as we will see shortly, fits perfectly alongside his philosophical practice of seeking consensus.

The suggestion that Socrates, by rejecting the *techné* model of practical rationality, begins to move toward a proto-phronesis model may sound strange to some readers, especially to those who are inclined to move in the direction of the theory of recollection with respect to moral knowledge. After all, is the theory of recollection not the direction Socrates himself explores with Meno's slave? Is not this interpretation of moral knowledge more natural in the context of the *Meno* as the kind of knowledge that cannot be taught? And is not the *phronesis* model of moral knowledge articulated by Aristotle much different from the recollection model of moral knowledge that Socrates explores in the dialogue? I want to suggest that if Plato's doctrine of recollection is sufficiently demythologized, then these two models are much closer than appears on the surface. I presuppose here that Plato employs elaborate mythical metaphors that are rich phenomenological descriptions of certain phenomena that can be translated (at least to a degree) into conceptual language. The phenomenon in question in the *Meno* is the knowledge known which cannot be taught, a radically different mode of knowing from techne. The relevant question, then, for understanding the idea of recollection, which is introduced as a myth in the *Meno*, is what it is like to experience the kind of knowledge that cannot be taught. On my reading, the doctrine of recollection is an early phenomenological exploration of what the experience of knowledge on the *phronesis* model would be like. I cannot fully defend this position here, but Gadamer has already provided a similar demythologization of the idea of recollection in the *Meno*.[36] What is significant for my argument is that, if we read the idea of recollection as a descriptive phenomenology of the knowledge known that cannot be taught, the doctrine of recollection can be read to be in fundamental continuity with an Aristotelian *phronesis* model of moral knowledge.

The position that becomes entirely clear only later with Aristotle's distinction between technical and practical reasonableness is in its nascent stages during the Socratic demonstrations of the inadequacy of the *techné* model.[37] One essential difference between technical and practical reasonableness is that, in the case of practical reason, one does not have recourse to an established body of general knowledge and procedures that can be methodically employed. Practical reasonableness is a non-methodical, insight-prudential model. On this model, one cannot merely appeal to a pre-established body of rules or knowledge or to a decision-making procedure. Knowledge about the right thing to do is a matter of insight into the particular practical situation, and thus, deciding reasonably in a specific, concrete case and providing a defense of that decision with reasons, is also characterized by the specificity and particularity of the practical situation.[38] However, even though one ultimately may not be able to "rely on previously acquired general knowledge" in the face of this particularity, if one is reasonable, then one will be able to provide a sufficient justification of one's decision with reasons that are "tailored to" or "right for" the particular case.[39] A significant part of the reasonableness here is the capacity "to summon the full range of considerations that are relevant in a particular case,"[40] a capacity that "cannot be taught in the abstract but only practiced from case to case, and is therefore more an ability like the senses."[41]

Returning to Socrates in the *Protagoras*, this conception of practical reasonableness is just the sort of position one would expect from someone claiming that virtue is knowledge, but is nevertheless unteachable; and it is just the sort of model in harmony with Meno's second possibility, namely, that virtue cannot be taught but it is the result of practice. As Gadamer maintains, a prudential capacity of this sort "is something that cannot be learned, because no demonstration from concepts can guide the applications of rules."[42] It is much more a capacity to be cultivated or formed (bildung).[43] Prudence is insight into the particular practical situation that is "not so much a techné—that is, an ability and knowledge—as a way of being."[44]

Socrates's rejection of the technical conception of moral knowledge most obviously applies to the case of the Sophists, but it also implicates the Autonomous position that tries to rise above situated moral practice and custom to the purely intellectual grasp of the good. Socrates does not attempt to escape the particularity of his moral identity, an identity which arises from his membership in a specific family, city, and community.[45] Rather, in his inquires into the good life for human beings, Socrates begins and ends with his own and his interlocutors' moral intuitions and the "consensual norms of valid reasoning"[46] present within his community. This is especially apparent in Socrates's dialectical method of consensus seeking. Far more than a mere strategy for getting his interlocutors to agree with him, Socrates's practice of consensus seeking is evidence of his recognition that broadly shared values and consensual standards of reasoning legitimately exercise authority over the members of a particular community. Socrates's method is so ubiquitous that it is actually easy to overlook and its significance, therefore, often goes unexamined. A few examples must suffice. In Book I of the *Republic*, a Socratic dialogue likely circulated independently,[47] Socrates contrasts his way of seeking consensus with Thrasymachus's sophistic way of giving parallel speeches. Socrates suggests, "But if, on the other hand, we investigate the question as we've been doing, *by seeking agreement with each other*, we ourselves can be both jury and advocates at once."[48] In this passage, Socrates draws Glaucon's attention explicitly to the way in which they have been engaged in their inquiry, namely, seeking and establishing common ground and common criteria from which they can adjudicate between various positions. It is significant that Socrates appeals to what appears to them, in common, to be correct. The standard of judgment is internal to their perspective as human knowers and internal to the communal standards achieved "so far" in their common practices of seeking justification.[49] Similar language emerges in the *Crito* where Socrates characterizes himself as "the kind of man who listens to nothing within me but the argument that on reflection seems best to me."[50] In other words, all Socrates can ever hope to do in exploring the truth of any given topic is to return again to his own best sense of things and allow himself to be addressed again by the question.

By insisting on the role of moral custom in Socratic moral reasoning here, it may appear that I am taking the bite out of the gadfly, ignoring the critical role of Socrates in challenging the conventional beliefs of the Athenians, and domesticating this oftentimes strident critic of the status quo. Referring back to the distinction between the Conservative and the Traditionalist should resolve this concern. Whereas the Conservative merely underwrites the prevailing, conventional view, often in the service of self-interest, the Traditionalist may be radically critical of the merely conventional in order to push the *hoi polloi* toward a more faithful and authentic embodiment of the *sensus communis*. For example, in the *Republic* Socrates pushes his interlocutors to reject certain conventional views about the gods based on a deeply shared intuition about the gods' perfection.[51] Here Socrates dialectically pushes his interlocutors to the next stage of their understanding of the divine by appealing to something they already know. Socrates accomplishes this by functioning as the negative element in the dialectic. The important thing to notice is that Socrates does this from within the confines of an ongoing tradition, from within the *sensus communis*. In this way, then, a Traditionalist working from a communal sense of what is fitting need not be supportive of the status quo.

Elsewhere in the *Crito* is another example of Socrates's consensus-seeking activity. When attempting to establish the position that one should never wrong another person no matter what the circumstance, Socrates counsels Crito:

And Crito, see that you do not agree to this, contrary to your belief. For I know that only a few people hold this view or will hold it, and there is no common ground between those who hold this view and those who do not, but they inevitably despise each other's views. So then consider very carefully whether we have this view in common, and whether you agree, and let this be the basis of our deliberation, that neither to do wrong nor to return a wrong is ever right, nor is bad treatment in return for bad treatment. Or do you disagree and do not share this view as a basis for discussion? I have held it for a long time and still hold it now, but if you think otherwise, tell me now. If, however, you stick to our former opinion, then listen to the next point.[52]

In this passage, we again see Socrates working from a standpoint within his and Crito's mutual sense of things based on the community they share with one another. These examples along with the recognition that Socrates continually appeals to what "we believe" or what "we say,"[53] a point which will be familiar to any reader of Plato, paint a picture of Socrates as one who explores the good life for the human via the overlapping consensus which is "always already pre-given in the traditional authority of language and customs (Sitten)."[54] Significantly, and in direct contrast with the Kantian Autonomous position so characteristic of the modern Enlightenment, Socrates does not attempt to strip his interlocutors of all their prior commitments, nor does he encourage them to abandon systematically the prejudices (i.e., prejudgments) embedded in what has been handed down to them in language and custom.[55] Rather he seeks to place his interlocutors into more authentic contact with their inherited moral identity in order that they might achieve an integrated moral self, ultimately eventuating in harmony of soul.

It is in the context of the authority of moral custom that one further aspect of the Sophist threat becomes particularly acute. Because Socrates grounds his own exploration of the good in the traditional authority of language and custom, whose life-blood is solidarity and community with one's fellow citizens, then any threat to that sense of political friendship would be a threat to the way in which "we" can seek the good. One of the chief characteristics of the Sophists is that they traveled from city to city teaching their knowledge. Socrates's unwillingness to travel from city to city is conspicuous by contrast, and I want to suggest that this is because Socrates roots his moral inquiry in the "we" of his Athenian community. In other words, Socrates's concern that, as travelers and strangers, the Sophists do not possess the organic ties of political friendship or the moral identity grounded in and through common participation in the Athenian community, makes sense in the context of a position that attempts to establish moral reasoning and moral knowledge on moral custom and the *sensus communis*.

Conclusion

As I have attempted to demonstrate, of the four positions that emerge from Meno's schematization of virtue's teachability, Socrates is best identified with the position that virtue cannot be taught but is the result of practice. I have characterized this position as Traditionalist, which stands as an alternative position on moral reasoning and moral knowledge to that of the Liberal Sophist, the Conservative Aristocrat, and to the Autonomous Kantian. If I am correct, then Socrates emerges not as a figure who pits reason against tradition, but as one who knows himself as a finite human being *in media res*, and as one who is dependent on the authority of tradition (i.e., what has been handed down to him) as the ground of his moral being.

Mount St. Mary's University

Notes

I would like to thank Bonnie Kent and Anne-Marie Bowery for their helpful comments on earlier drafts of this article.

1. I by no means wish to be read as making a claim about the historical Socrates over against the dramatic Socrates, who is merely a literary production of Plato. In this I follow Charles H. Kahn, who maintains, "in order to do justice to Plato's genius as a philosophical writer, one must first free him from the shadow, or rather the ghost, of the historical Socrates. Once we have recognized the fictional element in all the Socratic literature, we can no longer hope to extract an historical kernel from Plato's representation." Instead I am concerned with uncovering certain aspects of Plato's Socrates that have been obscured as a result of one dominant tradition of reading Plato. For a clear articulation of the position that distinguishes between an early-dialogue, historical Socrates and a middle and late dialogue, dramatic Socrates who represents Plato, see Gregory Vlastos, "Socrates *contra* Socrates in Plato," *Socrates: Ironist and Moral Philosopher* (Cambridge: Cambridge University Press, 1991), 45–80.

2. David Roochnik is a recent example of the pervasiveness of this view. He maintains, "[Muthos] is a powerful intellectual option, one which has never ceased to be attractive and compelling to human beings eager to express their own experience of life. It is not, however, philosophical" *Retrieving the Ancients: An Introduction to Greek Philosophy* (Malden: Blackwell, 2004), 17. Hans Georg-Gadamer draws attention to the way in which the schema of "the abstract contrast between myth and reason" is a distinctly modern Enlightenment philosophy of history. He asserts, "This can be seen with particular clarity in the fundamental schema of the philosophy of history that romanticism shares with the Enlightenment and that precisely through the romantic reaction to the Enlightenment became an unshakable, premise: the schema of the conquest of mythos by logos" *Truth and Method* (New York: Continuum, 2003), 273.

3. Peter Gay, "Greece: From Myth to Reason," in *The Enlightenment: An Interpretation* (New York: Alfred A Knopf, 1967), 73.

4. W. K .C. Guthrie, *The Sophists* (Cambridge: Cambridge University Press, 1971), 17.

5. For challenges to the anti-tradition Socrates, see for example, Roslyn Weiss, *The Socratic Paradox and Its Enemies* (Chicago: The University of Chicago Press, 2006); and Francisco J. Gonzalez, "The Socratic Hermeneutics of Heidegger and Gadamer," *A Companion to Socrates*, ed. Sara Ahbel-Rappe and Rachana Kamtekar (Oxford: Blackwell, 2006), 426–441. For the way in which the autonomous reason view persists, see for example, Richard Janko, "Socrates the Freethinker," *A Companion to Socrates*, 48–62; and Martha Nussbaum, *Cultivating Humanity* (Cambridge: Harvard University Press, 1997).

6. Immanuel Kant, *Foundations of the Metaphysics of Morals and What is Enlightenment?* (Indianapolis: Bobs-Merrill Educational Publishing, 1959), 85, emphasis added.

7. Plato, "Protagoras," in *Plato: Complete Works*, ed. John M. Cooper (Indianapolis: Hackett Publishing Company, 1997), 319. Unless otherwise noted, all references to Plato come from this edition.

8. P. Christopher Smith, "Introduction," in Hans Georg-Gadamer, *The Idea of the Good in Platonic-Aristotelian Philosophy* (New Haven: Yale University Press, 1986), xiii. Smith is here explicating the position of Gadamer.

9. Ibid., emphasis added. This is once again Smith's characterization of Gadamer's thesis pertaining to Plato.

10. Jacqueline De Romilly, *The Great Sophists in Periclean Athens* (Oxford: Clarendon Press, 1992), 44.

11. *Meno*, 70a.

12. Ibid., 70b–c.

13. De Romilly, *The Great Sophists in Periclean Athens*, 4.

14. *Meno*, 92e.

15. Ibid., 93a–95a.

16. *Protagoras*, 361a–362a.

17. Sextus Empiricus, *Selections from the Major Writings on Scepticism, Man, and God*, (Indianapolis: Hackett, 1985), 90.

18. In this fundamentally manipulative context, it is no surprise that a perceptive realist like Thrasymachus would come to view justice as "the advantage of the stronger." See *Republic*, 339a.

19. P. Christopher Smith makes this point when discussing Heidegger and Gadamer on the circularity of understanding: "the 'condition of the possibility' (Kant) of my understanding my world is not so much consciousness's interpretive acts or performances as it is consciousness *of* and recollection *of*, what is always already pre-given in the traditional authority of language and customs (Sitten)" (Gadamer, *The Idea of the Good*, nn. 19, 57). Making a related point from a Wittgensteinian, linguistic perspective, Sabina Lovibond asserts, "rationality in general—and hence, *a fortiori*, moral rationality—rests upon a shared practice which is *embodied* in institutions;" and further, "it is only as a member of some community that I exist as a moral being," *Realism and Imagination in Ethics* (Minneapolis: University of Minnesota Press, 1983), 82, 85.

20. Lovibond, *Realism and Imagination in Ethics*, 43. An analogous point is made by Alasdair MacIntyre during his discussion of tradition constituted inquiry in *Whose Justice? Which Rationality?* He maintains, "Because every such rational tradition begins from the

contingency and positivity of some set of established beliefs, the rationality of tradition is inescapably anti-Cartesian. . . . The kind of rational justification which they receive is at once dialectical and historical. They are justified insofar as in the history of this tradition they have, by surviving the process of dialectical questioning, vindicated themselves as superior to their historical predecessors. Hence such first principles are not self-sufficient, self-justifying epistemological first principles. They may indeed be regarded as both necessary and evident, but their necessity and their evidentness will be characterizable as such only to and by those whose thought is framed by the kind of conceptual scheme from which they emerge as a key element, in the formulation and reformulation of the theories informed by that historically developing conceptual scheme" (Notre Dame: University of Notre Dame Press, 1988), 360.

21. Lovibond, *Realism and Imagination in Ethics*, 45.

22. *Protagoras*, 361b–c.

23. 361d.

24. See Gadamer, *The Idea of the Good*, 23.

25. Terry Penner, "Socrates and the Early Dialogues," *The Cambridge Companion to Plato*, ed. Richard Kraut (Cambridge: Cambridge University Press, 1992), 126.

26. Gadamer, *The Idea of the Good*, 28, 35.

27. David Roochnik, *Of Art and Wisdom: Plato's Understanding of Techne* (University Park: Pennsylvania State University Press, 1996), xii.

28. See Penny, "Socrates and the Early Dialogues," 125–126; and Terence Irwin, *Plato's Moral Theory: The Early and Middle Dialogues* (Oxford: Clarendon Press, 1977), 71–101. For an account of the prevalence of this view, see Roochnik, *Of Art and Wisdom*, 1–15.

29. Ibid., 22.

30. Ibid., 50–51.

31. For a similar suggestion, see ibid., 50.

32. For a similar claim, see ibid., 33, 60–61.

33. 318d–319a.

34. *Nicomachean Ethics*, trans. Terence Irwin, second edition (Indianapolis: Hackett, 1999), Bk. VI, cc. 12, 98.

35. For example, see *Republic*, 401d–402a. Some may object to my use of Book III of the *Republic* as evidence for Socrates's attention to character formation. For example, on certain developmental accounts of the dialogues, the *Republic* is a middle dialogue and thus should be read as Plato's development of authentic Socratic thought, which is found in the early dialogues. See Vlastos, "Socrates *contra* Socrates in Plato," 45–80; and "Socratic Knowledge and Platonic 'Pessimism,'" *The Philosophical Review* 66.2 (1957): 226–238. However, I follow Kahn's alternative, unitarian interpretive strategy, which he defines as, "a proposal to read all the dialogues—and in particular all the early ones—as the work of an author whose world-view is defined by the *Phaedo* and *Republic*. But Plato did not believe that any doctrine or formula could successfully communicate this view to a reader in any direct way, so all of his most constructive statements are provisional, incomplete and subject to criticism and correction. Instead of fixed doctrines we have large and flexible schemata" Charles H. Kahn, "Response to Christopher Rowe," http://www.nd.edu/~plato/plato2issue/kahn.htm, accessed August 31, 2010. Nevertheless, my reading of Socrates as a Traditionalist does not rest on

this interpretive strategy or this evidence alone. For some of the contemporary options on the issue of interpretive strategies and related matters see the following: Christopher Rowe, "Just how Socratic Are Plato's 'Socratic' Dialogues?" http://www.nd.edu/~plato/plato2issue/rowe2.htm, accessed August 31, 2010; Charles H. Kahn, "Did Plato Write Socratic Dialogues?" *The Classical Quarterly* New Series 31.2 (1981): 305–320; Richard Kraut, "Virtue as a Means: Socrates in *Plato's Ethics* by T. Irwin," *Classical Philology* 91.3 (1996): 261–273; and Alexander Nehamas, "Socratic Intellectualism," in *Virtues of Authenticity: Essays on Plato and Socrates* (Princeton: Princeton University Press, 1998), 27–58.

36. See Gadamer, *The Idea of the Good*, 33–62.

37. See Gadamer's distinction between technical-theoretical reasonableness and practical reasonableness in, ibid., 35–36.

38. On ethical particularism, see Jonathan Dancy, *Ethics Without Principles* (New York: Oxford University Press, 2004). Especially relevant to Gadamer's particularlism is Dancy's discussion of holism and particularism. Dancy defines "*Holism* in the theory of reasons: a feature that is a reason in one case may be no reason at all, or an opposite reason, in another." He also claims that holism in the theory of reasons is the "main argument for particularlism in ethics," suggesting that particularlism maintains that "the possibility of moral thought and judgment does not depend on the provision of a suitable supply of moral principles" 73.

39. See Stanley Rosen's comments on the importance of doing "our best to articulate what we take to be the merits of our perceptions" without succumbing to the "illusion that these arguments, or others of a greater technical ingenuity, can succeed in transforming my perceptions into logical theorems" *The Ancients and the Moderns: Rethinking Modernity* (New Haven: Yale University Press, 1989), 19.

40. I borrow this apt phrase from Robert C. Miner. "Verum-factum and Practical Wisdom in the Early Writings of Giambattista Vico," *Journal of the History of Ideas* 59.1 (1998): 58.

41. Gadamer, *Truth and Method*, 31.

42. Ibid.

43. It is in this context that Vico and Gadamer insist on the importance of the *ars topica* in an educational curriculum. The polemical context for Vico is the Cartesian rejection of the *ars topica* for the *ars critica*, and similarly for Gadamer it is the hegemony that the model of the natural sciences exercises over truth, especially truth in the human sciences. See Gaeamer, *Truth and Method*, especially 19–30; and Robert C. Miner, *Vico: Genealogist of Modernity* (Notre Dame: University of Notre Dame Press, 2002), especially 3–19.

44. Gadamer, *The Idea of the Good*, 39.

45. This understanding of moral identity is especially evident in Socrates's defense of Athens and the laws in the *Crito*. Socrates, via the personified laws, suggests, "Did we not, first, bring you to birth, . . . and after you were born and nurtured and educated, could you, in the first place, deny that you are our offspring and servant, both you and your forefathers? . . . You were not on an equal footing with your father as regards the right, nor with your master if you had one, so as to retaliate for anything they did to you, to revile them if they reviled you, to beat them if they beat you, and so with many other things. Do you think you have this right to retaliation against your country and its laws? . . . We have given you birth, nurtured you, educated you; we have given you and all other citizens a share of all the good things we could," 50d–51d. For a similar exploration of moral identity as grounded "in and through its membership in communities such as those of the family, the neighborhood, the

city and the tribe," see Alasdair MacIntyre, *After Virtue* (Notre Dame: University of Notre Dame Press, 1984), 221.

46. Ibid., 45.

47. See for example, Penner, "Socrates and the Early Dialogues," 124.

48. *Republic*, 348b. Emphasis added.

49. I borrow the language of "so far" from MacIntyre's habitual way of speaking about "a kind of rational inquiry which is inseparable from the intellectual and social tradition in which it is embodied." For example, he asserts, "the concept of rational justification which is at home in that form of enquiry is essentially historical. To justify is to narrate how the argument has gone *so far*" (*Whose Justice? Which Rationality?*, 8; emphasis added). See especially "The Rationality of Traditions," 349–369.

50. Ibid., 46b.

51. *Republic*, 379a—383c.

52. *Crito*, 49d–e.

53. This "flight into the *logoi* (ways of saying things)" is of fundamental significance to Gadamer's interpretation of Plato and especially to his thesis that Platonic-Aristotelian philosophy represents a "unitary effect" in that they start "with the *legomena* (things we say)" *The Idea of the Good*, 15.

54. Smith in *The Idea of the Good*, 57.

55. On the transformation/distortion of the concept of "prejudice" by Enlightenment thinkers, see Gadamer, *Truth and Method*, 265–277.

Plato's Mimetic Art: The Power of the Mimetic and Complexity of Reading Plato

Gene Fendt

Abstract: Plato's dialogues are self-defined as works of mimetic art, and the ancients clearly consider mimesis as working naturally before reason and beneath it. Such a view connects with two contemporary ideas—Rene Girard's idea of the mimetic basis of culture and neurophysiological research into mirror neurons. Individuality arises out of, and can collapse back into our mimetic origin. This para-rational notion of mimesis as that in which and by which all our knowledge is framed requires we not only concern ourselves with Socrates's arguments and distinctions, but also see how the dramatic interaction of the characters is working (or not) on/in the characters, and consider how watching the interaction, hearing the parables and myths, and thinking through the arguments and interactions is meant to effect us. That Plato creates mimeses means he aims at passional conversion not merely argumentative worth, since mimesis aims to (and does) work on the passions.

> *For we have no common name to give to the mimes of*
> *Sophron and Xenarchus and to Socratic dialogues;*
> *nor even to any mimesis that might be produced in*
> *iambic trimeters or elegiac couplets*
>
> —*Poetics* 1447b

That Plato wrote dialogues is the commonest of knowledge. That these dialogues fall into the category of mimetic art, rather than scientific or philosophical treatise, has been an undeniable truth since antiquity. What that means for our reading of the dialogues, for getting Plato's point(s): doctrinal, philosophical, moral, passional—that is the question. Given the long history of such debates anyone daring to say anything further on philosophy's greatest mimetic artist ought to set out in brief his idea of what mimesis is and how it functions and then how this understanding shapes the reading and understanding of Platonic dialogue.

I will begin by briefly setting out a problem in the interpretation of ancient mimesis between the received view and an explanation I think is more adequate to the Platonic and Aristotelian language as well as the social-political problematic in which they unfailingly speak of mimesis. I will then show, even more briefly, how that better view of ancient mimesis ties into language acquisition, findings in contemporary neuroscience, and Rene Girard's theory about the origin (and plausible destruction) of culture. Those matters together set forth anew the power of the mimetic and place the ancient, and particularly Platonic, philosophical machinery on firm anthropological and cultural ground, where—even today—it finds significant real world traction.

In the second part of the paper I will show that even if one disagrees with my interpretation of the mimetic, reading a Platonic dialogue requires attention to at least three levels of discourse: the arguments at the philosophical surface, the interaction of the interlocutors, and what those interactions aim to incite, invite or require of the readers.[1]

1. The Mimetic Arts

The received view for quite some time was that our modern notion of art has little if anything in common with antiquity's concepts of *mimêsis*, or of *technê*.[2] The modern narrowing of mimesis to representation, of the mimetic to things that are representational of other things, and so considering the mimetic as intellectually or cognitively oriented rather than operating emotively is a further conclusion within the received view. But this cognitivist and at times thoroughly rationalist prejudice ("this persona represents that kind of person"), is also arguably not the whole story for both Plato and Aristotle. While it is true that *technê* extends far beyond what we ordinarily consider "the arts" on the other hand, it is undeniable that there is a *technê*, or art, for making such mimetic things; that they are constructed for an end as well as being from nature, and that mimetic constructions have some generalizable rules certainly underlies the argument of Aristotle's *Poetics*.[3] So, while *technê* is too wide a term for our understanding of the arts, mimesis has usually been considered to narrowly.

This last point has been powerfully called into question by Stephen Halliwell, who argued that the mimetic gave the ancients "a unified conception of art" which gathered together a wide variety of practices sharing "a representational-cum-expressive character" legitimately regarded as a coherent group.[4] Halliwell's argument begins our reconsideration of the status of the mimetic among the ancients. There are several elements of Platonic and Aristotelian thought which allow us to call the thoroughgoing intellectualism of the modern view into question. In *Republic*, Socrates is clearly concerned with some non-rationalist working of the arts, since his concern with them is primarily in regard to what surrounds the children. He says that music, poetry, painting, architecture and all other like crafts work on the young "like a breeze bringing health from salubrious places; and, beginning in childhood, it will, *without their awareness*, lead them . . . to likeness and friendship as well as accord;"[5] the works of the artists "flow . . . into dispositions and practices, and from there it emerges bigger in men's contracts with one another."[6] In *Laws*, where the language is rather of tuning, consonance, and drawing or pulling of strings[7] the Athenian Stranger says that all laws (*nomoi*) are like kithara melodies (*nomoi*) in needing preludes—among which he places all the arts of the muses—to set the souls of citizens up in a harmony which *tunes them to hear* the speech of the laws (and keeps them there); without such preludes he thinks even the best laws will fail.[8] In all of this it becomes apparent that the mimetic keeps company with the non-rational part of the soul[9] precisely because mimesis is a non-rational process. Mimesis certainly begins that way: before reason.

Plato's language in these places is biological or mechanical, not intellectual—the mimetic flows, blows, pulls, has a natural *ergon* working through eyes and ears;[10] in fact it works *lanthanê*, unawares, escaping the notice or knowledge of those it works on;[11] it works "before reason."[12] Even for those with reason songs "are really incantations for souls."[13] Aristotle, too, uses such language, and makes clear that we take a natural pleasure in the mimetic and our first learning is mimetic.[14] But our first learning can't be representational identifications (this is a that); our first learning has to be beneath such intellectual comparison, thereby allowing it. Indeed, Aristotle clearly distinguishes 'signs of' moral qualities from 'likenesses' of them in the art of painting.[15] Both Plato and Aristotle regard music as a mimetic art par excellence; one which works not only on infants, but even on some higher animals and some who suffer madness.[16] Thus, the argument that mimesis proceeds by some mechanical or biological process, and is not merely intellectual or conceptual activity, seems inescapable. As something that is both natural to us and made by us, we experience pleasure both *in* mimesis (for it is an unimpeded activity of nature[17] and *through* mimetic works.

So, whereas the received view's more intellectualist understanding of Aristotle explains that "the impulse unshackling the cathartic process did not come to the spectator 'from below' . . . —from his viscera and humors . . . but 'from above,' from the dianoetic enlightenment elicited from the logos of the poem,"[18] the Platonic and Aristotelian language, on the contrary, *requires us* to think both sorts of process may well be going on, but more significantly and certainly, that if the more basic biological and mechanical, pre-cognitive mimetic functioning is not drawn in and properly attuned or purified (catharsized), the cognitive will not be able to be heard, or to be heard correctly: all of our *nomoi* that are *logoi* need *nomoi* that are not *logoi* to prepare the way. Similarly, we must be moved in virtuous ways by nature or the mimetic (which is our nature) before we can know what virtue is.[19] Of course, the mimetic can work the other way too—or rather, any way; one is "inundated, . . . swept away and borne by the flood wherever it tends."[20] And this is how we first become what we are—whatever we are.

Just so, we learn speech first by becoming attuned to the sounds around us; in this attunement we first learn that speech is distinct from all other sounds. We are *in* speech not only before we are *of* speech, but we must be in it unknowing (and miming it) *before it can become* our way of knowing: if there were no pleasure in mimesis that is pre-cognitive we would never achieve cognition. And if mimesis is natural to us before reason there is no reason to suspect that this natural pre-cognitive activity ever ceases, certainly not since it is the root of that very thing through which we think—our mother tongue, which we know by heart. That mimetic heart is ever active, unspoken, in the language of the head. And perhaps it is not really the head that is speaking, but our speeches themselves are mere mimesis; as Kierkegaard says somewhere "some think human beings have language to hide their thoughts, but I think it is to hide that they have no thoughts." Perhaps he is being dialectically extreme; it was a favorite trope of his. Be that as it may, excluding the mimetic from the human soul or city (as *Republic* 10 argues) is impossible, just as it is impossible to exclude it from language—it is the delusional dream of rationalism to wish so (and that dream has proven mimetically infectious).

Contemporary Echoes of Ancient Mimesis

This understanding of mimesis is not merely an ancient artifact. It is in line with some contemporary strands of thought about how we become—or are—such complicated social creatures. It seems for Plato and Aristotle that we grow from (but never out of) mimesis into rationality and cognition. In *De Motu* Aristotle says "sense perceptions are *at once* a kind of alteration, and phantasia and thinking have the power of actual things. . . . That is why we shudder and are frightened just thinking about something."[21] So thought, phantasia and sense perception *each* change the body; the way bodies respond sounds literally mimetic; Aristotle's analogies for mimesis are infectious and mechanical rather than the cognitivist or conceptualist 'representative of.'[22] This understanding enables a rapprochement between the ancients and contemporary biology on two sides. The first is to what we know about the developing baby. In at least the first five years of their lives the pre-frontal lobe, which allows internally driven intention, is undeveloped (it isn't fully developed until one's twenties—they say). What is active are the occipital and parietal cortexes (which are also highly active—if that's the right word—in adults watching tv and movies, when the pre-frontal lobe dims). The attention of children is *taken up* by what surrounds them; indeed, to say they have intentions is ratiopomorphizing.[23] Their intentions are not made by them; rather, the body is changed by sense perception.

We should relate this to other contemporary neurological studies about the workings of the brain. Neurologists have discovered that so-called mirror neurons fire both when we watch and when we perform the same act (there is a further group that fires as well when we are the actor). According to neuroscientists, the working of such cells gives a physiological basis to the dissolution "of the barrier between the self and others."[24] Recent studies have shown that some mirror neurons fire when listening to certain kinds of music and when feeling emotions like those frequently said to be expressed by or in the music.[25] We are being taken up and shaped by what we see and hear around us; these studies give some organic basis to the ancient thesis that mimesis *builds up into* cognition, behavior, and habitual emotions, that perception is an immediate infectious change.

In addition, the ancient and the modern biological accounts can be tied to Rene Girard's theorization of the mimetic foundation of culture. According to Girard, culture arises out of a disaster brought on through the process of mimetic rivalry; religion institutionalizes a form of the mimetic disaster, which allows the group to successfully avoid its full blown repetition. So both culture and individuality *arise out of* mimetic indifferentiation—and sometimes dissolves back into it. The dissolution of the barrier between oneself and others which is tied to mirror neurons and a lack of one's own intentionality are precisely what the ancient view of mimesis held. This dissolution is not only the central issue of Girard's anthropological theory, but connects with a major effect of public popular artistic performances. Interestingly, Girard, thinking the ancients intellectualist, regards their notion of the mimetic as wrongheaded.[26] These modern researches agree with the ancient view that individuality arises out of, and can collapse back into, our mimetic origin. These mimetic connections give a more than political and economic ring to Socrates's first principle that no human being is self-sufficient.[27]

All this should not be taken to say that the arts do not work at all cognitively or through cognition; indeed all of the arts using language *must* do so (unless Kierkegaard is telling the truth).[28] The point I wish to insist upon is that for the ancients (and in reality) we grow into intellectual cognition through something that lies deeper. What lies deeper is what the ancients called 'the mimetic'—in which we participate by nature, that through which we first learn, that which we pick up from our surroundings unawares, that which is always active in the arts—even in those unequivocally highly intellectual arts which use language: drama, movies, Platonic dialogue. The arts are the place where our first emotional communion, our first learning—a learning which takes place without our notice, perhaps even in a state which cannot be properly called "mine," for the barrier between oneself and others *is* not—is renewed. It is at least partly for this reason that we frequently speak of aesthetic experience as producing an experience of transcendence: our own ego is dissolved. To speak of what is going on in such cases as involving a recognition of intentionality or an intentionality of one's own, to think of any art as merely signals or signs 'representing' some content or action misses the point and affectiveness of the mimetic, which takes us up into something not ourselves in which all our knowledge is framed.[29] The mimetic *takes us up into* an order (a *kosmos*)—visible or hearable[30]—and this order is that in which any intentions are given shape. It provides a pre-cognitive and extra-cognitive attunement without which cognition can never begin nor intentionality ever take place. Perhaps reason breaks us from permanent subsumption under the power of the mimetic; perhaps it does so as Girard theorizes, through the catastrophe mimesis itself brings on. This break, however, is never clean or permanent—all of our arts are *eikastic* and *mimetic*, the Athenian stranger says; even a logical representation of the world engenders (and is engendered by) a mimesis.[31] Our mimetic nature is both a blessing and a curse; mimesis is, as Plato saw, a permanent human issue—about which we can become aware, and which we can turn toward the good, but from which we can never escape.[32] Mimesis is the *archê* of *anthrôpos*. Even if the play or music or ritual is new, the state of passional communion is part of what is being renewed. Being brought into such a state could well be cathartic—if it is not delusive, polluting, or soul (and city) destroying. From that latter communion we might prefer not to wake, as, unfortunately, Agave does, after one such mimetic infection vividly produced before us in Euripides's *Bacchae*.

That Plato writes dialogues, works of mimetic art, is because he is aware of this power of mimesis, a power which, as Eva Brann says, will "draw [us] helplessly into a fictive world of vivid but spuriously attributed speech" to be sure. It not only "invites us," but *charms* us into the world of the speakers, as a hearer and possible interlocutor ourselves. The Athenian Stranger calls the arts "incantations" for the soul,[33] and Aristotle says that "since actors are making the mimesis, of necessity some part [of the poem] will be the *opseôs kosmos*—the visible ordering"—which they are creating around or before us.[34] So that Socrates is "present and responsible as the teller of the tale" does not in any way make *Republic* (nor any Platonic dialogue) something which "overcomes the dangers of poetry"—rather it *employs* exactly those dangerous powers. In *Republic*'s case, the person we are imitating from the beginning is Socrates (who imitates all the others), but it is the only poem of Plato's in which we do so, and Socrates makes up further *mythoi* within it. Nor is (Plato's or any artist's) mimetic power "nothing but an artificially heightened appearance."[35] We are rather being enchanted,[36] shaped and turned by the work of art, one aspect of which (in Platonic dialogue) is the arguments presented. Put another way, the first meta-philosophical condition (or condition for the possibility of) philosophy[37] is the proper upbringing and tuning. Socrates and the Athenian Stranger both argue for this position, and Plato is *constantly carrying it out* in precisely the way they suggest—through mimesis. It is not only the arguments that move us, not only representations, but we move in the world of the dialogue *as* the world moves, carried by it into motion ourselves.

2. Plato: The Difficulty of Reading Three Things at Once

Even allowing possible disagreements about the interpretation of the mimetic among the ancients and the Platonic (at least) disagreement with many contemporaries—like Freud—about the uses of the arts, Plato, Aristotle and the mainstream of contemporary philosophy affirm the following matters: (a) that there is no civilization without the arts, (b) that the arts are important elements society uses to advance the happiness of its members, as well as (c) that society has to limit and direct the unrestricted drive for pleasure which seems to be natural to human beings and (d) that art has some function in achieving this socially requisite task. A longer project could show that the distinction between delusion and illusion is one about which Plato and the moderns have a basic agreement and that it is Plato rather than modern psychology which exhibits their social and political influence (for good and for ill) most perspicuously.[38] For our purposes it is enough to outline three points: (1) that *in Republic* Socrates makes this important modern psychological distinction (it is equivalent to the true lie/verbal lie distinction). (2) *Through* his discussion Socrates is attempting to cure his interlocutors of some of their most dangerous political and social delusions. (3) *By* writing the dialogue Plato is both revealing the depth of political and individual delusion *and* setting up an artistic mimetic therapy for future readers in his work of art: the illusion of *Republic* is to cure the delusions of republics. More exactly, the poem titled *Politeia* is to cure the delusions of polities, both literal (of cities) and figurative (of souls). Of course if art (like the natural mimesis of which it is born) can be helpful or curative, one should also be open to the suspicion that its power can work the other way as well—to entrance into delusion. For Plato, art is much more complex than mere satisfying illusion, for the illusion of art is to effect a real cure of certain psychic delusions—or else it introduces and strengthens them. *Republic* not only *provides* direct *arguments* for this thesis (a telling), but also is a *performance of it* upon the souls of Socrates's interlocutors (a showing)—and on Plato's readers (an entrancing).[39]

That brief outline already sets out one of the great contrasts between reading Plato and reading Freud and almost every other philosopher or psychologist. To read *Republic* well we must not only concern ourselves with Socrates's arguments and distinctions, like (1), but we must also see how the dramatic interaction of the characters is working (or not) on/in the characters (2), and (as scholars and teachers) consider how watching the interaction, and thinking through the arguments, parables, quotations, myths, histories, interactions, etc. effects, or is meant to effect, us (3). These three depths may well exist in all texts,[40] but they are built into Plato's texts by Plato, who is not writing to transfer information about *psyche*, politics, theology, or ethics as textbooks in philosophy, psychology or theology might.[41] In fact, Aristotle explicitly differentiates Socratic dialogue both from the kind of writing that makes scientific truth claims, which kinds of writing he takes up in the *Organon*, as well as differentiating it from *Rhetoric*, which he calls dialectic's antistrophe, when he discusses Socratic dialogue in *Poetics*. As mimeses are of action and agents, who of necessity have a certain character expressed in their speech and thought,[42] such dialogues may (and do) include both the kinds of speech or writing the *Organon* and the *Rhetoric* analyze, but a Socratic conversation is never merely that. If Homer and Empedocles really have "nothing in common except their meter,"[43] then we are less rhetorically radical than Aristotle if we say that Platonic dialogue has more in common with Homer or Shakespeare than with Vlastos or Quine.

The first of these three depths to the reading of Plato (and *Republic*) is admitted and practiced by everyone; it has to do with what Plato shares with Quine. It is, we might say, the philosophical surface of Plato, and it is itself intricate and multifaceted, ranging from the seemingly simple description, distinction and syllogism to those distinctions and arguments about which there is unlikely ever to be precise scholarly agreement. Aristotle and several millennia of philosophers can (and do) exhibit propositions within a dialogue as examples of certain kinds of argument (sophistical or otherwise), and understanding how these work (or fail) and what they prove (or not) is a necessary beginning for all readers of Plato, but that is all it is. The second and third depths have their common source in the fact that Plato is a maker of *mimesês*, itself a term of art and scholarly debate in philosophy and *Republic*. The *fact* is recognized by almost all readers,[44] but not all give the interactions of the characters their due in attempting to figure out why a certain argument is given, or story told, or distinction made, much less what its acceptance, denial or fluffing indicates about the character who does so (2), and still fewer attempt to discern (3) what *Plato's* mimesis may be attempting with its audience as distinct from what *Socrates* may be attempting in what he says (including both narrative and dramatic mimeses as well as argument) to his audience. This last scholarly failure is most particularly pertinent when one considers what mimesis is supposed to accomplish and how it is supposed to accomplish it, rather than merely considering the issue as one about discerning the difference between Socratic and Platonic irony, or Socratic vs. Platonic teaching. For, according to both Plato and Aristotle, mimesis aims to (and does) work on the passions; the crucial questions of which passions, and how, and to what end have a wide variety of answers—even among those who recognize that Platonic dialogues, as mimeses, must be considered in line with this third depth in reading. Socrates's own definitions in *Republic* (392d–394e) agree with Aristotle's mention of Socratic dialogue in *Poetics* that all Plato's dialogues are mimeses. I propose that this three level view of reading a Platonic dialogue is more directly adequate to working with the dialogues as mimetic works than more rationalist or epistemologically concerned distinctions, such as reading *Republic* against the divided line, or particular concerns with Plato's development, etc.)[45] I propose that such reading is what their ancient recognition as mimeses requires. Such reading, particularly of the third level, will certainly pick out different problems for analysis than traditional exposition of Plato's arguments, and even some distinctly different issues than the growing number of 'dramatic readers' of Plato (who orient their work around the second level).[46]

Several Exemplary Aporiai

To give a small example of how these depths multiply the difficulties of reading Plato, consider a term originating in the philosophical surface: *aporia*. (1) An argument or distinction may present a logical *aporia* or difficulty; Meno famously presents one. On a deeper level (2), a number of dialogues end aporetically—*Euthyphro* and *Hippias Major*, for example, do not seem to come to any conclusion; Socrates and his interlocutor can find no way to come to agreement; they seem at odds and the interlocutor runs off. Between these two levels one may see that an aporetic argument challenges the interlocutor to contrive some new distinction or story, so that an *aporia* on the first level may allow or produce an at least partial agreement between the characters (level two); in book One of *Republic* Socrates produces *aporiai* out of Cephalus,' Polemarchus,' and Thrasymachus's original definitions of justice such that they at least agree that they "didn't mean it that way" though they do not know exactly what they did mean either.[47] That is not much of an agreement, and if *Republic* One were an independent dialogue—as some scholars think it originally was, no doubt it would be called an aporetic one.

On the third hand, though the characters in a dialogue may end not coming to agreement, perhaps between Plato and the reader (level three) there is no *aporia*. For example, one could argue that *Euthyphro* is philosophically or theologically aporetic at level two (between Socrates and Euthyphro), but between the reader and Plato there is no such *aporia*: Plato's *drama shows us* that the Socratic dilemma presented to Euthyphro is false, and a true theologian would see (and feel) that the right way to begin working through the issue is to say that justice is the *ratio cognoscendi* of holiness or piety and holiness or piety is the *ratio essendi* of justice, rather than allowing the strict causal separation of these terms in the hard disjunction Socrates offers Euthyphro. Plato's doctrine might well be called secret, then, because this is the only way to come to it—by becoming a philosopher oneself, and a philosopher about the dialogic form and its purpose, not merely an analyst of the arguments given by the characters. So, sensitivity to the drama (level two) and to its poetic effect (level three) need not necessarily leave us with skepticism about philosophy or about Plato's position.[48] Improper passion, improper response, missing the teaching—which is secreted from such a character.[49]

If an *aporia* at any one level, as just seen, does not imply an *aporia* at succeeding levels, we should expect that agreement on one level does not imply no *aporia* on another. It may sound foolish that an argument is aporetic, but that the characters agree about some further conclusion that pretends to follow from it, but this happens frequently in politics, where people may agree on a conclusion while disputing on the argument that leads to it. Similarly, just as an agreement between two characters on a conclusion does not imply that the characters have a real agreement—as is exhibited frequently, we should not expect that an agreement among several characters, including Socrates, is always something we readers should agree to. For example, one might argue that despite Meno's concluding agreement with Socrates's eliminative argument that virtue must be a gift of the gods, Plato means his readers to see that this conclusion is a noble lie. The false conclusion will disable Meno's prejudice against slaves (or other lower class, less sophistically trained people) having virtue and thereby put him on the road of *practicing* virtue by requiring he treat all others as possibly having the gift; and it is by this *practicing* that virtue comes to be in human beings—maybe even Meno.[50]

So, for example, when we come upon an argument of Socrates's that seems faulty the reader on the first level will point out how it fails and perhaps adjust premises or invent a distinction which will help the argument go through to its (presumed) conclusion. The reader on the second level will consider who this argument is addressed to, and what Socrates is trying to get him to agree to by giving it in the particular dramatic and argumentative situation where it appears. And not only arguments; Socrates tells stories, invents poetic images and myths; clearly these must be for some purpose in regard to the person spoken to.[51] He has to give several different kinds of speech to Phaedrus (who reveals he has an unshakable fixation on them), finally giving him a myth in the hopes of curing the fixation by having him quit cold turkey. Whether Socrates believes the story he tells about writing is not a question we can well answer, but it is clear that writing and memorizing speeches has taken Phaedrus's mind away! On the third level, the reader must attempt to become aware of what Plato's mimesis of the discussion among the interlocutors is trying to accomplish in us: perhaps spark us into this question—why have these characters agreed to nonsense? And then, what does our laughter at Phaedrus's interactions with Socrates reveal about us? What, in fact, might that laughter already be curing? Perhaps it is possible to write in such a way as not to cause mental and passional defects.

So, finally, we must double this number of ways (one on each level) of producing *aporiai*: for—as mimeses—Platonic dialogues are not merely intellectual enterprises, but emotional or passional ones, and as the mimeses in the dialogue may (and do) move the passions of the characters differently, the mimesis *of* a dialogue may be moving us (or be meant to move us) on a completely different—even opposing—vector to that the characters *in* the dialogue move on at their level. For example, Socrates's aporealizing of Cephalus's definition of justice as telling the truth and paying debts via his example of the madman at the door[52] moves Polemarchus, by filial piety, to paternal defense. The resulting aporetic discussion of Polemarchus's definition moves Thrasymachus to a mad rage at both Polemarchus and Socrates. I doubt that Plato means us to be moved to either emotion through his mimesis, rather he means us to be moved as Glaucon is after all this argument—to wonder about what justice really is, and perhaps to be somewhat surprised at Thrasymachus's violence. In any case, it will prove to be dangerous to pick up such a work, for as a lesser mimetic artist has said: "such works are mirrors, when an ape peers in, no apostle can be looking out."[53] In fact a quite deluded soul might reveal itself by looking in—but the wonder of great works of mimetic art is that they can help the would-be apostle out of his delusion—unless he mistakes them for a book of logical problems.

University of Nebraska-Kearney

Notes

1. I would like to thank Fr. Ross Romero, S.J. for his comments on this paper at the ACPA meetings; I have incorporated a number of his suggestions in this version of the paper. I would also like to thank the University of Nebraska-Kearney for a year long sabbatical during which time I wrote this article and the book on *Republic* for which it is a part of the Introduction.

2. Cf. Paul Kristeller, "The Modern System of the Fine Arts," in *Renaissance Thought and the Arts* (Princeton: University Press, 1980),163–227; R. G. Collingwood, *The Principles of Art* (Oxford: Clarendon Press, 1938), 5–56.

3. I have previously argued how Aristotle's *Poetics* is an outline for the entire field modernly called aesthetics in "The Others in/of *Poetics*," *Journal of Philosophical Research* 22 (1997): 245–260. See also the explication of mimetic objects as sharing the way of being of both natural and made things in *Love Song for the Life of the Mind: An Essay on the Purpose of Comedy* (Washington, D.C.: Catholic University of America Press, 2007), 17–22.

4. Stephen Halliwell, *The Aesthetics of Mimesis: Ancient Texts and Modern Problems* (Princeton: University Press, 2002), 7.

5. *Rep.* 401cd.

6. *Rep.* 424d.

7. E.g., *Laws* 653b, 659d–e.

8. *Laws* 722d–723c.

9. *Rep.* 603b–d.

10. *Rep.* 401c9.

11. *Rep.* 401d.

12. *Rep.* 402a; *Laws* 653b.

13. *Laws* 659e, 665c.

14. *Poetics* 1448b4–9.

15. *Politics* 1340a33.

16. *Politics* 1342a.

17. *NE* 1153a13–16.

18. The quote is from Pedro Lian Entralgo, *The Therapy of the Word in Classical Antiquity* (New Haven: Yale University Press, 1970), 234. It is quoted by Leon Golden as decisive against the view I am defending in *Love Song*, and in favor of the intellectualist view Golden himself prefers. See *Classical Philology* 103.4 (October, 2008): 449–454; the quotation is from page 452.

19. Hallvard Fossheim puts the matter strongly when he says "practical reason is in ineradicable debt to something that isn't in itself entirely reasonable." See "Mimesis in Aristotle's Ethics," in *Making Sense of Aristotle: Essays in Poetics*, ed. Øivind Andersen and Jon Haarberg (London: Duckworth, 2001), 84.

20. *Rep.* 492c.

21. *De Motu Animalium* 701b17–23. The effects are immediate and mechanical: "just as, if the rudder shifts a hair, the shift in the prow is considerable" (701b27–28).

22. Certain kinds of music will raise the heartbeat, heat the blood and raise up passions (like anger) which make the animal move faster, and certain kinds of music calm the passions (as Aristotle said in *Politics* 1342a10–17), by doing the opposite. Cf. *De motu* 701a5, b1–33.

23. A wide ranging discussion of these matters can be found in Alison Gropnik's *The Philosophical Baby: What Children's Minds Tell Us about Truth, Love and the Meaning of Life* (New York: Farrar, Straus and Giroux, 2009).

24. V. S. Ramachandran, "Mirror Neurons and the Brain in the Vat" [1.10.06]; accessible online at http://www.edge.org/3rd_culture/ramachandran06/ramachandran06_index.html.

25. Istvan Molnar-Szakacs and Katy Overy, "Music and Mirror Neurons: From Motion To 'E'motion," *Social, Cognitive and Affective Neuroscience* (2006) 1.3: 235–241.

26. For Girard's (mis)understanding of Aristotelian mimesis (he accepts what I am calling the received view), see *Job: The Victim of his People* (London: Athlone, 1987). See also, *Things Hidden Since the Foundation of the World*, trans. Michael Metteer and Stephen Bann (Stanford: University Press, 1987), 8. "Already in Plato the problematic of imitation is severely curtailed. . . . The examples he selects for us are consistently limited to *representation*" (italics original). The examples I have already quoted from Plato exhibit that this idea is false about the ancients.

27. *Rep.* 369b.

28. One 'can' about this 'must': I think the reason "A" keeps moving further away from the inside of the theatre when listening to *Don Giovanni* is precisely because he wants *not* to hear the words; he has a feeling that language brings one into a moral community—the actors and the words get in the way of his pure (would that it were!) arational aesthesis—of music (to say nothing of women). One *can* attempt to make even arts using language into pure mimetic flow. This would probably miss the artist's intention (or at least the intentionality the work carries within it when it uses language—whether the artist means it or not). See Kierkegaard's *Either/Or*, vol. 1.

29. So, someone like Jurgen Habermas, who thinks that the task of criticism is to translate "the experiential content of the work of art into normal [i.e., informationally communicative] language," will always be missing, quite precisely and exactly, the experience of mimetic art in doing so. See *The Philosophical Discourse of Modernity: Twelve Lectures*, trans. Frederick G. Lawrence (Cambridge: MIT Press, 1990), 208.

30. *Poetics* 1449b32.

31. I have previously exhibited how the Athenian Stranger's claim that all the arts of the muses are *eikastic* and *mimetic* (*Laws* 668a) is distinguishing between the representative or intentional and the mimetic, and how the second half of this distinction is (perennially) pushed out into the intentional in philosophy (though it still leaves a supplemental mimetic effect as its trace). See my "Intentionality and Mimesis: Canonic Variations on an Ancient Grudge, Scored for New Mutinies," *Sub/stance* 75 (1994): 46–74.

32. One great benefit of Joshua Mitchell's *Plato's Fable* (Princeton: University Press, 2006), is that he sees that "mimesis—the Socratic provocation as it is set forth in the fable of the *Republic*—precedes . . . [in the sense of lying deeper than, the modern] understandings of the relationship between imitation and reason" (11).

33. *Laws* 664b, 665c.

34. *Poetics* 1449b32.

35. All of the unlabeled quotes in this paragraph are from Eva Brann's "Introduction to Reading the *Republic*" in *The Music of the Republic* (Philadelphia: Paul Dry Books, 2004), 89–90.

36. *Laws* 773d, 812c.

37. Charles Griswold argues that the construction of dialogues is a solution to the meta-philosophical problem; Plato "seduces the reader" into philosophy and "poetry and mimesis are indispensable" for this purpose. See "Plato's Metaphilosophy: Why Plato Wrote Dialogues," in *Platonic Readings/Platonic Writings*, ed. Charles Griswold (London: Routledge, 1988): 143–167; the quotations are from p. 160.

38. One purpose of the book from which this is taken, *Plato's* Republic*: Comic Cure for Delusional Democracy* (forthcoming), is to prove this thesis.

39 In this I almost agree with Kenneth Sayre that reading a dialogue is supposed to produce "a similar effect in the mind of the reader" as an encounter with Socrates would have produced in the streets of Athens; he should have said 'soul' instead of mind. The same corrective is needed for the analogy to a "literary garden" which "produces fruit in the mind of a reader [that] contributes to his or her immortality." See *Plato's Literary Garden: How to Read a Platonic Dialogue* (Notre Dame: University of Notre Dame Press, 1995), 26 and 20. I am in much more agreement with Gerald Press, who, in "Plato's Dialogues as Enactments," in *The Third Way: New Directions in Platonic Studies*, ed. Francisco Gonzalez (Lanham, Md.:

Rowman & Littlefield, 1995), 133–154, says "whatever statements they make, whatever doctrines they may assert [including by enacting a doctrine that is essentially propositional, the dialogues] also create effects that are distinguishable from those statements and may even contradict them. They create these effects in a precisely poetic manner: by creating a world into which the reader enters and in which she sees and experiences" (140). "These other effects operate through the imaginations and emotions" (141). Press goes on to show how this view dissolves many of the traditional scholarly dilemmas about approaches to Plato.

40. "All the arts of the muses are *eikastic* and *mimetic*," but insofar as mimesis is natural to us, perhaps we should allow that simply all of our writing and speaking is so—even in science. See my abovementioned article from *Sub/Stance*.

41. As Joshua Mitchell puts it, "the philosopher's task is not to *hand down* a luminous and unspeakable 'knowledge of the Good'—Socrates makes light of those who claim to possess such a thing as this—but rather to awaken souls that yet slumber. Not by mortal generation is philosophy born; the mid-wife to *this* event comes prepared with palliatives of a different sort," in *Plato's Fable*, xi.

42. *Po.* 1448a, 1450a.

43. *Po.* 1447b17–18.

44. We might have good reason to deny recognition of the fact that Plato's dialogues are mimeses to Cornford, who at least in his translation of *Parmenides* cuts out the fact that there is an Aristotle responding to Socrates's speeches (London: Routledge and Kegan Paul, 1939). The fact has little significance for us if, like Richard Kraut, we think "Plato's aim in writing is to create an instrument that can, if properly used, guide others to the truth and . . . then it may serve his purpose to create a leading speaker who represents the sincere convictions of Plato himself." See "Introduction to the Study of Plato," in *The Cambridge Companion to Plato*, ed. R. Kraut (Cambridge, 1992), 25. I agree with Kraut's premise about creating a certain kind of instrument, but his conclusion about a mouthpiece tends to practically abrogate the fact that Plato creates mimeses; 'proper use' cannot be reduction to that character's philosophical theses.

45. As, for instance the widespread use of the distinction between Platonic and Socratic irony, or Kenneth Sayre's suggestion of four ways of reading a dialogue based on the divided line. Both are far too rationalist or epistemologically concerned divisions; there is more to poetry than irony, or knowing. See *Plato's Literary Garden*, 29–31.

46. Perhaps the fairest way to introduce the large number of such readers is to point out a few edited books which contain numerous such scholars: *Who Speaks for Plato: Studies in Platonic Anonymity*, ed. Gerald Press (Lanham, Md.: Rowman and Littlefield, 2000); Gonzalez, *The Third Way*; Griswold, *Platonic Readings/Platonic Writings*.

47. E.g., *Rep* 334b.

48. Nor does it leave us to trace merely "unphilosophical and dilettantish meanderings about this or that literarily cast 'teaching,'" as Charles Griswold (rightly) complains about some dramatic readers of the dialogues. See "Reading and Writing Plato," *Philosophy and Literature* 32 (2008): 205–216; the quote is from page 206.

49. Or perhaps I should say 'hidden' from such a character, following a distinction insisted upon by Thomas Slezak in *Reading Plato*, trans. Graham Zanker (NewYork: Routledge, 1999), 85–86.

50. An extended defense of this reading may be found in my "Forgetfulness in *Meno* or, Plato Invents the Art of the Fugue," in *Platonic Errors* (Westport, Conn.: Greenwood Press, 1998), 79–109.

51. As Catherine Zuckert proposes, "To show how the characteristics and interests of the interlocutors affect the argument, . . . the arguments [should be taken up] in the order in which they occur and [we should look] at each step of the results, which are not always logical" *Plato's Philosophers: The Coherence of the Dialogues* (Chicago: University Press, 2009), 6.

52. *Rep.* 331c.

53. The remark is Lichtenberg's, but I have it three or four removes from the truth: Hilarius Bookbinder uses it as an epigram for *Stages on Life's Way*, a collection of variously authored texts, at least one of which was stolen; the whole is generally accredited to S. Kierkegaard.

It Depends on What One Means by "Eternal": Why Boethius Is Not an Eternalist

Michael Wiitala

Abstract: Objections to the traditional view that God knows all of time eternally stand or fall on what one means by "eternally." The widely held supposition, shared by both eternalists and those who oppose them, such as Open Theists, is that to say God knows all of time eternally entails that he cannot know all of time from a temporal perspective. In this paper I show that Boethius's characterization of God's eternal knowledge employs a different meaning of "eternal," which is incompatible with this supposition. I argue that Boethius's claim that "the most excellent knowledge is that which by its own nature knows not only its own proper object but also the objects of all lower kinds of knowledge" entails that God is not limited by perspective and so eternally and simultaneously knows every temporal event from a temporal as well as a timeless perspective.

Boethius's solution to the dilemma of human freedom and Divine foreknowledge at the end of the *Consolation of Philosophy* is well known. It was highly influential in subsequent medieval solutions to the dilemma, and most contemporary "eternalist" solutions use Boethius's definition of eternity as "the whole, perfect, and simultaneous possession of endless life"[1] as a kind of first principle. Although the dominant solution to the foreknowledge and freedom dilemma throughout most of the Western philosophical and theological tradition has been some form of what we would now call "eternalism," many contemporary philosophers of religion reject eternalism for various reasons.[2]

The objection against eternalism that will be relevant for what I plan to do in this paper is one raised by William Hasker and other Open Theists: if God only knows time from an eternal perspective, he cannot know a whole host of temporal facts and events.[3] From an eternal perspective, for example, God could not know the fact that final examinations are over. As Arthur Prior puts it: "What we know when we know that . . . final examinations are over can't be just a timeless relation between dates because this isn't the thing we're *pleased* about when we're pleased that the examinations are over."[4] While this temporal fact is rather mundane, certain other temporal facts, and God's knowledge of them, are of utmost importance for most Christians. Most Christians tend to think that God desires to have a loving personal relationship with them and knows each of them more intimately than they know themselves. Yet how can God know each of us more intimately than we know ourselves when he cannot understand our hopes, our dreams, and our desires, all of which have to do with the future and are unintelligible without reference to temporal facts? Furthermore, many Christians believe that the primary purpose of their liturgies or religious ceremonies is to give praise and glory to God. But an eternalist God could not know most of the beauty in a liturgy or a religious ceremony, since the beauty of the words, the music, the liturgical actions, etc., would be unintelligible outside of a temporal perspective.[5]

These kinds of objections against the traditional view that God knows all of time eternally, however, stand or fall on the meaning that one gives to "eternally." The widely held supposition, shared by both the eternalists and those who oppose them, is that to say God knows all of time eternally entails that he does not know all of time temporally as well. In other words, objections against the traditional view that God knows all of time eternally are based on the supposition that to know time eternally means knowing every temporal event from an "eternal perspective" which is incompatible with a "temporal perspective"—a perspective that includes past, present, and future. Although this supposition certainly sounds reasonable and is shared by most contemporary eternalists, and perhaps even by some medieval "eternalists," my goal in this paper is to show how Boethius's characterization of God's eternal knowledge employs a different meaning of "eternal," which is incompatible with this supposition. I will argue that Boethius's claim that "the most excellent knowledge is that which by its own nature knows not only its own proper object but also the objects of all lower kinds of knowledge"[6] in Book V of the *Consolation*, leading up to the discussion of Divine eternity, entails that God eternally and simultaneously knows every temporal event from a temporal as well as a timeless perspective.[7]

In the first section of this paper I will briefly present Boethius's characterization of God's knowledge of time. In the second section, I will differentiate what I take to be Boethius's position on God's knowledge of time from Katherin Rogers's four-dimensionalist eternalism. I will conclude by showing how Boethius's characterization of God's knowledge of time is more adequate than the one offered by either Rogers's eternalism or Hasker's Open Theism.

Before proceeding, however, I would like to point out a few things that I will not do in this paper. First, I will not directly deal with the metaphysical debate between eternalism and presentism about whether all of time exists or whether only the present moment exists. I do not think that Boethius is necessarily committed to either one of those two positions.[8] Secondly, I will not discuss the role that God's Providence plays in Boethius's account, but rather simply focus on God's knowledge. Thirdly, I will not discuss whether or not Boethius's solution to the foreknowledge and human freedom problem can adequately account for libertarian freedom. Rogers does not think that it can. But whether one accepts my interpretation of Boethius's characterization of God's knowledge of time or sticks with the standard reading is not relevant to that debate, unless one thinks that God's knowledge is propositional, which Rogers does not.

Boethius and the Meaning of God's Eternal Knowledge

Philosophers who want to present the Boethian solution to the foreknowledge and human freedom dilemma will often begin with his definition of eternity as "the whole, perfect, and simultaneous possession of endless life." Boethius, however, does not have Lady Philosophy introduce this definition until the last of the three Prose sections that contain his solution to the dilemma. By starting with Boethius's definition of eternity, therefore, many interpretations in effect ignore the first two-thirds of his solution that serve to contextualize his characterization of God's eternity. If one goes back and looks carefully at the discussions in the first two Prose sections that deal with the solution to the foreknowledge and freedom dilemma, one will find that Boethius's characterization of God's knowledge of time is more subtle than most interpretations lead one to believe.

Near the beginning of Prose 4, Lady Philosophy explains why the foreknowledge and freedom dilemma arises in the first place and what a complete solution to it would entail. "The cause of the obscurity" that motivates the dilemma, she argues, "is that the process of human reason cannot comprehend the simplicity of divine foreknowledge. If in any way we could understand that, no further doubt would remain."[9] The dilemma arises because the human mind cannot comprehend God in his simplicity and as a result must break this simplicity into parts which then appear to be inconsistent with one another. These apparent inconsistencies, however, do not, for Boethius, so much reveal that our conception of God as eternal is fundamentally mistaken, as many contemporary philosophers, such as Hasker, conclude, but rather that "everything which is known is known not according to its own power but rather according to the capacity (*facultatem*) of the knower."[10] Our capacity or way of knowing differs from God's and cannot comprehend his. Consequently a complete solution to the foreknowledge and freedom dilemma in which "no further doubt would remain" is impossible. A partial solution, however, is possible insofar as we can understand Divine simplicity in some way, and Lady Philosophy promises to offer such a solution.[11]

One important ingredient for her solution is her explanation of the principle that everything that is known is known according to the capacity of the knower. Her explanation both serves as the basis for her later discussion of God's eternity and gives her characterization of eternity an apophatic character. Lady Philosophy explains the principle by means of some examples. She says:

> The roundness of a body is known in one way by the sense of touch and in another by sight. . . . A man himself is comprehended in different ways by the senses (*sensus*), imagination (*imaginatio*), reason (*ratio*), and intelligence (*intellegentia*). The senses grasp the figure of the thing as it is constituted in matter; the imagination, however, grasps the figure alone without the matter. Reason, on the other hand, goes beyond this and investigates by

universal consideration the species itself which is in particular things. The vision of intelligence is higher yet, and it goes beyond the bounds of the universal and sees with the clear eye of the mind the pure form itself.[12]

Through each faculty, the same being, man, is known in different ways. Thus, the principle that a thing is not known according to its own power but according to the capacity or power of the knower is vindicated. Furthermore, as Lady Philosophy immediately points out, the example reveals an asymmetry in the relationship of each mode of knowing to the others. "In all this," she says, "we chiefly observe that the higher power of knowing includes the lower, but the lower can in no way rise to the higher."[13] The senses, for instance, cannot apprehend what reason grasps. Reason, however, grasps not only the universal, which the senses cannot apprehend, but the material as well, which the senses do apprehend. In order to offer further evidence for this asymmetry, Lady Philosophy extends her analogy to the whole order of living things. Some animals such as shellfish and other similar creatures only have the power of sensation. Higher order animals, in contrast, which "have the impulse to seek and avoid certain things," possess both sense and imagination. "Reason," however, "is characteristic of the human race alone, just as pure intelligence belongs to God alone."[14] We sense the world in a way similar to other animals, but our reason allows us to grasp the things that we sense in terms of a universal—to grasp different things as instances of a certain *kind* of thing—and thus to use language. Like my dog, I can look around and perceive things. Yet I perceive things *as* certain kinds of things—*as* cars, trees, houses, etc.—which is something that presumably my dog cannot do, since he does not use language. Lady Philosophy concludes, therefore, that "the most excellent knowledge is that which by its own nature knows not only its own proper object but also the objects of all the lower kinds of knowledge."[15]

Whether or not one is fully "on board" with Boethius's epistemological distinctions, the claim that the most excellent knowledge—the kind that God presumably possesses—would include "not only its own proper object but also the objects of all the lower kinds of knowledge" is at the very least plausible; as is the claim that lower modes of knowing, such as our own, cannot fully comprehend higher ones, such as God's. If one grants these two claims, then although we are limited in our ability to comprehend God, God is not limited in comprehending us and our modes of knowing. Thus, although God knows time from an eternal perspective in a way that is beyond our comprehension, he also knows it from our temporal perspective, since his higher way of knowing time includes within itself all the lower ways of knowing time. What exactly this entails, however, is still in need of clarification.

Katherin Rogers's "Eternalism" and God's Eternity According to Boethius

In order to more clearly articulate what Boethius's characterization of God's eternal knowledge entails, I will contrast it with Katherin Rogers's eternalism. While Rogers considers herself an Anselmian, she recognizes that Anselm's solution to the foreknowledge and human freedom dilemma is based in large part on and has a lot in common with Boethius's solution. She of course interprets Boethius as an "eternalist" and hence as a close ally of hers, although she does disagree with him about the sense in which our free choices cause God's knowledge,[16] a problem that goes beyond the scope of this paper. While I will be arguing that Rogers ultimately misinterprets Boethius's characterization of God's knowledge of time, overall I think that their respective positions are fairly similar. Both Rogers and Boethius hold that God is outside of time, at least in the sense that he is not limited by time. Similarly, both believe that all of time is simultaneously eternally present to God. The two differ from each other, I argue, in that while Rogers espouses a four-dimensionalist, tenseless notion of time, Boethius does not.

Rogers's four-dimensionalist, tenseless notion of time is the belief that, to use her words, "past, present, and future are subjective and relative to temporal observers, though the temporal relations of 'before', 'after', and 'at the same time as' are objectively real."[17] From our perspective, some moments in time are past, while others are present, and still others future. From the "God's eye point of view," however, from a "divine perspective,"[18] all moments are simultaneously eternally present, and hence can only be ordered in terms of "before" and "after." God knows that on December 5th I went to the grocery store and on December 6th I went to church, and hence knows that I went to the grocery store *before* I went to church and went to church *after* I went to the grocery store. But he does not know these events as past, nor did he ever know them as future, nor did he know them as present in the temporal sense, that is, as a present which is preceded by a future and followed by a past. Rather God knows these events in an eternal present, a present that is not preceded by a future or followed by a past. According to Rogers, this eternal present "is analogous to our temporal present only in the sense that what any temporal perceiver has immediate causal and cognitive access to is what is temporally present to it."[19] God's eternal present, then, is like our temporal present insofar as he has "immediate causal and cognitive access to" what is contained in it. Unlike our temporal present, however, God's eternal present simultaneously contains "every place and every time."[20] Each moment of time, then, according to Rogers, has "the same ontological status,"[21] just as every point in space does. Our temporal perspective gives us a limited subjective view of time in which some moments appear as past, some as temporally present, and some as future; whereas God's eternal perspective is objective, since, on Rogers's view, it allows him to see each moment of time as it really is, as a part of a series—arranged according to "before" and "after"—in which each moment has the same ontological status.

Yet the idea that God is limited to one "divine perspective," even if it is the most objective, is problematic. As Hasker and others have pointed out, it seems to limit God's omniscience, since he cannot know a host of temporal facts or events. And even more basically, to speak of a "perspective" presupposes a previously existing framework. Yet God cannot be dependent upon any previously existing framework, because if that were the case, the framework would itself be God. So why should we conceive of God as being limited by perspective? As we have already begun to see, on Boethius's account, God would not be limited to a perspective on reality.

For Boethius, God not only sees all of time from what we could call an atemporal perspective in which there is only "before," "at the same time as," and "after," but from a temporal perspective, such as our own, as well, since "the most excellent knowledge is that which by its own nature knows not only its own proper object but also the objects of all the lower kinds of knowledge." God's eternity, for Boethius, does not limit him to a particular "God's eye point of view," but rather allows him to simultaneously know reality from every perspective, whether eternal, temporal, spatial, etc., that there could be.

According to Boethius's account, then, God would know event E at time t both eternally and temporally. Thus God would eternally know event E in a way similar to the one articulated by Rogers. But he would also know event E from every perspective within time. Let me try to clarify what his knowledge of event E from every temporal perspective entails. Let us say that God knows event E as temporally present. For God to know E as temporally present entails that he must know the events that preceded E, say B, C, and D, as past, and the events which will come after E, say F, G, and H as future, since the temporal present is defined as a present preceded by the future and followed by the past. Yet, since God is not limited by time and thus simultaneously knows every temporal perspective, he would not only know E as temporally present, but would also simultaneously know every event, including B, C, D, E, F, G, and H, as temporally present. This further entails, however, that in a way beyond anything we can imagine, he would also simultaneously know every event, including B, C, D, E, F, G, and H, as past and as future. Clearly we are no longer using the word "simultaneously" in any temporal sense, since we are claiming that God knows each event B, C, D, E, F, G, and H, "simultaneously" as eternally present and as temporally past, present, and future.

Perhaps a variation of Aquinas's well known metaphor for God's knowledge of time from the *Summa Theologiae*[22] can help to clarify what it means to say that God knows each moment as eternally present and simultaneously as past, temporally present, and future. Aquinas compares God's eternal knowledge to the view that a person would have from a height, from a mountain top for instance, of travelers walking on a winding road below. Although the travelers, like us temporal creatures, cannot see very far down the road and thus do not know what lies ahead of them as they continue their journey, the person on the mountain top, like God, can see what lies ahead for the travelers, since that person sees the whole road. While Rogers limits God's knowledge of time to the perspective of the person on the mountain, Boethius's characterization of God's knowledge entails that God would not only know time in a way analogous to the way in which the person on the mountain knows the road, but also in a way analogous to the way in which each traveler knows the road. God's knowledge, since it is not limited by perspective, would simultaneously encompass all of these perspectives. This is impossible for us to imagine because we can only see and know things from one perspective at a time. But if God is not limited by time, then he would not be limited to having one perspective *at a time*.

If we accept Boethius's characterization of God's knowledge of time, we will want to modify Rogers's eternalism in the following way. Rogers characterizes God's knowledge of every moment of time as "cognitively immediate to God."[23] According to Boethius's account of God's knowledge of time, however, both this statement and its denial are true. On the one hand, each moment would be "cognitively immediate to God" insofar as he would know each moment as both eternally and temporally present. On the other hand, however, each moment would not be "cognitively immediate to God" insofar as his simultaneous knowledge of every moment as temporally present entails that he must also simultaneously know every moment as past and as future, and therefore as "cognitively distant" or "absent" rather than "immediate." Yet once we have differentiated the reasons why the statement that "every moment of time is cognitively immediate to God" is true in one way, while the statement that "every moment of time is cognitively distant or absent to God" is true in another, there is no contradiction between the two statements. If we apply Boethius's principle that "the most excellent knowledge is that which by its own nature knows not only its own proper object but also the objects of all the lower kinds of knowledge," then God is not limited by perspective and hence can simultaneously know something, event E for instance, as both "cognitively immediate" and "cognitively distant" or "absent."

Conclusion

The standard for measuring the adequacy of a philosophical or theological conception of God has traditionally been whether or not that conception is the one that best glorifies him and manifests his perfection. My two primary contemporary interlocutors in this paper, Rogers and Hasker, also take this as the standard for their philosophical discourse about God. Since Anselm enshrined this standard by defining God as something-than-which-nothing-greater-can-be-thought, Rogers, as a good Anselmian, provides justification for her eternalism by saying that it "is entailed by the most robust conception of divine perfection."[24] Hasker, likewise, although not an Anselmian, argues for Open Theism by claiming that it portrays "God in a way that shows him to be fully worthy of . . . praise and honor."[25]

If one will follow Rogers, Hasker, and the tradition, and grant that whatever conception of God shows him to be more perfect and praiseworthy is the conception that is most philosophically adequate, then Boethius's characterization of God's knowledge of time is more adequate than the one offered by either eternalism or Open Theism. Open Theists argue that God is more perfect and worthy of praise if he can know temporal events and experiences, since he cannot have a loving personal relationship with temporal creatures like ourselves without such knowledge. Yet Rogers claims that God is more perfect and worthy of praise if he is not limited by time, but rather can know all of time—including what we would call the future—simultaneously, since only through such knowledge would he have the power to "*bring about* what happens at [time] *t*."[26] In one way the Open Theist conception of God's knowledge of time portrays him as more praiseworthy, while in another way the eternalist conception does. Boethius's conception of God's knowledge of time, however, allows us to take what makes God most praiseworthy and perfect in both

Open Theism and eternalism and put them together, since God's "most excellent knowledge is that which by its own nature knows not only its own proper object but also the objects of all the lower kinds of knowledge." The only difficulty with Boethius's characterization of God's knowledge of time is that we cannot imagine what it would be like to simultaneously know the same event as eternally present, temporally present, past, and future. But why should we think that we can imagine God's "mental states"? The reason that we cannot imagine what it would be like to simultaneously know the same event as eternally present, temporally present, past, and future is that, since we are limited by time, we can only imagine things from one perspective at a time. Since there is no reason to think that God is limited by time and perspective, however, and since God would be more praiseworthy and perfect if he were not limited by time and perspective, Boethius's characterization of God's knowledge of time is more philosophically adequate than the one offered by either eternalism or Open Theism.

University of Kentucky

Notes

1. Boethius, *The Consolation of Philosophy*, trans. Richard Green (New York: The Macmillan Company, 1962), V.6.

2. For a discussion of some contemporary objections to eternalism or "the timeless solution" see Linda Trinkaus Zagzebski, *The Dilemma of Freedom and Foreknowledge* (Oxford: Oxford University Press, 1991), 43–65.

3. See William Hasker, "The Absence of a Timeless God," in *God and Time: Essays on the Divine Nature*, ed. Gregory E. Ganssle and David M. Woodruff (Oxford: Oxford University Press, 2002), 182–206; Hasker, "Open Theism: An Introduction" (The Society of Christian Philosophers, Eastern Regional Conference, December 2003).

4. Arthur N. Prior, "The Formalities of Omniscience," in *Papers on Time and Tense*, ed. Per Hasle, Peter Ohrstrom, Torben Brauner, Jack and Copeland (Oxford: Oxford University Press, 2003), 42.

5. Hasker, "Open Theism," 3. Hasker points out the liturgical problem that a timeless God posses: "As the liturgy has it, 'Christ *has* died, Christ *has* risen, Christ *will* come again'—but when we say this, we are saying something that is indeed true, but something that God himself does not *know* to be true."

6. Boethius, *Consolation*, V.5.

7. In an article published in 1968, Lewis Ford offered an interpretation of Boethius's characterization of God's eternity very similar to the one that I am giving here. He develops his interpretation, however, using a conceptual framework that is significantly different from the one that I will be using in this paper, since the intent of his article was to make a comparison between Boethius and Alfred North Whitehead, whereas my intent is to show how Boethius's position differs from contemporary eternalism. See Lewis S. Ford, "Boethius and Whitehead on Time and Eternity," *International Philosophical Quarterly* 8.1 (1968): 38–67.

8. Although one can read Boethius as committed to the eternalist position, his characterization of God's knowledge of time is also compatible with the view that in one sense only the present moment exists, while in another sense all of time exists simultaneously. Since the word "exists" can have multiple senses, the idea that all of time "exists" and that only the present "exists" are not necessarily mutually exclusive.

9. Boethius, *Consolation*, V.4. "Cuius caliginis causa est, quod humanae ratiocinationis motus ad divinae praescientiae simplicitatem non potest admoveri, quae si ullo modo cogitari queat, nihil prorsus relinquetur ambigui."

10. Ibid.

11. Ibid.

12. Ibid.

13. Ibid.

14. Ibid., V.5.

15. Ibid. "Quo fit ut ea notitia ceteris praestet quae suapte natura non modo proprium sed ceterarum quoque notitiarum subiecta cognoscit."

16. Katherin A. Rogers, "The Necessity of the Present and Anselm's Eternalist Response to the Problem of Theological Fatalism," *Religious Studies* 43 (2007): 31.

17. Ibid., 28.

18. Rogers speaks of both a "God's eye point of view" and of a "divine perspective." See Katherin A. Rogers, "Anselm on Eternity as the Fifth Dimension," *Saint Anselm Journal* 3.2 (2006): 1–8; "The Necessity of the Present and Anselm's Eternalist Response to the Problem of Theological Fatalism."

19. Rogers, "The Necessity of the Present," 29.

20. Ibid.

21. Ibid., 28.

22. Thomas Aquinas, *Summa Theologiae*, Ia, Q. 14, A. 13, ad. 2.

23. Rogers, "The Necessity of the Present," 29.

24. Katherin A. Rogers, "Anselmian Eternalism: The Presence of a Timeless God," *Faith and Philosophy* 24.1 (2007): 23.

25. Hasker, "Open Theism," 5.

26. Rogers, "Anselmian Eternalism," 19–23.

The Meaning of the Word *Art*:
A Neothomistic Investigation

Abstract: In this paper I investigate how works of fine art differ from products of craft. I argue that historical and institutional definitions are incomplete because they fail to explain what is common to everything we call *art*. I then consider the way in which Francis J. Kovach and Jacques Maritain define *art*. I argue that Kovach's four-fold division fails on logical grounds. Maritain's division, however, makes the distinction between fine and useful art a matter of degree, not a division into separate species. This does reflect our use of the word *art*, and means that, when we call something a work of fine art, we are not designating it as part of a species. Rather we signify that it possesses a particular attribute which, in some way, belongs to every product of human making, but is more clearly present, or more attended to, in works of fine art.

Before discussing what art is, I want to briefly explain what I am trying to do by defining art. I want to formulate a definition which expresses something essential about art; but at the same time, I do not want to dictate how the word *should* be used, but rather reflect how we really *do* use it. Thus, a good definition will be explanatory, making us think: "Of course! That's exactly what that means," and not prescriptive, making us think: "So you're telling me that I should only use the word to mean. . . ."[1] But, of course, trying to figure out what is both common and fundamental to all the different ways that a word is used is never an easy task. Even in areas such as biology, where at least the things being defined appear more clearly distinguished than in areas such as aesthetics or ethics, there are disagreements about matters as seemingly straightforward, at least to non-biologists, as the relations between bison, cows, yaks, and other similar animals.[2] When discussing the meaning of the word *art*, the difficulties are greater.

One reason why defining *art* is especially difficult is that, while there is at least some general agreement about which animals are cows or cow-like and which are not, there is no such agreement about which things are works of art and which are not. It seems fairly clear that at least some plays, poems, paintings, novels, symphonies, and ballets are works of art. But it is far less clear whether every novel or every painting is a work of art: R. G. Collingwood, for example, claims that detective stories and many of the paintings produced for religious or patriotic purposes are not, properly speaking, art; and Arthur C. Danto makes the same claim about the drawings and paintings of children.[3]

Before going further, I should, perhaps, make a few preliminary and not especially controversial distinctions. The first distinction is between the three ways in which the word *art* is commonly used. First, art is the habit, ability, or talent—I don't plan to discuss which of these is most appropriate here—because of which an artist is called an artist. Second, and my focus in this paper, art is some *thing* produced by an artist. Third, art is the shared endeavor of all those engaged in a particular art in the first sense. This third sense is often referred to in the plural: "the arts."[4]

The second distinction—perhaps slightly controversial—is between art in the ancient sense, τέχνη or *ars*, and the modern use of the word *art* to refer primarily to what is sometimes called fine art. In the ancient and medieval use of the word, no consistent distinction was made between things which we regard as arts, such as painting, sculpting, and architecture, and things which we regard as crafts or mechanical arts, such as bricklaying, brewing, and metalworking. Although we call the latter mechanical *arts*, we generally do not refer to their products as works of art, simply speaking. In the ancient and medieval use of the term *art*, however, the products of all these mechanical arts were regarded simply as works of art, because they are all products of τέχνη, which Aristotle defines as "a state concerned with making, involving a true course of reasoning."[5]

On the other hand, Plato and Aristotle did regard poetry, including all of what we now call fiction, as well as drama, as somehow distinctive. And Aristotle, at least, saw music, dance, and painting as special in the same way, because all these arts are in some way imitative.[6] However, Aristotle's distinction between imitative arts and the other arts does not correspond nicely with our modern distinction between fine art and mechanical art: Much modern sculpture and painting is deliberately not imitative. Moreover, architecture, like purely instrumental music, is often not obviously imitative. Looking at a building, we are, at least sometimes, hard pressed to answer the question: "What is it about?" We might not even find the question meaningful. So, in contrast with Aristotle's distinction between the imitative and the non-imitative, not all those things which today we call "art" have the property of being imitative.

Now, since I am using language and trusting it as a means of arriving at truth, I am, at least initially, assuming that we are not completely mistaken about our modern use of the word art. So if there is something in reality corresponding to this use, then we should make an attempt to discover what distinguishes art in this modern sense from all the other things which would have been called *art* by the ancients and medievals.

Of course, philosophers have been trying to define *art* for quite a while now, and with a rather embarrassing lack of success. In fact, some philosophers seem to have given up the attempt altogether, and have shifted the focus to a discussion of individual arts, or of the differences between them, rather than the definition common to all arts.[7] But, while discussing the differences between particular arts is certainly a fruitful endeavor, it would be even more fruitful if we knew what made them all arts in the first place.

Since my main focus is the difference between fine art and mechanical art, I need to first briefly discuss the genus to which both sorts of art belong. I have so far been assuming that a work of fine art is a particular kind of work of art in the broad sense, in what I have been calling the ancient and medieval use of the word. This broad sense, following Aristotle, is the product of human making, as the result of a habit of making in accord with true reason.[8]

The reason I am convinced that fine art should be placed within the genus of human making—aside from etymology—is that everything we call *art* is, in fact, the product of human making. Things such as the sun, wild animals in their natural habitats, and oceans, are not referred to as *art* (except in the extended sense in which they are looked at as God's art—as the product of making, but not human making). What all these things which are not art have in common is that they are very clearly not something we produce. In contrast, all of the things which we do call *art* are human products in some way or another. We are never tempted to call even the most beautiful sunset or landscape a work of art until we have acted on it, tamed it into a garden or painted a picture of it. For this reason, fine art seems clearly to belong to the category of art in the broad sense.[9]

So, the next thing to do is take up the troubled question of what makes works of fine art different from other works of art. Over the years, attempts to identify this difference have generally been of two sorts: they have claimed that there is either some intrinsic property common to all works of fine art, or else that there is something extrinsic to the work itself that makes it fine art. Those who have attempted to define art in the first way have proposed specific differences which include single properties, such as beauty or imitativeness, clusters of such properties, and functions, such as expressiveness or exhibition of aesthetic properties.[10] Those who have attempted to define art in the second way, in terms of something extrinsic, have proposed differences which include participation in a cultural endeavor or in an enterprise with historical continuity. Defining *art* by its connection with a cultural enterprise is called institutionalism, and the cultural institution is called the artworld. Another example of an extrinsic definition of art would be to claim that, while we do not agree with the ancient Greeks about exactly what makes certain things art and others not, there is historical continuity between the enterprise which both we and they call art.[11]

Theories of this last sort have one important thing in their favor: they have no trouble explaining how we can treat some can openers and snow shovels as fine art, and others merely as tools. On the other hand, they do not give the kind of account that we want from a definition of art. One could make an analogy between the institution of art and that of philosophy: Who counts as a philosopher, as opposed to a journalist, a scientist, or an intellectual historian, depends on what tradition one is part of, as well as on one's national and historical viewpoint, not to mention one's personal tastes and prejudices. Similarly, which works of art count as art and which artists are really artists both depend on many or all of these same circumstances. But if, in addition to this institution of philosophy—the philosophy-world, if you like—there were not some activity which everyone who was part of the philosophy-world had to connect to in some way, then there would be no such thing as philosophy. Or at most, being called a philosopher would be simply a name, and not an activity. It would say no more about what one actually does than having the last name Jones.[12]

If we continue our analogy between philosophy and art, we find that some who were not part of the institutional philosophy-world, G. K. Chesterton, Orestes Brownson, or possibly—at least if we are talking about institutionalized academic philosophy—even Socrates, clearly did engage in philosophy. And others who are part of the philosophy-world spend much of their time doing things other than philosophy: intellectual history, textual criticism, or writing detective stories, for example. Yet, unless there were something more intrinsic to philosophy than only connection with a cultural institution or historical enterprise, the claim that someone might be taking part in the philosophy world without actually philosophizing would not be meaningful. In fact, there would be no reason for there to be a philosophy-world at all.

We can extend our analogy between art and philosophy to historical definitions of art as well. It is only because there is something common to what Hume did, what Heidegger did, and what Heraclitus did that we can talk about historical continuity and an ongoing endeavor. If Socrates had written metered verses about the history of Athens, and if Plato had followed Socrates around and then begun to make wooden wheels for oxcarts, and if Aristotle, after long study with Plato, had begun to lend money at interest, we would not say they were all engaged in the same enterprise. The historical continuity of an endeavor, as opposed to a last name, only makes sense if there is something the same about what everyone is doing.

So, since we definitely do not talk about art as if it were only a nationality, a club, or a family name, there must be something intrinsic which makes it the same for all those involved, in addition to participation in the artworld. As Jerrold Levinson says: "If another culture has art, it must have art in our sense, more or less—whatever the inevitable differences between its art and ours in terms of materials, structure, expressiveness, ritual-embeddedness, object-orientedness, and so on. Otherwise the claim, assuming we have not switched languages, has no clear content."[13]

Of course, the issue here is exactly what our sense of the word *art* is. And, while it is not possible to discuss every single definition of art, there are two ways of distinguishing fine art from craft which I would like to consider, both of them advanced by twentieth-century Thomists. While neither of these definitions is completely satisfying, each of them points out something worthwhile about what art is.

The first of these was proposed by Francis J. Kovach:

[The] fundamental role of the artwork's final cause . . . justifies the most basic and most important division into useful, beautiful, useful and beautiful, and novel work of art. The first kind is technological; the second, fine; the third, mixed (being per se both useful and beautiful); and the fourth, the product of twentieth century artists, experimental (being per se neither useful nor beautiful but only interestingly novel).[14]

So, Kovach distinguishes four different kinds of art, and his distinction is based on what each kind is for: The work of fine art is made to be beautiful, the technological artwork is made to be useful, the mixed work of art is made to be both useful and beautiful, and the experimental artwork is made to be different and interesting.

Now, one interesting but ultimately problematic feature of this four-fold division is that it splits up into parts what we generally regard as one and the same art. Some music would undoubtedly be categorized as fine art, while some would be experimental—much of John Cage's music, for example. But quite a lot of music, quite a lot of very fine music, would seem to fall into the mixed category. Dance music, commercial music, and above all, religious music all have some purpose in addition to simply being beautiful. So all these sorts of music, as well as similar sorts of painting and sculpture, not to mention all, or at least most, architecture would be classified not as works of fine art, but rather as mixed.

Now we tend to think that when we split up art into fine and not fine, we are doing something similar to the biologist who begins a classification by splitting up animals into vertebrates and invertebrates. The biologist would be very surprised to find some of the more particular classes of animals divided between these two, as if, for example, some mammals were found to be vertebrates and others invertebrates. But this is just what we are doing if we have to claim that particular kinds of art, such as painting, music, and sculpture, do not fall exclusively into only one of what seem to be the highest genera of art.

The sort of things which cut across genera in this way seem, in fact, to be accidents. If you classify living things by color, you can have a group of green living things which includes plants and animals, vertebrates and invertebrates, but it is a division of living things *as colored*, not as living. Being a plant, a fungus, or a mammal is a way of being a living thing, and painting, sculpture, and music are different ways of being the product of human making. Being green, in contrast, is not essentially a way of being a living thing, but rather a way of being colored, even if there is a definite reason why certain living things are green and others not. Similarly, being beautiful, or useful, or beautiful and useful, or interestingly novel is not an essentially different way of being made, even if the beauty, novelty, or usefulness of an artwork is not at all arbitrary or irrelevant.

At the same time, this quadruple distinction does seem to reflect reality to a great extent, precisely because so many works of fine art seem to have a definite useful purpose in addition to whatever beauty they might have. Furthermore, many things which we normally tend not to regard as works of fine art, urns, spoons, and furniture, for example, have at least some examples which are treated like fine art, and even displayed in art museums.

The second definition of art which I will consider is from Jacques Maritain's *Art and Scholasticism*:

> Art in general tends to make a work. But certain arts tend to make a *beautiful* work and in this they differ essentially from all the others. The work to which all the other arts tend is itself ordered to the service of man, and is therefore a simple means. . . . The work to which the fine arts tend is ordered to beauty; as beautiful, it is an end, an absolute. . . . They aim at producing an intellectual delight, that is to say, a kind of contemplation.[15]

Like Kovach, Maritain associates fine art with beauty. However, there are three significant differences between Kovach and Maritain. First, while Maritain holds that the fine arts are ordered towards beauty, he does not mean this in quite the same sense as Kovach. I will expand on this in a minute. Second, because Maritain restricts himself to a twofold division, he has to deal with works of art which seem both useful and beautiful differently from Kovach. And third, he connects the beauty of the work of art with contemplation.[16]

The first of these differences is that, while Maritain holds that works of fine art are ordered towards beauty, he sees that beauty cannot, strictly speaking, be their specific difference. In a note to *Art and Scholasticism*, he admits as much:

> To tell the truth the division of the arts into the arts of the beautiful (the fine arts) and the useful arts, however important it may be in other respects, is not what the logicians call an "essential" division; it is taken from the end pursued, and the same art can very well pursue utility and beauty at one and the same time. Such is, above all, the case with architecture.[17]

And in a later work, *Creative Intuition in Art and Poetry*, he explains that:

> No transcendental, even aesthetic beauty, can be used to define a genus, since transcendentals permeate all genera. Thus in a rigorous use of terms it would be better to define the fine arts with respect to some particular difference in that generic quality, the good of the work, which pertains to the artifact as artifact, or as object of making . . . I would say that the good of the work, which is the aim of every art, depends *more*, in certain arts, on its relations to the needs of human life, and on the fact of the work being *good for something else*; and that, in certain other arts, the good of the work succeeds *more* in being a *good in itself and for itself*. . . . When the good of the work reaches self-interiority, the art involved is not subservient, but free, as is the case with architecture and still more with painting and sculpture . . . and still more in music and poetry.[18]

Maritain holds (as does Kovach) that beauty is a transcendental, one of those things, like being, which can be said in some way or other about everything. Thus, since beauty can be said of everything, it cannot explain the *difference* between things, any more than life, belonging to all living things, could be the difference between living things of one species and another.[19]

Rather, Maritain says that the difference between a servile and a fine work of art is that the former is *more* useful, *more* directed towards the satisfaction of human need, while the latter is *more* for its own sake. (Ultimately—and unfortunately I do not have enough time to address this important point—this makes the fine art a special kind of liberal art for Maritain.) Furthermore not only is beauty not the specific difference of the fine arts, but Maritain goes on to say that "during long periods in human history, it was by men who did not claim to be artists creating in beauty, and who had no awareness that they were at the service of the beautiful, that masterworks in beauty were produced. . . . Neither the Chinese *artist* nor the Medieval *artist* were consciously seeking after beauty; they considered themselves craftsmen, and they consciously sought only to do a good work."[20] So, according to Maritain, even the conscious desire to make something beautiful is not essential. Rather, the artist, when making a work of fine art, must be focused primarily on the good of the work. That is, fine art, while beautiful, is distinguished by being made to be a good thing of its kind, with less concern for use than is the case with mechanical art.[21]

Second, while Maritain does not place the work of art which is both beautiful and useful in a separate genus like Kovach, he does admit that such a thing can exist, and classifies it as a work of fine art. A work of architecture is useful, at least in most cases, providing fitting shelter for whatever it is designed to house. Yet, as he says, a building, however useful, is fine art, although it does not exemplify the character of being-for-itself rather than being-useful as much as painting or poetry. This means, as Maritain himself admits, that the difference between art and fine art is not perfectly clear. It seems, in fact, that it is something of a matter of degree, with some works of art being more works of fine art than others.[22]

Third and finally, Maritain connects works of fine art with contemplation. This insight does, in fact, seem to reflect what we do with fine art. Yet, again, it seems to be a matter of degree, and not a clear division. Tools, weapons, furniture—all manner of things, in fact—are put in museums or hung on walls, and made objects of contemplation, enjoyed for their beauty rather than their use. So, Maritain's explanation of fine art, as he himself recognizes, does not permit a definite, water-tight distinction between fine art and mechanical art.[23]

This lack of precision in the distinction between fine and useful works of art is explicitly pointed out and nicely explained by Eric Gill:

> The line of division between arts and fine arts . . . is not so clear in practice as it is in theory. In theory we may lay it down, glibly enough, that the servile arts are those which serve the body and the fine arts those which serve the mind. . . . But in practice . . . the two spheres are hardly sepa-rable. There is an element of delightfulness deliberately contrived by the workman in nearly all the things men make to serve their bodily needs, and there is an element of physical serviceableness in many works which seem to owe their existence to the needs of the mind alone. Consider for example the art of architecture. What art could be more obviously servile than that which keeps the rain out of our houses, or more free and

therefore "fine" than that which contrived the high-pointed roof which keeps the rain off the tower of Salisbury? Nevertheless, the categories are distinct. . . . It remains true that a drainage system and a musical symphony belong to different orders of things.[24]

Here Gill expresses the difference between fine and servile art in a way similar to Maritain—after all, Gill published, and wrote an introduction to the first translation of Maritain's *Art and Scholasticism* under the title of *Philosophy of Art*. Yet, while agreeing with Maritain about the way in which fine and useful arts are distinguished, he explains that in practice *no* art is unmixed. Not even poetry, which he calls the most purely spiritual of the arts, is completely without concern for the material. And not even chair-making, which he uses to represent the useful arts as a counterpart to poetry, is without concern for beauty. In his words, "If the chair-maker has a spiritual soul, so the poet has a physical body."[25]

So if, as I have argued, fine art and useful art are not mutually exclusive, as Kovach treats them, but rather, as Gill says of poetry and chair-making, opposite poles in both of which all works of art share in some degree or another, what can we say about the distinction between fine art and useful art?[26]

It seems that, strictly speaking, my claims require that fine and useful works of art not be, strictly speaking, species. Fine as opposed to mechanical art would be something like a chair as opposed to a bed, rather than like animals as opposed to plants. We can, for the most part, distinguish the beds and chairs, but with the daybed, futon, chaise lounge, and other such ambiguous pieces of furniture, the distinction is not perfectly clear. Making fineness and usefulness properties rather than species allows one and the same art to include examples belonging to each of the extremes of fine and useful. For example, music includes compositions directed exclusively to advertising soap and others with no utilitarian purpose at all. Yet all of these are music, even though some are much more fine than others.

Furthermore, it seems very suggestive that the best examples of such ambiguity which I can think of come from the world of artifice, and not from the natural world. After all, as Aquinas says in the *De Principiis Naturae*, artificial things, works of art, are not substances, and consequently do not have natures properly speaking, but only what are sometimes called quasi-natures. Consequently, it seems that, because they only have quasi-natures, they also have only quasi-species. That is, the thing which we call a statue is, in its substance, actually a collection of minerals and crystals, and the fact that they are shaped into a statue is an accident. Thus, its essential definition is that of the substance or substances which compose it, and its definition as a statue is accidental to its real being, even though, to us, the fact of its being a statue is both more evident and more important than its natural existence as stone.[27]

And finally, identifying fineness as a characteristic more evident in, but not exclusive to, certain works of art both explains and clarifies the way that we do actually use the term *art*. It permits us to look at certain works of art as fine, and thus as especially fitting for contemplation. At the same time, it allows us to include as objects of this sort of contemplation all of the different artifacts that make their way into art museums, even urinals and Brillo boxes, since no work of art is completely free from the spiritual concern of the poet, and even the most utilitarian artifact bears at least some faint imprint of the human soul of its maker.

Ohio Dominican University

Notes

1. I am here following Aristotle's example in the *Posterior Analytics* (trans. G. R. G. Mure, in *The Basic Works of Aristotle*, ed. Richard McKeon [New York: Random House, 1941]), 2, 10, 94a5, where he provides a final definition of thunder as "the noise of fire being quenched in the clouds," which definition includes everything we call thunder while also explaining what thunder is. For discussions of how to define art, see Paul Ziff, "The Task of Defining a Work of Art," *The Philosophical Review* 62 (1953): 58–78; Roger Scruton, "Replies to Critics," *British Journal of Aesthetics* 49.4 (2009): 458–459; Robert Stecker, "Definition of Art," in *The Oxford Handbook of Aesthetics*, ed. Jerrold Levinson (Oxford: Oxford University Press, 2003); and Jeffrey T. Dean, "The Nature of Concepts and the Definition of Art," *Journal of Aesthetics and Art Criticism* 61.1 (2003): 29–35. For proposed definitions, see *Theories of Art Today*, ed. Noel Carroll (Madison: University of Wisconsin Press, 2000); Peter Kivy, *Philosophies of Arts: An Essay in Differences* (Cambridge: Cambridge University Press, 1997), 3–54; and Stephen Davies, *Philosophical Perspectives on Art* (Oxford: Oxford University Press, 2007).

2. C. P. Groves, "Systematic Relationships in the Bovini (Artiodactyla, Bovidae)," *Zeitschrift für Zoologische Systematik und Evolutionsforschung* 19.4 (1981): 264–278; *Mammal Species of the World: A Taxonomic and Geographic Reference*, 3rd edition, ed. Don E. Wilson and DeeAnn M. Reeder (Baltimore: Johns Hopkins University Press, 2005), 1: 689–690. For a discussion of the difficulty in identifying works of art, see Stephen David Ross, "Some Ambiguities in Identifying the Work of Art," *Journal of Aesthetics and Art Criticism* 36 (1977): 137–145.

3. R. G. Collingwood, *The Principles of Art* (London: Oxford University Press, 1938), 65–73, 86; Arthur C. Danto, "Artworks and Real Things," *Theoria* 39 (1973): 1–17.

4. Stecker, "Definition of Art," 136–137.

5. Aristotle, *Nicomachean Ethics*, trans. W. D. Ross, in *Basic Works*, 6, 4, 1104a20. Modern discussions and interpretations of τέχνη in Aristotle include Jan Edward Garrett, "Aristotle's Nontechnical Conception of 'Techne,'" *Modern Schoolman: A Quarterly Journal of Philosophy* 64 (1987): 283–294; Peter Goldie, "Towards a Virtue Theory of Art," *British Journal of Aesthetics* 47.4 (2007): 372–387; Sarah Broadie, *Ethics with Aristotle* (New York: Oxford University Press, 1991), 185–198, 202–212; Collingwood, *The Principles of Art*, 17–20; and Jacques Maritain, *Art and Scholasticism and The Frontiers of Poetry*, trans. Joseph W. Evans (New York: Charles Scribner's Sons, 1962; reprint, Notre Dame: University of Notre Dame Press, 1974), 7–22.

6. Aristotle discusses this in *Poetics* 1, 1–2; For similar discussions in Plato, see *Ion*; and especially *Republic*, books 3 and 10. For modern evaluations, see W. Tatarkiewicz, "Classification of Arts in Antiquity," in *Essays on the History of Aesthetics*, ed. Peter Kivy (Rochester: University of Rochester Press, 1992), 89; Maritain, *Art and Scholasticism*, 3–4, 21–22; Kivy, *Philosophies of Arts*, 6–29; and Lok Chong Hoe, "Plato and Aristotle: Their

Views on 'Mimesis' and Its Relevance to the Arts," *Philosophia: International Journal of Philosophy* 36.2 (2007): 119–140. Collingwood (*The Principles of Art*, 50–52), however, claims that Aristotle does not treat all poetry as representational, although I do not find justification for his claims in Aristotle's texts.

7. See, for example, Kivy, *Philosophies of Arts*, 30–54; Kendall Walton, "Aesthetics— What? Why? And Wherefore?," *Journal of Aesthetics and Art Criticism* 65.2 (2007): 147–160; Dominic McIver Lopes, "Nobody Needs a Theory of Art," *Journal of Philosophy* 105.3 (2008): 109–127; DeWitt H. Parker, "The Nature of Art," *Revue Internationale de Philosophie* 1.4 (July 1939): 684–685.

8. Aristotle, *Nicomachean Ethics*, 6, 4; cf. Francis J. Kovach, "Some Issues in a Neothomist Philosophy of Art," in *Philosophy and Art*, Studies in Philosophy and the History of Philosophy, vol. 23 (Washington, D. C.: Catholic University of America Press, 1991), 100.

9. Here, I am not using making in the very narrow sense in which it is taken to mean only the manipulation of some pre-existing material. Such an understanding of making would exclude not only driftwood art, but also orally transmitted poetry, music not written down, and perhaps other things which I do not intend to exclude from being works of art. An extended sense of making and artifactuality seems more appropriate to the way in which we speak about works of art than such a very narrow sense, and I think that such an extended sense is defensible, although I am not attempting to defend it here. On this, see Morris Weitz, "The Role of Theory in Aesthetics," *The Journal of Aesthetics and Art Criticism* 15 (1956): 27–35; Stephen Davies, *Definitions of Art* (Ithaca, N.Y.: Cornell University Press, 1991), 120–141; George Dickie, "The New Institutional Theory of Art," in *Aesthetics: Proceedings of the Eighth International Wittgenstein Symposium, Part 1*, ed. R. Haller (Vienna: Hőlder-Pichler-Tempsky, 1984), 57–64; idem., *The Art Circle* (Evanston, Ill.: Chicago Spectrum Press, 1997), chap. 3; Amie Thomasson, *Fiction and Metaphysics* (Cambridge: Cambridge University Press, 1999).

10. Monroe Beardsley, *The Aesthetic Point of View* (Ithaca, N.Y.: Cornell University Press, 1982); Rafael DeClerq, "The Concept of an Aesthetic Property," *Journal of Aesthetics and Art Criticism* 60 (2002): 167–172; Denis Dutton, "A Naturalist Definition of Art," *Journal of Aesthetics and Art Criticism* 64 (2006): 367–377; Aaron Meskin, "The Cluster Account of Art Reconsidered," *British Journal of Aesthetics* 47.4 (2007): 388–400.

11. Arthur Danto, "The Artworld," *The Journal of Philosophy*, 61.19 American Philosophical Association Eastern Division Sixty-First Annual Meeting (1964): 571–584; Dickie, *The Art Circle*, 49–86; Jerrold Levinson, "Defining Art Historically," *British Journal of Aesthetics* 19 (1979): 235–250.

12. Bohdan Dziemidok, "The Social Status of Art: Why the Institutional Approach is not Sufficient," in *Proceedings of the XIth International Congress in Aesthetics*, ed. Richard Woodfield (Nottingham: Nottingham Polytechnic Press, 1990), 42–44. For a defense of institutionalist definitions, see Derek Matravers, "Institutional Definitions and Reasons," *British Journal of Aesthetics* 47.3 (2007): 251–257; and James O. Young, "Defining Art Responsibly," *British Journal of Aesthetics* 37.1 (1997): 57–65.

13. Jerrold Levinson, "Extending Art Historically," in *The Pleasures of Aesthetics: Philosophical Essays* (Ithaca, N.Y.: Cornell University Press, 1996), 154.

14. Kovach, "Neothomist Philosophy of Art," 100–101.

15. Maritain, *Art and Scholasticism*, 33–34. Emphasis in the original.

16. Thomas Dominic Rover, *The Poetics of Maritain: A Thomistic Critique* (Washington, D.C.: The Thomist Press, 1965), 30–31; Maritain, *Art and Scholasticism*, 33–63; Maritain, *Creative Intuition in Art and Poetry* (New York: Pantheon Books, 1953), 175; Kovach, "Neothomist Philosophy of Art," 101. Interested readers may also consult John W. Hanke, *Maritain's Ontology of the Work of Art* (The Hague: Nijhoff, 1973); Paul J. Marcotte, "Maritain's Distinction Between Free and Subservient Art," in *Jacques Maritain: A Philosopher in the World*, ed. Jean-Louis Allard (Ottawa: University of Ottawa Press, 1985), 173–186; Mary Carmen Rose, "The Aesthetics of Jacques Maritain: A Retrospective and Prospective Assessment," in *Jacques Maritain: A Philosopher in the World*, 187–196.

17. Maritain, *Art and Scholasticism*, 158 n40.

18. Maritain, *Creative Intuition*, 175. Emphasis in original.

19. Ibid.; Rover, *The Poetics of Maritain*, 30–31; Hanke, *Maritain's Ontology*, 30–37. Kovach discuss beauty as a transcendental in "The Transcendentality of Beauty in Thomas Aquinas," in *Scholastic Challenges: To Some Medieval and Modern Ideas* (Stillwater, Okla.: Western Publications, 1987), 83–90.

20. Maritain, *Creative Intuition*, 175–176. Emphasis in original.

21. Rover, *The Poetics of Maritain*, 30–31; Maritain, *Creative Intuition*, 55, 63, 175; Maritain, *Art and Scholasticism*, 34.

22. Maritain, *Art and Scholasticism*, 34–36, 63–73; Maritain, *Creative Intuition*, 61, 174.

23. Maritain, *Creative Intuition*, 61; Maritain, *Art and Scholasticism*, 33–34. Also of interest on this topic are the works of Josef Pieper, especially *Only the Lover Sings: Art and Contemplation*, trans. Lothar Krauth (San Francisco: Ignatius, 1990).

24. Eric Gill, "Beauty Looks After Herself, in *Beauty Looks After Herself: Essays by Eric Gill* (New York: Sheed and Ward, 1933), 236–237.

25. Ibid., 236–245.

26. Ibid.

27. Aquinas, *De Principiis Naturae*, c. 1. For other views about the ontological state of the work of art, see Frank Sibley, "Why the Mona Lisa May Not be a Painting," in *Approaches to Aesthetics*, ed. John Benson, Betty Redfern, and Jeremy Roxbee Cox (Oxford: Oxford University Press, 2001), 256–272; Paul Thom, "Works, Pieces, and Objects Performed," *Journal of Aesthetic Education* 43.3 (2009): 67–79; Timothy Binkley, "Piece: Contra Aesthetics," *Journal of Aesthetics and Art Criticism* 35 (1977): 265–277; Scruton, "Replies to Critics," 458–459; David Davies, "The Primacy of Practice in the Ontology of Art," *Journal of Aesthetics and Art Criticism* 67.2 (2009): 159–171; and Kovach, "NeoThomist Philosophy of Art."

Is Anyone Else Thinking My Thoughts?
Aquinas's Response to the Too-Many-Thinkers Problem

Eric W. Hagedorn

Abstract: It has been recently argued by a number of metaphysicians—Trenton Merricks and Eric Olson among them—that any variety of dualism that claims that human persons have souls as proper parts (rather than simply being identical to souls) will face a *too-many-thinker* problem. In this paper, I examine whether this objection applies to the views of Aquinas, who famously claims that human persons are soul-body composites. I go on to argue that a straightforward reading of Aquinas's texts might lead us to believe that he falls prey to Merricks and Olson's objection, but that a more heterodox interpretation reveals a way to avoid this problem.

Introduction[1]

It has been recently argued by a number of metaphysicians that any variety of dualism that claims that human persons have souls as proper parts (rather than simply being identical to souls) will face a *Too-Many-Thinker* problem. Such a view, they argue, entails that for any given human person S, for every single thought that S has, a corresponding thought will be had by S's soul, thus resulting in twice as many thinkers as we would have pre-theoretically suspected, along with a host of problematic consequences.

Prima facie, if anyone falls prey to this objection, the Christian Scholastics of the thirteenth and fourteenth centuries do. Philosopher-theologians such as Aquinas repeatedly and straightforwardly claim that a soul is not a human being but is merely part of a human being. These thinkers also casually attribute thought both to the human person and to that person's soul; they also tend to move freely from talk of what our soul knows to talk of what we know (and vice-versa).

I begin this paper by discussing this objection in detail and noting several key assumptions that it depends on. I will then briefly argue that on a cursory reading Aquinas appears to be committed to these assumptions. But this is not the end of the story; I will go on to argue that on one (admittedly heterodox) interpretation, Aquinas does in fact resist one of the key assumptions of the objection. So then, to the extent we find the objection compelling, we have a reason to prefer this kind of interpretation of Aquinas's account to more orthodox readings.

The Merricks-Olson Objection

In his book, *What Are We*, Eric Olson claims that compound dualists (i.e., those who believe that human persons[2] are beings composed of an immaterial soul and a material body) face what we may call the "Too-Many-Thinkers" problem:

> If our souls think, yet we are not our souls, then we are not the beings that think our thoughts. We merely have thinking parts. That might make it true to say, in the right context, that we think, just as it might be true to say in the right context that my house is made of glass owing to the fact that it has glass windows. But we are not thinkers in the strictest sense. And the idea that we don't strictly think, whereas things other than us think our thoughts, is hard to warm to. If I believe that I am the compound, doesn't my soul believe that it is the compound? How do I know that I'm not making that mistake? What justifies my belief that I am the compound and not the soul?[3]

Olson seems to vacillate between two worries for compound dualism; if we have souls as parts, then either (1) we aren't the things doing "our" thinking, or (2) there are too many thinkers. The first of these worries is grounded in the conviction that, whatever we are, we are essentially thinking things. Now, if we respond to this first worry by claiming that both souls and persons think, Olson claims this leads to the even more incredible consequence that there are two thinkers for every human person; that is, for every human being, there will be a soul that is thinking in addition to the human being that is thinking.

Trenton Merricks agrees with the substance of Olson's objection, providing a compressed version of the same critique in his *Objects and Persons*:

> If the soul has the same mental properties as the 'compound' person, then we have twice as many thinkers as persons. Moreover, this view implies that I cannot tell whether I am a soul or a compound; after all, things seem exactly the same to both; thus I can't tell whether or not I am a person or even whether I am spatially extended.[4]

Call the objection common to these two passages the *Merricks-Olson Objection*. Now what precisely is the Merricks-Olson objection, and what assumptions does it depend on? To begin, according to compound dualism, in addition to human persons there are also human souls. A person is not identical to a soul,[5] but is something that has a soul as a proper part. But what is it that thinks, according to the compound dualist? It is philosophical commonplace to assume that we are persons (perhaps essentially so), and since we seem to be the sort of things that have mental states and act on account of those states, we take it for granted that persons are able to think.[6] But most dualists posit the existence of souls because they deny that any material thing could think. So, the thrust of the Merricks-Olson objection is that the compound dualist has to bite one of two bullets here; either (1) she must deny that we are thinkers (properly speaking), or (2) her view leads to a kind of overpopulation of human thinkers.

The unpleasant nature of the first horn of this dilemma is relatively clear; it seems clear on reflection that we are the sort of things that think, are conscious, and the like. Olson appears to assume that the compound dualist won't want to seize this horn; Merricks appears to ignore the possibility altogether. So that leaves the second horn, that compound dualism leads to an overpopulation of thinkers. But it isn't immediately obvious why such overpopulation should be so bad. (Consider the case of a materialist who believes that human bodies have organs as proper parts; such a materialist will likely believe that I am a thing that digests and that my stomach is also a thing that digests. Nevertheless, I'm not aware of any literature on the "Too-Many-Digesters" problem.) If we assume that every thought I have is had in virtue of my soul having a similar thought,[7] then there turn out to be two thinkers and two thoughts where we otherwise would have thought there was only one thinker and one thought (for instance, when I am thinking that grass is green, my soul is also thinking that grass is green). Again, though this sounds strange, it doesn't even seem worthy of incredulous stares, let alone of being taken as a decisive objection. But both Olson and Merricks point out that first-person beliefs appear to be particularly problematic on this account: when I form the belief that I am a thing composed of a soul and a body, my soul is also having a belief with the same content. But my belief is true while my soul's belief is false. (Conversely, when I read Descartes's *Meditations* in an unduly credulous mindset, I and my soul both believe that I am soul, but only my soul believes this truly.) And it doesn't seem that I have any way to tell whether I am the soul or the person, whether I am the thing that survives death or the thing that is destroyed.[8]

This then is the Merricks-Olson objection: A Too-Many-Thinker problem will arise for anyone who accepts the following four assumptions:

1. Human persons are things with a soul as a proper part,

2. Human persons are things that think,

3. Souls are things that think,

4. For any human person S, there is some p such that S thinks that p if and only if S's (embodied) soul thinks that p.[9]

Aquinas and the Merricks-Olson Objection

At this point, the reader of this paper may be wondering what all this has to do with Aquinas and his Scholastic contemporaries. Though the Too-Many-Thinkers problem might have some purchase on contemporary dualists influenced by Descartes, surely someone like Aquinas is free of such Cartesian influences. Olson and Merricks both aim their critiques at a view on which souls are immaterial substances—ultimate subjects of predication—but, it is often said, Aquinas denies that human souls are substances.[10] Despite this, I think that Aquinas's own presentation of his view makes it seem that he does fall prey to this objection (or some very close analogue), for he appears to openly endorse all four assumptions of the Merricks-Olson objection.

Begin with the first assumption: that human persons are things with souls as a proper part. Now, Aquinas frequently says that a human being is a thing composed from a body and a soul.[11] Taken at face value, such statements clearly suggest that a human being is a composite entity with two proper parts (namely, a body and a soul), each of which is at least conceptually prior to the entity that they come together to compose.[12] That is, provided that the explication of what it is to be a human being is given in terms of these two proper parts, it must be possible (at least in principle) to specify what each of these parts is independently of the whole that they compose.[13]

Someone might say in Aquinas's defense that Aquinas's conception of the soul as substantial form makes it improper to speak of the soul as a proper part of the human person. Yet when Aquinas himself speaks of the human soul, he tells us that it is incorporeal, subsistent, incorruptible, a "this-something" [hoc aliquid] that both operates on its own and exists on its own.[14] Indeed, the soul will continue to exist and can still engage in cognition (though in a somewhat different fashion) even after the human being it is a part of has died.[15] These sorts of claims do suggest that Aquinas is a substance dualist (though not exactly in the orthodox Cartesian archetype).[16] That is, Aquinas appears to state in such passages that there are such things as immaterial souls, that they are substances in their own right, and that they are one component of human beings.[17] So, to conclude, Aquinas appears to affirm the first assumption of the Merricks-Olson objection.

Turn now to the second and third assumptions: that human persons and human souls are both things that think. Here, I claim, an examination of Aquinas's texts will show that he attributes thought to both human persons and human souls. Before looking at any texts, however, there seems to be a quick argument from premises that Aquinas accepts to the conclusion that only the human being thinks. First, it is a fundamental principle of Aristotelian metaphysics that only substances can bear accidents.[18] But acts of thinking are accidents. So, whatever thinks must be a substance; if it weren't a substance, it couldn't bear the accidents that are acts of thought. Since, as mentioned above, Aquinas denies in *Summa theologiae* I that human souls are substances, it must be the person that thinks.[19]

Though I have found no evidence that Aquinas ever offers such an argument, he does claim in a number of passages that, properly speaking, it is the composite human person that undergoes mental states like thinking and believing. So, he says that it is "more appropriate to say that a human being understands by means of their soul" than it is to say that the soul understands.[20] I take the "by means of" here to mean that the soul is something like an instrument of thought; just as we couldn't see if we didn't have eyes, so we couldn't think if we didn't have souls. But that is entirely compatible with the human person being the one actually performing the thinking. He emphasizes this in his Disputed Questions on the *De anima*, where he states that "a human being understands by means of the possible intellect . . . so if there were one possible intellect in all human beings, it would follow that whatever one human being understood would also be understood by others."[21] Finally, in his commentary on the *De anima* he points out the unpleasant consequences that would follow upon a denial that the composite human person thinks:

> It is clear that it is the human being that understands. And if this is denied, then the person asserting this view doesn't understand anything, and so we should not listen to them.[22]

Yet despite all these passages that speak of thinking as an activity performed by human beings, Aquinas *also* asserts that thinking is something that is principally done by souls. Indeed, the lengthy discussion of human cognition in the *Summa theologiae* begins by asking "how a soul conjoined to a body understands" material things, immaterial substances, and itself.[23] And throughout this discussion he regularly and quite explicitly attributes acts of intellectual cognition to the soul. For instance, he tells us that

> A thing principally operates due to a form of that to which the operation is attributed. For example, that by which a body is principally healthy is health, and that by which the soul principally knows is knowledge. So, health is a form of the body and knowledge is a form of the soul.[24]

The principle appealed to here is that whatever object bears the form of *F*-ness is the object that is most properly said to be *F*. But, since every instance of knowledge is a form that is borne by the soul, it is the soul that principally knows.

Likewise, while explicating the difference between sensory and intellectual cognition, Aquinas attributes the latter to the soul rather than to the composite entity:

> [Aristotle] claimed that sense does not have a proper operation that the body does not share, and so sensing is an act of the conjoined being and not of the soul alone. . . . In contrast, Aristotle did claim that the intellect has an operation that it does not share with the body, [namely, intellectual cognition].[25]

He affirms this point—that acts of sensation belong to the composite but acts of intellection belong to the soul alone—in several other places as well, though perhaps nowhere else so explicitly.[26]

Finally, the fact that some kinds of cognition continue after death, when the composite no longer exists, provides additional evidence that Aquinas takes souls to be performing these cognitive acts.[27] Since it is clearly the soul performing these kinds of cognition after death, it seems reasonable to also attribute these acts to the soul when it is embodied. Given all these texts then, Aquinas seems to affirm the second and third assumptions of the Merricks-Olson objection as well.

Finally, in at least one text, Aquinas gives an argument that appears to implicitly rely on the truth of the fourth assumption of the Merricks-Olson objection:

If the soul has a natural knowledge of all things, it does not appear possible
that such great forgetfulness of this natural knowledge could occur that it
would not know that it has this kind of knowledge. *For no human being
forgets the things that he knows naturally.*[28]

The particular argument here shouldn't concern us; what should concern us is the
way that Aquinas smoothly moves from attributing an instance of knowledge to
the soul to attributing that knowledge to the human being. By pointing out that
the composite person does not have a certain epistemic property—that of naturally
knowing a particular proposition—Aquinas takes it as demonstrated that the person's
soul also doesn't possess that epistemic property. Assuming that knowledge entails
belief, then, Aquinas commits himself here to the claim that S's (embodied) soul
believes that p only if S believes that p. This is, of course, logically weaker than the
fourth assumption of the Merricks-Olson objection, but I take the ease with which
Aquinas makes this particular inference as evidence that he endorses the fourth assumption (or something very much like it).

A Possible Response for Aquinas

I have argued to this point that Aquinas affirms all four assumptions that lead
to the Too-Many-Thinker problem. That is, he believes that every human person
has a soul as a proper part, that both souls and persons think, and that there are at
least some thoughts had by both souls and persons. Now, one could try to resist
the problem on Aquinas's behalf by arguing that Aquinas really rejects (4). Such a
strategy might first note that my textual argument for (4) was the weakest of all; it
would also note that in arguing for (3) I provided evidence that Aquinas does think
there is a difference between the person's thoughts and the soul's thoughts. Recall
again the passage from *Summa theologiae* I.84 that I quoted above:

[Aristotle] claimed that sense does not have a proper operation that the
body does not share, and so sensing is an act of the conjoined being
and not of the soul alone. . . . In contrast, Aristotle did claim that the
intellect has an operation that it does not share with the body, [namely,
intellectual cognition].[29]

Here Aquinas draws a distinction between sensitive cognition and intellectual cognition, where the former includes perception and knowledge of particular truths,
the latter cognition of universals and general truths. Sensation, he seems to say, is
to be attributed to the composite being that is the person, while intellection is to
be attributed to the soul. With this distinction in hand, it might seem that Aquinas
can resist the worst implications of the Too-Many-Thinker problem. The person
has some thoughts and her soul has others, so there are still two thinkers where we
would have expected one; however, since there are no thoughts *shared* by both the
person and her soul, the problematic epistemic consequences that Merricks and
Olson draw from the existence of paired thinkers melt away.[30]

Perhaps this will be the most successful strategy for resisting the Merricks-Olson objection on Aquinas's behalf. But I have my doubts regarding the possibility of cleanly drawing the distinction between sensitive and intellectual cognition at the level of propositions,[31] and I find compelling Aquinas's conviction, quoted earlier, that the human being is what understands if anything does. So, in what remains, I will attempt to map out a different strategy for resisting the Too-Many-Thinker objection on Aquinas's behalf, a strategy according to which Aquinas denies the first assumption, namely that human beings are things with a soul as a proper part.

To begin, it must be remembered that human souls are, for Aquinas, the *substantial forms of human bodies*. As such, souls are necessary for there to be human bodies at all. It is easy while skimming the passages in which Aquinas speaks of the human person being composed of body and soul to take 'body' for a human-shaped material object with arms, legs, organs, arteries, neurons, and the like.[32] But this is deeply misguided; we must remember that, for Aquinas, the existence of a human-shaped material object with the relevant kind of structure *requires* that there be a substantial form giving that object that kind of structure. In the absence of substantial form (*per impossibile*), matter is entirely undifferentiated. So, when Aquinas says that the human being is a composite of soul and body—since there is nothing but entirely undifferentiated matter prior to the coming of the human soul—the term 'body' in these contexts must be taken to refer to *prime matter*. Aquinas says exactly this in his commentary on Aristotle's *De anima*:

> Soul must be understood as something existing in a subject. *And here 'subject' is taken broadly*, not so only an actual being is called a subject— which is the way in which an accident is said to be in a subject—but *so that prime matter, which is a potential being, is called a subject*.[33]

Here Aquinas is explaining that when he says that a human soul informs a body, he really means that a soul informs prime matter. He repeats this point a few paragraphs later:

> A substantial form does not come to an already preexisting subject, but only to one potentially existing—that is, to prime matter.[34]

We now have a rather different picture of the human person: rather than being composed of body and soul (where 'body' is taken for a human-shaped material object), we should say that a human being is composed of a human soul along with a parcel of undifferentiated matter.

But here a problem arises. According to Aquinas, it is never the case that there is such a thing as entirely undifferentiated matter. Prime matter does not actually exist; there is no actual object that counts as undifferentiated matter.[35] This is so because prime matter is matter entirely without form, matter without any specifiable feature at all. For prime matter to actually exist there would have to be some actual object that had absolutely no features whatsoever. But anything that occupies a given region of space or has some determinate shape has that shape or occupies that region precisely in virtue of a form that brings about those properties. So, Aquinas thinks the actual existence of prime matter is impossible; there simply can't be such a thing. (In addition, Aquinas thinks we can't even form a distinct concept of prime matter, for anything that is conceivable is only conceivable under some feature or other.[36] And this inability to cognize prime matter is not simply due to human cognitive limitations; Aquinas argues that not even God himself could have cognition of prime matter on its own.[37])

What are we then left with? If we take Aquinas's own language seriously, human beings are composed of soul and body, where the reference of 'body' is a chunk of prime matter underlying the human being.[38] But, of course, it's not even possible to *think* about prime matter apart from the composite, let alone possible for such matter to *exist* prior to the composite. The only way I can find to gloss Aquinas's meaning here is to say that a human being is a composite, one component of which depends upon the existence of the composite.[39]

Yet if this is correct, then Aquinas's insistence that human beings are entities composed of form and matter seems to be literally false. Saying that the matter of the composite depends upon the composite for its existence appears to be the denial that matter counts as a component at all (if it is not simply incoherent).[40] For surely, composites depend on their components, not vice-versa! But in that case, Aquinas looks to be very far from being a composite dualist; though he plainly says that souls are parts of human beings, he appears to be committed to denying that human beings have any parts other than their souls.

Nevertheless, though (on this reading) Aquinas thinks human beings have only one part, he still seems to think of it as a proper part. For, he insists, Abraham's soul is something less than Abraham.[41] And this should not be thought of as merely a claim about the patriarch; Aquinas is clear that this is a general truth about human beings:

> The soul, since it is part of the human body, is not the whole human being. My soul is not me. Even if [my] soul were to obtain salvation in another life, neither I nor any other human being would obtain it.[42]

Yet, despite his insistence that the separated soul is something other than the human being and that the existence of the former is not sufficient for the existence of the latter, Aquinas simultaneously maintains that the being of the embodied soul is not something other than the being of the composite.[43] That is, though the soul is not identical to the person, the soul's being just is the person's being.

Indeed, in one early text Aquinas goes so far as to say that "the soul is not something other than the human being."[44] Now, perhaps this statement was a youthful indiscretion that Aquinas later abandoned, but I think that a promising line of interpretation can begin here, according to which Aquinas turns out to be a kind of monist. Robert Pasnau has already given one such interpretation; his Aquinas believes that forms are the only things that exist.[45] On this reading, Aquinas's claims that "material substances are composed of matter and form . . . cannot be taken literally."[46] Form and matter are not "separate constituents making separate causal contributions to the composite substance"; rather, "matter united to form is no different from matter's actually existing,"[47] which is just for there to be an existent thing "subject to alternation, generation, and corruption."[48]

On this kind of monist-interpretation of Aquinas, then, it may be possible after all to deny the first assumption of the Merricks-Olsen objection. For even if the soul and the human person are not identical, this alone does not entail (1), provided that the human person be, say, only a mode of the soul's existence (rather than being something with the soul as a part). If matter turns out not to be an existent but rather a mode of existing, then Aquinas's talk of souls informing matter turns out to be just a way of talking about the manner of the soul's existence. So then, human persons do think, as do their souls; but since the person turns out to be the soul as it presently exists (i.e., in the material way), there is only one thinker. And one thinker is neither too many nor too few.[49]

University of Notre Dame, South Bend, Indiana

Notes

1. In this paper, I use the following abbreviations for Aquinas's texts: *Summa theologiae* (*ST*), *Summa contra gentiles* (*SCG*), *Scriptum super Sententiis* (*Sent*), *De principiis naturae* (*DPN*), *Quaestiones disputatae de spiritualibus creaturis* (*QDSC*), *Quaestiones disputatae de anima* (*QDDA*), *Sententia libri de anima* (*InDA*), *Super 1 ad Corinthios* (*In1Cor*). All translations are my own.

2. In this essay, I take 'human person' and 'human being' to be synonymous expressions, and will freely switch between them.

3. Eric Olson, *What We Are* (New York, N.Y.: Oxford University Press, 2007), 169.

4. Trenton Merricks, *Objects and Persons* (New York, N.Y.: Clarendon Press, 2001), 48n9.

5. As on more orthodox versions of substance dualism.

6. It is also commonly held (though not as common as that we are persons) that cognition, consciousness, or some closely-related condition is sufficient for personhood. Obviously, if the compound dualist holds that souls think, she must deny that any such condition is sufficient for personhood, on pain of regress.

7. That is, I am thinking that p iff my soul is thinking that p.

8. Olson and Merricks both go on to ask how it could be that any of these first-person beliefs could count as knowledge, given that the soul and the person seem to have identical justification. I ignore this question as I have no interest in introducing epistemology into this paper. Brueckner and Buford, however, point out that this stage of the argument is only valid if justification entails truth, a condition that few impose upon justification. See Anthony Brueckner and Christopher T. Buford, "Thinking Animals and Epistemology," *Pacific Philosophical Quarterly* 90.3 (2009): 310–314.

9. The parenthetical on the right-hand side of the biconditional is there since most compound dualists will believe that the soul can survive the death of the person, and thus

there can be cases when the (disembodied) soul thinks though the person does not. The principle is stated in terms of "some p" since the Too-Many-Thinker problem arises so long as there is *some* proposition that both the soul and the person occurrently think.

10. In *ST* 1.75.2, Aquinas says that human souls are merely "subsistent things," where being a subsistent is necessary but not sufficient for being a substance. I have strong suspicions that those who cite this as evidence that Aquinas is not a substance dualist are equivocating; just because human souls aren't substances according to Aquinas's usage of 'substance' doesn't entail that such souls don't count as substances in our own, comparatively looser, sense of that term. Also, it should be pointed out that Aquinas does call the soul a substance in other texts (I take him to be using 'substance' in a broad sense more akin to contemporary usage in such passages). See, for instance, *QDSC* 2.resp: "It seems evident that the form of a human body must be a substance . . . to the degree that it exceeds the being of corporeal matter, being able to subsist and operate on its own, the human soul is a spiritual substance." Similar statements can be found throughout *SCG* 2; see especially *SCG* 2.68: "How an Intellectual Substance can be the Form of a Body." It may be suggested that Aquinas's view changed between *SCG* and *ST*; in reply, I point out that *QDSC* is contemporaneous with the first part of *ST*.

11. For instance, see *ST* 1.75.4.resp: "A human being is not only a soul, but is a thing composed of soul and body."

12. Aquinas thinks that, insofar as they are causes of it, the components of a composite entity must be prior to it. See *DPN* 4.

13. I argue below that this reading of Aquinas is deeply mistaken.

14. See especially *ST* 1.75, articles 2 and 6.

15. See *ST* 1.89. Aquinas says there that even though the separated soul lacks certain bodily functions that are typically required for human cognition, souls can continue to cognize after death provided that God provides acceptable substitutes for these requisite bodily functions.

16. On this reading, Aquinas's major departure from Cartesian orthodoxy is that he assigns acts of sensation and perception to the composite rather than to the soul alone. See *ST* 1.75.4.resp.

17. As pointed out in n. 10, especially in *ST* 1, Aquinas refrains from explicitly labeling human souls as substances, choosing instead to only call them "subsistent things." The contemporary reader of Aquinas may well wonder whether anything substantive (pun non intended) really turns on this choice.

18. Thus Aquinas: "Actions belong to supposits and wholes, and not, properly speaking, to parts, forms, or powers . . . " *ST* 2-2.58.2.resp. (My thanks to Therese Scarpelli Cory for pointing me to this passage.)

19. The fact that Aquinas offers no such argument seems to me additional evidence that he does regard souls as substances in the sense that they are among the ultimate bearers of properties.

20. *ST* 1.75.2.ad 2.

21. *QDDA* 3.sed contra.

22. *InDA* 3.7.20 (n. 690).

23. *ST* 1.85.prooemium.

24. *ST* 1.76.1.resp.

25. *ST* 1.84.6.resp. Though in this article Aquinas speaks as if he is merely reporting the views of Democritus, Plato, and Aristotle, context makes it clear that he favors Aristotle's answer to the question.

26. For instance, he clearly has this in mind in *ST* 1.75.4, where he argues that if sensation were an operation of the soul rather than of the whole person, then "every operation which is attributed to a human being would belong to the soul alone." The implication here being, of course, that intellectual operations *do* belong to the soul alone.

27. See *ST* 1.79, as well as *QDDA* 17-21.

28. *ST* 1.84.3.resp (emphasis added).

29. *ST* 1.84.6.resp.

30. Another possibility, which I don't have space to address here, is that one might also deny (4) by claiming that Aquinas holds that only disembodied souls think (and consequently that all of Aquinas's talk of the thoughts of embodied souls is a kind of shorthand). My thanks to Michael Rota for raising, and Therese Scarpelli Cory for pressing, this point.

31. I do not have the space here to defend this claim at length, but such a defense would begin with the observation that every thought with the content *x is an F* appears to bring together the cognition of a particular with that of a universal.

32. Or, for the compositional nihilists in the audience, for collections of atoms arranged armly, legly, organly, neuronally, and so on.

33. *InDA* 2.1.10 (n. 220). (Emphasis added).

34. *InDA* 2.1.14 (n. 224).

35. "It must be known that matter does not have in its own nature any form or privation. . . . Nevertheless, matter is never stripped from [all] form and privation, for it is under one form at one time and under another form at another time. Rather, matter can never exist on its own. For since it doesn't have any form in its own definition, it doesn't have actual being, because actual being is had only by form. . . . Anything that actually exists can not be called prime matter" (*DPN* 2).

In addition, when commenting upon Genesis 1:2, Aquinas says that the existence of prime matter is not just metaphysically impossible but is logically contradictory: "Saying that matter once existed without form is to say that a being was actual without being actual, which is a contradiction" (*ST* 1.66.1.resp).

36. "The intellect only cognizes prime matter as it is related to form" (*ST* 1.87.1.resp).

37. "Since we believe that matter has been created by God (though not without form), there is indeed an idea of matter in God, but this idea is not something distinct from the idea of a composite [of form and matter]. For matter in itself does not have being and is not cognizable" (*ST* 1.15.3.ad 3).

38. It might be suggested that 'body' does pick out something other than prime matter (the human-shaped material object, the whole person insofar as it is subject to quantity, the quantified matter underlying the whole person, etc.), but this is to admit that saying that the human being is *composed* of body and soul is radically misleading, since all the relevant suggestions are ultimately posterior to the human person itself. Surely it can't be correct to say that some entity *x* has as a component some *y*, where *y* is (conceptually and ontologically) posterior to *x*.

39. John O'Callaghan has pointed out to me that human beings are unique to some extent here; for all other material creatures, the corresponding claim would be that *both* components (that is, the form and the matter) depend upon the composite.

40. Simona Massobrio argues much the same point: "If in effect all of the composite's actuality and being is given to it by the form and none by the matter, and if the matter considered in itself is pure passive potentiality (and indeed non-being, if considered apart from form and in itself), it seems that the composite is not really a composite at all since it is 'composed' of form and something which in itself does not exist and acquires all its being from the form" *Aristotelian Matter as Understood by St. Thomas Aquinas and John Duns Scotus* (unpublished doctoral dissertation, McGill University, 1991), 141–142.

41. "The soul of Abraham is not, strictly speaking, Abraham himself, but is a part of him (and the same is true for everyone else). So the life of Abraham's soul would not suffice for Abraham to be alive or for the God of Abraham to be the God of the living. The life of the whole conjoined being is required; that is, [the life of] the soul and the body" (*Sent* 4. d. 43.1.1.1.ad 2).

42. *In1Cor* 15.2.

43. "The soul communicates the being in which it itself subsists to the corporeal matter that, along with the intellective soul, makes up one thing, so that the being that belongs to the whole composite is also the being of the soul itself" (*ST* 1.76.1.ad 5). See also *ST* 1-2.4.5.ad 2.

44. "The species that is understood in actuality completes an intellect that is in potentiality. From their conjunction, one complete thing is brought about, which is an intellect in actuality. This is just like how from a soul and body one thing is brought about, which is a human being having human operations. And just as the soul is not something other than the human being, so the intellect in actuality is not something other than the intellect actually understanding, but is the very same" (*Sent* 1. d. 35.1.1.ad 3).

45. See his *Thomas Aquinas on Human Nature* (New York, N.Y.: Cambridge University Press, 2002), 131-140. As Pasnau has noted elsewhere, many of the Scholastics after Aquinas (Scotus, Ockham, Suarez, et al.) thought Aquinas's account of prime matter too deflationary to be consistent with his hylomorphism (in particular, that Aquinas's prime matter is too thin to function as the ultimate substratum of change); but where those Scholastics uniformly chose to "thicken" their own accounts of prime matter, Pasnau's Aquinas makes his account consistent by watering down the hylomorphism.

46. Ibid., 132.

47. Ibid., 133.

48. Ibid., 136.

49. I thank John O'Callaghan, Michael Rota, and Therese Scarpelli Cory for providing helpful comments on earlier versions of this paper.

American Catholic Philosophical Association
Eighty-Fourth Annual Meeting

Minutes of the 2010 Executive Council Meeting

Loyola University of Maryland, Baltimore MD
5 November 2010

The meeting was called to order at 10:00, and began with a prayer. In attendance were: Thérèse Druart (President), Dominic Balestra (Vice President), Thomas Osborne (Secretary), Steven Jensen (Treasurer), Catherine A.J. Deavel, Colleen McCluskey, Richard Taylor(3rd year Executive Council Members), Christopher Cullen, Tobias Hoffmann, Michael Tkacz (2nd year Executive e Council Members), , Paul Bagley, Michael Dougherty, Atherton Lowry, Christopher Lutz, Bernard Pruzak (1st year Executive Council Members). Also attending as non-voting members were David Clemenson (ACPQ Editor), David Foster, David Clemenson, Jorge Garcia, Liz Murray, Jack Carlson (incoming Executive Council Members).

The Secretary presented the Secretary's Report, and the Council voted to accept it as presented.

R. Edward Houser was elected to a four-year term as National Secretary.

The Treasurer presented the Treasurer's Report, and the Council voted to accept it.

Jason Eberl was elected as a three-year member of the Finance Committee.

David Clemenson gave a report on the *ACPQ*

Bernard Pruzak moved that we accept David Clemenson's proposal that we include new submission and editorial information as links in our Website, as well as guidelines for book reviews, referees, and special issues. Dominic Balestra seconded the motion. The motion passed.

Dominc Balestra moved that we accept David Clemenson's proposal of a special issue, edited by Richard Taylor, called "Aquinas and the Arabic Philosophical Tradition." Bernard Pruzak seconded the motion. The motion passed.

There was a discussion of the current Editorial Consultants. The Council asked David Clemenson for a detailed proposal on Editorial Consultants for the next meeting. There should be a clear proposal on whether to separate the referee and editorial board separated, and about what the Editorial Consultants should do. This proposal is connected with the issue of whether to commission papers form the Editorial Consultants.

Michael Tcaz moved that the Council commission the Editor of the *ACPQ* to develop a proposal for an *ACPQ* early-career scholar's award and present it to the Council next year. Dominic Balestra seconded the motion. The motion passed.

The Council asked that the following questions be addressed: How many early career scholars already submit? How many are accepted?

Anthony Lisska gave a presentation on a proposal to find money for a junior faculty fellowship program. The proposal was submitted to the Lilly endowment. But there is a necessary condition that someone be connected to a theological school.

Catherine Deavel moved that Anthony Lisska have the authority to do preparatory work with looking for funding for the ACPA junior faculty fellowship program. Colleen McCluskey seconded the motion. The motion passed.

Colleen McCluskey moved to accept the new applicants to the ACPA. Steven Jensen seconded the motion. The motion passed.

J. L. A. Garcia was elected as Aquinas Medalist.

There was a discussion of future locations for future ACPA Annual Meetings, and there was general agreement that next year's meeting should be in St. Louis.

Tobias Hoffmann and Christopher Cullen were elected to the ACPA Executive Committee.

Dominc Balestra moved to adjourn the meeting. The motion was seconded, and the meeting adjourned at 12:30.

American Catholic Philosophical Association

Secretary's Report (2009)

I. News from the National Office

A. Future Annual Meetings of the ACPA

The ACPA continues to encourage inquiries and offers from individuals who think that their institutions may be willing and able to sponsor a future Annual Meeting of the ACPA. In response to a generous offer from Saint Louis University, the Executive Committee of the ACPA determined that the Association's 2011 Annual Meeting will take place in Saint Louis, Missouri, and will be hosted by Saint Louis University. We are looking for volunteers for 2012 and 2013.

B. Details Regarding the 2011 Annual Meeting in Saint Louis, Missouri

President-Elect Dominic J. Balestra announced (and the Executive Committee of the Association approved) the following theme for the Association's upcoming Annual Meeting, to be held October 27–30 in Saint Louis: "Science, Reason, and Religion"; An announcement of this theme, along with the submission guidelines, was mailed to all members in the May 2010 mailing. The call for papers for the 2011 Annual Meeting is also posted on the ACPA's website: http://www.acpaweb.org. Papers should be received at the ACPA Office, University of St. Thomas, 3800 Montrose, Houston, TX 77006, no later than April 2, 2011.

II. ACPA Membership

In 2009, the ACPA roster included **1113** *active* members. The *active* members in 2000 through 2009 (all segregated according to membership category) is as follows:

Membership Category	2009	2008	2007	2006	2005	2004	2003	2002	2001	2000
Professor	159	176	176	183	201	209	198	185	198	198
Associate Professor	120	134	118	126	122	131	137	124	153	160
Assistant Professor	222	167	170	155	155	142	147	125	152	142
Instructor	0	41	59	67	74	73	68	53	64	63

Membership Category	2009	2008	2007	2006	2005	2004	2003	2002	2001	2000
Lecturer	0	36	31	33	38	39	41	37	43	41
Student	235	238	236	216	208	181	152	132	173	154
Emeritus/Emerita	110	125	126	132	131	132	129	122	139	134
Associate	78	81	92	98	97	97	91	80	100	99
Institutional	76	14	13	16	15	21	13	11	14	13
Library	0	60	61	60	60	66	60	58	63	62
Life	77	79	79	80	81	83	88	86	96	90
Exchanges	36	34	34	49	49	34	35	36	35	35
Totals	1113	1185	1195	1215	1231	1208	1159	1049	1230	1191

New Membership

2009	2008	2007	2006	2005	2004
92	101	98	113	108	53

III. ACPA Publications

A. ACPQ

In 2009, four issues of the *American Catholic Philosophical Quarterly* (volume 83) were published. The journal is edited by Dr. David Clemenson, assisted by Drs. W. Matthews Grant, Christopher Toner, and Ann M. Hale.

The 2000–2009 distribution to *active* members, etc., are as follows:

Distribution Type	2009	2008	2007	2006	2005	2004	2003	2002	2001	2000
ACPA Members	1077	1151	1161	1166	1182	1174	1124	1013	1195	1156
Subscribers	485	487	453	488	531	469	516	501	508	493
Exchanges	36	37	34	49	49	34	35	36	35	35
Totals	1598	1675	1648	1703	1762	1677	1675	1550	1738	1684

B. Proceedings

Drs. Edward Houser and Christopher Martin edited volume 83 of the *Proceedings of the ACPA*, entitled *Reason in Context*.

The 2000–2009 distribution to *active* members, etc. are as follows:

Distribution Type	2009	2008	2007	2006	2005	2004	2003	2002	2001	2000
ACPA Members	1077	1151	1161	1166	1182	1174	1124	1013	1195	1156
Subscribers	88	133	148	129	120	129	132	147	143	150
Exchanges	27	27	27	42	43	47	66	75	39	35
Totals	1192	1311	1336	1337	1345	1350	1322	1235	1377	1341

C. Acknowledgments

On behalf of the ACPA, I would like to thank Dr. David Clemenson and all at the University of St. Thomas (MN) for their work in producing the *American Catholic*

Philosophical Quarterly. I would also like to thank the University of St. Thomas (MN) for its ongoing institutional support of the *American Catholic Philosophical Quarterly.*

IV. ACPA Annual Meetings

A. Eighty-Third Annual Meeting (2009)

The Eighty-Third Annual Meeting of the ACPA was held November 13–15 in New Orleans, Louisiana. The conference theme, selected by ACPA President Sr. Mary Beth Ingham, CSJ, was "Reason in Context." The winner of the 2009 Young Scholar's Award was Br. James Dominic Rooney, OP, for his paper, "Reconsidering the Place of Teleological Arguments for the Existence of God in Light of the ID/ Evolution Controversy." On behalf of the Association, I would like to thank the 2009 Program Committee: Bonnie Kent, Christopher Kaczor, and John Hittinger. Loyola University of New Orleans gave very considerable financial support, as did Loyola Marymount University of Los Angeles.

B. Eighty-Fourth Annual Meeting (2010)

The Eighty-Fourth Annual Meeting of the ACPA will be held November 5–7 in Baltimore, MD, NE and will be sponsored by Loyola University Maryland. The conference theme, selected by ACPA President Thérèse-Anne Druart, will be: "Philosophy and Language." On behalf of the Association, I would like to thank the 2010 Program Committee: Nadja Germann, John Greco, Christopher Kaczor, and Christopher Martin. The winner of the 2010 Young Scholar's Award is Daniel De Haan, of University of St. Thomas (TX), for his paper, "Linguistic Apprehension as Incidental Sensation in Thomas Aquinas." Loyola University Maryland gave financial support.

V. ACPA Elections

The complete results of this year's ACPA election (concluded April 1, 2010) are as follows:

Vice-President / President-Elect:
    Richard C. Taylor (Marquette University)
Executive Council Members:
    John W. (Jack) Carlson (Creighton University)
    David Foster (Seton Hall)
    J. L. A. Garcia (Boston College)
    Bonnie Kent (University of California, Irvine)
    Elizabeth A. Murray (Loyola Marymount University)

On behalf of the Association, I would like to thank these newly-elected individuals, and to thank all who were willing to stand for election.

VI. Thanks and Acknowledgments

On behalf of the ACPA, I would first like to thank Messrs. John Boyer, John Macias, and Ms. Jessi Jacobs, for their work as graduate students who are sponsored by the University of St. Thomas. Finally, I would like to thank the University of St. Thomas (Houston, TX) for its very generous financial and institutional support. Since this is the last year of my four-year term, I would also like to thank the Association for allowing me to serve as National Secretary.

Respectfully submitted,

Thomas M. Osborne, Jr.
ACPA Secretary

American Catholic Philosophical Association

Treasurer's Report (2009)

I. Financial Statement

The Financial Statement shows that 2009 was a positive year for the ACPA. In 2009, the ACPA's total net gain of revenues over losses was $70,707 (compared to a deficit of $66,407 in 2008). The Financial Statement shows that at the end of 2009, the Association's total liabilities and net assets were $432,802 (compared to $367,514 in 2008). Of this amount, $426,409 represents net (unrestricted) assets (compared to $355,702 in unrestricted assets in 2008). The difference of $6,393 arises from bills for the 2009 conference that were paid in 2009. In 2009, therefore, the ACPA's net assets increased by $70,707 (as compared to a decrease of $66,407 in 2008).

II. Annual Revenues and Expenses

Between 2008 and 2009, total annual revenues increased by $149,318 (total revenues in 2009 were $125,603, while in 2008 they were negative $23,715), and total annual expenses increased by $12,204 (total expenses in 2009 were $54,896, while in 2008 they were $42,692).

III. Annual Meeting

A summary of revenues and expenses in connection with the 2009 Annual Meeting is attached. The Association is very grateful to the local host institution **Loyola University** for its direct donation of cash ($10,000) in connection with the meeting. The Association would also like to thank Loyola Marymount University for a donation of $3000 toward the expenses of invited speakers. The attached financial statements show that the 2009 Annual Meeting resulted in a $5,660 deficit of expenses over revenues (compared to an excess of $3617 in 2008).

IV. Assets and Investments—Total: $432,802

The Statement of Financial Position lists our assets on December 31, 2009, as follows:

A. Cash and Cash Equivalents: $105,505

On December 31, 2009, the Association held $105,505 in a Chase Manhattan checking and savings account.

B. Inventory and Supplies: $724

C. Non-cash Investments: $303,157

On December 31, 2009, the Association's non-cash investment holdings with TIAA-CREF were valued at $303,157

V. Liabilities—Total: $6,393

Account Payable: $11,812

The amount of $6,393 represents expenses incurred by the ACPA in 2009 (such as fees attributable to work performed in 2009), but not yet paid for until after December 31, 2009, i.e., after the closing date for 2009 statements from the ACPA's bank and investment manager. Accordingly, the ACPA carries these not-yet-paid expenses as a liability.

VI. Reminder

The Association depends heavily for revenue on membership dues and subscription payments. Therefore, the National Office reminds members to be prompt in paying their dues and/or subscription charges.

VII. Donations

As always, the Association welcomes donations. Since the ACPA is a tax-exempt organization under section 501(c)(3) of the Internal Revenue Code, all donations to Association are tax-deductible to the full extent allowed by law.

VIII. Acknowledgements

On the behalf of the Association, the Treasurer would like to thank the University of St. Thomas in Houston for its generous financial support of the Association throughout 2009. In 2009, the Association received $9,000 in cash donations and $15,400 in-kind donations from the University of St. Thomas, for a total of $24,500.

Appendix: Proposal for the Disbursement of Individual Travel Stipends

The finance committee has been asked to propose criteria for distributing funds for individual travel stipends to the annual meeting. The monies available are determined by the following formula (as decided in 2007):

The amount available is the lesser of the following two:

$$.5E \; B \; I$$
$$.05T \; B \; I$$

Where E is the average earnings on the ACPA's investment assets over the past three years; I is the amount of money devoted in the current year to help host the annual meeting, and T is the ACPA's total investment assets averaged over the past three years.

The finance committee recommends that these monies be distributed according to the following criteria:

Monies are to be given to refereed speakers who have had papers accepted for the ACPA program. If sufficient funds are available, then monies will also be given to commentators within ACPA sessions.

Monies will first be distributed according to need, based upon the applicants' status. Students will have the highest need, then adjunct professors, then assistant professors, then associate professors, and finally full professors.

Within each of these groups, monies will then be distributed based upon the merit of their presentation, as determined by the Program Committee's evaluations of their papers. The highest ranked student paper will be funded first, then the next highest ranking student paper, and so on. The same procedure will then apply to adjunct professors, then to a assistant professors, and so on.

When available, monies will be distributed to commentators based first upon need, once again using the standard of the applicants' status. Within any need group (student, adjunct Professor, etc.), monies will be distributed based upon a first come, first-serve basis. Those who apply earlier will receive the funds first.

Each individual will receive a maximum of $500, applied to travel expenses and to room and board expenses. Receipts for all expenses will be required for reimbursement.

The committee also recommends that the limit of $500 be open to change, given the fluctuations of inflation, based upon the recommendations of the treasurer and the approval of the Executive Council.

American Catholic Philosophical Association
Financial Statements

Years Ended December 31, 2009 and 2008

American Catholic Philosophical Association
Accountants' Compilation Report

Years Ended December 31, 2009 and 2008

TABLE OF CONTENTS

American Catholic Philosophical Association
Accountants' Compilation Report

Years Ended December 31, 2009 and 2008

To the Executive Council
American Catholic Philosophical Association
Bronx, New York

We have compiled the accompanying statements of financial position of American Catholic Philosophical Association (the Association) as of December 31, 2009 and 2008, and the related statements of activities and changes in net assets and cash flows for the years then ended, and the accompanying supplementary information contained in Schedule I, in accordance with Statements on Standards for Accounting and Review Services issued by the American Institute of Certified Public Accountants.

A compilation is limited to presenting in the form of financial statements information that is the representation of management. We have not audited or reviewed the accompanying financial statements and, accordingly, do not express an opinion or any other form of assurance on them.

Management has elected to omit substantially all of the disclosures required by accounting principles generally accepted in the United States of America. If the omitted disclosures were included in the financial statements, they might influence the user's conclusions about the Association's financial position, results of operations, and cash flows. Accordingly, these financial statements are not designed for those who are not informed about such matters.

Hutchinson and Bloodgood LLP

May 21, 2010

American Catholic Philosophical Association
Statements of Financial Position

Years Ended December 31, 2009 and 2008

ASSETS	2009	2008
Current assets		
Cash—checking and savings	$ 105,505	$ 153,154
Accounts receivable—PDC Royalty	23,416	11,290
Inventory and supplies	724	762
Investments, at market value	303,157	202,308
Total assets	$ 432,802	$ 367,514

LIABILITIES AND NET ASSETS		
Current liabilities		
Accounts payable and accrued expenses	$ 6,393	$ 11,812
Unrestricted net assets	426,409	355,702
Total liabilities and net assets	$ 432,802	$ 367,514

See accountants' compilation report.

American Catholic Philosophical Association
Statements of Activities and Changes in Net Assets

Years Ended December 31, 2009 and 2008

SUPPORT AND REVENUES	2009	2008
Annual meeting	$ 27,378	$ 24,715
Royalties	20,812	28,060
Donations from University of St. Thomas	24,500	25,800
Miscellaneous income	—	59
Interest and dividends	3,970	9,357
Net realized and unrealized gains (losses) in investments	48,943	(111,706)
Total support and revenues	125,603	(23,715)
EXPENSES		
Annual meeting	33,038	21,098
Subscription expense	1,120	—
Salaries and wages	15,500	16,800
Postage	441	336
Office supplies and expenses	—	260
Insurance	936	898
Accounting services	2,900	2,900
Web service charges	72	234
Miscellaneous	889	166
Total expenses	54,896	42,692
Increase in unrestricted net assets	70,707	(66,407)
NET ASSETS, BEGINNING OF YEAR	355,702	422,109
NET ASSETS, END OF YEAR	$ 426,409	$ 355,702

See accountants' compilation report.

American Catholic Philosophical Association
Statements of Cash Flow

Years Ended December 31, 2009 and 2008

CASH FLOWS FROM OPERATING ACTIVITIES	2009	2008
Increase (decrease) in unrestricted net assets	$ 70,707	$ (66,407)
Adjustments to reconcile increase in unrestricted to net assets to net cash provided by operating activities		
Net realized and unrealized loss (gains) in investments	(48,943)	111,706
Net change in:		
Accounts receivable		(5,023)
Inventory and supplies	38	38
Accounts payable and accrued expenses	(5,420)	11,748
Net cash provided by operating activities	4,256	52,062
CASH FLOWS FROM INVESTING ACTIVITIES		
Net change in investments	(51,905)	(7,642)
Net cash used in investing activities	(51,905)	(7,642)
Net increase in cash and cash equivalents	(47,649)	44,420
CASH AND CASH EQUIVALENTS AT BEGINNING OF YEAR	153,154	108,734
CASH AND CASH EQUIVALENTS AT END OF YEAR	$ 105,505	$ 153,154

See accountants' compilation report.

American Catholic Philosophical Association
Supplementary Information

Years Ended December 31, 2009 and 2008

American Catholic Philosophical Association
Schedule I: Revenues and Expenses of Annual Meeting

Years Ended December 31, 2009 and 2008

REVENUES	2009	2008
Registration and banquet	$ 14,378	$ 10,870
Book exchange, exhibits and advertising	—	1,845
Donations:		
Creighton University	—	6,000
Villanova University	—	6,000
Loyola University	10,000	—
Loyola Marymount University	3,000	—
	27,378	24,715
EXPENSES		
Banquet expenses	22,104	11,699
Invited speakers costs	1,500	2,500
Young scholar award	450	250
Aquinas medal and engraving	198	115
Meeting registration services	3,349	3,555
Printing and duplicating expenses	—	1,625
Postage expenses	2,178	153
Travel	3,259	1,201
	33,038	21,098
Excess (shortage) of revenues over expenses	$ (5,660)	$ 3,617

See accountants' compilation report.

American Catholic Philosophical Association

ACPQ Editor's Report

1. Summary of ACPQ *article submissions*

    a. Submissions (not counting special issues): 90–95/year

    b. Approximate turn-around times

        i. Accepted articles: 12 weeks (down from 14 last year)

        ii. Rejected articles: 8 weeks (down from 13 last year)

        iii. Published articles: 13 weeks (down from 28 last year)

        iv. Referees: 11 weeks (down from 15 last year)

        v. Editors: 6 weeks (up from 5 last year)

2. Request changes to ACPA Publications site and PDC site for the ACPQ

    a. Dallas version obsolete (refers to outdated Chicago 14).

    b. Would like a page (ACPA Publications and PDC) with links to our documents

        i. "Article Submission Guidelines"

        ii. "Style and Formatting Guidelines for Accepted Articles"

        iii. "Book Review Guidelines"

        iv. "Guidelines for Referees"

        v. "Guidelines for Special Issue Editors"

3. Special issues

    a. Request for clarification of procedure for approval of issues (e.g., does the Council or the Committee decide on the topics/editors?)

    b. Proposal: Richard Taylor: "Aquinas and the Arabs"

4. Ideas for increasing number and quality of submissions

    a. Award (not monetary) for early-career scholars whose articles are published.

        i. Members of editorial board could be asked to review prize submissions.

       ii. To ensure blind review, only after article accepted would author be asked whether wishes this to be considered for young scholar award.

    b. Issue invitations to members of the editorial board, or to other prominent members of the profession, for submissions; ask members of the editorial board to encourage submissions

    c. Commission articles or discussion/conversation of topics

Necrology (2010–2011)

Rev. Stephen Ernest, SVD, Santa Rosa College and
    Dominican School of Philosophy (Berkeley)

Dr. Richard Francis, CU-Colorado Springs

Rev. Albert Jenemann, SJ, St Joseph's University

Rev. Kurt Pritzl, OP, The Catholic University of America

Dr. James Ross, University of Pennsylvania

Requiescant in pace

Available Back Issues of the Proceedings

72	1998	*Texts and Their Interpretation*
73	1999	*Insight and Inference*
74	2000	*Philosophical Theology*
75	2001	*Person, Soul, and Immortality*
76	2002	*Philosophy at the Boundary of Reason*
77	2003	*Philosophy and Intercultural Understanding*
78	2004	*Reckoning with the Tradition*
79	2005	*Social Justice: Its Theory and Practice*
80	2006	*Intelligence and the Philosophy of Mind*
81	2007	*Freedom, Will, and Nature*
82	2008	*Forgiveness*
83	2009	*Reason in Context*

Please send orders to:
Philosophy Documentation Center
P.O. Box 7147
Charlottesville, VA 22906-7147
800-444-2419 (U.S. & Canada), or 434-220-3300
Fax: 434-220-3301
E-mail: order@pdcnet.org
Web: www.pdcnet.org

All back issues of the *Proceedings* are $30 each, plus shipping (see rates below). Make checks payable to the Philosophy Documentation Center. Please send checks in U.S. dollars only. Visa, MasterCard, and Discover are accepted for your convenience.

Shipping and handling charges for book orders are as follows:

Total Price	Delivery within U.S.	Delivery outside U.S.
$ .01–$ 50.00	$ 5.00	$ 8.00
$ 50.01–$ 100.00	$ 7.50	$ 12.00
$ 100.01–$ 200.00	$ 10.00	$ 16.00
$ 200.01–$ 300.00	$ 13.00	$ 19.00
$ 301.00–$ 400.00	$ 16.00	$ 22.00
$ 400.01–$ 500.00	$ 19.00	$ 25.00
$ 500.01–$ 1000.00	$ 22.00	$ 28.00
Over $ 1000.00	$ 25.00	$ 31.00

For international airmail rates, please contact the PDC.